D1511049

INTRODUCING BOOKPLOTS 3

INTRODUCING BOOKPLOTS 3

A Book Talk Guide
for Use with Readers Ages 8–12

By DIANA L. SPIRT

R. R. BOWKER COMPANY
New York & London, 1988

Published by R. R. Bowker Company
a division of Reed Publishing (USA) Inc.
Copyright © 1988 by Reed Publishing USA
All rights reserved
Printed and bound in the United States of America

Library of Congress Cataloging-in-Publication Data

Spirt, Diana L.
  Introducing bookplots 3.

  Bibliography: p.
  Includes index.
  1. Children's literature—Stories, plots, etc.
2. Children's literature—Book reviews.   3. Children—
Books and reading.   4. Book talks.   I. Title.
II. Title: Introducing bookplots three.
Z1037.A1S7   1988   011'.62   87-37513
ISBN 0-8352-2345-0

To Stephen

Contents

Foreword

CHILDREN's book people must be pleased by the current, widespread enthusiasm for introducing very young children to books. As individuals who appreciate the ability of good books to enrich the life of the young child as well as to deepen the caregiver/child relationship, we must continue to do everything we can to support and strengthen this initiative. It is gratifying indeed for those of us who work with children's literature to suddenly find a legion of educators, parents, and caregivers clamoring about the importance of the book in the life of the young child, but there are dangers, too. How seductive it is to read aloud to enraptured toddlers and preschoolers from beautiful picture books, while we bask in the warm appreciation of the book-loving adults who are involved with these children.

However, as important as it is for us to respond positively to the interest in early childhood, it is equally vital that we be aware of and work energetically to satisfy the reading needs of children in their middle years. Joyous as the preschool storytimes are, they will not lead children into lifelong reading if we fail to work with them as they grow older to help them develop and maintain the habit of reading widely for pleasure and self-education. Too often children in their middle years are left to struggle on their own to find engaging books, and frequently they turn away from reading to more easily accessible but less rewarding and sustaining pastimes.

As children mature they grope for understanding, meaning, and values. They may have the help of caring friends or they may struggle in isolation. Whatever their family and social situation provides they can find in good books characters and situations that are more clearly delineated and understandable than those they encounter in their daily lives. Characters who are searching for a sense of identity, who are trying to understand their place in the family or in society, who are making important choices, and charting future directions are clearly, movingly present. A child who learns that these kinds of people are waiting for him or her in

books, to share cares, fears, and insights, can never be alone or without
resources again. It is up to us to ensure that children of the middle years
find such friends on their reading and developmental levels.

As a child I read anything and everything I found in my tiny public
library without adult intervention or advice, and the memory of the
wonderful characters I came to know has stayed with me. Perhaps it was
easier then to choose books as companions. As a children's librarian now,
with almost a quarter of a century of work in a public library, I am
passionately convinced that we can no longer depend on the persever-
ance and luck of individual children to find the books that will speak to
them and comfort them and give them models for life. How many times
has a child already 11 or 12 and a "good reader" admitted to never
having heard of a classic such as *Charlotte's Web?* It is a dismaying but
common phenomenon. If a knowledgeable adult is not there to earn a
child's confidence with appropriate, convincingly presented suggestions
the child may miss the perfect time to read books that could be important
in his or her life.

Less well known but distinguished titles can also be perfect for a particular child. Often I am surprised by which of my recommendations
children embrace. My Japanese-American friend, who is 13 now, still
asks her father to read aloud to her from Yoshiko Uchida's warm family
story, *A Jar of Dreams,* when she is worried about something. Uchida's
Journey to Topaz, which I also gave her, is about a courageous Japanese-
American family in an internment camp during World War II. It seems
to be too powerful for this particular child. She started to read it, I know,
because she reads everything I give her by this author, but she never
speaks of the second title.

Another friend, who is 11, lifted my heart recently when he discussed
the titles from the Prydain Chronicles by Lloyd Alexander, which he had
borrowed from me. He told me how much he liked Taran's decision to
stay in this "messed up world" to try to make things better, when he
could have gone off to "a perfect place." This is the kind of sustaining
message we hope young people will find in books.

Everything we suggest will not prove to be the right book for a particular child, but if we know enough to suggest books that move the heart
and enrich the spirit we will be successful some of the time. A successful
recommendation can be enough to make a child understand that it is
worth the effort to spend time with books.

In our continuing efforts to help children of the middle years find books that they will treasure, we are fortunate to be able to turn to *Introducing Bookplots 3.* This volume guides the adult adviser to exemplary titles. The reading level for the books cited is given as ages eight to twelve, and shows an admirable range in level of difficulty, but many of the titles will interest readers both younger and older. The author's selection of books shows imagination and sensitivity. Using the same well-conceived developmental topics for the nine chapters as in her previous volume, *Introducing More Books,* the author has provided a completely new collection of book titles published mainly in the latter part of this decade. Plot summaries introduce the reader to each featured book. The suggestions of passages for introducing titles to children provide chapter and often page citations, and will help generate ideas for booktalks, displays, programs, classroom discussions, and other activities. Related materials are given for each featured book to provide additional print and nonprint titles appropriate for a range of developmental and reading levels.

Children slip so quickly from childhood to the brink of maturity. During those few critical years, as they are becoming increasingly independent, we must be certain they have the tools they need to form healthy and positive values. If we lecture, condescend, or try to impose our views on them they are unlikely to be receptive. However, if we introduce them to good books and the people in them, children will have access to resources with which they can help themselves for years to come.

While we help them we help ourselves to a richer life. Children ages eight to twelve are a remarkably varied and engaging group of individuals. The literature which has been created for them includes a wealth of delights. Using reader guidance skills to bring these children and their books together is the most challenging and satisfying work a children's literature specialist can do. We are fortunate when we have the opportunity to undertake the task and we should miss no opportunity to embark on this joyous and stimulating endeavor.

MARILYN BERG IARUSSO
Assistant Coordinator
Children's Services
The New York Public Library

Preface

THIS volume, *Introducing Bookplots 3,* like its earlier companions, *Introducing Books* and *Introducing More Books* (both Bowker, 1970; 1978), is designed to help the person who is working in an elementary, middle, or junior high school or a public library to give booktalks, to read aloud, or to engage in other types of reading guidance with children between the ages of eight and twelve (grades 3–7). *Introducing Bookplots 3* continues the series' tradition of usefulness for those who try heroically amidst voluminous materials and books to introduce the pleasure of reading to middle-graders.

Essentially similar to its predecessors, *Introducing Bookplots 3* has some useful additions. An important change is a new book title that signifies an added benefit for the reader. This series for middle-graders is now part of the larger . . . *Plots* series that R. R. Bowker has inaugurated covering childhood from preschool to young adulthood. *Introducing Bookplots 3* assumes the vital task of providing a key to reading guidance and booktalking for the middle-grade audience. The majority of the more than 1,225 titles mentioned in this book are suitable for youngsters in this age range. Although each title will have some appeal to some youngsters, together they reflect the wide range of conceptualization, readability, and interest levels that are common among middle-age children.

Another significant addition to this book is the Reading Ladder—a listing of the featured titles within each developmental goal (chapter). The Reading Ladder, which follows the Preface, lists the titles within each chapter by range of difficulty for middle-graders; page numbers are included for easy access. Helpful adults—parents, care givers, teachers, and librarians—now can use the traditional alphabetical listing by author for each developmental goal (chapter) that appears in the Table of Contents (the developmental goals appear in ascending developmental order), or the Reading Ladder, beginning on page xix.

In this volume there are lengthy plot summaries of 81 books that have been carefully selected and read. They are arranged equally under nine developmental goals for middle childhood. The developmental goals also serve as chapter headings: (1) Getting Along in the Family; (2) Making Friends; (3) Developing Values; (4) Understanding Physical and Emotional Problems; (5) Forming a View of the World; (6) Respecting Living Creatures; (7) Understanding Social Problems; (8) Identifying Adult Roles; and (9) Appreciating Books. These goals help to explain the rhythmic nature of child development through the various stages of growth, as well as within each stage, which may also demonstrate considerable variation. This underscores the usefulness of the new Reading Ladder. For those who prefer a different approach, there is also a subject index at the back of the book that categorizes the titles under conventional headings; types of literature, geographical locations, and values that the books represent and reinforce; e.g., Adventure and Adventurers, Cousins, Friendship, and Survival.

More than 1,225 titles appear in this volume for the use of the individual who arranges the reading program. Together with the 81 featured books, about 890 related materials are suggested (an average of at least 11 related media suggestions, including books, posters, recordings, computer software, and films and videos for each featured book). Additional suggested titles that relate to the developmental goal of the chapter, about 155 in total, including audiovisual media, are included at the end of each chapter. Each of the 81 featured book discussions is divided into these sections:

1. *Plot Summary.* The story is analyzed emphasizing the main characters by name and age and situation, where appropriate, while hopefully retaining some of the author's flavor. Brief introductory material, including the age of the child to whom the book may appeal, is mentioned in the first paragraph.

2. *Thematic Analysis.* Secondary, as well as primary, themes are listed to encourage ways to present the title.

3. *Discussion Materials.* Different methods of introducing the book are indicated. Specific pages and illustrations that are suitable for reading aloud, booktalking, discussing, or displaying are noted.

4. *Related Materials.* Included are books and audiovisual titles on similar themes or topics that may interest the same readers.

The detailed treatment of the featured titles is meant as an aide-mémoire; this author definitely recommends complete familiarity with a book that is introduced. This book is likewise not a volume of literary criticism nor a compilation of the best books for children. Rather, it is representative of titles that the author thinks will be useful in reading guidance for middle-graders, based on middle-grade developmental goals.

To select the titles in this volume from among the large number of children's books published from 1979 to 1986, the same types of sources used in the first two volumes of this series were employed as a starting point (reading reference polls, bibliographies, and selection aids). Fiction titles primarily were isolated; however, a few nonfiction works emerged toward the final stages of the selection process both because they are outstanding and are directly related to the particular developmental goal. Additionally in the selection process for this volume, a heavy reliance was placed on *Elementary School Library Collection,* 15th ed. (Brodart), *Booklist,* and *School Library Journal* to keep the choices as current as possible. The selection process for the many titles that resulted from these steps then included a comparison of a recommended title among local polls, bibliographies such as "Children's Choices," *The Reading Teacher,* and *Children's Books, 1985—One Hundred Titles for Reading and Sharing* (New York Public Library), and other selection aids such as "Children's Editors' Choice" and *Adventuring with Books: A Booklist for Pre-K—Grade 6,* 1985 ed. (National Council of Teachers of English), plus the recommendation in the already mentioned magazines *Horn Book* and the *Bulletin for the Center for Children's Books.* If the suggested title was also recommended by at least three of these and other reputable sources, it was read or reread by this author. The final criterion, however, although subjective, involved personal reading and the relationship of the title to the developmental goal (chapter). Both the Library of Congress subject headings in some selection aids and in the Cataloging-in-Publication in many books themselves helped in this part of the process. Especially helpful were the developmental values listed for each title in the *Bulletin for the Center for Children's Books.* The final choices in this systematic deductive-inductive process should appeal to a broad spectrum of readers with definite developmental reading abilities and interests. All of the featured titles are likely to be available in school or public libraries.

This book also includes, as did the earlier volume, the following: an index of biographical entries on the authors and illustrators that uses the newest biographical sources; a title-author-illustrator index, which now includes audiovisual titles; and a subject index. New to this volume is a directory of audiovisual publishers and distributors that is intended to aid in locating and obtaining materials.

One of the objectives of this book is to help everyone who deals with middle-graders to reinforce the books they have read and encourage them to read the selected titles. Another objective is to encourage young-sters to read, view, listen, and simply enjoy. *Introducing Bookplots 3* contin-ues to espouse another objective of this series: to encourage middle-graders to use more of their time reading by introducing books that will appeal.

This book is dedicated to my son, Stephen Jonathan Lembo, M.D., the eldest of my small brood. He and his wife, Sandra, are alive and well in their new house in Berkeley, California, where Stephen continues his practice. My older daughter, Jarron, and her husband, Jim, are parents of my granddaughter, Jaeme Samantha, a lovely child who appreciates picture books and is the delight of my life. Deirdre, my younger daugh-ter, is an enterprising businesswoman; one to make a mother proud. And so time passes!

I am indebted to Marion Sader, the Executive Editor of Professional and Reference Books at Bowker, who skillfully brought this volume from initiation to fruition. I am also indebted to Olga S. Weber, formerly of Bowker, who was my first editor. Above all, however, the gentle guidance of Nancy Bucenec, my Production Editor, enabled everyone to bring this book into print within a demanding schedule. Finally, my thanks to a former colleague and coauthor, John Gillespie, who was instrumental in seeing that this volume was initiated.

I used several locations for my work and I would like to thank the staffs for wonderful library service: the LIS Library of the C. Davis Schwartz Memorial Library of C.W. Post/LIU and its director, Professor Ellen Weinstein; Emily Lehrman, Maria Zarycky, and Joanne L. Gerber of the Instructional Materials Center of the Schwartz Library, C.W. Post/ LIU; and the Bayville Free Library, its director, Lorna Bertino, and staff, including its participants in the Nassau Library System's central-ized computer service delivery. And to you, the reader, who continues to find this work valuable, my grateful thanks. You are embracing a con-cept in which I deeply believe.

> DIANA L. SPIRT
> Emeritus Professor of Children's
>   Books and Materials
> Palmer School of Library and
>   Information Science
> C.W. Post College/Long Island University
> Brookville, New York

Reading Ladder

1

Getting Along in the Family

CHILDREN in the middle grades, or those from ages 8 to 14, have hopefully resolved one of the primary developmental tasks of infancy and childhood—learning to relate comfortably to their family unit. It is an essential point in everyone's mental growth and if not resolved can recur in other guises, sometimes throughout a lifetime. The task becomes ever more complex in these changing times: Rapidly changed family structures, from the traditional family of mother and father to such alternate styles as single parenting of either sex and foster parents, are all in a state of flux in societal valuation; only the resilience of the youngster prevails. It is naturally more beneficial for future development if an infant can resolve this developmental task neatly. However, the resolution can be accomplished at any young age. Competent venturing outside the home into a larger society is easier if this early developmental task has been successfully resolved.

The books in this chapter pay close attention to two cardinal principles. Younger boys identify in their quest for independence with a juvenile hero; girls relate well to youngsters, especially females, who win against outrageous odds. This has not changed, although life-styles have. The books here have been chosen on the basis of literary and artistic excellence, as well as popularity with middle-graders. They represent a great variety of family situations from the typical to the different or the traditional to the modern, illustrating with fond recollection the way things were, and the way they are. All, however, deal with the needs of middle-graders, hopefully offering insight and identification for those who need help, or enjoyment for those who already have resolved, "getting along in the family."

Beatty, Patricia. *Eight Mules from Monterey*
Morrow, 1982, 192 pp.

This well-known author of exciting fiction for young people concentrates mainly on adventure tales set in the West in the 1800s. Patricia Beatty is a prolific writer (see *Introducing Books*, Bowker, 1970, p. 242; and *Introducing More Books*, Bowker, 1978, pp. 22–26) who has received many honors. She researches thoroughly and writes with an ever-present submerged hilarity line. This novel was chosen by the National Council of Social Studies (NCSS) as a notable book for 1982. Youngsters aged 10–12 (grades 5–7) will enjoy the merry adventures of the Ashmores— Mother (Lettie), Fayette, and younger brother, Eubie—as they drive a "mulemobile" from Monterey to Big Tree Junction, California, in the mountains to the east. Along the way, the reader learns about the terrain, both physical and social, of that back country in 1916, as well as a lot about mules. The adventures are exotic, the characters well developed, and the story line taut.

The front jacket by Ronald Himmler portrays the mule train, with the riders in sepia tones, coming through an antique picture frame. Looming in the immediate background is the bearded and fierce-looking leader, Mr. Turlock. In the far background are the steep cliffs of one of the canyons they traverse. With calm determination, the young heroine, Fayette, sits astride the lead animal.

When Fayette, who is around 13, realizes that her mother, who is studying librarianship at the Monterey Public Library under the director, Mr. Wallace, would like to take books to the mountain outpost Big Tree Junction, in answer to the outpost ladies' letter, Fayette tries to make it happen. She would like to get her mother a job away from Mr. Herbert, her recently deceased father's stuffy law partner, who wants to marry her immediately. Of course, she would also like to spend the summer doing something interesting, so she can tell those rich twins the Hillmans about it. When the library assistant, Mr. Embleton, is injured getting a book for Fayette, she seizes the moment and suggests to Mrs. Wallace, who was her teacher, that she intercede in getting a job for her mother.

Soon they are "booted, and ready to ride." Eubie, who has just completed sixth grade, packs his father's Spanish-American War army bugle. Denver Murfree, the muleteer, finally agrees to take "two hers and a him," provided Eubie doesn't blow the horn. As they leave the livery stables at the edge of town, eight mules and one white mare, Hagar, are in the procession. Four of the mules—Noah, an old army issue, Ham, Shem, and Japeth—carry library books in their saddlebags.

After climbing for a couple of days, they reach the MacKenzies' cabin. Murfree, who had jilted the MacKenzies' daughter many years before, is still accepted by them. He helps out by chopping wood while the father, Silas, is out getting the cows. Because he is so full of alcohol—he put 24 bottles in with the books—Murfree hardly feels anything as he chops his foot. When the Mackenzies hire Mr. Turlock—known as "the Possum" because he sleeps in trees—Fayette knows for sure that the book that had felled the library assistant, *The Fall of the House of Usher,* now in their saddlebags, is bringing them bad luck.

As soon as she can, Fayette puts the book in her own saddlebag. The injured Murfree stays with the MacKenzies, and to help him recuperate, Malindy, now a widow, decides to shoot all but two whiskey bottles, which she keeps for medicinal purposes for both families. Malindy MacKenzie Culpepper also becomes the librarian for her hill neighbors. Turlock slowly begins to tell Eubie about himself, especially when they come to the old family burial plot. When he was younger than Eubie, he was sent to help his uncle, and while he was away, some bad folks killed his entire family. Every now and then he must come back, he admits.

Soon after Turlock's revelation to Eubie, the mule train arrives at Pickett's Crossing, where Mr. and Mrs. Pickett sort their share of books and agree to distribute and keep track of them. As the journey continues, they help bury the Rogers boy, who dies of typhoid, and also promise to telegraph for help at the next possible place. Next they come to the Phipenny homestead with its crowd of youngsters, including Joshua, an orphan who has been badly treated there for the last three years. Fayette leaves *The Fall of the House of Usher* with him, both because she wants to be rid of the bad luck and because he can read. But Joshua decides to follow them, to join them and to return the book.

Not long afterward, they come upon two moonshiners who know Turlock and want him to drink with them. Although a fight ensues, they eventually do leave, but Turlock then heads for one of the medicinal whiskey bottles. Mrs. Ashmore decides to intervene. Silas MacKenzie had told her that Turlock when he had been drinking was responsible for his brother-in-law's death. While Fayette takes the rifle from Turlock's bedroll, her mother confronts Turlock with her pistol and tells him to leave.

Being muleteer, however, turns out to be too much for all of them—even for Eubie, who learned from Turlock, and for Joshua, who is used to hard work. When their lead mare, Hagar, becomes ill, they manage to cure her with the aid of a book on animal diseases and some of the medicinal whiskey. No sooner does Hagar recover, however, than Shem falls over a cliff. Luckily Turlock, who is now clearly grateful for Mrs. Ashmore's earlier intervention, is close by to help them.

They finally reach Big Tree Junction where they meet Addie Parsons and Marie Simkins, who had originally written requesting books. In spite of the five signatures on the letter, the two women had done all of the planning themselves. One would dispense the books from the post office, the other from the saloon. Dedicated literary ladies, they had been sharing the six books they owned one month at a time in each other's homes. From now on, however, they would have plenty of books, including *The Fall of the House of Usher*. As Eubie blows his bugle no one notices Mrs. Simkins running after the departing mule train, yelling that they already own a copy.

Thematic Analysis

Two themes throughout the story are essential in getting along with immediate family members and people in the surrounding community. Fayette's reactions to each event and character show an increasing awareness of self, permitting her to be a staunch family member and a trusted traveler. Eubie receives some similar attention. The secondary theme is just as fundamental: the growing independence of Fayette in her understanding of herself and the roles society places indiscriminately on individuals. Incidents that show a young person's ability to surmount restrictive attitudes in 1916, a bygone era, are eye-opening.

Discussion Materials

After introducing the main characters—the Ashmores and the Possum—and paraphrasing the plot, one can choose from among the numerous anecdotes: woman to woman talk between Fayette and Mrs. Wallace (pp. 21–24); Pickett's Crossing (pp. 94–104); Joshua (pp. 107–110); the hot springs bath (pp. 111–114); the Rogers' burial (pp. 117–122); Hagar's cure (pp. 152–156). "Booted, and ready to ride," describing the scene at the livery stables would also make a good introduction (pp. 35–46).

Related Materials

Of special interest to female readers is the 16mm film *California Gold: Stories of Two Women* (Barr Films, 1986), about westward expansion based on two settlers' diaries. The following family stories are suitable for this audience of boys and girls: *Sea Change* (Farrar, 1984) by Peter Burchard, about how family members deal with each other in different situations; *Muskrat War* (Little, 1980) by Larry Callen, about two boys and their dad in a rural area during hard times; *Shepherd Avenue* (Atlantic-Monthly Pr./ Little, 1986) by Charles Carillo, about ten-year-old Joey who adjusts to living with his grandparents after the abandonment and death of his parents; *Margaret in the Middle* (Scholastic-TAB, 1986) by Bernice Thurman Hunter, about the recovered heroine who returns to her Toronto family only to realize that farm life with her aunt and uncle is really her place.

The recording *The Courage of Sarah Noble* by Alice Dagliesh is available from Random. The film *Molly's Pilgrim* (Phoenix Films and Video, 1986), based on Barbara Cohen's story, also stresses the trek and freedom theme. Two books that treat child abuse are *Maddy's War* (Houghton, 1985) by Margaret Dickson and *The Girl Who Lived on the Ferris Wheel* (Dutton, 1980) by Louise Moeri. Two other books to suggest, especially to boys, are *War on Villa Street* (Delacorte, 1978) by Harry Mazer and *So Long, Grandpa* (Crown, 1981) by Elfie Donnelly. *Emma and Grandpa: Adventures on the Farm* (Video Assoc., 1986) explores the seasons and nature in poetry and prose. A voice-over narration and live-action footage are sure to delight young viewers. Available in a film or video, *Families* (WMPT Studios, 1986) has six live-action episodes that treat the subtleties of family relationships, and is suitable for the more advanced.

Byars, Betsy.   *The Blossoms Meet the Vulture Lady*
Illus. by Jacqueline Rogers. Delacorte, 1986, 160 pp.

The author has been honored with the Newbery Award for *Summer of the Swans* and the American Book Award for children's books (formerly NBA) for *The Night Swimmers*. She has written more than 20 books, all of them popular (see *Introducing Books*, Bowker, 1970, p. 23, and *Introducing More Books*, Bowker, 1978, pp. 144–147). Betsy Byars not only has great literary talent, but also a perceptive awareness of the thoughts and activities of youngsters. In this book, a sequel to *The Not-Just-Anybody Family*, Junior Blossom builds a coyote trap, is rescued by Mad Mary, the Vulture Lady, who takes him to her mountain lair, and finally is reunited with his family. The adventure story will appeal to both boys and girls between 8 and 11 (grades 3–6), who will find the warm family atmosphere compelling.

Eight full-page pencil drawings by Jacqueline Rogers are beautiful portraits of family members and Mad Mary that emphasize the comfortable family environment. The full-color front jacket shows the family dog, Mud, licking Junior, while the two elder children, Maggie and Vern, wrestle for a soccer ball in the meadow surrounding the Blossom farm. This picture provides an enticing prelude to the adventures within.

Junior Blossom, the youngest member of his "not just anybody" family, doggedly constructs a coyote trap in the barn out of sight of Pap, the grandfather with whom he lives, his mother, Vickie, a former rodeo rider who is now home, his older sister, Maggie, and his even older brother, Vern. Hoping to make a lot of reward money by catching coyotes, instead Junior gets trapped in the cage when he takes it to the woods. Mud follows him during his secretive trip to the woods because he smells the hamburger meat to be used to set the trap. But once Mud gets the hamburger, he then leaves, in response to Pap's impatient honking signaling his departure on his regular Monday trek to collect trash with Vern and Maggie.

Junior definitely seems stranded, but Mad Mary, a recluse who is known in the area to collect DORs (dead on roads varmints) for her stew, rescues him and takes him to her mountaintop cave near a vulture's nest. This alone seems incredible to Junior because he has seen her chase vultures away from her DORs. The cave is even more unusual because of the many books that Mad Mary, the former Mary Cantrell, reads. She treats Junior gently and lovingly.

Meanwhile, the Blossom family searches frantically for Junior. Ralphie, a leg amputee who knows Junior from an earlier hospital visit (in an earlier book), has a crush on Maggie and joins her in the search. When they find Mud, who has gotten himself caught in the coyote trap, and release him, he leads them to Mad Mary's cave. Pap, who has known Mary Cantrell since fifth grade, suspected that she had taken Junior, but he also knew that she would take good care of him. Pap is pleased to be a witness to Junior's rescue and Mary's return from her self-imposed isolation. Vickie, who has been distraught, is happy to have Junior home, but wise enough to know on a subsequent Monday when Pap and his crew go trashing that she should go out to the barn and find out what Junior is up to now. "Junior . . . you and I are going to have a little talk," she says.

Thematic Analysis

Mad Mary's release from her cave—from her isolation from others to a reconciliation with society—is contrasted with Junior's escape from the double travail of the coyote trap and Mad Mary's cave. This theme occurs within the strong, loving bonds of a family with three youngsters, a mother, and a staunch grandfather. The relationships between and among the various family members are sure and comforting. They signify a reassuring place in the sun for the youngest, and for all the others.

Discussion Materials

An excellent book-talk device for this story is a brief retelling of the plot while displaying the jacket, or the eight illustrations as enlarged overheads or transparencies, as a background for the story (frontispiece, pp. 6, 25, 52; same picture as frontispiece, pp. 72, 100, 119, 133). Many anecdotes can be "talked," for example, the trap springs (pp. 28–30), in the trap (pp. 36–38), Mud—Junior's last chance (pp. 39–44), the trap springs for Mud (pp. 76+, 108–109), or you can combine them all. Mad Mary and the cave adventure will also serve (use the frontispiece to introduce this highlight, pp. 49–51, 59–61, 64–65, 73–75, 80–83, 94–101, 104–106, 114–120, 123–124).

Related Materials

All of Byars's stories are suggested, especially *Glory Girl* (Viking, 1983); *Two-Thousand Pound Goldfish* (Harper, 1982); *Good-bye, Chicken Little* (Harper, 1979). A kit with a cassette and paperback of *Trouble River* is available from Listening Library; a record of *The TV Kid* from Viking/Live Oak Media. Also of use are the following: *Willie Bea and the Time the Martians Landed* (Greenwillow, 1983) by Virginia Hamilton, about a 12-year-old who strains the extended family with his Halloween antics; *Jar of Dreams* (Atheneum, 1981) by Yoshiko Ucida, about a sensitive young girl and the strength of her Japanese-American family, further developed in *The Best Bad Thing* (Atheneum, 1983); *Kissimmee Kid* (Lothrop, 1981) by Vera Cleaver and Bill Cleaver, about adventuresome 12-year-old Evelyn, who uncovers some cattle rustling on her older sister's Florida farm; and *Tobias Goes Ice Fishing* (Carolrhoda, 1984) by Ole Hertz, about a 12-year-old Greenlander accomplishing his daily activities—the illustrations are worthy of note. Four records from Random should not be overlooked: Joseph Krumgold's *Onion John*, about Andy's friendship with an old vagrant; Laurence Yep's *Dragonwings*, about a Chinese-American father and son who live between two cultures and through the 1906 earthquake in San Francisco; Natalie Savage Carlson's *Family under the Bridge*, about an old French hobo and the three children he meets; and Virginia Hamilton's *M. C. Higgins, the Great*, about a young boy who discovers that leaving home does not necessarily bring comfort and safety.

Cameron, Eleanor. *That Julia Redfern*
Illus. by Gail Owens. Dutton, 1982, 144 pp.

This author has written many distinguished books for young people from the early Mushroom Planet series to *The Court of the Stone Children*, winner of the National Book Award for children's books (now ABA). She is also well known for her adult essays on children's books. In this title, the heroine is once again younger than in the previously published titles *Julia and the Hand of God* (*Introducing More Books*, Bowker, 1978, pp. 197–201) and *A Room Made of Windows*. The fourth and subsequent title in the Julia series, *Julia's Magic* (Dutton, 1984), describes an even younger Julia.

In *That Julia Redfern* the feisty girl has deep affection for her father and his hoped-for career as a writer which is cut short by his death in World War I. Her own imagination and her motivation to carry on as a writer herself provide the continuity that runs throughout the series. Although primarily of interest to females who are good readers, both boys and girls ages 9–11 (grades 4–6) will find numerous adventures that involve the vivacious Julia, her brother Greg, Patchy-cat, and Felony, the doll.

Gail Owens's front jacket picture in pastels and pen shows a youngster in dungarees on an out-of-control bike heading for an upset, mirroring "Greg's Bike," the first of 15 short chapters. The illustrator also drew 11 pen-and-pencil full-page sketches of the main characters—Celia (Mom), Dad, Greg, Patchy-cat, Felony, and Julia. The characters' clothing, set around World War I (probably 1922), does not limit the story, because children's activities and concerns at this age have changed little over the years. The story could be contemporary.

Julia, observing that older brother Greg and his friend Bob are out of sight, gives in to her desire to ride his bike. Across the street, Julia's friend Maisie taunts her as she wobbles and speeds down the sidewalk slope and almost bumps into Aunt Alex and Uncle Hugh, who rescue her. Aunt Alex's recriminating remarks to Julia and her later complaints to Celia, her sister-in-law, show that she is definitely Greg's champion, and things do not improve for Julia during her aunt's Saturday visit. Aunt Alex insists that Greg is slated to be a writer, but she is not impressed with Julia's reading ability. The day ends for Julia with an upset stomach, a hurried trip to the bathroom, and the demise of her imaginary playmate, Sister, after Aunt Alex seats herself in Sister's special chair and Sister no longer appears to Julia.

Soon after, however, Daddy, who is leaving for service in World War I, makes Julia a handcrafted desk, which she treasures. She is so happy that her father not only accepts Greg's wish to choose his own career (presently he wants to be a car inspector) but also recognizes her literary potential. It doesn't matter to Julia that both Aunt Alex and Gramma tell Daddy that the desk is too big for her. Nor does it matter that Greg will get to use Daddy's desk and typewriter. Now Julia has her own.

When Aunt Alex and Uncle Hugh give Julia a doll to make up for Sister's disappearance, she promptly names her Felony Franklinburg and thinks of ways to be rid of her. Felony is a shallow replacement for her imaginary Sister. Julia's disdain for the doll and her behavior when she helps a mouse escape from Aunt Alex's house do little to endear her to her aunt.

When Julia says good-bye to her Daddy at the railroad station, she hands him a letter mentioning the Grimling in the garden. She writes him many other letters before he arrives in Great Britain, all the while remembering his last few sequestered days at the typewriter. Meanwhile, Julia gets the inspired idea to put Felony in the garden with the Grimling.

Having settled that, Julia goes off to play with Maisie at the playground. Just after Maisie goes home Julia climbs too high and falls, landing unconscious on the pavement. While she is lying there all alone, she dreams that she and her father are walking and floating all over Berkeley and San Francisco. As he kisses her and leaves, he says, "Remember to tell Mama to go through my papers." When she regains consciousness, she hears a strange voice saying "Be still, little lady." A nightmarish episode follows during which a reclusive older brother and sister hold her captive, but she is finally rescued by her mother, her brother, and a policeman. After x rays are taken, all her relatives and friends visit her in the hospital and Julia decides that she has become famous.

Recovered and at home, Julia, to her delight, discovers that Maisie has found Felony and likes her, and she talks Mrs. Woollard into allowing Maisie to keep her. At about the same time, Julia learns from Uncle Hugh that her father's airplane was shot down, and her mother confirms the sad news.

Overcome by the news, Celia gets the flu. Both Gramma and Patchy-cat, who will not leave the patient's room, try to help out. The cat alerts Gramma and Julia when Celia loses consciousness, and fortunately they are able to "talk" her back. During Celia's recovery, Julia remembers her father's admonition in the dream, and after some problems, they find the papers, which prove to be a story, "In the Hot Golden Berry Garden." Julia's Mom works on her husband's written suggestions, then sends the story to a publisher.

When Uncle Hugh takes Celia, Greg, and Julia camping at Yosemite to give them a change, Julia experiences a series of wonders: the firefall at Glacier Point; the afterglow from Bridalveil Fall; an adventure with bears and a King snake; and a hill of boulders. But the excitement of the vacation is only a prelude for what is in the mail for them at home—an acceptance of Dad's story. Julia couldn't be happier. She and Patchy-cat are home and hungry and everything looks so much better.

Thematic Analysis

A rich and varied assortment of family members and friends—who well may exist for youngsters today—appear in this story. Julia's interaction with each is a blueprint that will be familiar to readers. This adventure in growing up also contains the traumatic event of a beloved parent's death and the child's reaction and eventual acceptance. Although the subtle theme of spirituality and intuitiveness is the essence of the story, with its familiar childhood events, the book may also be just plain enjoyed by young people.

Discussion Materials

After a brief introduction, some of the adventures can be highlighted: Julia on Greg's bike (transparency of the book jacket; pp. 1–7); Julia saves Mrs. Tittlemouse (pp. 27–30; picture p. 29); Felony is placed in the garden (pp. 41–43); Julia's accident and captivity (pp. 46–48); Julia and Greg (pp. 63–69); Julia experiences Yosemite's wonders (Chapter 14). Other growing-up experiences can be presented: Julia's desk (pp. 18–22, frontispiece, picture p. 20); Julia's letters to Dad (pp. 33, 36–39, 43); Julia learns of her father's death (pp. 76–80); and Julia's dream (pp. 49–53). Julia's understanding of the literary aspirations of her Dad and herself also can be explored: Julia's confrontation with Aunt Alex (pp. 10–11); Dad's pronouncement (p. 16); Dad's story (pp. 33–34); Julia and the promise (pp. 89–97, Chapter 13); and the publication of Dad's story (pp. 123–128). An especially poignant segment involves Julia, her mother and Gramma, and Patchy-cat during the serious flu incident (pp. 81–86).

Related Materials

In addition to the other titles in Beverly Cleary's Ramona series, another suggested book by Cleary is *Dear Mr. Henshaw* (Morrow, 1983). Books by others are: *Gift for Mama* (Viking, 1981) by Esther Hautzig; *Circle of Gold* (Scholastic, 1984) by Candy Dawson Boyd; *The Mother's Day Mice* (Clarion, 1986) by Eve Bunting; *Hand-Me-Down Kid* (Viking, 1980) by Francine Pascal; and *Annabelle Starr, E.S.P.* (Clarion, 1983) by Lila Perl.

Some audiovisual materials also can be used: A recording of Cleary's *Dear Mr. Henshaw* is available as a cassette from Random; Eleanor Estes's *Pinky Pye* is both a cassette and a record from Miller-Brody/Random; Robert Burch's *Queenie Peavey* is available as a record from Viking/Live Oak Media; Sharon Bell Mathis's *Hundred Penny Box* also comes as a record from Random; Mary Rodgers's *Billion for Boris*—a sequel to *Freaky Friday*—can be obtained from Listening Library as a paperback and cassette; *Ben's Dream*, a film of Chris Van Allsburgh's book available from Made-to-Order Library, displays notable film images through fine cinematic techniques. A filmstrip that shows the childhood recollections of Jean Fritz, *Homesick: My Own Story*, and recordings of Zilpha Keatley Snyder's two popular stories *Headless Cupid* and *Witches of Worm* are all available from Random.

Carris, Joan. *When the Boys Ran the House*
Illus. by Carol Newsom. Lippincott, 1982, 150 pp.

The author has fashioned a humorous book chock full of incidents with which youngsters from 9 to 12 (grades 4–7) will identify. In an engaging style, Joan Carris has written about four boys from 2 to 12½ who undertake the responsibility of keeping things going while their father is overseas on a business trip, their mother is ill, and their Aunt Martha who has been helping has to return home. Even though the family responsibility only lasts several weeks, Jut (Justin), the eldest, is kept busy and wonders what made him think he could handle it. The book will be useful with slower readers; episodes deal with basketball, insect collecting, goldfish swallowing, and a persistent quest for "the awful smell." The beloved family cat and dog are also interwoven into the story. The author's own experience with a crewful of boys shines through the book.

The nine pencil drawings by Carol Newsom—five full and four one-half pages—are expressive renderings of the family members. The full-color front jacket portrays the three younger boys—studious Marty, 10; lively Nick, 7; and Gus, a typical two-year-old—sitting at the kitchen table supervised by the smiling visiting nurse, "Amazon Brown," and serious Jut, 12½. Pierpont, the basset hound, and Eleanore, the furry cat, lap up spilt milk in the foreground. The back jacket carries a color illustration of Eleanore, who serves as the "fifth piece of business" in this story. The pictures enhance the story by introducing the characters with appropriate facial expressions.

When Aunt Martha has to leave unexpectedly, the four Howard boys have to run the house for several weeks while Mom is recovering from encephalitis. Dr. Collins agrees that while Mrs. Howard rests, Nurse Brown can visit. Meanwhile, Mrs. Thomas will come regularly to take care of Gus until Jut gets home and takes over the chores. In that way, Mr. Howard, who is on a vital European business trip for his new computer company, can be spared from knowing about the problem at home.

Jut feels proud—at least until Gus makes a puddle and he has to wipe it up. He makes a deal with Marty to diaper Gus, but from then on, each ordinary situation seems frustrating to him. Things begin to look up to basketball hopeful Jut when Nurse Brown, a very tall former basketball star whose "free throws" are spectacular, arrives. Jut learns a lot from her about basketball. He also learns a lot about running a house and managing youngsters. But when on his mother's advice, he gives Marty codirectorship, at least in name, Marty, a budding entomologist, is not able to get rid of the bees that take over the kitchen. Fortunately, the exterminators do. Then Nick decorates Eleanore with graffiti. Jut grits his teeth, patiently tells the younger boy to put his Magic Markers away, and proceeds to clean the cat. He even acquiesces to his mother's request that he substitute at Nick's second-grade Parents' Night—a difficult experience as it turns out, except for a friendly new resident who compliments him. Nick's expertise on junk food contributes further to Jut's discomfort during a supermarket visit.

Meanwhile, Gus swallows a goldfish while the others are trying to locate a bad odor that keeps getting worse. Some relief comes when Amazon Brown (as the boys dub the visiting nurse) takes them to a baseball game. Even Gus's disappearance there seems tolerable, especially when the scorebox announces that he is found. However, the smell near the fireplace continues to permeate the house no matter how well they clean. Then Marty finds out about secret passageways through the librarian.

In the midst of all this excitement, Mrs. Howard convinces Jut to take Marty on a hunting expedition as a special family birthday celebration. Marty is thrilled, especially when they bring home an assortment of squirrels and crows which they cook as a special dinner for Nurse Brown. Amazon Brown finds the fowl somewhat tough, even though she is a former farm girl, but when Nick blurts out that it is crow she politely does not speak out.

The boys finally find a secret panel by the fireplace when Nick unknowingly springs the hinge. There they discover Eleanore's kittens and a pile of dead mice that she had provided as food for them. Mrs. Howard—who is much better—is incensed. Although she loves the kittens, she was told Eleanore was spayed.

To the delight of all, Mr. Howard arrives home and finds his wife recovered, his sons well, and Jut resplendent with news of making the school basketball team. Jut also is proud of a job well done, but basically he's just plain happy to be a son again.

Thematic Analysis

Taking on the roles of mother and father with younger siblings, no matter how part-time, gives a youngster a tremendous sense of pride and motivation until reality sets in and a sense of retaining one's own role and growing up takes over. This theme, which is the core of the story, treats the growth of independence and the correlative necessity of getting along with family members according to their needs. The incidents cleverly demonstrate the unique characteristics of the various ages and the different personality of each individual.

Discussion Materials

Any episode dealing with the fundamental theme or any well-developed incident can be used in a presentation, perhaps beginning with a brief introduction (pp. 1–7) and including Gus making a puddle. Or a series of humorous episodes can be paraphrased: bees in the kitchen (pp. 22–25, 27–33); Eleanore and the Magic Markers (pp. 34–40); the supermarket adventure (pp. 50–62; picture p. 56); Gus's goldfish (pp. 63–71; picture p. 67); or the hunting party (pp. 96–105). Or a series involving Amazon Brown and basketball can include Nurse Brown (pp. 16–18; front jacket) and the baseball game (pp. 72–84, 106–122; pictures pp. 110, 119). For the recurring "awful smell" episodes use pages 85–95, 123–135, and the picture on page 127. To highlight Jut, you can paraphrase Parents' Night (pp. 41–49) or his basketball tryouts (pp. 138–142).

Related Materials

Sisters Impossible (Knopf, 1979) by James David Landis describes the developing interest of an older sister in ballet. A kit is available from Listening Library. In Tom Birdseye's title *I'm Going to Be Famous* (Holiday, 1986), fifth-grader Arlo tries to enter the *Guinness Book of Records* by gobbling 17 bananas in less than two minutes. His practice sessions on lemons are funny. *Jill the Pill* (Atheneum, 1980) by Julie Castiglia shows what it is like to be a nine-year-old sibling. Esther Hautzig's title *Life with Working Parents* (Macmillan, 1976, o.p.), offering realistic help for children in these circumstances, probably can be obtained through your library. Richard Peck's *The Ghost Belonged to Me* (Viking, 1975), available from Live Oak Media as a recording and a cassette, has one of the classic comediennes in recent children's literature as its heroine. Tom Davenport Films has produced a 16mm film, *Bearskin*, that also will be useful here. Two titles by Judy Delton can be suggested: *Back Yard Angel* and *Angel in Charge* (Houghton, 1983; 1985). *Sweet Whispers, Brother Rush* (Philomel, 1982), also available from Miller-Brody/Random as two filmstrips, is a fine suggestion for good readers and those who like secret passageways.

Cleary, Beverly. *Ramona, Forever*
Illus. by Alan Tiegreen. Morrow, 1984, 192 pp.

This award-winning author, whose titles are extremely popular with youngsters, continues to write interesting stories for young people. When *Ramona and Her Father* was highlighted in *Introducing More Books* (Bowker, 1978, pp. 171–174), Beverly Cleary had written 22 books. Today she has more than 28. Her heroine in the Ramona series has become a classic character whom we have watched grow. Ramona is the epitome of a feisty, young female with everyday concerns and fears that she is able to overcome in her progress toward getting along in the family. *Ramona, Forever*, the sixth in the series, will appeal to the many fans and youngsters ages 7– 9 (grades 2–4). The large-size type details the activities of the lovable Ramona and her family in ten chapters. The heroine, now a third-grader concerned with the coming baby and her father's employment, will strike a responsive chord in the reader.

Once again Alan Tiegreen illustrates with attractive, sharp pen-and-ink drawings. Each of the 11 full-page sketches of the main characters and the 22 one-half or three-quarter page illustrations captures the essence of the corresponding text with its facial expressions and lines of action. Children who don't already know what Ramona looks like will delight in the portraits. The colorful front jacket displays four portraits of Ramona of varying size: wearing sneakers; in red shorts with hands on hips; wearing a blue-and-white horizontally striped T-shirt; sporting the typical Ramona smile (read grimace) and Dutch-bobbed almost black hair. The background against which the small to large Ramona appears is reminiscent of the familiar wall yardstick for measuring height during childhood, or while "growing up!"

As the story opens on Klickitat Street in January, Ramona, a third-grader, is sitting down for supper with her family—Mother, who is still working; Father, who will graduate in June and is looking for a job as an art teacher; sister Beatrice (Beezus), who is in junior high; and Aunt Beatrice, who is Mom's younger sister and also a third-grade teacher. Ramona mentions that her friends' (Howie and Willa Jean's) "rich uncle" from Saudi Arabia is coming to visit the Kemps, and Aunt Bea immediately realizes that the same Hobart Kemp was her high school classmate.

At supper the following evening, the tearful Ramona recounts, at her father's urging, the day's tragedies with their babysitter, Mrs. Kemp, who babysits for Beezus and Ramona and her grandchildren, Howie and Willa Jean, after school, had reprimanded Ramona for her many misadventures with the unicycle and for playing the accordion Uncle Hobart had brought for his niece and nephew. Ramona never liked going to Mrs. Kemp's after school, but now she really resents it. To make matters worse, she can't stand Uncle Hobart and his insistence on serenading her by singing the song "Ramona." When Beezus agrees to babysit for them at home, the situation seems resolved. But staying home after school presents its problems, too. When Ramona gets bloodied riding Howie's bike (while he is riding his new unicycle), Beezus refuses to help because she overheard Ramona commenting that her face looks like an old pizza. The two sisters do bury their old cat, Picky-picky, together, however, sparing their mother and father the ordeal and hard work. Another afternoon at home, Beezus tells Ramona that she thinks Mother is going to have a baby around Thanksgiving, and Ramona then confirms the news with her father.

Soon after Mom announces that she expects the baby in July. Beezus hopes for a girl, Ramona a boy. Dad, who says he'll be happy with either, brings home a book of names. At first naming the baby becomes all important, but interest subsides after they refer to Mother's bulge as Algie. Then Father's employment becomes a pressing concern, when he gets a letter from a one-room schoolhouse quite far from Portland. Much as he would like to try teaching there, he decides that uprooting the family just now is out of the question. Ramona is secretly very happy.

She is, that is, until Aunt Bea and Hobart announce their impending July marriage after classes end. But Ramona perks up when she learns that they are leaving immediately afterward for Alaska where Aunt Bea already has a teaching job. Then when Aunt Bea says that they are not going to replace her in the Portland schools, Father saves the day with the news that he has become manager where he has been moonlighting.

With the wedding only two weeks away, everyone pitches in. Hobart takes Beezus and Ramona, the two bridesmaids, Willa Jean, the flower girl, and Howie, the protesting ring bearer, in tow to get the outfits, flowers, and sundries, and father promises food from his store. During this time, Ramona gains respect for gentle Hobart and his skill in accomplishing things. She also thinks highly of his ice cream treats. Grandpa Day arrives from California and hires a limousine. The ceremony goes off without a hitch, except that Howie drops the ring. Ramona, shoeless because the hand-me-downs are too tight, valiantly retrieves it and saves the day. After the wedding couple leaves, Grandpa Day suggests that they settle down to a pizza.

Within a few weeks, Roberta Day Quimby weighs in at six pounds four ounces. Ramona almost thinks that she really doesn't like cross-eyed Roberta, but when her Mother tells her how much she has missed her and how much Roberta resembles Ramona when she was a baby, in a flash Ramona becomes her wonderful self again.

Thematic Analysis

Four events interrupt Ramona's young existence—the arrival of Hobart and his marriage to Aunt Bea; the death and burial by the two sisters of the cat, Picky-picky; the hectic preparations for the madcap wedding; and the arrival of her baby sister, Roberta. The underlying theme in each is a youngster's coming to terms with difficulties that are part and parcel of family living. The story relates the vagaries of getting along with family members honestly and with deep understanding. A secondary theme—that of getting along with a sibling—is also clear.

Discussion Materials

Because the book works independently of the other titles in the Ramona series, it is not necessary for the reader to know Ramona in the preceding stories. Nonetheless, a brief retelling of the Quimby main characters will be useful. Any of the events can be employed for anecdotal material: the arrival of "the rich uncle" (pp. 2–16; pictures pp. 8, 18); the hustle-bustle preceding the wedding (pp. 98–138; pictures pp. 100, 104, 114, 117, 121, 127, 133); the wedding day (pp. 139, 159; pictures pp. 140, 144, 147, 157, 158; highlight pp. 151–153); Picky-picky's burial (pp. 61–75; pictures pp. 63, 70); the new baby (pp. 38–41, 42, 76, 77, 81–90, 160–161, 182; pictures pp. 43, 77, 84, 89, 163, 167, 172, 178); Ramona's interactions with Beezus (pp. 44–60; pictures pp. 49, 58); Ramona's bicycle adventures (pp. 50–54; picture p. 52). Include the pictures on p. 15 and the frontispiece. You can also use Ramona's problem (pp. 27–37; pictures pp. 24, 30, 31). An enlarged front jacket or a transparency or poster from Morrow will serve well here.

Related Materials

Be sure to mention the other books in the series: *Beezus and Ramona; Ramona the Pest; Ramona and Her Father; Ramona and Her Mother; Ramona Quimby, Age 8;* and *Ramona the Brave,* which are also available as paperbacks; records and cassettes can be obtained from Random. *Ramona, Forever* has just been released as a filmstrip, too. *Me, My Goat, and My Sister's Wedding* (Clarion, 1985) by Stella Pevsner about a young boy would be good to suggest here, as would *Sisters* (Harcourt, 1984) by David McPhail, a perfect picture book for the younger ones, illustrating well how individual likes and differences can generate love in a family. Another heroine to suggest is the main character in the following titles by Lois Lowry: *Anastasia Krupnik* (Houghton, 1979); *Anastasia Again* (Houghton, 1981); *Anastasia, Ask Your Analyst* (Houghton, 1984); and *Anastasia on Her Own* (Houghton, 1985). The series covers the events in a 10 to 13-year-old's everyday life.

For younger readers, suggest *Whatever Happened to Beverly Bigler's Birthday* by Barbara Williams (Harcourt, 1979), which tells how the seven-year-old feels when she thinks her birthday has been forgotten because of her sister's wedding. For older readers, there are Judy Blume's *Tales of a Fourth Grade Nothing* (Dutton, 1972) and *Superfudge* (Dutton, 1980), both of which are also available as a filmstrip or cassette from Pied Piper. Some may enjoy the hero in the following titles: *Case of the Missing Rattles* (Troll, 1982) by Robyn Supraner (kit of book, 48 pp., cassette, and four spirit masters available); *The Bungalo Boys* (Bungalo Books, 1986) by John Bianchi, a sequel to the popular Canadian title *The Dingles;* and *Malcolm Yucca Seed* (Harvey, 1977) by Lynne Gessner. The video *To Tell the Truth* (Churchill Films, 1986), scripted by Patricia Reilly Giff for grades 3–5, about some of the ordinary life situations in which youngsters find themselves, is bound to have a profound effect.

Jukes, Mavis.   *Like Jake and Me*
Pictures by Lloyd Bloom. Knopf, 1984, 32 pp.

For her first book for children, Mavis Jukes received the prestigious Newbery Honor Award for 1985. Her adult novel *No One Is Going to Nashville* (Knopf, 1983), also illustrated by Lloyd Bloom, received fine reviews as well. She employs a similarly subtle touch to describe young Alex's adoring relationship with his stepfather, Jake, and other relationships in this deceptively simple story. The author explores the youngster's desire to be like his stepfather through to his discovery that he can be of real help to Jake when a spider crawls on his neck. This vivid slice of a youngster's life is set in a calm farm-life atmosphere, with his pregnant mother, Virginia, quietly present. Because of the author's haunting style, Alex's life assumes an almost dreamlike quality, and youngsters ages 6–9 (grades 1–4) will find the story and pictures compelling.

Lloyd Boom's special way of painting with pastels—first discovered while working on this book—resulted in 15 full-page drawings of the three characters in the book. Bloom used muted shades of every color in nature—witness the purple shaded clouds, the golden brown pears, and the green glass bottle hanging from the tree in the frontispiece. The illustrator's drawings treat the author's gentle probing of deep relationships between the young and their parents in a reverential way that beautifully augments the text. Bloom's elongated figures are a sophisticated artistic touch for viewers.

Alex, around seven, idolizes his stepfather, Jake, a former cowboy. He is impressed, for example, with Jake's strong ax-swinging when he splits logs. At the same time, small boy that he is, he loves his Mom, Virginia, and is interested in her anticipated present to Aunt Caroline—the pears in a bottle that Virginia put over a twig on the pear tree in the spring. It is practically autumn, and the pears will soon be ready to pluck—at about the same time the birth of the twins is expected. When Alex asks Mom if the twins will be like Jake, he is somewhat surprised to hear Mom reply that they may be a little like both Jake and her. This new thought is very satisfying, and Alex can barely contain himself. He then shows Mom the jump step that he learned in the ballet lessons that his entomologist father had signed him up for.

Later, while he is helping Jake fill the wood stove, Alex tells Jake about his loose tooth, confessing that he is "too chicken" to pull it out. As he is explaining this, he comments on the wolf spider on Jake's neck. In Jake's ensuing panic, to the point of stripping down to his shorts with Alex's help, Alex realizes that Jake is as much afraid of bugs as Alex is of pulling his tooth. When Jake thanks Alex for his help in getting rid of the spider, Jake and Alex dance and twirl around in triumph. Jake's dancing relieves Alex's own feelings of embarrassment about his ballet lessons. As Virginia rubs her belly and announces that the twins are dancing, too, it is another important moment in young Alex's life. As they whirl around the porch, he truly feels part of a family.

Thematic Analysis

A youngster's discovery that he can be truly related to all his immediate family is the ultimate lesson of getting along in the family. That you can be like an adored stepfather (mother), and that he can be like you, is personified in the title *Like Jake and Me*. That new siblings (or stepsiblings) can share the same strengths and fears as Mom and Dad or stepparents is a wonderful revelation. Learning about yourself and human potential is important for growing youngsters. As a secondary theme, getting along in a stepfamily is treated humanely and realistically by an understanding Mom.

Discussion Materials

This complex story, which is simple on the surface, can be introduced in many ways. For the youngest or slower readers, display the oversize picture pages and paraphrase the story. For those who are in more advanced grades or better readers, after briefly announcing the three characters, choose a strand of the story and paraphrase it while displaying the appropriate pictures: how to put growing pears in a bottle (frontispiece, back jacket, pp. 3–4); Jake swings an ax (pp. 2, 7–8, 9–10); Alex finds a wolf spider on Jake (pp. 11–26). At the end, hint at the final page and picture (pp. 27–28). Or for older readers, the jacket can be used to introduce the book, stressing a quiet mood.

Related Materials

Here are a few of the many related materials: *The New Baby* (Putnam, 1985) by Fred Rodgers discusses soothingly the feelings that children of expectant mothers harbor. Lauren Krasny and Marc Brown also have written a comforting book, *Dinosaur's Divorce: A Guide for Changing Families* (Atlantic/Little, 1986). The 16mm film *I Know a Secret* (Beacon Films, 1983), about a young girl who mistakenly thinks she is a local peddler's daughter, can be shown. The filmstrip *Ben's Trumpet* (Random), based on Rachel Isador's 1980 ALA Notable Honor Book, also will be useful. Pat Hutchins's title *The Very Worst Monster* (Greenwillow, 1985), about monster sibling rivalry, will be effective for the youngest. *Mouse and His Child* can be obtained from Caedmon as a record and a cassette, read by Peter Ustinov and abridged from Russell Hoban's book. Three titles that can be suggested to the older crowd are: *A Book for Jodan* (Atheneum, 1975, o.p.) by Marcia Newfield, about a youngster who thinks he is responsible for his parents' divorce; *Don't Make Me Smile* (Knopf, 1981) by Barbara Park, about 11-year-old Charles and his agonized feelings at his parents' divorce; and *Things Won't Be the Same* (Harcourt, 1980) by Kathryn Ewing, about Marcy's adjustment to the divorce in her family. Random has both

Thimble Summer by Elizabeth Enright and *The Fledgling* by Jane Langton available in record and cassette. The famous title by Elizabeth Enright describes Garnet's happiness on a farm in Wisconsin; the second—a Newbery Honor Award-winner—tells about eight-year-old Georgie and her extended family. Random has just released a read-along cassette and hardcover of *Like Jake and Me*. Parts of it will be helpful as a segment in the book talk.

McCully, Emily Arnold. *Picnic*
Illus. by the author. Harper, 1984, 32 pp.

Although she has written adult fiction and illustrated more than 100 books for children, this is the first book for children for which this well-known illustrator is solely responsible. Emily McCully's poster "Book Power," commissioned by the Children's Book Council, was well recognized in the 1970s. She is responsible for the distinctive illustrations in numerous award books, as well as many books that are popular with youngsters (see *Introducing More Books*, Bowker, 1978, p. 32). Watercolors outlined in broken pen lines appear throughout this warm, wordless story about family solidarity, which can be used as a picture book for the youngest, as a discussion aid for those in grades K–3 (ages 5–8), and also can be helpful with the reluctant and special reader.

Fully opened, the jacket portrays a mouse family's arrival at a lake. The red truck that brings them and the green rolling hills surrounding the meadow are a lush backdrop for the frolicking mice who are unaware that the youngest is missing. The title page shows five of the nine mouse youngsters (including the baby holding a pink doll mouse) helping Mama fix the wicker hamper, while Papa tunes the truck. This introduction invites one to turn the page to the double-page frontispiece, which shows the family climbing helter-skelter into their truck and leaving their cottage home.

As the journey begins, the viewer is treated to three pictures of the backless truck careening over a rutty, boulder-filled road. In the third picture, the mouse baby and pink doll are flung skyward and both land, as the next double spread shows, squarely in the road unharmed, but sadly watching a disappearing truck. The next double spread shows the family arriving at its destination. Everybody goes about their business:

Mama and Papa look for a place to spread the picnic, one mouse tests the lake's diving board, one picks flowers, and two cavort. This activity continues in the next full-page illustration as Mama and Papa watch contentedly. But, on the following page, the viewer sees the tiny mouse clutching the doll while big tears fall on the gravel road, and the next two full-page illustrations show the baby mouse walking until some raspberry bushes loom nearby.

Then the food is spread on the checkered tablecloth. Mama pours the milk and one of the older children rounds up the others—one of the younger ones sticks a finger in the salad. Meanwhile, as the next illustrations show, the littlest mouse is busily stuffing raspberries into his mouth. When Grandma, Grandpa, Mama, and Papa line up everybody beside the picnic cloth to start, they count only eight children. Everyone looks high and low for the youngest mouse, until finally they put everything away and return to the truck. Back at the raspberry bushes, Baby has finished all but two raspberries and rested before he returns to the road and is reunited with his happy family. After all the kisses and hugs, Baby scurries back to the raspberry bushes to rescue his missing doll. Happily the restored family parks the truck once again and celebrates with a picnic.

Thematic Analysis

Being lost or abandoned is one of childhood's earliest and strongest fears. This wordless picture book reassuringly presents the comfort of caring among parents, grandparents, and siblings. The soft watercolors, and the strong story line that they evoke, provoke a sense of reassurance. Family strength and love is implicit in the story, which is told magnificently in the illustrations.

Discussion Materials

A typical picture-book presentation is one way to introduce this book. Another is to show the extended jacket and tell the children that this family of grandparents, parents, and nine brother and sister mice has gone on a picnic, but doesn't know yet that baby mouse and his pink doll have flown out of the truck (p. 3); leave the resolution unstated, but suggest that it is happy. After introducing the story line, you can display the pages showing baby mouse alone and hunting raspberries (pp. 4, 5, 11, 12, 13, 16, 17, 23, 25, 26, 27, 28, and 29). Or you might show the family scenes prior to the discovery that baby mouse is missing (pp. 6, 7, 8, 9, 10, 14, 15, 18, 19).

Related Materials

Sunshine (Lothrop, 1981) by Jan Ormerod is a notable wordless picture book that describes a family's morning activities. *Max's Christmas* (Dial, 1986) by Rosemary Wells, the latest in a popular series that deals with familiar childhood experiences, should appeal to the same youngsters who like *Picnic*. *Benny Bakes a Cake* (Greenwillow, 1981) by Eve Rice tells about the family rallying around when the dog eats the cake. Mordecai Gerstein's *The Room* (Harper, 1984) humorously describes zany characters. *Anna and the Seven Swans* (Morrow, 1984) by Maida Silverman retells the rescue of baby Ivan by Anna from the witch Baba Yaga. David Small's illustrations help to make it a captivating experience for children. *Bunnicula . . .* (Atheneum, 1980) by Deborah Howe and James Howe is a funny story purportedly written by Harold, the dog; Chester, the cat; and Bunnicula, the rabbit; a newcomer in the Monroe family. An abridged LP record and cassette read by Lou Jacobi (60 min.) can be obtained from Caedmon. *Corduroy* (Weston Woods, 1985), based on Don Freeman's popular book, is available as both a 16mm film and a videocassette. *John Jacob Jingleheimer Schmidt: The Songs We Sang at Summer Camp* (Filmakers Library, 1985), an exhilarating melodic experience of childhood that doesn't change, is available in both 16mm film and videocassette. Two pictures from *Paddington Bear* (Eden Toys/dist. by Caedmon) by Michael Bond; a recording read by Michael Bond of *Paddington Soundbook* (Caedmon, 1979); and filmstrips of *Paddington at Large* and *Paddington on Top* (both Learning Tree, 1983) will definitely enhance this book presentation, as will the filmstrip *Picnic* (Weston Woods, 1986).

MacLachlan, Patricia.   *Sarah, Plain and Tall*
Harper, 1985, 58 pp.

This Newbery Award-winner is a gentle story about the hopes and fears of a motherless prairie farm family that welcomes Sarah, a spinster from Maine, as a prospective mother. Youngsters ages 8–10 (grades 3–5) will find the story appealing, both for its gentle probing of the feelings of a young boy and his older sister, and also for its slim size. The economy of words and the fluid writing style are hallmarks of the author's writing that can also be enjoyed in her several picture books and novels for young people: *Arthur, for the Very First Time; Cassie Binegar;* and *Unclaimed Treasures.*

Although this book is devoid of illustrations—the descriptions of place are so vivid that they might be superfluous anyway—it has a fine pencil sketch by Marcia Sewall on the jacket. The softness of the artistic medium and the artist's ability to portray the feelings of the three main characters through their expressions create an arresting image. Sitting on the porch steps, plain Sarah cuts young Caleb's hair, happily overseen by older sister Anna. Sarah's cat, Seal, lies contentedly on a step.

Anna, who is preparing the evening supper stew, replies for the ten thousandth time to Caleb's request to tell what their mother said when he was born, because she realizes that they both are hurt. Caleb because he never knew his mother, who died the day after he was born, and she because she didn't even say good night before she died. When their father, Jacob Witting, tells them that he has written a letter for a new bride the way his neighbor Matthew did, they are pleasantly surprised. Now their neighbor family is Matthew, Maggie, and two small girls, Rose and Violet, and they like Maggie from Tennessee. They are even more hopeful when their father shows them a reply from Sarah Elizabeth Wheaton, saying that she will come for a trial month and bring her cat, Seal. When Jacob replies, he includes the children's question "Does she sing?" Anna has told Caleb often that their Mama and Papa used to sing all the time.

Sarah writes to all of them: to Anna she writes that she does braid hair and describes her fisherman brother, William; to Caleb she writes that her cat is not as large as their dogs, Lottie and Nick, and that she can make fires, and that she doesn't know if she snores; to Papa she writes that she will be wearing a yellow bonnet on arrival, and that she is plain and tall—at the bottom she says simply, "Tell them I sing." In the spring, Papa hitches up Old Bess and Wild Jack to go to town to fetch her.

When Sarah arrives, everyone loves her. They hope she will stay and make them a family, instead of returning to her beloved Maine sea. They pick wildflowers and walk through the prairie grass. Sarah cuts their hair and teaches them to scatter it for the birds' nests; she teaches them to sing "Summer Is Icumen In"; she tells them about her three old aunts; she draws pictures to send back to Maine; she even starts a charcoal drawing of the prairie grass; and she takes them swimming in the waterin' hole in the cow pasture. Jacob makes her a dune of hay and brings her bunches of June roses. Maggie and her girls come to visit and suggest that she plant a garden. In fact, as soon as Sarah learns to ride, Maggie invites her over to get some tansy for her garden. Meanwhile,

Sarah helps Papa plow the fields and fix the roof (she had announced early on that she was both rugged and independent), as well as helping Anna with the cooking and chores. In return she insists that Papa teach her to hitch up the wagon and ride Wild Jack.

Then one day, almost a month later, she announces that she is going into town and hitches the wagon. While she is gone, Caleb wonders what she is doing. Anna and he are so fearful that she is leaving to go back to Maine. After a long day of worry by all three Wittings, Sarah comes back with three colored pencils—blue, gray, and green—to make her drawings of the prairie grass look more like the sea, the way it did after a local squall. Everybody is so happy that Sarah will stay. In honor of Sarah, Jacob will even say "ayuh" for "yes" during the wedding ceremony. Caleb and Anna will say "ayuh" silently, too.

Thematic Analysis

The importance of a mother or mother-surrogate in the lives of the young is shown simply in this appealing story. The necessary ingredients of the family unit, regardless of the time, are stressed. Also treated is the young's ability to manage in a family with or without all the requisite members. A pervading secondary theme to which all human beings can relate, regardless of age, is the feeling of longing and loneliness. The difference between locales (seacoast and farmland in this example) is also a tertiary theme, and the subtle imposition on one's thoughts and attitudes of a given locale serves as a thread of continuity for the story.

Discussion Materials

This title with its nine short chapters only needs a simple introduction. A transparency of the front jacket makes a good background while you introduce the prairie farmer Jacob Witting, his children, Anna and Caleb, his Maine-bred mail-order bride, Sarah Elizabeth Wheaton, and her cat, Seal (pp. 1–15; the letters, pp. 9, 11–13, 15). The squall is a good anecdote to illustrate the family in an emergency. If you are book talking to a group of readers, little persuading will be needed; for slower readers, the book will make a good read-aloud.

Related Materials

Of particular interest is the author's *Arthur, for the Very First Time* (Harper, 1980), about a ten-year-old boy who has a most unusual summer. Also worth suggesting is MacLachlan's *Seven Kisses in a Row* (Harper, 1983), about seven-year-old Emma and her older brother, Zach, who are being cared for by a young aunt and uncle. Robert Burch's *Ida Early Comes over the Mountain* (Viking, 1980), about the Suttons, who are relieved from their aunt's bossiness when Ida appears to take care of them, and its successor, *Christmas with Ida Early* (Viking, 1983), are both appropriate. *Stairstep Farm: Anna Rose's Story* (Philomel, 1981) by Anne Pellowski will also be useful. *Farm Animals* (Holiday, 1984) by Dorothy Hinshaw Patent is a nonfiction account with photographs. Two titles for the younger group are *Superduper Teddy* (Morrow, 1980) by Johanna Hurwitz, about five-year-old Teddy and his seven-year-old sister, Nora, and *The Story of Jumping Mouse* (Lothrop, 1982) by John Steptoe, which is also available as a filmstrip from Random, with Jamake Highwater as narrator.

Rylant, Cynthia. *When I Was Young in the Mountains*
Illus. by Diane Goode. Dutton, 1982, 32 pp.

The author rates a Caldecott Honor Award for this, her first book. Cynthia Rylant has since written others—the most recent, *Night in the Country* (Bradbury, 1986). In her award-winning title, the author's reminiscences of the countryside around Grandpa and Grandma's Appalachian home are appealing. She captures the joy in ordinary experiences that each reader remembers or is experiencing. This evocative style makes the work noteworthy. A young mountain girl about eight and her younger brother live with their grandparents in rural Appalachia. Their savoring of everyday opportunities and their love of their grandparents will appeal to youngsters between 5 and 10 (grades K–5).

The illustrations, which are an integral part of this oversize book, add to the love of place and family that suffuses the story. In muted shades of blue, green, and brown, shaded with pencil and highlighted with white pastel, Diane Goode presents a soft, loving look about a young girl and boy in their comfortable way of life and with their wonderful grandparents. She has captured a special slow-paced way of life that, although departed for most, closely resembles childhood for some.

The story actually opens on the front jacket, which portrays the two youngsters with a dog standing beside a large tree. They are smiling contentedly at a small cabin in which they live with their grandparents;

the cabin is snuggled peacefully on a nearby hill drenched in the moon and stars. A small, framed picture of a bare-branched tree bathed in night lights and shadows decorates the back jacket. A small drawing on the title page shows the cabin visible through the branches of a tree, rooted in a winter setting, while the dedication page displays some common table implements of the time—a hurricane lamp and a few flowers. The reader is now ready to enter the electricity-less world of the youngsters who describe their ordinary experiences.

The remembered events begin with Grandfather who, returning from the coal mines covered with soot, places a kiss on top of the young girl's head, and receives a pitcher of water from the young boy. They all sit around the kitchen table at supper devouring the usual steaming hot corn bread, pinto beans, and fried okra. Because everything tastes so good, the young girl eats too much and later that night her Grandmother accompanies her to the outhouse. The two youngsters engage in such everyday activities as going to the swimming hole, stopping at the Crawford's general store to smell the sweet milk, pumping well water for their baths in tin buckets, sipping cocoa from the old black wood stove afterward, going to church on Sundays, standing on the river bank for baptisms, watching Grandmother kill a black snake with a hoe, posing with young friends with the dead snake draped across their necks for a traveling photographer, and shelling beans at night on the porch swing with Grandmother, while Grandfather whittles and brother plays with the dogs. Contentment is the core of her life. As the young girl sits on a ladder reading, she comments that her home in the mountains is always enough.

Thematic Analysis

A deep strand in this story is the young girl's realization that what she has is wonderful. The special relationship between the grandparents, who are really the parents, and the youngsters is part of this. The warmth and gentleness of each childhood moment will not be lost on the child reader and viewer, who will respond positively to the assurance and love that surround the children in the story.

Discussion Materials

This story is easy to present in the usual picture-book style. The wonderfully evocative full- and double-page spreads tell the story well to any viewer. A discussion can be held afterward, showing the scenes that revolve around life as it was in Appalachia when the audience's parents and grandparents were young: a general store (pp. 9–10); an outhouse (p. 6); the "ole swimmin' hole" (pp. 7–8); pumping well water (p. 12); the black wood stove (p. 14); and many others will provide a raft of questions. A general presentation of the main characters and locale also makes a good introduction (front of book jacket; Grandfather, p. 2; Grandmother, p. 4). If family companionship is highlighted, use the family table (p. 4) and in the evenings (p. 24). For fun and excitement, use Grandmother and her hoe attacking the snake (pp. 19–20), and the youngsters photographed with the snake (p. 22).

Related Materials

A filmstrip adaptation of this lyric title is available from Random. Two other titles by Cynthia Rylant are *Waiting to Waltz: A Childhood* and *The Relatives Came* (both Bradbury, 1984; 1985), both illustrated by Stephen Gammell. The former describes adolescence in Appalachia; the second enlarges the family. Vera B. Williams's *Something Special for Me; Music, Music for Everyone;* and *A Chair for My Mother* (all Greenwillow, 1983; 1984; 1982) are strong family stories. The latter title received a Caldecott Honor designation in 1983; it is also a filmstrip from Random. *Cathy Fink and Friends: Grandma Slid Down the Mountain,* which fits well here, is available from Rounder Records as a disc and cassette. Dylan Thomas's *A Child's Christmas in Wales,* a breathtaking recollection of the family holiday with all its foibles and tenderness, can be obtained from Films, Inc., as a 16mm film or videocassette, or as a book (Holiday, 1985) illustrated by Trina Schart Hyman for grades 3–6. Two titles not to be overlooked for this group are Thomas Locker's *Where the River Begins* (Dial, 1984), which shows the companionship between grandfather and grandson as they explore the river, and Amy Hest's *The Purple Coat* (Macmillan, 1986), about a young girl and her tailor grandfather who devises a way to make her a desired coat. Locker's gorgeous illustrations evoke feelings of the wonders of the earth and its inhabitants. Transparencies of some of the fine illustrations in all of the books mentioned are a great aid.

Getting Along in the Family: Additional Titles

Bawden, Nina. *Kept in the Dark.* Lothrop, 1982, 160 pp. (Gr. 4–6)
The Cap. Film, 26 min., also available on video. Beacon Films, 1986. (Gr. 3–5)

Children of the Tribe. Japan series. Film, 28 min., also available on video. National Film Board of Canada, 1981. (Gr. 5–up)

Cleaver, Vera. *Sugar Blue.* Lothrop, 1984, 155 pp. (Gr. 4–6)

Cross, Gillian. *On the Edge.* Holiday, 1985, 170 pp. (Gr. 5–8)

Gaines, Ernest. *Long Day in November.* Drawings by Don Bolognese. Dial, 1971, 137 pp. (Gr. 5–6)

Gerson, Corinne. *Tread Softly.* Dial, 1979, 133 pp. (Gr. 4–6)

Heyn, Jean. *Tessie C. Price.* Illus. by Claude Howell. John F. Blair, 1979, 210 pp. (Gr. 5–6)

Howe, Fanny. *Race of the Radical.* Viking, 1985, 144 pp. (Gr. 5–8)

Howjadoo. Recording or cassette. Rounder Records, 1985. (all ages)

Kessler, Ethel, and Kessler, Leonard. *The Sweeneys from 9D.* Macmillan, 1985, 56 pp. (Gr. 1–4)

Langton, Jane. *Her Majesty, Grace Jones.* Illus. by Emily Arnold McCully. Harper, 1972, 189 pp. (Gr. 4–6)

Lewin, Hugh. *Jafta—The Journey.* Illus. by Lisa Kopper. Carolrhoda, 1984, 24 pp. (Gr. 1–4)

Little Dragon and Other Stories by Jay O'Callahan. Recording, 2s 33rpm. Weston Woods, 1982. (Gr. 2–4)

Little, Jean. *From Anna.* Pictures by Joan Sandin. Harper, 1972, 201 pp. (Gr. 4–6)

Lord, Athena V. *Today's Special: Z.A.P. and ZOE.* Illus. by Jean Jenkins. Macmillan, 1984, 150 pp. (Gr. 3–5)

Mahy, Margaret. *Haunting.* Atheneum, 1982, 135 pp. (Gr. 4–6)

Michael, Mark. *Toba.* Illus. by Neil Waldman. Bradbury, 1984, 112 pp. (Gr. 5–up)

Milton, Hilary. *Mayday, Mayday.* Watts, 1979, 152 pp. (Gr. 4–6)

Nelson, Theresa. *The Twenty-Five Cent Miracle.* Bradbury, 1986, 224 pp. (Gr. 5–8)

Perl, Lila. *That Crazy April.* Clarion, 1974, 188 pp. (Gr. 5–6)

Pfeffer, Susan Beth. *Kid Power.* Illus. by Leigh Grant. Watts, 1977, 121 pp. (Gr. 4–6)

Pippi Longstocking. Recording, 2s 33rpm, also available as a kit (fs & pap.) from Listening Library. Live Oak Media, 1973. (Gr. 3–5)

Robinson, Nancy K. *Oh Honestly, Angela!* Scholastic, 1985, 128 pp. (Gr. 4–6)

Rodowsky, Colby. *Hi, My Name Is Henley.* Farrar, 1982, 183 pp. (Gr. 4–6)

The Silver Cow. Filmstrip. Weston Woods, 1986. (Gr. 1–4)

Smith, Alison. *Help! There's a Cat Washing in Here!* Illus. by Amy Rowen. Dutton, 1981, 152 pp. (Gr. 4–6)

Stanek, Muriel. *All Alone after School.* Illus. by Gay Owens. Albert Whitman, 1985, 32 pp. (Gr. 1–4)

Voigt, Cynthia. *Dicey's Song.* Atheneum, 1982, 196 pp. (Gr. 5–6)

———. *Homecoming.* Atheneum, 1981, 312 pp. (Gr. 5–6)

Williams, Barbara. *Mitzi and the Terrible Tyrannosaurus Rex.* Illus. by Emily Arnold McCully. Dutton, 1982, 112 pp. (Gr. 3–5)

2

Making Friends

FRIENDSHIP is so natural a quality that most people tend to forget that it is an acquired trait. For many it is hard won, difficult for all. Children reach the developmental stage for making friends early in their life—as young as three for many—just as they are hopefully making progress toward getting along in their family group. These tasks are somewhat dependent on each other in the sense that an easy and early resolution of the latter helps in making friends. Because of such myriad factors as personality and various social and economic circumstances, youngsters are not always able to achieve a satisfactory conclusion. The difficulties that may arise as a result may cause varying degrees of emotional turmoil.

Adults can often observe a young person making friends one day and withdrawing the next. This retrogression is customary, with each step toward the ultimate goal of making friends a victory. These early accomplishments, which are easier for the child who has a secure footing in the family unit, can facilitate later sexual ones. The ability to cooperate or share within a group, another consequence of making friends, is vital for the future citizens of American democracy, as well as for the entire planet.

The books that follow stress a wide variety of situations in which the young person may find identification and comfort in his quest. These heroes range from the very young, who are just beginning to discover how to make friends, to the older youngster who still has to proceed through the years of puberty, when sexual attraction will complicate the procedure. There are books of prose and poetry for beginning readers, of learning to evaluate and interpret friendship, of historical practices in Europe and America in the 1800s, of friendship for horse lovers, and of the making of friends in all the tragic proportions that haunt humanity. They should provide enjoyment and a fine vicarious experience for youngsters who are already able to make friends, for those who are in unusual circumstances, and for those who are just beginning to try to make friends.

Bank Street College of Education. Child Study Children's Book Committee, comp. *Friends Are Like That! Stories to Read to Yourself*
Crowell, 1979, 114 pp.

With friendship as its theme, this title has stories by such famous authors as Charlotte Zolotow, John Steptoe, Carolyn Haywood, and others—ten in all. Selected by a committee of educators, librarians, authors, illustrators, and others, these stories will appeal to children ages 8–10 (grades 3–5), either as independent reading or as read-aloud. The Committee has functioned for more than half a century as a division of the Child Study Association of America and is now affiliated with Bank Street College. It is responsible for an annual publication, as well as more than a dozen books that started as the well-known Read-to-Me series.

Eighteen full black-and-white pen drawings by the well-recognized Leigh Grant are accompanied by a framed two-color vignette on the book jacket of three young friends playing ball. The pen sketches—two for each story but the first and last—are wonderful examples of pointillism, which, by the artistic style of shading, indicates well the nonprejudicial nature for which the association has long been known.

James Flora's selection, "Why I Like Charlie," from his book *My Friend Charlie,* opens this title and in 2½ pages lists the qualities of friendship that one little boy about nine or ten values in his friend. The episode from *I Need a Friend* by Sherry Kafka closes the book with a 2½-page poem that enunciates all of the things that the androgynous youngster pictured can do alone, concluding in each verse that it is better done with a friend. Three stories illustrate a pertinent way of looking at friendship. The "Me and Neesie" selection, from the book with the same title by Eloise Greenfield, treats Janell, a small black girl, and her imaginary friend, just before she looks forward to going to a new school and playing with new friends the next day. In "Tim and Mr. B," the young boy spends a happy summer making a "gran-friend," Mr. B, who dies in a fall at age 86 after school has started. Tim is saddened but realizes that he will never forget what he learned from his friend. "Ann Aurelia and Dorothy" by Natalie Savage Carlson, from a book of the same title, is about two young girls who meet and become friends over a pair of broken glasses, only to discover that they will be in the same grade.

Thematic Analysis

Each of the slices from the chosen books illustrates friendship between two children or a significant other person. In addition to the different sexes of the protagonists, there are rural and urban settings, varying economic levels, and a variety of situations involving different ages and the many aspects of friendship.

Discussion Materials

Although the book talker can use any of the stories to advantage in introducing the book, the following choices are suggested. "Boys Just Can't Keep a Secret," from Astrid Lindgren's book *Happy Times in Noisy Village*, bears retelling. One can either read pages 20–31 or paraphrase the story of the three young girls and the three young boys in Middle Farm, Sweden, who play together but separately. The girls find the boys' secret—a tunnel in the hay—but will the boys find the girls'—strawberry patches? Be sure to display and perhaps enlarge the two illustrations that accompany this middle-grade story of group or "gang" friendship. Roberta Greene's *Two and Me Makes Three* gives the reader the selection "Two and Me Makes Three," listing the many activities a multiethnic group of three urban boys can do, even to saying "I'm sorry," in the interest of making and keeping friends. The two illustrations that accompany this selection will add to the retelling, if displayed. The poem "I Need a Friend," from a book of the same title by Sherry Kafka, will also make an excellent introduction to this title. In lovely verse it states the theme of friendship, which is the essence of the selection and the book. "All by myself/ I can play alone/ But I need a friend for sharing."

Related Materials

A collection of poetry by Lee Bennett Hopkins, *Surprises* (Harper, 1984), is for beginning readers and others who are entranced by poetry. *Best Friends* (Dial, 1986) by Steven Kellogg, a picture book worth looking at, is about some of the high and low spots of friendship in childhood. *Three Ducks Went Wandering* (Houghton/Clarion, 1980) by Ron Roy is an amusing fantasy about an interracial group of friends. *Beany* (Pantheon,

1980) by Jane Feder tells about a small boy and his beloved cat. E. W. Hildick, a popular author in the middle grades, has written a title in his McGurk series, *The Case of the Phantom Frog* (Macmillan, 1980), about the McGurk Organization and how it solves the mystery of a "werefrog" while babysitting a seven-year-old Hungarian boy. It can also be obtained as a motivational (without ending) cassette (Listening Library, 1984). The filmstrip *Two Roman Mice* (Educational Enrichment Materials, 1982) will appeal to some middle-graders. *A Treasury of Hans Christian Andersen* (nine tales; Miller-Brody, 1973) and *The Ugly Duckling* (Weston Woods, 1977) can be obtained as filmstrips. The latter title is also available as a record from Caedmon. The information and black-and-white photographs in Joan Anderson's *The First Thanksgiving Feast* (Clarion, 1984) are strikingly illustrative of friendship in bygone times as seen here in the Plimouth Plantation.

Beatty, Patricia. *Behave Yourself, Bethany Brant*
Morrow, 1986, 172 pp.

This award-winning author—the Jane Addams Children's Book honor book designation for *Lupita Manana* and the author of several NCSS notable titles—is noted for her exhilarating adventure stories set in a historical background, generally in the Wild West (see pp. 1.19+ in *Behave Yourself, Bethany Brant*). (One of her earlier works, *How Many Miles to Sundown*, is condensed in *Introducing More Books*, Bowker, 1978, pp. 22–26.) In the title under discussion—another of Patricia Beatty's commendable books—two youngsters in Texas during the turn of the century lose their mother. They go to live on a farm with their uncle, aunt, and cousins until their circuit-riding preacher father collects sufficient funds to build a new manse in which to dwell as minister. It is also the story of an independent 13-year-old and her brother, 11, who learn to accommodate to life among strangers and become best friends with an equally independent cousin. The rip-roaring story, with the ambience of Texas at the turn of the century, will appeal to all from age 9 to 13 (grades 4–8). Beatty's deft characterizations, strong plot, and thorough research into the place and time carry the story once again. She outlines the research in her customary "Note," which should be read both before and after the book.

The three main characters, Bethany, Abel, and their father, Minister Nathaniel Brant, appear in full-color tones of yellow, brown, and blue in the front jacket illustration by Daniel San Souci. The patient and determined Brants sit on a wooden plank at the Prineville, Texas, railroad station waiting for their relatives. In the background, the prefabricated and unfinished town rises behind them. The artist's rendering illustrates the family's solidarity well.

Eleven-year-old Bethany Clarinda Brant and her brother, nine-year-old Abel, accompany their parents, Nathaniel and Dulcie, to a county fair in their hometown, Blue Fork, during the summer of 1898. Although Pa is a local minister, and Bethany knows that a preacher's kid, especially a female, is expected to be holier than most, she also knows that she has a plain-wicked part. This is her fourth fair and once her family has split up, she hightails it to the fortune-teller's tent, which costs her 5 cents of her precious total of 15 cents. Queen Fareeta tells Bethany that she will move soon, have some bad and good news, have a friend-in-need in a one-eyed man, and have elephants in her future. With her usual oath, "Frog Warts," Bethany wonders how she can avoid telling Pa that she went to a fortune-teller.

When they get home, Mama is feeling poorly. Bethany learns that she is going to have a baby around the New Year. But, as fall begins with Bethany in fifth grade and Abel in third, Mama continues to lose strength. Soon after New Year, Mama and the new baby brother die. Everybody can cry, except Bethany. Queen Fareeta's fortune starts to come true. Because the Blue Fork manse holds too many memories, Pa returns to circuit riding. Bethany and Abel go to live with Mama's only brother, Uncle Luke Morris, in Prineville, about 100 miles west in cattle country. His wife, Aunt Reva, is delighted. Bethany not only can help care for their new baby boy, Billy Bob, who is about the same age as the dead baby, but will also be able to tutor their unschooled daughter, Mattywill, who is about Bethany's age, so that she can be in the sixth grade with Bethany. Abel can help Uncle Luke tend the cattle. Meanwhile, Pa can settle as a minister in Prineville as soon as the deacon raises funds to build the manse.

At the beginning of summer, the Brants leave on a train to Prineville. It takes them two days to get to the newly settled land. Mattywill, at first mistaken for a boy, picks them up. She comments that wearing trousers makes doing chores easier. She also expresses enthusiasm about learning to read better so that she can be in the sixth rather than fourth grade in the fall. Two of Queen Fareeta's prophecies have come true.

During the summer, while Deacon Cass, a ne'er-do-well and the mayor's son, collects money for the manse, Bethany helps Aunt Reva with the household chores while Mattywill and Abel help Uncle Luke with the cattle. Bethany also spends time each evening trying to tutor Mattywill. Each is trying in her own way to be friends. However, Bethany resents doing all the "female" chores and Mattywill wishes she could be perfect like Bethany.

When the circus (with elephants) arrives in Prineville, Bethany knows that Queen Fareeta's fortune-telling is close to being three-quarters correct. Lady Peaches, an elephant who has been trained by a bareback rider, plucks Bethany onto her back and keeps her in the river with the herd while a crowd gathers on the bank. When she is safe again, there is little doubt that the courageous Bethany will be the July Fourth "Miss Columbia: The Gem of the Ocean." As a bonus for her courage, folks take up a special collection for the manse. As an extra bonus, Billy Bob gets to be the "best-looking baby" at the fair.

When school opens, Mattywill is put in the fifth grade by the new teacher, Miss Penny, who is being pursued by Deacon Cass. Bethany finds a new friend in sixth grade, Callie Stark, the daughter of the bartender at the Dutchman Saloon where the deacon spends a lot of time, who gives her an unexpected gift of lice. With Mattywill sullen and the Mack family furious because their brother, Benjamin, didn't win the best-looking baby contest at the circus, Bethany forgives Callie and brings her some kerosene for her hair, too. But things get more difficult. Mattywill throws a spitball at Bethany, and the Mack kids continue their shenanigans in the schoolhouse. In November, midway between Bethany's and Mattywill's birthdays, the Morris's give them a joint party. Each girl gives the other a dress of identical material in a different, horrible shade. Nevertheless, each wears her ugly dress to school the next day. Things couldn't be worse!

During the Christmas pageant, which is slated to have Pa as minister, Bethany as the flying angel, Mattywill as a shepherd, and Billy Bob as baby Jesus, everything starts to get better. Mattywill and Bethany withdraw from the pageant so that the Macks can salvage their pride. They become friends again. Everyone is pleased, except Bethany who is still worried about the manse collection. She realizes that it will be 1900 before the building can start now. Bethany finds Deacon Cass in the saloon playing poker with the $5,000 collection fund. Since he is inebriated, she takes over and wins the total by drawing a one-eyed jack. Her fortune has come true; everyone is happy! Even Pa, who starts to court Miss Penny after she chooses him as her dance partner. With her new spirit of friendliness, Mattywill suggests that Bethany tell Miss Penny how much is expected of a preacher's wife. Mattywill knows now what Bethany has known all along—it's tough to be a preacher's kid.

Thematic Analysis

Throughout the story, the pressing need of youngsters for a friend is ever-present. Further, the book expresses the sensitive feelings that must be interpreted and understood before friendships can be established. A secondary theme of male and female roles as they were across the country at the turn of the century is well stated. The stereotypical judgment about "preacher's kids, especially female" is also explored.

Discussion Materials

A good introduction would be to paraphrase the "Author's Note" (pp. 167–172), then display the front cover while paraphrasing the story of the Brant family's arrival in Prineville (pp. 26–28). Several anecdotes will explain the heroine's hopes and the realities: Queen Fareeta's predictions (pp. 2–6); Pa tells the children about their new temporary life (pp. 24–25); life for Bethany in Prineville (pp. 38–40; 108; 134–136); and Deacon Cass and the church money (pp. 44–48; 94–95). The story of the exotic elephant, Lady Peaches, and Bethany's courageous ride bears retelling (pp. 56–81). The theme of the tough road to friendship can be book talked by using the scuffle and resolution between Bethany and Mattywill (pp. 82–86; 90–91; 112–115; 119–126; 129–136; 163–166). What it was like to be in Bethany's shoes at the turn of the century would also be an interesting subject (pp. 140–150).

Related Materials

The author's other titles are all recommended; however, two are especially suggested for those who like this title: *Lacy Makes a Match* and *Wait for Me, Watch for Me, Eula Bee* (both Morrow, 1979). The first title, set in California at the turn of the century, is a romp with another persevering 13-year-old female who cares for a family of four grown men. Also suggested are *King Kong and Other Poets* (Viking, 1986) by Robert Burch, about two sixth-graders; *The Dark behind the Curtain* (Oxford, 1984) by Gillian Cross, about a school production; and *Tikhon* (Harper, 1984) by Ilse-Margaret Vogel, about a friendship between a young German girl and a homesick Russian soldier during World War II. For older readers, suggest *This Old Man* (Houghton, 1984) by Lois Ruby, about a teenager who learns, with help, to understand friendship. Two audiovisual productions that are useful here are *Pies* (Direct Cinema, 1985), in 16mm or video, about an amusing controversy between two peasant women over cow manure, and *Taking a Chance* (Great Plains Instructional TV Library, 1983), about three teenagers who try to run a small TV station. Leonard Everett Fisher's recent title *The Alamo* (Holiday, 1987), which treats a large event in Texas history in 1836, will make a fine informational source in this segment. Also suggested is *The Legend of the Bluebonnet: An Old Tale of Texas* (Putnam, 1983) by Tomie dePaola, which can also be obtained from Listening Library, 1985, as a filmstrip.

Danziger, Paula.   *It's an Aardvark-Eat-Turtle World*
Delacorte, 1985, 132 pp.

Five books, from the pen of Paula Danziger, all popular with young people, preceded this title: *The Cat Ate My Gymsuit; The Pistachio Prescription; Can You Sue Your Parents for Malpractice; There's a Bat in Bunk Five;* and *The Divorce Express.* The author's keen ear for the conversation and understanding of the feelings of young people shows in the popularity of her stories. She lives in Woodstock, New York, the locale of this story, which adds to its wonderful feeling of atmosphere.

The two teenagers in this story, each with divorced parents, were first introduced by the author in *The Divorce Express,* where they became fast friends. In this story, the two young females learn to be family members as well as friends when Rosie's mother and Phoebe's father marry. Young females from 10 to 14 (grades 5–8) will find the story of the realistic mix-ups and the complexities of adapting to a new family relationship fascinating. The book jacket drawing portrays the interracial Rosie—her mother, Mindy, is white; her father, black—in her jeans leaning against a playground pole while Phoebe—whose dad, Jim, is moving in with Rosie's mom—is in her jeans sitting on a swing. It serves well to introduce the two protagonists.

Rosie, the heroine, is a displaced person with uncommon good sense and stability. She used to visit her father until he and his new wife and kids moved to California. Although she enjoys seeing her father, she doesn't shed any tears over her situation. Nor does she think much about being interracial, chiefly because her mother, Mindy, makes it so acceptable. But becoming a family with Jim and his daughter and her friend, Phoebe, is a little more difficult.

Rosie is a responsible young female and babysits for three-year-old Donny (whom she refers to affectionately as the "little Nerlet"). During one of her visits, Aardvark, the Donners' dog, eats the turtle that has just arrived by mail from the "Pet of the Month Club." It seems an appropriate slogan for what occurs when Jim and Phoebe move in and they try to become a family. First, Rosie and Phoebe share the bedroom that used to be Rosie's. Because Rosie is neat and Phoebe messy, even sharing a bedroom is a problem. Then Phoebe has a steady, Dave, on whom she dotes and flaunts. The mailbox with three names—Brooks, Kovacs (Mindy), and Wilson (Rosie)—suggests the complexities and stresses.

When Mindy reprimands Phoebe for "making out" with Dave in the car in front of their house, the resulting blowup almost ends Rosie's willingness to go to Canada with Phoebe, her mother and stepfather, and Kathy and Duane Carson, to visit Duane's brother and youngsters, Aviva and Jason. But they finally do go. During the visit, Rosie is attracted to Jason, but sees Phoebe flirting with him. Jason, however, makes his preference clear when after a wonderful touring trip with Aviva, her mother, Phoebe and her mother, and Rosie to the Eaton Centre in Toronto, he takes Rosie to see the famous Casa Loma. They fast become friends, and Rosie even invites him to visit her in Woodstock.

At last Rosie is also part of a pair; she doesn't have to make her choice between friendship and family membership any more. Rosie has enlarged her ring of friendship. Phoebe's anger and her decision to live with her mother in New York City don't last too long. She returns from her mother's more than willing to be Rosie's sister and friend. Soon, Jason arrives for Christmas in Woodstock. Rosie concludes that despite the many trials, it's not a dog-eat-dog world, not even an aardvark-eat-turtle world.

Thematic Analysis

Friendship as a basis for family relationships and love is the basic theme of this story, interspersed with the complexities of growing up for youngsters. Divorce and its problems, interracial youngsters and their feelings, the interactions between people of different generations, and the tenuousness of young love are also all explored. A charming relationship is also suggested between Rosie and Donny in the babysitting episodes.

Discussion Materials

A simple retelling of the story, identifying the main characters (pp. 1–2) and displaying Rosie and Phoebe on the front of the book jacket, is a good way to introduce the book. Other episodes that can be used to present themes from the book are: babysitting (pp. 3–7; 27–31; 122–124); the Canadian highlights (pp. 65–72, Eaton Centre; pp. 85–90, Casa Loma; and pp. 91–95, harbor front conversation about being interracial). Phoebe's decision to return to the family (pp. 124–128) can serve as an epilogue to the preceding incidents. A special anecdote about Christmas with Jason in Woodstock (pp. 129–132) will give a particular glow to the presentation.

Related Materials

The author's other books are suggested, especially *The Divorce Express* (Delacorte, 1982), which tells about Rosie and Phoebe's life before they became a family. Two appropriate records are *Up a Road Slowly* (Random, 1972) and *Confessions of an Only Child* (Caedmon, 1978). Both have female heroines who deal with growing up in a household run by an aunt and with a mother who is expecting a new baby. Two titles that treat youngsters dealing with the turmoil of divorce are also suggested: *With a Wave of the Wand* (Lothrop, 1980) by Mark Jonathon Harris and *Wicked Stepdog* (Crowell, 1982) by Carol Lea Benjamin. Johanna Hurwitz's *Law of Gravity* (Morrow, 1978) is a story about Margot from a traditional family in an urban society who is able to solve her mother's unwillingness to leave their apartment home; it will appeal to this audience. Elaine L. Konigsburg's title *Journey to an 800 Number* (Atheneum, 1982), which is about a young boy who spends his mother's second honeymoon renewing his friendship with his father and learning about loyalty from him, is recommended. The new title by Jeanne Betancourt, *Sweet Sixteen and Never Been . . .* (Bantam, 1987), is also suggested for the audience.

Fleischman, Sid.   *The Whipping Boy*
Illus. by Peter Sis. Greenwillow, 1986, 90 pp.

In this rousing adventure tale, which is the 1986 Newbery Award winner, the author again demonstrates his ability to write an exceptional story for youngsters. This title about the travails of Prince Brat and the boy who stands in for him for corporal punishment will appeal to children ages 10–12 (grades 5–7). Another successful comic novel, this book follows in the tradition of many of the author's popular novels, for example, *Chauncey and the Grand Rascal* and *Mr. Mysterious and Company*. It is distinctive, however, in its resemblance to nineteenth-century novels, with such chapter headings as "In Which the Plot Thickens." Sid Fleischman's flair for the spare style, character development, and heightened sense of adventure subtly illuminate his treatment of universal themes, whether set in the past or present.

The book is illustrated by Peter Sis with numerous pen-and-ink sketches that are shaded with crosshatch lines and dots: 8 full-page illustrations, 20 chapter heads, a dedicatory sketch, a frontispiece, and an endnote decoration. The sketches capture the grotesquely comic nature of the four main characters. Sis also did the book jacket painting, which shows the palace runaways on horseback in the background, with the two villain highwaymen hiding behind two trees in the foreground. A large mellow moon shrouded in fog glows quietly in the sky; shades of dark blue and green with swirling white ground fog complete the scene.

Prince Brat (Horace), who refuses to learn to read and write, is a mischievous fellow. He can be as insolent as he wishes because when his father, the king, reprimands him with "Give him twenty whacks," servants bring the latest whipping boy, the common boy Jemmy, from the North Tower to receive the whacks. Jemmy, an orphan whose father was a rat catcher in the nearby medieval town, never cries, to the prince's consternation. The most Jemmy exclaims, after being summoned repeatedly, is "Gaw."

When Prince Brat, who is bored, conscripts Jemmy with a plan to run away, Jemmy formulates the first of his plans to slip away to the sewers to escape his present onerous life. The two set off on a royal charger with Jemmy carrying the prince's basket of food. In the fog they are captured by two highwaymen, Hold-Your-Nose Billy and Cutwater. The large and bushy-bearded Billy is famous in song for his habit of eating garlic.

Cutwater, who willingly plays second fiddle, discovers that they really have a royal package, verifying Prince Brat's loud protestations.

After they get to the villains' hut, Jemmy prepares his second plan as the highwaymen ask the prince to write a ransom note. Knowing that the prince can't write, Jemmy says that he will write to his papa, the king, over the strenuous denials of his serving boy, Prince Brat. Jemmy even increases the ransom to a wagonload of gold and jewels. After reading his note backward to the dubious villains, Jemmy suggests that his whipping boy deliver the message. Prince Brat declares he won't. Thwarted, Jemmy has to amend his plan. He tries to hide under a bed of straw, but flies out the door when Prince Brat betrays him. The prince and villains follow.

Jemmy, who takes refuge from a bear in a hollow root, meets the prince again, and they begin to form a friendship. Prince Brat follows Jemmy as he goes through the woods until they meet young Betsy, who is searching for her dancing bear, Petunia, and she gives Jemmy directions to the river. Jemmy wants to get back to the safe sewers and catch rats. Meanwhile, however, though grimy and disheveled, Prince Brat has begun to have the time of his life, and Jemmy can't get rid of him.

Jemmy looks for firewood in the trash—mudlarking—giving in to his better instincts by including the prince. When he finds a bent bird cage in which he can keep sewer rats, things seem to be looking up. He even gets Cap'n Nips, the hot-potato man, to stop his coach for them, and the Cap'n tries to save them when the highwaymen attack the coach. However, Billy whips the prince, who bravely doesn't let a sound escape. Betsy has to send Petunia to stop the cruel affair. Betsy and Petunia then join Jemmy and Prince Brat in the coach ride to the bustling town.

Once they are in town, Smudge, an old male friend, recognizes Jemmy and shakes hands with him and the prince—much to the prince's delight. Hot potatoes, new milk, and everyone calling him Prince Brat, not Prince Horace, are some of the prince's pleasant new experiences. They hear some of the ballad seller's verses about Billy and a sensational broadside announcing that the whipping boy has abducted and sold the prince to the gypsies. With that, Jemmy hightails it for the sewers, with the prince in full pursuit. On the way they see Billy and Cutwater following them. When they reach the sewers, the prince tosses the bird cage against a wall in the direction of the town brewery to make the villains head that way. Covered with rats from the brewery grain, Jemmy and the prince flee.

Prince Brat insists that Cap'n Nips take them back to his father, the

king, and collect the reward. In spite of Jemmy's worst fears of returning, the king extends the prince's protection to him. He also makes
Petunia the "Official Dancing Bear to Your Royal Majesty." Prince Horace promises to do his lessons and behave himself. Finally, the king tells
them that if they run away again, he wants to go along. Someone sees the
two villains on a ship headed, unknown to them (for they boarded surreptitiously), for a distant convict island.

Thematic Analysis

This title has deep social themes; the endnote sets the story squarely
on social justice. However, for the young person for whom the book is
intended, the theme of friendship across different styles of life is well
delineated. The historical setting and the satiric strand take second
place for the younger reader who will delight in the adventures. Nevertheless, the readers are sensitized to the different ways of looking at
things as the broad comedic plot progresses. Finally, the importance of
sharing with another—in ordinary or dangerous times—is prominently
expressed.

Discussion Materials

This book can be presented in multiple ways. It can be presented with
sketches, briefly suggesting what they mean: the protagonists (frontispiece); the whipping boy's role (p. 3); the runaways (p. 10); caught
(p. 17); a reversal of roles in the hut (p. 24); the boys argue over the
ransom note (p. 35); saved by Petunia (p. 43); Betsy (p. 47); Prince Brat
gets whipped (p. 59); the waterside fair (p. 71); and a last ghastly look at
Billy and Cutwater (p. 82). It can be presented by reading the chapter
headings and dropping a plot hint, or by introducing the characters (pp.
1–6; 12–15) and presenting the highlights: runaways (pp. 7–11); caught
(pp. 12–21); the ransom note (pp. 22–26); delivering the note (pp. 29–
38); Betsy and the bear (pp. 42–49; 60–62); Cap'n Harry Nips (pp. 52–
54); in the city (pp. 63–70; 72–73); and the sewers (pp. 74–84). Reading
the note is suggested before any introduction.

Related Materials

The Swing (Bradbury, 1980) by Emily Hanlon, about Beth, 11, and
Danny, 14, who become friends when they resolve her possessiveness
over a swing, and *If This Is Love, I'll Take Spaghetti* (Macmillan, 1983) by
Ellen Conford, about a girl from a single-parent home who finally

realizes that life has its ups and downs, are good choices for a youngster of the same age. The following titles will be enjoyable to those in grades 4–6: *Chip Rogers, Computer Whiz* (Morrow, 1984) by Seymour Simon; *The Magic of the Glits* (Macmillan, 1980) by C. S. Adler; and *Strange New World across the Street* (Camelot/Avon, 1979) by Nan Gilbert. For younger readers in grades 2–5, three authors have suitable titles: Johanna Hurwitz's *Hot and Cold Summer* and *Aldo Applesauce* (both Morrow, 1984; 1980); George Selden's *Chester Cricket's Pigeon Ride* and *Chester Cricket's New Home* (both Farrar, 1981; 1983); and Pat Hutchin's *Curse of the Egyptian Mummy* (Greenwillow, 1983). Selden's titles are excellent as read-alouds.

A record of *The Prince and the Pauper* (Caedmon, 1977) by Mark Twain is a natural for *The Whipping Boy*. It is read by Ian Richardson. Four cassettes, *The Best of Encyclopedia Brown* (Miller-Brody/Random, 1977), are suitable for the younger audience. They use Donald J. Sobol's stories: *Encyclopedia Brown; Encyclopedia Brown and the Case of the Secret Pitch;* and *Encyclopedia Brown Gets His Man.*

Hughes, Shirley. *Alfie Gives a Hand*
Illus. by the author. Lothrop, 1984 (Bodley Head, 1983), 32 pp.

Written and illustrated by an author-illustrator who is respected for her Alfie series, this title eloquently describes a birthday party for a small boy. Alfie extends his hand to a young companion during his first appearance alone during a party and so takes another step toward maturity. This distinguished picture book will appeal to young folk from ages 3 to 8 (grades pre-K–3). The inviting book is preceded by *Alfie's Feet* and *Alfie Gets in First*. Another title, *An Evening at Alfie's* (Lothrop, 1985), is an ALA Notable Book for children.

The full-color drawings are enticing, redolent of childhood with charming swiggly pencil outlines around drawings of the characters and events, allowing the viewer an intimate view. They vary from vignettes interspersed around the brief text to double- and full-page drawings with outlined or free-standing text. The colors are bright, but portray well what is actually seen in nature. The facial expressions are natural and reflect those seen on everyday people. Each page has both an illustration and minimal text. The book jacket on the square-shaped book shows the eight birthday-party participants playing "Ring-around-a-Rosie" and sitting at the outdoor birthday table under festive balloons.

The half-title page introduces nursery school age Alfie running to his mom and younger sister Annie Rose with a note in his hand. The written invitation decorates the verso; such typical birthday party fare as a cake appears on the title page. Mom opens and reads the note. Annie Rose stands wobbily at her knee, while she and Alfie sit in a comfortable chair. When he recognizes his name on the birthday party invitation from his nursery school friend Bernard, Alfie helped by mom and Annie Rose bathes and dresses. After he learns that his mom and Annie Rose are going to wait for him in the park while he is at the party, Alfie retrieves the battered old piece of blanket from his bed. Although his nursery school acquaintances will all be at the party, only his security blanket gives him the courage to step inside alone when Bernard's mom greets him and his mom and Annie Rose leave. Then Bernard's mom escorts him to the backyard of their attached row house, where Alfie sees Bernard, Min, Sam, and Daniel—all from nursery school—playing joyfully with each other in the brightly festooned yard.

The excited birthday boy opens Alfie's present of crayons and throws them in the air. Then Bernard's mom introduces a soap bubble activity. In spite of her gentle reprimand, Bernard bursts more bubbles than anyone. Alfie bursts few because he is so busy holding his blanket. Min tries to hold one large bubble that lands on her arm, but in his exuberance, Bernard comes up and bursts it. Quiet Min, a little interracial girl, starts to cry and refuses to sit down without holding on to Alfie. During lunch, Bernard continues to blow through his lemonade and throw his Jello until his mom makes him stop. Then Bernard puts on his favorite gift—a tiger mask—and crawls around trying to scare everyone. When Min starts to cry, Bernard's mom tries to save the moment by introducing a circle of "Ring-around-a-Rosie." Bernard grabs Alfie's hand and won't join the circle without him. Surrounded by friends—Bernard, the bad actor, and the crying Min—Alfie puts his food encrusted blanket in a safe place under the table and joins the circle, taking both Bernard's and Min's hands. After "all fall down," they play and eat some more. Soon it's time to go home with mom, Annie Rose, and his blanket. Before they leave, Bernard's mom compliments Alfie for being such a helpful guest. Moreover, Alfie has taken a first and decisive step outside his immediate family.

Thematic Analysis

The depth of a youngster's feelings when he makes a gradual yet decisive step toward a newer stage of development, together with the courage behind such an act, is the underlying theme of this book. The main theme of this honest story about a youngster's feelings is the reassuring act of friendship or compassionate understanding of another's distress and how one person helps another. The story also shows a deep understanding of the different and unique rates of growth among children. When his mom wistfully knows that Bernard's obstreperous behavior may one day change, it is underlined.

Discussion Materials

This lovely picture book can be presented through its pictures or as a read-aloud, or it can be introduced with many anecdotes. The book jacket can serve as background for the birthday party, and specific incidents can then be highlighted: Alfie gets ready (pp. 3–4); Alfie's first glimpse of the backyard (pp. 9–10); bubbles abound (pp. 13–14); and "Ring-around-a-Rosie" (pp. 25–26). Alfie's act of bravery also can be developed: Alfie brings his blanket (pp. 5–6); Alfie takes the first tentative step (pp. 7–8); Min begins to cry (pp. 17–18); and Alfie's act of friendship (pp. 23–24). The youngest will want to look at the pictures; older youngsters will look at them as they read.

Related Materials

Many stories can be suggested: *Hippos Go Berserk* (Little, 1980) by Sandra Boynton tells in counting rhyme about a lonely hippo; *Clancy's Coat* (Warner, 1984) by Eve Bunting tells in an Irish lilt about a grudge between a tailor and a farmer; *Bert and Barney* (Houghton, 1980) by Ned Delaney is about two best friends—an alligator and a frog. The 16mm film *Angus Lost* (Phoenix Films and Video, 1983) retells the beloved story of the small Scottish terrier. Gabrielle Vincent's titles about Ernest and Celestine (all Greenwillow), about a female child mouse and her guardian, a bear, are child-oriented: *Ernest and Celestine* (1982); *Ernest and Celestine's Picnic* (1982); *Merry Christmas, Ernest and Celestine* (1984); and *Breakfast Time, Ernest and Celestine* (1985). *The Snowman* (Weston Woods, 1984) is a good film for this age. Inspired by Raymond Briggs's captivating book, it is also available as a record from CBS, Inc. Donna Guthrie's *The Witch Who Lives down the Hall* (Harcourt, 1985) is a good addition, especially at Halloween.

Lowry, Lois. *Us and Uncle Fraud*
Houghton, 1984, 148 pp.

Well known for her series on Anastasia, Lois Lowry has written other stories, many of them prizewinners. This popular title with youngsters ages 9–12 (grades 4–7) demonstrates the author's ability to capture the feelings and expressions of the young. The author's writing style is clean and crisp, much like the oral style of the young, with edges of humor in such lively situations as the young are often engaged. The insight that a visiting uncle provides for the short time he is with the heroine, 11-year-old Louise, and her 10-year-old brother, Marcus (Matt), helps them through subsequent dangers and reaffirms their family love and friendship.

Both sides of the jacket display a compelling full-color rendition by George Hughes of Louise and Matt in their yellow slickers locked in an embrace while the waters of the flooded river around them rise, and the cemetery tombstones on the far bank slide ominously into the river. The drawing graphically illustrates the dramatic high point of the book and will attract readers.

Louise Amanda Cunningham (Lulu to her father and 14-year-old brother, Tom; Louisa to herself; and Louisamanda to Uncle Claude) is just a year older than brother Marcus. It has been three years since Claude Newbold, also a year younger than his sister, Hallie Cunningham, visited her and her husband, Matt. He has never met 2½-year-old Stephie (Stephanie), the youngest Cunningham. Father, the editor of the local paper, doesn't think highly of mother's younger brother, and Tom just plain calls him Uncle Fraud. Mother patiently explains that in spite of being a drifter, Claude has a sweet nature full of imagination and love. Practical father and Tom, who is beginning to ape him, barely tolerate the visit, but Louise and Marcus are fascinated, particularly with the "priceless and fragile" contents—purportedly Fabergé eggs—of the smaller of his two boxes; the other is a shabby suitcase that Marcus carries to Louise's room, which she has vacated for Uncle Claude.

Uncle Claude, who surreptitiously drinks father's whiskey, doesn't stay too long, but while he is there he escorts Louise, Marcus, and Stephie to the Leboff mansion on the riverbank. Marcus gets the key from fifth-grader Kenny Stratton, who knows where it is hidden. (Kenny's father is caretaker while the Leboffs are summering and the housekeeper, Mrs.

Shaw, is on vacation in Kansas City.) Once they go inside, Uncle Claude spins romantic tales and dreams for them as they tour, and tells them that he is going to hide gifts for them to find. Louise is sure that they are the Russian eggs, especially as he repeatedly says to them, "Ya tebya lyublyu." Even mother's overheard admonition to her brother to stop filling their heads with fanciful stories doesn't make him stop. He teaches them the heritage behind their given names, and that anything worth having is worth searching for. According to him, that is what makes him a traveling man. Typically, he leaves one evening without notice.

Louise and Marcus keep looking unsuccessfully for their gifts. When just after Uncle Claude's departure they hear of a robbery of silverware at the Leboffs', Louise suspects that the gifts might be silverware, not Fabergé eggs. The children don't know what to believe; they don't know what is real. When Louise asks her mother about Uncle Claude, she says that Claude has always been a dreamer, much like Marcus. Later when she reads a note from Uncle Claude, who is now in Denver, she decides only that he is a poor speller.

While Louise has been thinking about Uncle Claude, it has continued to rain. Soon the National Guard is called out because of the rising flood-water. Although the school and library are closed, Mr. Mueller conducts a fine search on Fabergé eggs at Louise's request. While father goes down to the river to help with the sandbagging, Louise decides to join Marcus down on the river bank, watching the headstones tumble into the water. She finds Marcus standing in the swirling water, unable to move because his foot is stuck. Louise tries to help but is battered by the rushing water. Tom finally rescues him, but is carried off by the flood-water in the effort. Louise, bloodied and skinned, runs through the cemetery to find a phone. When she sees Kenny's dad, Mr. Stratton, busily digging, she tells him what has happened. As Mr. Stratton goes to phone for help, Louise picks up a muddy remnant of what he was burying and puts it in her pocket.

Tom is rescued, but spends a long time in a coma afterward. Mother encourages Louise and Marcus to talk to him, a difficult task. Louise, meanwhile, tells her mother that she should hate her brother, Uncle Claude, because he didn't leave any Fabergé eggs. Even the librarian Mr. Mueller's wonderful pictures of them are better gifts. But Mrs. Cunning-ham answers simply, "He's my brother. I've always loved him."

After Tom recovers, they discover that Mr. Stratton had stolen the silverware—a muddy piece of which Louise had picked up—but Louise testifies on his behalf, because he saved her brother. Louise finally recognizes that Marcus is very much like Uncle Claude was as a youngster, and that she loves Marcus very much. She also realizes that Uncle Claude's real gift—a priceless one—is not fragile at all; it is the essence of family life and of the love that binds family members together.

Thematic Analysis

Love among family members—the fragile thread that holds humanity together—is discussed here against the typical peculiarities of a traditional family unit. Developing the ability to distinguish between reality and nonreality and appreciate both at appropriate times is also treated. Acceptance of each individual's uniqueness and ability to contribute is an important and tertiary theme.

Discussion Materials

This book provides a good introduction of the main characters (pp. 1–8). To introduce Uncle Claude further, one can use pages 8–13, 16–19, 40–42, 43–48. The trip to the Leboff mansion, an interesting episode that is pivotal to the plot (pp. 19–38), should be paraphrased. One can also paraphrase Tom's admonition to Louise and Marcus (pp. 75–78). A reading of mother's reminiscences of her younger brother is appropriate (pp. 81–82), and the library visit also bears retelling (pp. 100–104). The flooded river scene at the cemetery makes a dramatic vignette, together with the book jacket illustration (pp. 105–117). Tom's coma will make an enlightening and interesting book talk (pp. 122–123; 127–131; 141; 147). The ending, of course, will be better left untold.

Related Materials

Some particularly useful titles here are *Oliver Button Is a Sissy* (Harcourt, 1980) by Tomie dePaola; *Hambone* (Tundra, 1980) by Caroline Fairless; *Cardboard Crown* (Crowell, 1984) by Clyde Robert Bulla; and *Hit-and-Run Connection* (Whitman, 1982) by Carole Smith. All are appealing to both sexes and the last three are good for reluctant readers. Others are *Great Easter Egg Mystery* (Troll, 1982) by Francine Sabin; *Saturdays in the City* (Houghton, 1979) by Ann Sharpless Bond; *Maggie and Me* (Kids Can Pr., 1986) by Ted Staunton; and *The Case of the Muttering Mummy* (Macmillan, 1986) by E. W. Hildick (the latest in the McGurk mystery series). For females, Astrid Lindgren's *Pippi on the Run* (Viking, 1976) and Ruth Yaffe Radin's *Tac's Island* (Macmillan, 1986) will be interesting. The Scholastic-TAB magazine's *Crackers*, intended for Canadian children, will entertain all children on the North American continent with its plethora of articles, pictures, games, cartoons, riddles, and recipes. Patricia Windsor's first title for middle-graders, *How a Weirdo and a Ghost Can Change Your Entire Life* (Delacorte, 1986), about Martha and Teddy who become best friends, can be suggested.

Morgenroth, Barbara. *Nicki & Wynne*
Atheneum, 1982, 139 pp.

Written by an author who has spent her life around horses, this rollicking story about two young girls who spend a summer living together at a boarding stable appeals to young females from 10 up (grade 5 up) who enjoy horse stories. Barbara Morgenroth writes with that sure knowledge about horses and youngsters that is guaranteed to attract readers. She has written many adventure books in this genre—just what the young female horse lover or riding afficionado enjoys. One adventure after another involving horses is the key.

Blanche Sim's full-color book jacket painting sets the scene nicely. It shows a gently rolling farm on the back and a picture of the two female protagonists on the front. Cautious Nicki is holding Quick by the mane, while exuberant Wynne is down on her hands and knees painting red apples on the horse's hoofs. Needless to say, Wynne Batchelder is covered with waterproof acrylic paint. The pig, Arnold Houdini, watches the tableau in the Batchelders' stables. The illustrator captured the scene in the book (pp. 33–35; 40).

When 12-year-old Nicki Geary learns that she has to leave her Ohio friends and weekly riding lessons at Foxfield Farm, she is upset. While her parents look for a place to live in Connecticut—her father's new company's home—they have arranged for her to be a summer boarder at the Batchelders' stables near Hartford. She is even more distressed when she arrives at the recently divorced Ceci Batchelder's small stables because she is sharing a room with Wynne Batchelder who is her age. Ceci is nice enough, as is Maura, Wynne's older sister, and the four female boarders who live with her above the garage. Maura gives daily classes in equestrienneship and shows horses—both of which Nicki likes. Wynne, who is a tomboy and expert horseperson, prefers rough and ready trail riding and jumping. Nicki begins to learn that Wynne is superb around horses. She is also a bit of a joker. Nicki is scared!

The Batchelders' stables are fortunately small, with eight stalls. Maura's showhorse, Timeless Flight, and Wynne's pony, Applesauce, occupy two; another is divided for Creampuff, the pony used for little kids, and Houdini.

Nicki's first experience presages the tremendous learning she can expect with Wynne. When Nicki leads Creampuff out of the stables, she disregards Wynne's advice not to let the pony get ahead of her shoulder. The minute she does, Creampuff takes off. Luckily, Ceci catches him.

Nicki thoroughly enjoys Maura's first lesson; afterward, Wynne talks her into a trail ride. Saddling up Quick (silver) and Bowen, Wynne and Nicki take to the trail where Wynne convinces the nervous Nicki to jump a stone wall, her first jump, not counting her tentative inside jumps in Ohio. Soon Nicki has no time to miss anyone or anything. Lessons, chores, and "Wynne to ride with" become the temper of her days.

The summer passes quickly with each event following the last in rapid succession. Nicki's first real horse show in the jumping class on Quick sees her scared witless. Nevertheless, she does just fine even with the riderless Creampuff running at her side. The judge compliments her on her composure and asks her to tell the mischievous Wynne not to decorate the horse's hoofs again. Nicki, who has always wanted a horse, wants one now even more.

Meanwhile, Wynne wants her mother to marry again—an outdoor man. To make it happen, she conspires first with the vet, Dr. Lucas, until he arrives with his fiancée. Her next target is the quarter horse trainer, Buzzy Kerrigan, at Bittersweet Farm. A cowboy whom she has seen ride, he can't get over how naturally Wynne rides western for the first time. Afterward, Wynne tells Nicki that she has only to arrange a meeting for her mother and Buzzy.

The passing days bring other moments of amusement: tracking and missing Houdini, who finally follows Nicki home, and learning another of Creampuff's tricks (lying down and rolling around while the rider struggles). The thought of the end-of-summer hunt brings pleasure and pain. Nicki has always wanted to go cubbing, but the hunt signals the end of her stay. Just before the hunt, Nicki and Wynne are caught in a torrential rain, but manage to get home. Nicki thanks her lucky stars and her mount, Applesauce. Wynne comments to Ceci that Nicki is now half a rider, having survived a trial by water.

On the big day, Wynne on Stanley Steamer, a newly bought horse, is stopped by the master of the foxhounds because the horse needs a stronger bit for control—something Wynne had told Maura. During the hunt, Nicki scratches her nose on a branch, drawing blood. Afterward, Wynne explains that Nicki has passed the second trial because of her injury and is now a real rider. If Nicki wants to show in the future, Wynne says she will join her, and she really wants Nicki to go with her to the minihorse trial in September. Nicki is confused and sad. She knows that she has a good friend but she doesn't know where she will be in September.

When the Gearys arrive to collect their daughter, they bring good news. Not only can Nicki have a horse of her own, but the Gearys' new home is less than three miles from the Batchelders' stables, on the other side of Bittersweet Farm. The two girls can even ride over there together to get to know Buzzy better. Ceci exclaims that both girls have changed for the better. Wynne has become calmer, Nicki more boisterous. The two friends part briefly.

Thematic Analysis

Although on the surface this horse story treats a natural phase of love of horses and riding that many young females go through, the theme of friendship between the two 12-year-olds is paramount. The concept of sharing between the two characters and their complementary personalities are well demonstrated with the normal give and take between them expressed naturally.

Discussion Materials

After introducing the characters and setting (Stepping-Stone Farm, pp. 3–13), show the book jacket. You can also present an inspiring book talk based on the horsemanship and riding incidents (pp. 26–29; 35–51; 72–75; 81–88; 102–104; 112–116; 117–124; 125–133). There are many entertaining sections: Creampuff's shenanigans (pp. 21–22; 82–84); painting Quick's hoofs (pp. 30–35); and Wynne's attempts at matchmaking (pp. 52–59; 65–77). Houdini's leave-taking and return are also good for highlighting, including an amusing account of little Timmie, a summer student, "watering the horses." The book lends itself to reading and paraphrasing.

Related Materials

The following books are useful for male readers: *Sometimes I Think I Can Hear My Name* (Pantheon, 1982) by Avi, about a boy and girl who both come from a divorced family and their hilarious adventures when they meet in New York City; *River Rats* (Dutton, 1979) by Jean Craighead George, about two boys who befriend a wild boy in their adventurous survival trek; *Fireball* (Dutton, 1981) by John Christopher, about Simon and his American cousin who are thrown back into Roman Britain. Three others especially for females are *That's What T. J. Says* (Holiday, 1982) by Betty Baker, about moving to a new house; *You're Allegro Dead* (Atheneum, 1981) by Barbara Corcoran, about a mystery at reactivated Camp Allegro; and *First the Good News* (Bradbury, 1983) by Judy Angell, about five ninth-graders who interview a rising TV star in a school newspaper contest. *Alan Mendelsohn, the Boy from Mars* (Dutton, 1979) by Daniel Manus Pinkwater, about the class creep and hilarious occult adventures, and *Prisoners of Vampires* (Farrar, 1984) by Nancy Garden, about two friends who stumble on a vampire while doing schoolwork, are two titles that will also appeal to your readers. For your better or older readers, suggest *Wonder Wheels* (Knopf, 1980) by Lee Bennett Hopkins and *Sisters by Rite* (St. Martin's, 1984) by Joan Lingard. The 16mm fine or video *Cornet at Night* (Beacon Films, 1985) is a wonderful adaptation of the Ross short story, which tells about a 12-year-old Canadian farm boy who has a brief friendship with a jazz musician.

Prelutsky, Jack. *The New Kid on the Block*
Poems by Jack Prelutsky, drawings by James Stevenson.
Greenwillow, 1984, 159 pp.

A man of many talents, the author, who has written 19 other titles for children, applied his creative ability here in 118 zany poems with his usual verve. This title will appeal to youngsters ages 8–10 (grades 3–5) and as a read-aloud to those who are younger. All of Prelutsky's titles are worthy of note; this one, however, was singled out by *Booklist* (ALA) and *School Library Journal* (Bowker), as well as being designated a 1984 ALA Notable Book. Youngsters who like poetry will be delighted; those who need to be introduced will find the humorous and short poems—some only a paragraph—funny and enjoyable.

Adults, especially those who regularly scan the *New Yorker* magazine, will recognize the squiggly line drawings of James Stevenson. Children will find them irresistible. With an irreverent pen and pencil, the illustrator adds to the merriment in the poems. For example, the grimacing cowboy holding his backside while standing beside a benign-looking cactus perfectly interprets the poem "You Need to Have an Iron Rear" (p. 15); the line drawing of a baby sitting in an expansive puddle aptly illustrates the description in the poem "My Baby Brother," by an older sibling as he looks at his baby brother who has only been around a week (p. 61); and Stevenson's prancing mice on the half-title page introduce the note of merriment that anticipates his drawing of a hand-held welcome mat on the title page. His fire-breathing dragon blowing on a birthday cake, illustrating the poem "Happy Birthday, Dear Dragon" (pp. 152–153), concludes the book joyously and with explosive force.

James Stevenson's full-color drawing on the book jacket of children in tenement windows and dogs on the street watching the new red-headed kid on the block march down the street makes an inviting entrance to this book. It highlights the first poem, "The New Kid on the Block" (p. 7), which says in the second and final paragraph that the ". . . New kid is really bad, I don't care for her at all," issuing an invitation to peek inside.

Although the poems are full of surprises, each contains a thought that will be immediately familiar to most youngsters. Together they deal with myriad characters—animal, vegetable, and mineral, real and imaginary. Everything that crosses a child's mind is here, and the humorous resolution of problems can be most helpful to youngsters. The poems also demonstrate a humorous didacticism toward resolving problems that can only be accomplished through poking fun. Perhaps the most important lesson that youngsters can learn about being friends is implicit in the poem "I'm the Single Most Wonderful Person I Know" (p. 137). Learning through humor what nobody likes in a person is an invaluable lesson. Another is in the poem "My Mother Says I'm Sickening" (p. 112), which lists the rules for good behavior. Each poem contains character sketches, jokes, and wordplay; everything that children love. Monsters and other imaginary characters are functionaries in gleeful slayings—so satisfying to young people. Finally, there are useful indexes, to titles and first lines, each decorated with prancing mice.

Thematic Analysis

These poems have so many themes that it would be improper to highlight just one. They treat the many fears and feelings that youngsters have, from bullies in the neighborhood, to the real fear of individual animal's threatening characteristics. However, the freedom a youngster has to express feelings and the confidence he feels in striking out with friends are overriding threads of continuity. "I'm the Single Most Wonderful Person I Know" (p. 137) is perhaps the most obvious example, although each poem in its own way helps a young person to get a better hold on the fine line between reality and nonreality at a young age. Becoming friends is a step on the road toward appropriate behavior and socialization.

Discussion Materials

This is an easy book to introduce among poetry lovers, and most children are. Just show the book, read one poem, and tell your audience that there are 117 more. It is also easy to use with the youngest or reluctant readers as a read-aloud. Pick a number of poems that best represent the concerns you are trying to illuminate. Also, a transparency can be made of the front cover and displayed on an overhead as background. Some of James Stevenson's drawings from the preliminary pages can also be handled in the same way. Two of the poems, "The New Kid on the Block," and "Happy Birthday, Dear Dragon (pp. 7; 152– 153), should be included as the alpha and omega lines in the book. A short reading of Jack Prelutsky's biography on the back jacket flap will make fascinating fare for your audience, and will also give you the opportunity to suggest further titles by this author. Include with the information the pen-and-ink sketch on the back cover by Pat Trujillo done in 1983. No matter what else you do, read the poem "I'm the Single Most Wonderful Person I Know" (p. 137), together with a display of the satisfied young man portrayed underneath it.

Related Materials

In addition to other titles by Prelutsky, be sure to suggest *The Sheriff of Rottenshot* (Greenwillow, 1982). You can also alert the group to the following: *The New Girl at School* (Dutton, 1980) by Judy Delton, about Marcia's first weeks at a new school; *Neighbors* (Harper, 1979) by M. B. Goffstein, about a new and an entrenched neighbor who become best friends; and *New Neighbors for Nora* (Morrow, 1979) by Johanna Hurwitz, about seven-year-old Nora and her friends, told in six brief stories. An earlier title about Nora, *Nora and Mrs. Mind-Your-Own-Business*, treats her when she was in first grade; *Mind Your Own Business* treats her when she is eight years old (both Morrow, 1977; 1982). The film-strip of Judy Blume's well-known *Freckle Juice* (Pied Piper, 1984) retells the story of three friends and their concern with freckles. A record of *Bridge of Terabithia* (see *Introducing More Books*, Bowker, 1978, pp. 38–40) can be obtained from Random. A cassette of the title under discussion, *The New Kid on the Block*, read by the author, is available from Listening Library. Kits of the following two titles are also available: *Secret Language* (Listening Library, 1978), about Vicky and Martha who become friends, and *Mystery of the Lost Ring* (Troll, 1982), an easy-to-read book about best friends Heather and Florence.

Three other titles will be useful: *Maggie and the Goodbye Gift* (Lothrop, 1980) by Jerry Milord describes moving and making new friends; *Harvey's Horrible Snake Disaster* (Houghton, 1984) by Eth Clifford tells about two cousins who become friends; *Lisa and Lotte* (Avon/Camelot, 1982) by Erick Kastner is a story of identical twins who become fast friends at camp and secretly switch identities (and homes) with their divorced parents, happily seeing them reunite.

Yolen, Jane. *Children of the Wolf*
Viking, 1984, 136 pp.

Jane Yolen writes thoughtfully for and about children. A prolific author, Dr. Yolen, who teaches children's literature, wrote more than 70 books before this one and has received many awards. Her deep interest in words and childhood combine again in this title which is based on an original missionary's diary. The author's imagination and her ability to enter the mind of the young, combined with her remarkable writing style, permit her to write this story about the capture of two feral or wild young girls in India in the 1920s and their subsequent brief life at the Christian mission. Yolen's own fascination with the development of the young boy—a fictional character—and his responses through words and love propel the story that will appeal to youngsters ages 10–14 (grades 5–8).

The arresting full-color jacket painting by Charles Mikolaycak is easily identifiable as that of this famous illustrator. The dark red shades of the sky and the intertwining exotic flower-vines provide a haunting background, as the young boy, Mohandis, crouches watching the girl children being nurtured by wolves—the younger one hunched and staring, the older baying to the full moon, while crouched on all fours. Both are shaggy-haired and fearsome to onlookers in their boniness.

Orphans, Mohandis, 14, and Rama, 16, share a room at the Christian mission (the Home) run by the British Reverend Welles outside the Indian village of Tantigoria. The other children there are Krithi, who has a shriveled leg and was abandoned; Veda, who speaks in whispers and was unclaimed in a nearby village; Preeti, who only has peripheral vision; and Indira, who was sent by her parents for schooling. Indira is continually hostile and angrily pinches the younger girls. Rama, who converses easily in Bengali, responds to the stern and religious Mr. Welles with an Indian head shake, which to Mr. Welles is "Yes," but to an Indian can mean "Maybe," "Yes," or "No." Now that Rama has reached manhood, he slips out at night to the back streets of the village. He boasts to the younger Mohandis (who keeps his fascination with words in a cypher hand of Bengali and English he learns from the reverend, in a diary away from prying eyes) that he is really the wolf of the region. Wolves howling on the edge of the great sal jungle make Mohandis shiver, even though he knows that the Home is separated from the jungle by the *maiden* (parade grounds) and the rice fields.

Supplicated by the ghost worshippers from the nearby village of Godamuri, Mr. Welles, a capable hunter, takes a small band into the forest to find the ghostly, shining, blue-eyed creatures that howl like wolves and have been seen at night by villagers. As part of the hunting party, the frightened Rama and Mohandis find a wolf's lair, from which they see wolves and finally the ghosts (*manush-bagha*) emerge. One of the bearers kills the female wolf who cares for the two dirty and disheveled creatures, and after two nights in the forest, the band returns with the creatures to the mission.

Mohandis is dismayed that the small wolf children must join civilization at the Home. Mrs. Welles, who supervises their daily baths and soakings for their scars hoping to make them healthy and presentable, quickly discovers that they are little girls, about three and nine. She holds her usual bedtime story hour dripping wet from their animal-like struggles. Mr. Welles, a lover of words and a religist, thinks of the feral children as a mandate from the Lord—a chance to witness a miracle by civilizing them and to learn about their previous life in the forest. The children at the Home howl and make fun of them, in spite of Mr. Welles's injunction to apply Christian kindness.

But Mohandis makes friends with them in their corner of the compound and names them Amala and Kamala. He tries to teach them their names and some other words, like "friends," but has only some success with Amala, who creeps into his lap, less with Kamala, who bites Indira during one of her taunting trips. Rama, on the other hand, gives up almost immediately after he slips out at night to visit Kamala and she does not even recognize him. Mr. Welles turns over their learning to Mohandis, who shares his appreciation for the power of naming things, and Mohandis becomes his *gillie* (gameskeeper).

Shortly after the monsoon rains arrive in June, however, Amala takes sick and dies in spite of medical treatment. Soon after the rains end, Kamala manages to say "Mmmmdah," while attempting to repeat Mohandis's name. She still runs on all fours, digs up dog bones, and refuses to eat cooked food. By September, however, she is able to walk upright and respond a little to Mohandis's attention. A smattering of words follows. Then Rama, who will be apprenticed soon, takes to visiting her at night. Indira is discovered one night secretly torturing Kamala in a jealous rage until she repeats that she is an evil *bhut*. Pinches and bruises are part of the torture. On a subsequent night Kamala retaliates by bloodying Indira, then runs into the forest. Mohandis finds her in a white ant mound similar to the one in which she was originally found.

Back at the Home, Kamala mumbles one word—the last she ever speaks—"Mmmmdah." From then on she only eats and plays with the dogs; she brings the attention of the press to the Home. Mohandis sees her for the last time as he leaves for Sandhurst—Mr. Welles's alma mater. When he returns on holiday, Kamala is dead from a parasite in one of the pigeons she ate. He mourns alone and though he eventually returns to study languages at Oxford, he never forgets the wolf children.

Thematic Analysis

On its deepest level, the thin line between human beings and beasts is suggested, as is the effect of civilization and the role of language in providing structure. On a surface level, however, the tenuous thread of friendship among persons from birth on is evident. The specific differences between children and adults are also presented, together with the salient effect of sensitivity, and the innate cruelty of youngsters and adults is well portrayed. Although many constructs can be ascribed to the poignant story, none is more important for middle-graders to recognize than the healing strength of friendship.

Discussion Materials

Against the background of an enlarged projection of the cover painting on an overhead projector, Mohandis—the narrator—and the principal members of the Home can be introduced (pp. 3—10). The following anecdotes will also be useful: the feral children come to the Home (pp. 12–14; 16); the trip to the great sal forest (pp. 18–45); Amala's and Kamala's first days at the Home (pp. 46–47; 48–59); and the naming (p. 60). A concentration on the feral children can also be intriguing: a description of the girls (pp. 62–72); Amala's death (pp. 74–82); Kamala and words (pp. 81–103); and Indira's mischief (pp. 107–113). The presenter could perhaps paraphrase Jane Yolen's afterword, "What Is True about the Book" (pp. 134–136).

Related Materials

Three suggestions for third- to fifth-graders are: *What's the Matter with Herbie Jones?* (Putnam, 1986) by Suzy Kline, about Herbie's infatuation and best friend Ray's reaction; *Your Former Friend, Matthew* (Dutton, 1984) by Lou Ann Gaeddert, about the changing boy-girl relationships at pre-puberty; and *Danby and George* (Greenwillow, 1981) by Betty Baker, about a deer mouse who learns to ask friends for help. Four titles for fourth- to sixth-graders are: *Case of the Horrible Swamp Monster* (Dodd, 1984) by Drew Stevenson; *Empty Window* (Warne, 1980) by Eve Bunting; *I and Sproggy* (Viking, 1978) by Constance C. Greene; and *The Great Ideas of Lila Fenwick* (Dial, 1986) by Kate McMullen. Each story emphasizes friendship among youngsters. Other titles for this group are: Ellen Conford's *Revenge of the Incredible Dr. Rancid and His Youthful Assistant, Jeffrey* (Little, 1980) and Patricia Reilly Giff's *Have You Seen Hyacinth Macaw?* (Delacorte, 1981), *Loretta P. Sweeney, Where Are You?* (Delacorte, 1983), *Winter Worm Business* (Delacorte, 1981), and *Love from the Fifth-grade Celebrity* (Delacorte, 1986). Conford's title is especially suggested for slower readers; the last is a sequel to *Fourth-grade Celebrity* and *The Girl Who Knew It All*. For older or better readers, try *Life Is Not Fair* (Clarion, 1984) by Gary Bargar, about prejudice surrounding two high school boys in the late 1950s. *The Accident* (Barr Films, 1986), in both 16mm and video cassette, explores the death of a beloved pet (for 8 to 13-year-olds). Ivy Ruckman's *Night of the Twisters* (Crowell, 1984) is a fictional account, based on an actual incident, of two young boys who go through a tornado.

Making Friends: Additional Titles

Allard, Harry. *Bumps in the Night*. Illus. by James Marshall. Doubleday, 1980, 32 pp. (Gr.1–3)

Baker, Betty. *Night Spider Case*. Macmillan, 1984, 113 pp. (Gr. 3–6)

Byars, Betsy. *The Cybil War*. Illus. by Gail Owens. Viking, 1982, 144 pp. (Gr. 3–6)

Carrick, Carol. *Some Friend*. Illus. by Donald Carrick. Houghton, 1979, 112 pp. (Gr. 3–5)

——. *What a Wimp*. Illus. by Donald Carrick. Clarion, 1983, 89 pp. (Gr. 4–6)

Cohen, Barbara. *Molly's Pilgrim*. Illus. by Michael J. Deraney. Lothrop, 1983, unp. (Gr. 1–3)

Conford, Ellen. *Anything for a Friend*. Little, Brown, 1979, 180 pp. (Gr. 5–6)

Cricket in Times Square, by George Selden. Recording, 2s 33rpm. Random, 1971. (Gr. 4–6)

Delaney, M. C. *Henry's Special Delivery*. Illus. by Lisa McCue. Dutton, 1984, 138 pp. (Gr. 4–6)

Garfield, Leon. *Fair's Fair*. Illus. by S. D. Schindler. Doubleday, 1983, unp. (Gr. 4–6)

Gerson, Corinne. *Oh, Brother*. Atheneum, 1982, 125 pp. (Gr. 4–6)

Godfrey, Marty. *Plan B Is Total Panic*. James Lorimer, 1986, 125 pp. (Gr. 4–6)

Greene, Constance C. *Dotty's Suitcase*. Viking, 1980, 147 pp. (Gr. 5–6)

Heidi, by Johanna Spyri. Recording, 2s 33 rpm. Caedmon, 1970. (Gr. 4–6)

Honey I Love, by Eloise Greenfield. Recording or cassette. Caedmon, 1985. (Gr. 5–6)

Just an Overnight Guest. Film. Phoenix/BFA Films, 1985. (Gr. 6–up)

Key, Alexander. *The Case of the Vanishing Boy*. Archway, 1980, 212 pp. (Gr. 5–7)

Klein, Norma. *Taking Sides*. Pantheon, 1974, 156 pp. (Gr. 5–up)

Lisle, Janet Taylor. *Sirens and Spies*. Bradbury, 1985, 169 pp. (Gr. 6–up)

Mahy, Margaret. *Aliens in the Family*. Scholastic, 1986, 174 pp. (Gr. 5–7)

Milton, Hilary. *Tornado*. Watts, 1983, 147 pp. (Gr. 4–6)

Newton, Suzanne. *An End to Perfect*. Viking, 1984, 216 pp. (Gr. 4–6)

Philip Hall Likes Me, I Reckon Maybe, by Bette Greene. Recording, 2s 33rpm. Random, 1976. (Gr. 5–6)

Pinkwater, Daniel M. *Alan Mendlesohn, the Boy from Mars*. Dutton, 1980, 240 pp. (Gr. 3–5)

Prince, Alison. *Sinister Airfield*. Illus. by Ellen Thompson. Morrow, 1983, 111 pp. (Gr. 4–6)

Rosenberg, Maxine. *Being Adopted*. Photos by George Ancona. Lothrop, 1984, 48 pp. (Gr. 1–4)

Sachs, Marilyn. *Bus Ride*. Drawings by Amy Rowen. Dutton, 1980, 107 pp. (Gr. 5–6)

Sargent, Sarah. *Weird Henry Berg*. Crown, 1980, 113 pp. (Gr. 4–6)

Skurzynski, Gloria. *Trapped in the Slickrock Canyon*. Illus. by Daniel San Souci. Lothrop, 1984, 123 pp. (Gr. 4–6)

Speare, Elizabeth George. *Sign of the Beaver.* Houghton, 1983, 135 pp. (Gr. 4–5)
Voigt, Cynthia. *Solitary Blue.* Atheneum, 1983, 189 pp. (Gr. 5–up)
Wilbur, Richard. *Loudmouse.* Illus. by Don Almquist. Harcourt, 1982 (1963), unp.
  (Gr. 2–4)

3

Developing Values

FUNDAMENTAL values are a person's cultural lifeline for making moral and ethical choices within the standards of civilization. Developing a set of values and a sense of responsibilities toward these beliefs begins in early childhood. This process coincides closely with the emergence of a healthy conscience. Early on this can be seen as an adamant sense of right and wrong in a young child's behavior, and as a critical attitude toward the more complex behavior of adults. As youngsters grow, however, they come to understand the complexities involved in most situations, so that by adolescence they have generally learned these subtleties and stand ultimately on the firm footing of their basic beliefs.

Although the process of developing values is long and continuous, no time is better than the infant and intermediate years to provide helpful vicarious experiences. Specific examples of political and personal freedom, honesty, and corrosive excessive vanity can help youngsters during this formative period. At no other time will children be as eager and able to learn rules for appropriate behavior. With their quiescent but awakening sense, children can be appropriately exposed to books and other media. Stories that show strong beliefs and value judgments with tenderness, and those with heroes who live successfully through the many phases of moral and ethical dilemmas, can help youngsters identify and substantiate their own values.

Each book in this chapter treats values through the main character's reaction to the problems he or she must face. A range of situations is represented, from compassion and education to a positive personal attitude and freedom, offering unique perspectives for the young person's consideration. All of the books are interesting, beautifully designed, and well written.

Bang, Molly. *The Grey Lady and the Strawberry Snatcher*
Illus. by the author. Macmillan, 1980, 46 pp.

This author, who is known and respected for her beautifully illustrated books, came to prominent attention when *Wiley and the Hairy Man* (Macmillan, 1976) was selected as an ALA Notable Book. Bang's most recent title to burst upon the scene is *The Paper Crane* (Greenwillow, 1985). The title under discussion, published in 1980, is a strikingly illustrated wordless allegory that superbly tells the story of a "strawberry snatcher" who pursues a "grey lady" and her box of strawberries through many intriguing adventures until by accident he discovers the delights of blackberries. Everyone will enjoy this visually told story, especially youngsters in the middle grades. Because of its particular usefulness in deepening visual literacy and mental acuity, it makes an excellent discussion title.

Twenty-three full-color double-spread illustrations skillfully integrate the fantasy, humor, and excitement of the travels of the grey lady with her box of strawberries from the market through the eerie swamp to the final enjoyment of the berries by her real family. A full-page illustration appears on the first and last pages of the book. The back book jacket reproduces the painting from the last page of the book of an empty strawberry box beside a sink littered with strawberry stems and the grey lady's crocheted shopping bag. A tiger lily in a pretty glass bottle stands behind the empty box. The front jacket displays loose cherries, boxes of strawberries, and nectarines in a wooden market bin, and the same illustration appears on the title page. The drawings are so realistic, especially the wood grain, that they could be mistaken for photographs. The verso of the title page portrays an elderly black man standing behind the fruit and vegetable bins extending a basket of luscious strawberries to the lady whose greyness denotes her unreality. Only her pinkish-brown face and hands are colorful. With these visual devices, the viewer enters a world of fantasy contrasted with reality. Molly Bang translates her creative ideas to introduce ethnic people with superb artistic skill. She uses sharp perspective in her double spreads to reinforce the abrupt changes in the allegory.

On her way home from the market through the corridors of the indoor mall, the grey lady passes a flower shop carrying a box of strawberries. An attractive young black woman is exiting carrying a large bunch of flowers to which a card bearing the book's dedication is attached. A green-mantled bluish-purple strawberry snatcher lurking nearby starts to follow the grey lady, but she fades into the background, leaving only the strawberries visible to him.

As they pass a series of lovely shops—pastries, toys, crafts, and oriental rugs—the grey lady turns sharply left, and an East Indian woman in native costume on a red skateboard, holding a bucket filled with snakes, bumps into the stalker. While the strawberry snatcher is entangled in snakes, the grey lady boards a bus. The strawberry snatcher jumps on the red skateboard and tries to catch up with the bus. Later, he waits for the grey lady beside the swamp through which she must pass when she gets off the bus. The eerie trip through the swamp nearly costs him his life as he flounders in the water.

Once through the swamp on the final leg of the journey to the grey lady's home they enter a flowering forest which seems friendly at first, that is, until the grey lady's greyness begins to increase. She becomes covered by the grey places in the forest and therefore less visible to him. Just as he is about to reach her, she hands him a cut birch tree and escapes into the greyness of blank pages. He looks everywhere but cannot find her. In his determination, however, he does find a clump of blackberry bushes and luxuriates in the delicious berries. As he takes off his purple straw hat, he displays a shock of radiant yellow curly hair.

Meanwhile the grey lady brings her strawberries home to a young grey boy and girl and banjo-playing husband, while a woman—reminiscent of a real (not imaginary) grey lady—feeds a bottle to a young grandchild. The woman and the grandchild are the only figures in the picture represented in full color, that is, aside from the cat, the parrot, and the furnishings.

Thematic Analysis

This allegory is wonderful for the many themes that are visually accessible to observers, depending on the experience and knowledge that they bring to it. Berries (rewards) for all are clearly shown. The small malcontent, or strawberry snatcher, in all can discover a satisfying berry along the way. The full line between reality and fantasy becomes more apparent, which is especially important for middle-graders. All viewers, from the older ones to the youngest, will enjoy the mementos that decorate the home of the grey lady, symbolizing a life of remembrance and love. Above all, the story incorporates values and beliefs, including an appreciation of multiracial persons, that the young person may adopt to make his or her role in society more comfortable and meaningful. Repeated readings will offer new insights, which discussion of the book will deepen.

Discussion Materials

This book can be presented as a wordless story by first showing the front jacket and the empty box on the back jacket, then the bluish-purple strawberry snatcher trailing the grey lady (pp. 4–5), asking the question "What happened?" Or use some of the eerie swamp pictures and the grey episodes in the woods (pp. 16–19; 20–26) to indicate the possible nature of the grey lady. As a special highlight, try a rebus-type activity by asking the questions "Which persons are real?" and "Is it possible that some have two representations?" to increase interest (pp. 44–45). This book can be presented fully or, for the more sophisticated audience, briefly. In either case, it deserves careful consideration from the viewer, whether independently or in a group.

Related Materials

Five well-known authors have written titles suitable for middle-graders: *The Gathering* (Greenwillow, 1981) by Virginia Hamilton; *Dragon's Blood* (Delacorte, 1982) by Jane Yolen; *Silent Voice* (Dutton, 1981) by Julia Cunningham; *Rescue of Ranor* (Atheneum, 1983) by Wilanne Schneider Belden; and *The Present Takers* (Harper, 1984) by Aidan Chambers. Two titles by Robin McKinley are good for more advanced readers: *Blue Sword* and *Hero and the Crown* (both Greenwillow, 1982; 1984), the latter is set several hundred years earlier than the first. For older readers who want an exciting story, suggest Dee Brown's *Killdeer Mountain* (Holt, 1983) and Bruce Brooks's *Midnight Hour Encores* (Harper, 1986).

The filmstrip *The Dream Child* (Random, 1986) is suggested as background. Also recommended are the following cassettes: *Two Hands Hold the Earth* (A Gentle Wind, 1985) by Sarah Pirtle; *Graveyard of Ghost Tales Told by Vincent Price* (Caedmon, 1973); *Graveyard Tales* (N.A.P.P.S., 1985); and *Transport of 7-41-R* (Viking, 1974) from the book by T. Degens. The film *John Brown, Rose and the Midnight Cat* (Weston Woods, 1982) will be useful here. The microcomputer software *Mindscape* (Story Book Starters, 1986), which correlates with the *Bank Street Story Book*, contains mystery pictures that will help youngsters deepen their curiosity. It is from the Apple II family of floppy disks.

Brittain, Bill. *Devil's Donkey*
Drawings by Andrew Glass. Harper, 1981, 120 pp.

The author's first title for children, *All the Money in the World* (Harper, 1979), was acclaimed a children's choice by the International Reading Association/Children's Book Council. *Devil's Donkey*, published two years later, is also popular with children, and recently Bill Brittain published *The Wish Giver: Three Tales of Coven Tree* and *Dr. Dredd's Wagon of Wonders* (Harper, 1983; 1987), which are more or less sequels.

Devil's Donkey, a properly scary witch story set in the New England town of Coven Tree, about Dan'l, a youngster who is turned into a donkey until he wins a bet with the Devil and attains his human form again, will appeal to young people in grades 2–6 (ages 7–11). The book has eight short chapters of approximately 35 pages each.

Nine black-and-white pencil illustrations by Andrew Glass, as well as his book jacket drawings, add to the eeriness of the story. The front jacket shows a bordered picture of a scary Dan'l, with large donkey ears and body fur, entangled in the bare branches of the coven tree as a partially hidden full moon peers down. A small rendition of the tree appears on the back jacket. The frontispiece portrays a rider (Stew Meat) on a donkey (Dan'l) near the coven tree as they approach the cottage of the witch (Old Magda) by moonlight.

Seven full-page drawings illuminate the story. The first shows a dungareed and scared Dan'l with his hair standing on end when the silhouette of Old Magda in her crone's cap appears in the doorway. In the final drawing, the smiling Dan'l, released from his donkey bondage, is still arrayed in the muzzle and harness. The other five portray Hecate, the owl, finding Dan'l in the woods; Jenny and Dan'l talking; Old Magda recovering from her magic efforts in the pantry; Dan'l talking with Mr. Beel (the Devil incarnate); and donkey-Dan'l pulling his load in the contest. A small picture within the text shows donkey-Dan'l spelling out the expletive "Dang blast" with hoof marks on the wall of the stall.

Stewart Meade (Stew Meat) is the narrator and owner of the general store in Coven Tree. His second cousin Daniel (Dan'l) Pitt, an orphan, comes to live with him at age nine. Dan'l acclimates easily, red hair and all, that is, in everything but the acceptance of tradition. His favorite question is "Why?" For example, he can't believe the old story about not chopping down branches from the coven tree that stands on the edge of town. Nor does he show any fear of Old Magda whom people call a witch. One day, when he is 14, Dan'l cuts some dead branches from the coven tree to save time when Stew Meat sends him to the orchard for firewood. Dan'l pays no attention when one limb strikes his ankle and draws blood, but later, when Old Magda appears at the general store and says the right words: "Who sheds his blood by Coven Tree / Under Old Magda's spell will be," Dan'l becomes a donkey.

Luckily, Stew Meat discovers what has happened, and they both go to Old Magda's cottage (see frontispiece). There he discovers that Dan'l's favorite expression, "Dang blast," is the proper completion to the magic rhyme, and Dan'l returns to human form. Although Stew Meat and Dan'l then go about their business, they keep a wary eye out for Old Magda, who has told Stew Meat that she promised a donkey as recompense to a Mr. Beel who is coming soon. But Stew Meat lets his guard down when he goes to the city for a weekend. Although Dan'l says he'll be fine, Hecate, the owl, finds him on the bank of Spider Creek. After Hecate mesmerizes him, Old Magda, disguised as a blackberry bush, changes Dan'l into a donkey again. To ensure his safe delivery until Mr. Beel arrives, she talks farmer Bingham (Paul) and his wife and daughter (Anna and Jenny) into using him. Although he minds being a donkey, Dan'l doesn't mind being with Jenny, who is about his own age. In fact, she is the one who sees "Dang blast" spelled out with hoof marks on the wall of the stall and repeats the words aloud to return Dan'l to human form again. Stark naked until Jenny gets some of her Pa's clothes, Dan'l talks with Jenny for awhile before he goes back to explain to Stew Meat that he didn't just run away.

But Hecate and Old Magda soon follow, and for the third time she changes Dan'l into a donkey. Even worse, Old Magda with her witchery chases the magic cure clean out of Stew Meat's head. Donkey-Dan'l frantically runs to Jenny, but she can't remember the term either. However, Stew Meat figures out that the old witch intends to pay tribute to her master, the devil (Mr. Beel), with the donkey but he also realizes that Dan'l has not yet sold his soul, and that gives him an idea.

When Mr. Beel, who resembles a peddler of old, arrives in his dark, red wagon, Stew Meat proposes that they wager on a pulling contest between Mr. Beel's off-donkey—Hercules, who in human form used to be a strong woodsman—and donkey-Dan'l for both Dan'l's and Stew Meat's souls. Fortunately, donkey-Dan'l wins. Mr. Beel leaves, freeing Old Magda in the bargain and making her happy for the first time in 300 years. Folks are much more friendly to her now. Everything is still the same, but somehow better. The coven tree still stands, but Dan'l is now much more respectful of heritage.

Thematic Analysis

The essential struggle between good and evil is presented with a humorous and pseudoscary outline for youngsters. Dan'l like many youngsters learns to value traditions the hard way (hopefully the youngsters reading the story will learn this value vicariously). Everything turns, however, on the devilish wager. The message is to pull your load and respect the complexities of man or lose your soul. Magic makes the story all the more appealing.

Discussion Materials

This book can be presented in many ways. To paraphrase briefly, summarize the eight chapter headings (p. vii). To introduce the main characters use: Stew Meat and Dan'l (pp. 4–6); Old Magda (p. 11); Hecate (pp. 39–40); the Binghams (pp. 52–53); and Mr. Beel (pp. 85–88). Or use the drawings in the same way: (frontispiece, pp. 15, 21, 38, 59, 63, 72, 87, 110, 117). A casual remark about the donkey-boy and the old witch will stimulate interest.

Related Materials

Natalie Babbitt's *Devil's Storybook: Stories and Pictures* (Weston Woods, 1974) is a suitable record or cassette, as is *Pinocchio* (Caedmon, 1969). The film *Getting Started* (L.C.A., 1981) satirically examines procrastination. Some suggestions for younger middle-graders are: *Pigs Might Fly* (Viking, 1982) and *Babe: The Gallant Pig* (Crown, 1985), both by Dick King-Smith; the records *Charlotte's Web* and *Stuart Little* (both Pathways of Sound); *Thaddeus* (Little, 1984) by Alison Cragin Hertiz; and *Fables You Shouldn't Have to Pay Any Attention To* (Lippincott, 1978) by Florence Parry Heide. Four other stories can also be used: *Bundles of Sticks* (Atheneum, 1982) by Pat Rhoads Mauser, about 11-year-old Ben; *My Secret Admirer* (Delacorte, 1984) by Stephen Roos, about 11-year-old Claire; *North of Danger* (Dutton, 1978) by Dale Fife, about 12-year-old Arne; and *George Midgett's War* (Scribner, 1985) by Sally Edwards, about young George and his father who are helping with the supply lines to Valley Forge. Also recommended are the Random record *Mrs. Frisby and the*

Rats of Nimh and a worthy successor, *Rasco and the Rats of Nimh* (Harper, 1986), by Jane Leslie Conly, which continues the story of Thorn Valley.

Cleaver, Vera, and Cleaver, Bill. *Hazel Rye*
Lippincott, 1983, 178 pp.

Since the authors' first book, *Ellen Grae*, was published in 1967, Vera Cleaver and Bill Cleaver have consistently given the young reading public more than a dozen excellent titles, some award-winners, all popular (see condensations in *Introducing Books*, Bowker, 1970, pp, 56–59, and *Introducing More Books*, Bowker, 1978, pp. 1–4, 201–204). The Cleavers are noted for their sensitive portrayal of youngsters, especially as they approach the discoveries of some of life's most fundamental and cosmic values. They have been recognized as well for their writing skill, which expresses a southeastern regional mind-set.

Hazel Rye is set in Florida ridge country where there are many orange groves. (Although Bill Cleaver died before it was completed, Vera Cleaver finished it for the great benefit of youngsters in grades 5–7 [ages 10–12], who will find it entertaining and enlightening.) The young heroine, who has been retained in sixth grade, is as content with her poor reading ability as is her family. Luckily, however, she learns from an intelligent young itinerant boy, who restores her orange grove, that the world around her is much larger and more expansive than the restricted space she inhabits.

Eleven-year-old Hazel is the daughter of Ona and Millard Rye. Her Missouri-born father is a good provider and successful carpenter who can't read and doesn't expect more of Hazel. Her Tennessee-born mother suffers from "nerves" and keeps herself aloof. Her older brother, Donnie, the cab owner-driver in the nearby town of Echo Springs, has been married for two years to Vannie Lee, who spends a lot of time on her appearance.

Hazel doesn't feel put out about being retained in school. She knows that her father, whom she calls Millard because she has a close relationship with him, will not object, and she feels confident in her restricted world. Even Mr. Bartlett—a town resident who grows plants—likes her. On one visit, he tells Hazel that he'd give $10,000 for a brain like hers and only $100 for one like Jimmy's. Jimmy is the smart youngster in

Hazel's former class who can read well. Millard never tells her that this is a backhanded compliment, so Hazel feels superior even without reading.

Meanwhile, Millard continues his bad habit of going into a rage when Hazel disagrees with him. Luckily, however, he doesn't hurt anyone. Hazel reacts by silently sulking, and at the end of one of her silent sulks, Millard scribbles a "legal deed" to his adjoining three-acre orange grove and gives it to Hazel. She is thrilled because she envisions selling the derelict grove to some northerners for a lot of money. Ona, meanwhile, decides that she has had enough and goes to Tennessee for a vacation.

One evening as Hazel and Millard assume their customary seats on the porch, the Pooles pull up in their run-down car. Josephine (Jo), the mother, asks politely if they may rent the shack in the orange grove. Her husband recently died and she is traveling with her elder daughter, Wanda, her son, Felder, about Hazel's age, and three-year-old baby daughter, Jewel. Jo and Wanda intend to get jobs in Echo Springs to pay the rent. Millard and Hazel have a big argument, but finally Millard agrees to let the Pooles move in after they clean the messy Rye kitchen and Felder who brought some budsticks with him promises to restore the orange grove.

Soon afterward, the Poole women get jobs and Felder sets about budding, cultivating, and fertilizing the orange trees. Felder, a nature lover who also reads well, wants very much to have a microscope. Millard tells Hazel that Felder will always get along, yet he objects to Hazel's interest in helping in the grove, until, that is, Hazel concocts a whopper about the TV shows she pretends to watch when she is grounded at home, and Millard decides that it would be better for her to be the boss of her grove. After that, Hazel and Jewel help with the cultivating and watering, while Felder buds the trees. When he runs out of budsticks, they get more from Mr. Bartlett who also agrees to have a plant sale from which they can have 25 percent of the profits.

When the budding is complete and they are ready to fertilize, Felder reminds Hazel that she agreed to buy the fertilizer in return for his promise of work. According to the agreement, the Pooles can also live in the shack rent-free and Felder will get 10 percent from the sale of the orange grove. To get busy on her end of the bargain, Hazel asks Donnie to drive her with the hauling cart to Mr. Bartlett's. Together, they pick up the plants and decorate the cart for the sale in the park.

The plant sale turns out to be a big success. They sell all but three plants, have their pictures taken, and are interviewed for the local newspaper after the mayor sees the little bit of Americana from her office near the park and telephones the newspaper. Just before they leave the park, however, a young man tries to steal their money. A crowd gathers as Felder fights valiantly and Hazel smashes a plant across his nose. When the police arrive the villain is apprehended and the mayor tells the policeman to empty the robber's pockets for the kids.

After the plant sale is over, things happen rapidly. Felder and Hazel realize that they need more fertilizer for the trees, but Millard refuses to let her go back to Mr. Bartlett, saying that he will go. Then, while Felder helps her place her plants in the grove for safekeeping, Hazel tells him that she doesn't want to sell, and that she hopes he will accept the rent-free cottage and a dollar a week from her allowance as recompense for their original deal. Felder tells her that he knew all along she wouldn't sell, then adds that when winter comes some of the trees will need covering. Hazel goes to see him the next day, but finds that the Pooles have gone taking only what they brought.

At first, Hazel thinks that maybe Millard made them go, but when she finds the jar of seeds Felder has left for her in her row of plants, the idea of change and growth stir within her. She remembers a time not long ago when Millard brought home a dictionary and a ship model—from where he was working—how Felder used the dictionary to find the nautical meaning for the word "reeve," something Hazel and Millard couldn't do. She determines to learn to read well and expand her horizons while still enjoying Florida ridge country and her orange grove.

Thematic Analysis

The independent spirit and the fulfillment and satisfaction that its first stirrings bring are the main theme. That the freedom that independence brings to people enables them to be the best they always wanted to be is comforting and enlightening to youngsters of this age. Other aspects also are good reading fare, for example, ideas that are acted upon, such as cleaning the slovenly kitchen and bedrooms, a plant sale to raise cash, and learning how to make an orange grove productive. The emphasis on nature—seeds, birds, trees—is appealing to youngsters as well.

Discussion Materials

The story can be told using Hazel's orange grove to indicate change, from her initial idea to sell it and make a lot of money to the arrival of the Pooles and Felder's work with the fruit trees until she wants to keep the grove. Introduce the characters: Millard (p. 7); Hazel (p. 8); the Pooles (p. 10); Ona (pp. 36–37). Then paraphrase the orange grove gift (pp. 5–7); Hazel's dream of making money (pp. 35–37); and finally Hazel's decision to keep the grove (pp. 172–173). Millard's monetary persuasions might also be shown: tempting Hazel (pp. 108–109); the earrings (pp. 95–97); and the Cadillac (155–157; 164–168). Special anecdotes to highlight are the plant sale (pp. 137–150) and budding the orange trees (pp. 59–61).

Related Materials

Some suggested books are: *Story for a Black Night* (Houghton, 1982) by Clayton Bess, about moral choices that must be made in a Liberian setting; *Fridays* (Putnam, 1980) by Patricia Lee Gauch, about a junior high female in today's world; *Beloved Benjamin Is Waiting* (Dutton, 1978) by Jean Karl, about Lucinda's courageous solutions to her problems; *Java Jack* (Crowell, 1980) by Luqman Keele, about Jack, the son of anthropologists, who has many adventurous and fantastic experiences in Java; *Dan Alone* (Lippincott, 1983) by John Rowe Townsend, about abandoned 11-year-old Dan, who takes to an English city's streets; *One-Eyed Cat* (Bradbury, 1984) by Paula Fox, about Ned, who disobeys his minister father, and the consequences of his behavior; and *Seaward* (Atheneum, 1983) by Susan Cooper, about two youngsters who in their search for their parents survive difficult obstacles. The book of poems *Class Dismissed II: More High School Poems* (Clarion, 1986) by Mel Glenn is also recommended together with its predecessor. The poems suggest pertinent themes for youngsters.

A few audiovisual titles are also suggested: the film *Revenge of the Nerd* (L.C.A., 1985); the records *Edgar Allan Poe Soundbook* (Caedmon, 1977), read by Basil Rathbone and Vincent Price, and *Caddie Woodlawn* (Random, also in video); the filmstrip *Silver Pony: A Story in Pictures* (Weston Woods, 1975) by Lynn Ward; and the kit *Phantom Tollbooth* (Listening Library, 1982) by Norton Juster.

Dahl, Roald.   *Boy: Tales of Childhood*
Farrar, 1984, 160 pp.

This much-admired author of wonderful seriocomic stories for children (see *Introducing Books*, Bowker, 1970, pp. 60–63) has produced his "autobiography" to age 20. Roald Dahl has never published a boring story—far from it—and in his author's note he says that he would never write a history of himself. Rather, he has put down the highlights of his childhood impressions. The result is an intriguing book of a child's impressions of childhood experiences that will appeal to all ages. Roald's progress through his fascinating early life will strike a responsive chord in many, especially middle-graders, for the universality of the young feelings that reside in each incident. As he says, "Some are funny, some painful. Some are unpleasant. I suppose that is why I have always remembered them so vividly. All are true." Mr. Dahl is a genius; he bridges the feelings of the young and their fantastic sense of fun (sometimes covering horror), so that adults can also tap their remembered feelings.

Quentin Blake, who also illustrated the author's recent titles *The Witches* and *The BFG* (both Farrar, 1983; 1982), drew the black-and-white pictures of the young author (about age 10) for the arresting front jacket. The title, *Boy*, appears in bright red letters at the bottom of the picture. The back jacket carries a full-length photograph of a current Roald leaning against an old Norwegian hay wagon. The endpapers are a compilation of a baker's dozen of charming small photographs of Roald at various ages with members of his family. The book is dedicated to his five siblings—two of whom he refers to as his ancient half brother and half sister (from his father's first marriage). His natural siblings are all female, although he sadly notes the death of a seven-year-old sister—Astri—and as an adult the death of his seven-year-old daughter.

The book is divided into four parts chronologically by his school attendance and corresponding ages: Starting Point; Llandaff Cathedral School, 1923–25 (ages 7–9); St. Peter's, 1925–29 (ages 9–13); Repton and Shell, 1929–36 (ages 13–20). Each of the seven or eight chapters—save two in the first part—are liberally illustrated with old photographs and small black-and-white childlike drawings of objects mentioned in the text, especially things that are no longer in everyday use. The second part contains mainly drawings, except for the chapter on the Norway visit.

Roald (Boy) is born, the only boy of four children, in Llandaff, Wales, to a Norwegian Papa and Mama who were married after Papa's first wife, a Frenchwoman, died leaving two other children. Boy's Papa, Harald, and his brother, Oscar, were both eager to make a fortune. They left their home near Oslo (then Christiana), Norway, and did. Harald and a partner became shipbrokers in Cardiff, Wales, and Uncle Oscar established a fishing fleet in La Rochelle, France. They each established a wealthy family replete with art and literature. Harald lost his left arm at the elbow as a boy, but was little impeded by its amputation. In fact, he became a prolific diarist.

When Boy is two, the large family moves to larger quarters in the Welsh village of Radyr. There, in 1920, when Boy is three, his eldest sister, Astri, seven, dies of appendicitis. Papa Harald dies soon after of pneumonia. The pregnant widow, who has a baby girl two months later, has to care for six children and herself. Fortunately, although reduced (they have to move back to Llandaff), she has the means. Because Papa believed strongly in education in general and English public schools in particular, Mama determines to carry out his wishes by moving eventually to England. Meanwhile, Boy goes to a local kindergarten, Elmtree House, for a year. The adult recalls little before age seven; however, Boy's excitement riding to and from school on his tricycle unaccompanied by adults and watching older youngsters whiz by on their bicycles remains clear in Roald's memory.

While at the Llandaff Cathedral School, which he attends from ages 7 to 9, Boy enjoys his three friends and their visits to Mrs. Pratchett's Sweetshop, but he resents her mean spirit and the soiled hands with which she retrieves their candy choices from the jars. To get even he puts a dead mouse—with the knowledge of his friends—in a jar of Gobstoppers. Mrs. Pratchett subsequently appears at school to identify them, and Mr. Coombs applies the "cane," the traditional method of punishment.

Boy also likes to go to Norway during the summer. Seeing Bestepapa and Bestemama and sharing an annual reunion with his Norwegian relatives are pure pleasures. The "skaal" ritual, boating, and swimming are wonderful experiences, and sailing the Oslofjord to the magic summer island of Tjöme is thrilling. The only unpleasant adventure is the surprising loss of his adenoids without anesthesia in the doctor's basin.

When he is nine, Boy goes across Bristol Channel from Cardiff to England and St. Peter's as a boarder. Dressed in his gray flannel school uniform and carrying his "tuck-box" filled with his favorite small possessions, he and Mama sail across the channel in a packet. Boy cries as Mama leaves, after which begins the required writing home once a week. (Fortunately, Mama kept the letters, as Roald found out after she died. Parts of them are reproduced on pages where they reinforce the text.)

In the second floor dormitory, the matron—well known throughout English literature—reigns supreme. Boy and his classmates are terrified by this person who seems so insensitive. Somehow he survives until the holidays, when he returns home, and his severe homesickness makes him feign an appendectomy attack. His kindly family doctor is not fooled, however, and tells him he must return. Before he goes back, the same doctor stitches his nose back on after the ancient half sister (with only two hours of instruction) drives them into an accident in their new motorcar. Mama finally gets Boy, the most seriously hurt, to the doctor for surgery. When he awakens from the ether, she gives him a gold sovereign.

Back at school, Hardcastle (one of the meanest masters) gives Boy a "stripe" for talking in "prep"—in truth he only asked another boy for a pen nib to replace his broken one. Boy receives six unmerciful strokes with the cane.

Meanwhile Boy's ancient half sister gets engaged. When her young man accompanies them to Norway during the summer, with natural high jinks, Boy puts goat droppings in the young man's pipe. All the children wait quietly until he smokes it. After a few minutes of explosive pain, the young man finds out from the littlest girl what happened. Soon, many small children are jumping in the water.

By the time he is 12, Boy and his family are living in Kent, England, and Boy chooses to go to Repton in the Midlands. After being outfitted in the school costume of tails and a panama sailor hat, Boy and Mama take a train from London to the school. Not long afterward Boy learns all about "Boazers" (prefects), who have the power of life and death over junior boys. Although the headmaster, who eventually becomes the archbishop of Canterbury, leaves a negative impression on the youngster, the custom of the Cadbury Company to submit their chocolate bars for surveys to the school stands Boy in good stead when 35 years later he uses his memories to write *Charlie and the Chocolate Factory* (condensed in *Introducing Books*, Bowker, 1970, pp. 60–63). Boy is intrigued by a curious math teacher who hates math, the system of "fagging" (or slave labor), which keeps him warming an older boy's bog seat (outdoor toilet) all winter, how good he is at some games, and photography. Although he becomes a captain of fives and of squash rackets, he does not become a Boazer, generally an automatic attainment. To quote Roald, "I'm awfully glad I didn't."

After Boy graduates, he lands a job with Shell, even though he was advised that he wouldn't, but soon joins the Royal Air Force in World War II. At that point, Roald ends the clear and sharply remembered experiences: "But all that is another story. It has nothing to do with childhood or school or Gobstoppers or dead mice or Boazers or summer holidays among the islands of Norway."

Thematic Analysis

The development of beliefs is a theme that flows strongly in these reminiscences. That the young Boy learns the lessons of getting along in his semiextended family, making friends along his path, is obvious as this story unfolds, for example, the three friends in the sweetshop episode. What is equally obvious is Mr. Dahl's position against excessive corporal punishment of children and child exploitation, for example, "fagging," and for the independence of youngsters to recognize and take pleasure in their special interests, for example, fives, squash racquets, and photography. He also clearly values his father's diary-writing ability and his mother's strength and courage. What Mr. Dahl now believes is instantly recognizable in the experiences he relates.

Discussion Materials

This is a good read-aloud book. It can also be book talked by displaying the front jacket and endpapers while setting the background (pp. 13–20), but read the brief author's note beforehand. Many episodes can be read or paraphrased: about candy (pp. 27–35; 70–71; 130–135); the schools (pp. 21–24; 40–41; 69–73; 123–127; 151); caning (pp. 45–50; 99–114); vacations in Norway (pp. 51–63; 115–120); medical encounters (pp. 14; 64–66; 75; 86–90; 91–98; 112–114). Some incidents about mischievousness can be highlighted: the great mouse plot (pp. 35–37); homesickness (pp. 86–90); and goat tobacco (pp. 115–120).

Related Materials

Eleanor Roosevelt, with Love: A Centenary Remembrance (Lodestar, 1984) by her son, Elliot Roosevelt, complements this title, even though it emphasizes her life during the White House years. Four other titles are useful with older youngsters: *Thursday's Children* (Viking, 1984) by Rumer Godden; *Sarah Will* (Harper, 1985) by Sue Ellen Bridgers; *Tancy* (Clarion, 1984) by Belinda Hurmence; and *Maroo of the Winter Caves* (Clarion, 1984) by Ann Turnbull. Some for younger people are *Quentin Corn* (Godine, 1985) by Mary Stolz; *Fifth Grade Magic* (Dutton, 1982) by Beatrice Gormley; *The Falcon Bow* (Macmillan, 1986) by Sid Campbell; and *Long Claws* and *Frozen Fire* (both Macmillan, 1981; 1977) by James Houston.

The cassette *And Now Miguel* by Joseph Krumgold is available from Random. Two suggested films or videos are *Quest* (Pyramid, 1985) and *I Promise to Remember* (Cinema Guild, 1985).

Godden, Rumer. *The Mousewife*
Illus. by Heidi Holder. Viking, 1982, 31 pp.

Well recognized and beloved by young readers over generations, the author has written many stories (see, for example, *Introducing Books*, Bowker, 1970, p. 284). Recently, she published *The Diddakoi, The Dragon of Og*, and *Aesop's Fables*, and many of her books have been reissued, *The Story of Holly and Ivy*, for example. *The Mousewife*, which first appeared in 1951, was renewed by the author in 1979 and published by Viking in 1982, for the first time with illustrations by Heidi Holder. The simple and direct story is about a mouse "housefrau" and an outdoor turtle-dove, which the owner of the house puts in a cage. Rumer Godden found the story in a journal of Dorothy Wordsworth, William's sister. The only difference—a significant one—is that Godden's dove is released by the mousewife to return to the wild. This allegorical tale will appeal to all ages, particularly to those in grades 3–5.

The artist, Heidi Holder, who is self-taught and also illustrated the author's *Aesop's Fables*, did six beautiful full-page black-and-white pencil drawings of the mousewife, her family, and the dove, each bordered decoratively or with a thin black pen line. In the last picture, the tip of the dove's wing extends onto the opposite page. Eleven half-page or smaller drawings follow the activities of the main characters. The title page shows the mousewife consoling the sorrowful sedentary dove. On the jacket Holder used soft watercolor washes over pastel pencil-and-ink renderings of the two main characters, with muted peach as the background color, within a flowered baroque wooden frame. The mousewife's curled tail extends over the frame. Lavender endpapers set a gentle mood. The well-designed book bears a legend noting the media used by the artist and the typefaces.

Although the mousewife lives comfortably with her husband in Miss Barbara Wilkinson's house, she wants more. When her husband asks her what, the mousewife says she doesn't know. Mice have always been the same throughout recorded history, but she is a little different. She does the usual things: She plays with the other mice, she makes a proper nest for the babies that she hopes to have someday, she keeps her home nice and neat, and she accepts her status as a house mouse, and not a garden or field mouse. But all winter and spring she looks out the upstairs window and sees things that she doesn't know about. Then her husband becomes ill from eating rich Christmas cake, and the mousewife's customary duties increase; now she has to gather all the food, too.

The mousewife soon discovers that Miss Wilkinson has put a turtle-dove in an elegant cage and added water, peas, and sugar for the captured bird to eat. Eager to get the peas—Miss Wilkinson keeps a very neat house, leaving little food for the mice to eat—the mousewife quickly steals a pea from the cage, and even though she suspects danger there, she returns for more peas the next day. The homesick dove, who will not eat them, lets her take them all. Meanwhile, Miss Wilkinson is so happy because she thinks the dove is eating.

Intrigued by the dove, the mousewife tries to entice it at least to drink some water, but the dove replies that it only drinks dew. When she asks what that is, it tells her about the grass, the leaves, and the morning freshness. Telling her, makes the dove long for its home and mate even more, and as it tries to tell the mousewife what flying is, it spreads its restricted wings against the bars of the cage. The mousewife continues to visit the dove daily, bringing it crumbs, and even a blackberry, to eat. The dove calls happily to her, "Roo coo, roo coo," and tells her more about the world beyond the house on the other side of the river each day.

Then the happy day comes when the mousewife has a nestfull of baby mice. The eldest, Flannelette, and her husband, who seems no better, keep her so busy that she is not able to visit the dove for some time. While her husband is visiting friends one day, however, she goes up to see the dove, whom she finds even more disconsolate now because it thinks she has gone away. Despite her husband's anger when he returns and finds her gone, she determines to creep up to the cage again to release the dove. Even though she doesn't think like a dove, she can empathize with it.

When the mousewife returns to the cage, she finds the dove sleeping and imagines that it is dreaming of flying free. Without hesitating, she releases the catch with her teeth and the door opens. As the dove spreads its wings and flies out of the cage, the mousewife drops to the floor and watches it fly out the window and over the trees. Not only does the mousewife see what it means to fly, but she also sees the distant stars, something most mice don't see. She proudly goes back to bed.

Much later in life, the mousewife's great-great-great grandchildren treat her with respect. Although she looks the same as other mice, they know she is a little different. She "knows something they do not."

Thematic Analysis

Although this simple story has many themes, freedom of the human spirit is foremost. Learning and knowing about foreign experiences intimately without actually having them can develop an attitude of understanding and personal freedom. That such an understanding can come as readily from sensitive feeling as from thinking is also implied. Sharing, women's rights, and other issues all find recognition here, but the human need to be with those who share common experiences and beliefs assumes primacy in the march to freedom.

Discussion Materials

This book can be presented as a picture book, or it can be paraphrased while displaying the pictures: gathering food (p. 2); mice in the attic (p. 6); meeting the caged turtledove (p. 10); a cradle of baby mice (p. 17); the mousewife ponders releasing the dove (p. 21); and the dove flies out the window (p. 26). Or the activities of the house mice can be paraphrased through illustrations: the mousewife decorates her hole (p. 4); she looks out the window (p. 7); the mouse husband takes to his bed (p. 8); the mousewife enters the cage to steal the peas (p. 13); the dove tries to spread its wings (p. 14); the mouse husband visits friends (p.18); the mousewife comforts the dove (p.19); the mousewife's journey to release the dove (p. 23); the mousewife sees the stars through the window (p. 28); and great-great-great Grandma (p. 29). For independent readers introduce the two main characters (title page); for all read the author's short epilogue (p. 31).

Related Materials

Two picture books worth investigating are *The Polar Express* (Houghton, 1985) by Chris Van Allsburg, about the long-lasting magic of Christmas, and *Brave Irene* (Farrar, 1986) by William Steig, about pluck and success in human endeavors. *Song of Pentecost* (Dutton, 1983) by W. J. Corbett, an allegory about the dangers facing the mice of Pentecost Farm, is suitable for older middle-graders. Four titles also for this age group are: *Night the Monster Came* (Morrow, 1982) by Mary Calhoun; *The Bionic Bunny Show* (Little, 1984) by Marc Brown and Laurene Brown; *Chin Chiang and the Dragon's Dance* (Atheneum, 1984) by Ian Wallace; and *I Know a Lady* (Greenwillow, 1984) by Charlotte Zolotow. Four records that also fit well are: *Watership Down* (The Mind's Eye, 1986); *Dark Is Rising; Grey King* (both Random, 1977); and *Knee-Knock Rise* (Random, 1971). Two films or videos suitable for older middle-graders are *To Bear Witness* (Phoenix, 1985) and *Deciso* (Churchill Films, 1982).

Hastings, Selina, retel.   *Sir Gawain and the Loathly Lady*
Illus. by Juan Wijngaard. Lothrop, 1985, 29 pp.

The author and illustrator of this title are also responsible for the earlier title *Sir Gawain and the Green Knight* (Lothrop, 1981). Like its predecessor, this title retells a folklore episode from the King Arthur epic. Selina Hastings gracefully retells the story of the horrible looking gnome-like lady who saves King Arthur from a malevolent knight by answering the riddle "What does every woman want?" in return for Arthur's promise to give her one of his knights as a husband. Youngsters in grades 4–6 will enjoy the retelling; all ages will appreciate the story and the beautiful illustrations.

The front cover with its library binding has one of the book's magnificent illustrations—Sir Gawain walking down the aisle with the horrible old hag (loathly lady) on his arm. On the back cover within a decorated frame with two heraldic-like inserts, the text is briefly summarized. Both covers have a navy blue background with a pattern of small yellow stars. The endpapers are small, covered with colored mosaics within a border, and the front endpapers also include an ex-libris device showing a monkey-man reading a book. The title page is bordered with three small asymmetrical traditional heraldic pictures: a metal statue of a mounted knight; a painting of a knight on a charger in malevolent black; and an ivory-like statuette of King Arthur holding a specter and an orb. Each page of text, beginning on page 6 and continuing to page 29, bears the same ¾-inch floral border, as well as a combination of illustration and heraldic device, perhaps a miniature detail of the main picture on the same or previous page. Some of the illustrations are arranged horizontally, some vertically; many are full pages, and two are double spreads. Each is full of authentic costumes and details of the period.

As Arthur Pendragon, the king, is riding in the Inglewood outside Carlisle Castle where he and the Knights of the Round Table are spending the Christmas holidays, he suddenly becomes lost. He finds himself on the edge of a brackish pond, where he sees a knight dressed in black armor approaching on a black charger to do battle. The king is helpless without his magic sword, Excalibur, which is far away in Camelot. At the last moment, however, the errant knight tells Arthur that if he can answer the riddle, "What does every woman want?" when they meet again on New Year's Day (three days later), he will let him go. On the way back to the castle, King Arthur asks every woman that he meets to answer the riddle, but he gets no uniform answer. Then, just before he reaches the castle, he sees an old hag dressed elegantly in red velvet, fur, and fine rings, who agrees to give him the correct answer if he will give her one of his knights as husband. He promises, and although he is sorry he did so after she whispers the answer to the riddle in his ear—that what most women desire is to have their own way—the errant knight does spare his life when he tells him the correct answer.

Back at the castle, King Arthur sorrowfully tells his wife, Guinevere, of his promise to the old hag. Sir Gawain asks that he may be the one to save the king's honor by marrying the old hag. Together they all set out with a paladin to find the loathly lady who is still on the stump in the forest where Arthur first saw her. Everyone but Guinevere and Sir Gawain, who can accept her difference, is aghast when they see her. Guinevere helps the bride prepare for the wedding and Sir Gawain calmly escorts her down the aisle.

After the ceremony, Guinevere kisses the bride on both haggard cheeks. Meanwhile, Sir Gawain goes to the bridal chamber, and in desperation holds his head in his hands. When he looks up, however, he is nonplussed to discover a beautiful young woman standing behind him— his wife. She tells him that she is now half-absolved from her spell, but that she still has to spend half of each 24 hours as a hag. She asks whether he wishes her to choose day or night. When he chooses night, she accuses him of being selfish. When he then changes his answer to daytime, she again complains, saying that he will find her very repellent at night. Sir Gawain, not knowing what to say, tells her to choose. "You have given me what every woman wants—her own way" she answers.

"And now the spell is broken." The celebration at the Castle of Carlisle goes on for many days, longer than any before.

Thematic Analysis

The moral of this tale can be interpreted in many ways. Although this retelling emphasizes women's rights, it is merely the mechanism for stating something more essential to the spirit of all human beings—the freedom of choice. The development of this value makes each person's journey toward adulthood smoother; however, an appreciation of the moral from this tale depends on such factors as the age, sex, and experience of the reader. Freedom of choice is hard-won, especially for middle-graders.

Discussion Materials

The best way to present this book in typical picture-book fashion is to paraphrase each page, ending with the double-spread illustration of the wedding procession (pp. 22–23), but first display the front cover and read the summary that appears on the back cover. For independent readers, use the following plan: the front cover illustration of the wedding procession; the back cover words verbatim; paraphrased pages 8–9 including the riddle "What is it that women desire the most?"; a picture of the loathly lady (p. 12); and her bargain with King Arthur (p. 13).

Related Materials

Middle-graders will enjoy *Acorn Quest* (Crowell, 1981), a spoof of the Arthurian legend by Jane Yolen. A cassette or kit of the title *Girl Who Cried Flowers and Other Tales* (Weston Woods, 1983) by the same author presents five old-fashioned fairy tale-like stories that will appeal to the same group. Another story of the transfiguring power of love, *Buffalo Woman* (Bradbury/Macmillan, 1984) by Paul Goble, retells the Plains Indian tale of the young hunter who marries a buffalo. Six other titles are also suggested—the first three for grades 4–6; the last three for grades 5–6: Alan Arkin's *Lemming Condition* (Harper, 1976); Johanna Hurwitz's *Tough-Luck Karen* (Morrow, 1982); Patricia MacLachlan's *To-morrow's Wizard* (Harper, 1982); Astrid Lindgren's *Brothers Lionheart* (Viking, 1975); Gregory Macguire's *Dream Stealer* (Harper, 1983); and Phillipa Pearce's *Shadow Cage and Other Tales of the Supernatural* (Crowell, 1977). Two records from Caedmon of Joan Aiken's *Wolves of Willoughby Chase* and *Necklace of Raindrops and Other Stories* are suitable here. The filmstrip of Hans Christian Andersen's *Swineherd* (Weston Woods, 1977) is also useful. A video or 16mm film of *The Mystery of Stonehenge* and *The Mystery of the Maya* (WNET/13) will provide a stimulating background.

Magnus, Erica. *The Boy and the Devil*
Illus. by the author. Carolrhoda, 1986, 27 pp.

The author, who previously wrote *Old Lars* (Carolrhoda, 1983), drew from her Norwegian heritage for this title—from the tales she heard from her father as a young girl. (She also adapted and illustrated another Norwegian folktale about a lad who outwits a stranger (the Devil) by flattering him.) The *Boy and the Devil* will appeal to youngsters ages 5–9 (grades K–4).

The illustrations are bright pastel paintings with superb fine line shadings. The feathery detailed lines give an impression of blowing breezes in many pictures, the construction of fabrics in others. The predominant shades of autumn—red, yellow, and gold in the deciduous leaves—and the green and blue of the native evergreens of Norway abound. The young boy, about 11, has the familiar white-blond hair color of Scandinavian children; the Lincolnesque figure (save for the somber, evil countenance) is dressed in shades of black. The 16 full-page color illustrations interpret the facing page of text bordered with a red or green line. In two places the full-page illustrations are opposite each other without text. The illustration on the half-title page shows a large framed portrait of the boy holding the crucial nut before his lips, while the evergreens and trees with brilliant yellow and red leaves of autumn appear as background. The front jacket portrays the sly youngster peering through the leaves with a threatening-looking black horse's hoof behind him. The painting is framed in an intricately scrolled heavy blond wood rectangle. The back jacket shows a round carved detail of light wood on which the cracked nut rests.

As a young boy dressed in a traditional Norwegian costume with tasseled cap goes nutting along a woodland path, he stoops to pick up a nut with a tiny worm hole. He continues walking until he meets a stranger, whom he knows to be the trickster (the Devil) because of the black horse's hoof extending from one of the stranger's trouser legs. Without hesitation, the boy asks the stranger if he can make himself as big as an elephant. Flattered, the stranger grows to gigantic height. Then the boy asks him if he can make himself as small as a flea, and when the stranger obliges, the boy asks him to creep into the hole in the nut. Sticking a twig in the hole, the boy takes his prize to the blacksmith, whistling all the way. Along the way all the animals—the deer and rabbits in the woods, the sheep, and the horse drawing the wagon that he passes—swiftly turn and run away.

When the boy gets to the blacksmith's wooden hut, he asks the blacksmith to crack open the nut. At first the blacksmith uses his smallest sledgehammer for the tiny nut, but the nut cries out and flies off the anvil. The blacksmith then tries a larger sledgehammer, but again the nut cries out and hurls itself across the shop. The astonished blacksmith takes his largest sledgehammer. As he smashes the nut through the roof, the roof, walls, and furniture tumble all around him. The blacksmith mutters "The Devil himself was in that nut," and the boy who stands smiling in the middle of the rubble knowingly answers that he was.

Thematic Analysis

In its adaptation the Norwegian folktale not only carries the culture and geography of the country, but also transmits a dual message. Vanity or self-aggrandizement can get one into trouble, but in a life-threatening situation, it can be used defensively. By humorously showing a young person that vanity is not a desirable characteristic, the tale reveals a development in values.

Discussion Materials

The title should work perfectly in a picture-book talk. If you choose to introduce it by highlighting a few episodes, try this outlined plan: the success of the ploy or the theme (front and back jacket); the boy and the nut (half-title page); the boy meets a stranger while nutting (the first four illustrations); and the nut lays broken (back jacket). One could also add the picture of the blacksmith watching the flying nut after hitting it with the small sledgehammer (p. 20 [unp.]).

Related Materials

Several titles will appeal to independent readers in grades 4–6: *Cave of Time* (Bantam, 1981) by Edward Packard; *Curse of the Blue Figurine* and *The Revenge of the Wizard's Ghost* (both Dial/Dutton, 1983; 1986). Many titles are recommended for older youngsters beginning in fifth grade: *This Time of Darkness* (Viking, 1980) by H. M. Hoover; *Howl's Moving Castle, Warlock at the Wheel, Archer's Goon,* and *Charmed Life* (all Greenwillow, 1986; 1984; 1984; 1977) by Diana Wynne Jones; *Magic Stone* and *Legacy of Magic* (Morrow, 1978; 1981) by Leonie Kooiker; *The Beggar Queen, The Kestrel,* and *Westmark* (Dutton, 1984; 1982; 1981) by Lloyd Alexander; and *This Place Has No Atmosphere* (Delacorte, 1986) by Paula Danziger. For more advanced science fiction fans, suggest *Young Mutants* (Harper, 1984) edited by Isaac Asimov, Martin Greenberg, and Charles Waugh. This title contains short stories about children who are mutants.

Two filmstrips apply here: *Clown of God* (Weston Woods, 1982) and *Magic Fishbone* (Listening Library, 1977) from the stories by Tomie de Paola and Charles Dickens. Another of Tomie dePaola's famous stories, *Strega Nona's Magic Lessons* (Caedmon, 1985), is available as a record narrated by Tammy Grimes. A record of the Newbery Award-winner *Cat Who Went to Heaven* can be obtained from Random. Two films are also excellent in this session: *The Magic Hat* (McGraw-Hill, 1981) and *Bearskin: Or the Man Who Didn't Wash for Seven Years* (Davenport Films, 1983). *Byte into Books* (Calico, 1986), computer software, will aid the young user to find books on the patron floppy disc as the librarian or other person adds title entries to the 24 categories. The discs are unprotected.

O'Dell, Scott. *Sarah Bishop*
Houghton, 1980, 184 pp.

An accomplished author, Scott O'Dell commands a secure place in the world of publishing and young readership. (See *Introducing Books,* Bowker, 1970, p. 56 and *Introducing More Books,* Bowker, 1978, pp. 111–114, 153–156.) He is a Newbery Award-winner, as well as an ALA Notable Book author, a winner of the Regina and De Grummond Medals, the German Jungenbuchpreis, and the International Hans Christian Andersen Author Medal for his body of work. All of his many exciting stories show exceptional and loving familiarity with the historical period against which they are set, and each story moves calmly in spite of its profound significance because of the author's excellent writing style. In this title, the heroine, Sarah, cast adrift at 15 in the war-torn New York countryside in 1776, slowly gains her independence as she bravely survives the chaos of her life. The front jacket illustration by Ted Lewin portrays Sarah in typical colonial garb with a "Brown Betsy" musket in her hands and a knapsack on her back. The forest is in the background, and her pet muskrat is at her feet. The forlorn yet determined look on her freckle-spattered face is gently expressive. Children in grades 5–7 (ages 10–12) will enjoy Sarah's adventures and be compelled by her strong beliefs as she bravely faces the trials that she undergoes.

As 15-year-old Sarah stands on the small family farm near Wallabout Bay across from Manhattan, she hears musket fire. Her father thinks it comes from Jim Quarme, one of miller Purdy's new hands. The Bishops—Father, Chad, and Sarah—have only been in the colonies a few years. They left England after Mother died on their English farm and the village business they moved to failed. Now the tension of imminent war and political division threatens the family. Her older brother, Chad, who works in the nearby village at the tavern, the Lion and the Lamb, is sympathetic to the rebels and tries to get his father to take down the picture of King George. Father won't; he is a confirmed Loyalist. Even though the picture disappears and miller Purdy tries to change his mind, he holds to his views. Meanwhile, Sarah stands in the midst of this dispute and swiftly culminating events.

Chad and David, a friend who is studying to be a minister, come to tell Father that they are headed for Fort Brooklyn to join the ranks for the coming battle. Upset, Chad's father refuses him the musket. Nevertheless, the two leave across the meadow as Sarah waves good-bye and her father watches. Shortly after, Ben Birdsall's riders who harass Loyalists torch the Bishop farm and tar and feather Mr. Bishop while Sarah, tied to a tree, watches. Mrs. Jessop and her family arrive after Birdsall's riders leave and bring Mr. Bishop to their farm. Although they heroically try to save him, he dies the next day. The War of Independence has already taken a heavy toll on Sarah.

Two weeks later, Sarah visits the ruined farm and fills a knapsack with her father's tools, a few clothes, and a blanket, and Mrs. Jessop gives Sarah her bible. With these scanty possessions, Sarah leaves to seek a job at the Lion and the Lamb. While at the tavern—Mr. and Mrs. Pennywell are only too happy to employ her—she serves many British officers and learns a lot about the war. Mr. Pennywell tells her about the recent big battle during which the British captured Fort Brooklyn. Hoping that Chad is a prisoner, Sarah asks Major Stirling, a tavern regular, to write a letter to Captain Cunningham, a British officer in New York City, then goes by ferry from Long Island to Manhattan to try to find him.

In lower Manhattan, she is first cheated of half her hard-earned money, then arrested by the British as a culprit in the Trinity Church steeple fire. Finally, however, she escapes and convinces a ferryman and a Hessian soldier to take her to the six hulks that the British are using as prisons. Along the way they pass ships from which many dead bodies are being lowered. From one of the ships the starving David shouts to her that Chad died that morning. Feeling utterly alone and destitute, Sarah escapes from the soldier and the boat and heads toward the Lion and the Lamb. The Pennywells hide her, but Sarah is afraid that the British will capture her again, so she decides to go as far from the war as possible.

On the road again, Sarah tries to find comfort in Mrs. Jessop's bible, but she is so angry at her fate that she rips the verse from Matthew, "Love thy neighbor," and burns it. She finally reaches the ferry from Long Island to White Plains, New York, where the ferryman takes pity on her and teaches her how to shoot the "Brown Betsy" musket she buys from him. When she arrives in White Plains, she takes a job at The Golden Arrow for one day, but decides to press on northward to Ridgeford, about a day's journey away. A man named Sam Goshen helps her get part way there, but when he bothers her during the night, Sarah doesn't waste a minute and takes off by herself. In Ridgeford, she buys an ax, some musket shot, a couple of blankets, and some staples at the Morton's general store with the rest of her money, determined to lose herself in the woods to the west. Young Isaac Morton tries to convince her that she needs more blankets because of the coming winter.

Afraid of civilization, Sarah sets out for the wilderness. She finds a cave not far from Long Pond (a lake) and the deep woods, yet not too far from Ridgeford. After chasing out the bats, except for a white one that she treats as a pet, Sarah makes it as homelike as possible. The Long-knifes—John, Helen, and Bertha, a young child—help her. Helen, a pregnant woman of mixed breed, teaches her how to collect natural food. John teaches her how to make a dugout canoe over the long winter and also helps her secure a cave door to protect her from marauding bears and other animals. The Longknifes then leave, but promise to return the following summer.

Meanwhile, Sam Goshen sets trap lines in the woods. When Sarah finds them she springs them, especially after she finds a muskrat who had chewed off one foot trying to escape. Expecting the muskrat to die, she takes it to her cave. It doesn't die after all, so she has a second pet.

Then she finds Goshen caught in a bear trap. She tries to leave him there, but can't, so she carts him to her cave. With her musket ever ready at her side, she nurses him back to health, but when he is finally well, she insists that he leave. During the winter she stares down a territorial native American whom she finds sniffing at her door, but that turns out to be nothing compared to the copperhead snakebite she receives in early spring. Unconscious for days with a swollen hand and arm, Sarah finally recovers. Fortunately, the Longknifes return unexpectedly and help her. They also tell her that young Mr. Morton (Isaac) hopes she will come to Ridgeford, and she decides to go.

In Ridgeford, Isaac convinces Sarah to attend the Quaker meeting that he and his father attend. When because of the "flux" only half of Ridgeford's Quakers remain, some people, including the elder Mr. Morton, think that Sarah is a witch and is responsible for the "curse." Things look especially bad for her when Sam Goshen testifies at the meeting that Sarah talks to a strange white bat. But Isaac Morton convinces Sarah to speak out, and that makes her feel better. Then someone who has been to Boston reports the consequences of the "flux" there, and she is completely exonerated. The restoration continues for Sarah.

Sarah then sees the same Hessian soldier who was her captor at Wallabout Bay. When he looks at her without recognition, she knows that she is safe once again and can return to Long Pond free from the fear of being hunted. Isaac gives her a torn replacement page from his bible and asks her to return in two weeks for the next Quaker meeting. When Sarah goes back to the cave and sees a copperhead drinking from the lake, she cannot kill it, even though she had previously been filled with vengeance. She looks down on the Ridgeford village and realizes that she has ". . . Forgotten how pretty friendly lights could be."

Thematic Analysis

The survival motif is spread liberally throughout this exciting story with the theme of acquiring independence by doing things on one's own. The story also stresses the difficulty of finding a place in the world under the most deprived circumstances—alone—and the feelings of fear, inability to trust, and wanting to withdraw that one can experience. But perhaps the deepest themes are the precarious quality of the Golden Rule and the life-giving energy that a restoration to civilization and its acceptance can bring.

Discussion Materials

After the main characters are introduced (p. 12), many incidents can be highlighted: Sarah, Mr. Purdy, and the missing picture (pp. 6–11); Chad and David join up (pp. 16–21); William Tyndale and the bible (pp. 29–30); Birdsall's visit and Father's death (pp. 31–36); the Lion and the Lamb (pp. 37–44); the New York City fire (pp. 45–57); Chad is dead (pp. 58–62); the ferry to White Plains (pp. 72–76); Sarah meets Sam Goshen (pp. 79–82); the "territorial" native American (pp. 99–102); Sarah meets the Mortons (pp. 87–88); the cave (pp. 93–99, 103–105); the Longknifes (pp. 106–112); the muskrat (pp. 113–115); Sam Goshen and the traps (pp. 116–132); Isaac Morton again (pp. 137–141); the Longknifes return (pp. 144–147); the snakebite (pp. 148–154); the Quaker meeting (pp. 155–181); and the bible (pp. 182–184). The author's foreword can be read word for word (pp. vii).

Related Materials

Here are some suggestions for the audience: *Cold Sassy Tree* (Ticknor & Fields, 1984) by Olive Ann Burns, about Will Tweedy's "growing up" at the turn of the century in Georgia; *The Wild Children* (Scribner, 1983) by Felice Holman, about a young boy separated from his family in Bolshevik Russia; *Footsteps* (Delacorte, 1980) by Leon Garfield, about young William Jones who tries to find his dead father's partner on the seamy side of London; *Place Called Ugly* (Random, 1981) by Avi about Owen's awakening; *S.O.R. Losers* (Bradbury, 1984) by Avi about 11 seventh-graders who find themselves on a soccer team, although disinterested in sports; and *Many Waters* (Farrar, 1986) by Madeline L'Engle, a fourth continuation of her time stories involving the Murry twins.

Records of the classic first title in L'Engle's time warp books, *Wrinkle in Time* and *Wind in the Door* are available from Random. Jean Craighead George's *Julie of the Wolves*, a classic survival story about a youngster, is also available. For younger tastes try *Brer Rabbit Stories* (Weston Woods, 1985) read by Jackie Torrance. *Graven Images* (Harper, 1982) by Paul Fleischman with its sophisticated stories will appeal to the better readers. All the youngsters should be directed to *Taking on the Press: Constitutional Rights in Conflict* (Crowell, 1986) by Melvyn Bernard Zerman, a nonfictional exploration of freedom of the press. *My Brother Sam Is Dead* by James Lincoln Collier and Christopher Collier, available from Random as a videocassette and a filmstrip, closely parallels *Sarah Bishop* as told from Chad's point of view and will be a good addition for the males.

Yorinks, Arthur. *Hey, Al*
Pictures by Richard Egielski. Farrar, 1986, 32 pp.

When Yorinks and Egielski published *Sid and Sol*, their first title together, in 1977, their magical blend of story and illustration first appeared. They followed in three-year intervals with *Louis the Fish* and *It Happened in Pinsk* (both Farrar, 1980; 1983). Both titles were well received, and the latter was selected as a New York Times Best Book of the Year for children. The promise of their collaborative ability came to fruition again in 1986 with the publication of *Hey, Al,* for which Richard Egielski received the 1986 Caldecott Award. As one of the Caldecott Award criteria is a faithful and excellent interpretation of the text, Arthur Yorink's words obviously convey a more than creditable experience as well. The two-character tale of Al, the janitor (sanitary engineer), and his little dog, Eddie—and multiple exotic birds in the fantasy sequence—will appeal to all ages, but is especially recommended for grades K–3, provided the presenter can familiarize the tale and minimize the drabness implied in the first few pages.

The book's design is noteworthy for its clear and easy-to-read type, the precise color separations, and the side-sewn binding, an especial pleasure when the book lays flat for reading or displaying. The extraordinary endpapers visually restate the moral of the story and set the mood at the beginning and end of the book. The sand-colored front endpapers reflect the drabness of Al's surroundings; the bright yellow back endpapers reinforce the concept of appreciating and working creatively with what exists and also echo the bright yellow paint spot on the wall of the humble room the main character is painting.

A decoration of a bucket, mop, and scrub brush appears on the half-title page. The verso illustrates Al in full color carrying the tools of his occupation, trailed by Eddie who is looking at three bluebirds flying overhead. In four framed full-page illustrations of Al's small room, a door in the room and a window in the bathroom on the two sides of the constricting frame cleverly suggest some openness. Three similarly framed pages appear at the end of the book showing six newspapers accumulated outside the door. In the illustration at the end, Al starts to paint the wall yellow.

Seven double-page spreads present the intriguing fantasy in the middle. The first and last fantasy pages portray the characters' arrival and escape from the island in softly muted blues and greens. The four middle pages show the surroundings with explosive force in bright colors with a profusion of foliage and birds. Significantly, the large bird that carries Al and Eddie away is present in each, carefully looking away. The tremendous force behind the story is brilliantly captured in totally integrated words and illustrations. The slightly chilling human hands issuing forth from one of the birds in the outer ring of birds in the centerfold is reminiscent of the illustrations in *Alice Through the Looking Glass.* The cane and the bird itself are also suggestive of *Alice.* . . .

In this simple tale, Al, a janitor, succumbs to the monotony of scrubbing the floors in a local old-fashioned school by becoming depressed. He returns to the small urban room and bath that he shares with his beloved dog, Eddie, who accompanies him to work. When a noncommittal exotic bird (which is presumably Al's imagination) sticks his beak in the bathroom, he is easily able to convince Al to pack a suitcase. The next day the bird returns to fly the two of them to an island in the sky, together with their suitcase, which unfortunately drops in flight.

When they reach the island and fly over it, they see lush foliage, waterfalls, and many different exotic birds. Soon Al is sitting in front of his own waterfall wearing a bright tropical shirt and lei and eating fruit served by a large duck. Eddie is just about to take a swim! Suddenly, Al sees feathers growing on his arms, his nose turning into a beak, and the same thing is happening to Eddie. Al quickly decides that he doesn't want to spend his life that way and the two try to fly home.

When Al awakens in his room, he is once again normal, but extremely sad. As they were approaching the city, Eddie had dropped into the nearby river. The dripping Eddie soon enters through the doorway, however, and Al is so happy that he and Eddie are back safe and sound that he starts to paint his room in a cheerful color. As the last line says, "Paradise lost is sometimes Heaven found."

Thematic Analysis

The fairly straightforward theme of appreciating selfhood can be stated colloquially as "The grass is always greener on the other side," or "There's no place like home." The fundamental message, however, involves not only appreciating where one is, but also doing something concrete to make it the best possible place to be. And it further involves the realization of one's own self-worth; that one is the most important person in the world and only one's own recognition of this will permit one to recognize the worth of others. An important theme, indeed!

Discussion Materials

The full book jacket with birds resplendent in their bright plumage following Al as he mops the school corridor and Eddie leans against his trouser leg while looking at the flock makes an attractive presentation with a brief paraphrase of the story's beginning. The book can be shown in many ways: as a typical picture book; through the four opening pictures and words; or through the double-spread dream sequence. Perhaps the best way is to display it as an independent visual experience with only a brief word about the intriguing endpapers or about the bird's "hands" in the centerfold.

Related Materials

The following titles will be enjoyed by a young crowd: *The Crane Wife* (Morrow, 1981), translated by Katherine Paterson, retells the Japanese folktale about a peasant who loses a beautiful wife and wealth to greed; *Oh, Kojo! How Could You* (Dial, 1984), retold by Verna Aardema from an Ashanti folktale, is about Ananse who cannot triumph against Kojo who has the help of a cat; *The King's Flower* (Philomel, 1980) by Mitsumasa Anno is about a king who discovers beauty in small things; and *The King at the Door* (Doubleday, 1980) by Brock Cole is about a king dressed as a beggar who rewards unselfishness in a servant boy. Two titles useful to girls in grades 2–4 are *City, Sing for Me: A Country Child Moves to the City* (Human Sciences, 1978) by Jane Jacobson and *Tink in a Tangle* (Albert Whitman, 1984) by Dorothy Haas. Also useful for middle-graders is *Yussel's Prayer: A Yom Kippur Story* (Lothrop, 1981) retold by Barbara Cohen, from the traditional tale of an orphan boy who learns how to say thanks to the Lord.

Three films are appropriate: *Paradise* (Direct Cinema, 1986) complements the main title perfectly with its lush images of foliage and birds that indicate in animation that one should appreciate his own existence; *How to Be a Perfect Person* (L.C.A., 1985) delivers the message in its title humorously; and *Love of Life* (L.C.A., 1982) is a dramatization of a Jack London story about a cynical abandonment after a gold strike. The last two titles are suggested for older youngsters. The filmstrip *Thumbelina* (Live Oak Media, 1979) by Andersen and the record of *Bat-Poet* (Caedmon, 1972) read by the author, Randall Jarrell, are also available.

Developing Values: Additional Titles

Aesop's Fables. Illus. by Heidi Holder. Viking, 1981, unp. (Gr. 3–5)

Avi. *History of Helpless Harry; to which is added a variety of amusing and entertaining adventures.* Illus. by Paul O. Zelinsky. Pantheon, 1980, 179 pp. (Gr. 4–6)

Baker, Betty. *Seven Spells to Farewell.* Macmillan, 1982, 123 pp. (Gr. 5–6)

Bartholomew, Barbara. *Great Gradepoint Mystery.* Illus. by Yuri Salzman. Macmillan, 1983, 106 pp. (Gr. 4–6)

Call It Courage, from the book by Armstrong Sperry. Recording, 2s 33rpm, also available as a video. Random, 1980. (Gr. 5–6)

Conford, Ellen. *We Interrupt This Semester for an Important Bulletin.* Little, 1980, 176 pp. (Gr. 3–5)

dePaola, Tomie, retell. *The Mysterious Giant of Barletta.* Illus. by the author. Harcourt, 1984, 32 pp. (Gr. 2–4)

Gee, Maurice. *Halfmen of O.* Oxford, 1982, 204 pp. (Gr. 5–6)

Gilson, Jamie. *Thirteen Ways to Sink a Sub.* Lothrop, 1983, 128 pp. (Gr. 3–5)

Girion, Barbara. *Joshua, the Czar, and the Chicken Bone Wish.* Illus. by Richard Cuffari. Scribner, 1978, 155 pp. (Gr. 4–6)

Green, Phyllis. *Eating Ice Cream with a Werewolf.* Illus. by Patti Stern. Harper, 1983, 121 pp. (Gr. 3–5)

The Hairyman and Other Wild Tales by David Holt. Recording, also available as a cassette. High Windy Productions, 1979.

Haller, Danita Ross. *Not Just Any Ring.* Illus. by Deborah Kogan. Knopf, 1982, unp. (Gr. 3–5)

Harris, Robie H. *Rosie's Razzle Dazzle Deal.* Illus. by Tony DeLuna. Knopf, 1982, 122 pp. (Gr. 2–4)

Haugaard, Erik Christian. *The Samurai's Tale.* Houghton, 1984, 256 pp. (Gr. 6–up)

Hyman, Trina Schart, retell. *Little Red Riding Hood.* Illus. by the author. Holiday, 1982, 32 pp. (Gr. K–3)

Johnson, Crockett. *Ellen's Lion.* Godine, 1984, 62 pp. (Gr. 2–4)

Kennedy, Richard. *Blue Stone.* Drawings by Ronald Himler. Holiday, 1976, 93 pp. (Gr. 4–6)

Levy, Elisabeth. *Dracula Is a Pain in the Neck.* Illus. by Mordicai Gerstein. Harper, 1983, 74 pp. (Gr. 3–5)

Light Princess, read by Glynis Johns. Recording, 2s 33rpm, also available as a cassette. Caedmon, 1981. (Gr. 3–5)

Lively, Penelope. *Revenge of Samuel Stokes.* Dutton, 1981, 122 pp. (Gr. 5–6)

McGowen, Tom. *The Magician's Apprentice.* Dutton, 1987, 118 pp. (Gr. 5–8)

Mayer, Mariana. *The Black Horse.* Dial, 1984, unp. (Gr. 2–4)

Platt, Kin. *Brogg's Brain.* Lippincott, 1981, 124 pp. (Gr. 4–6)

Rogasky, Barbara, retell. *The Water of Life.* Holiday, 1986, unp. (Gr. K–6)

The Treasure. Filmstrip. Weston Woods, 1982. (Gr. 2–up)

The Velveteen Rabbit, narrated by Meryl Streep. Video. Rabbit Ears and Random, 1985. (Gr. 2–up)

Wilde, Oscar. *Selfish Giant.* Illus. by Lisbeth Zwerger. Picture Book Studio/ Alphabet Pr., 1984, unp. (Gr. 2–4)

Zelinsky, Paul O., retell. *Rumpelstiltskin.* Illus. by the author. Dutton, 1986, 40 pp. (Gr. K–4)

Zhang Xiu Shi, adapt. *Monkey and the White Bone Demon.* Illus. by Lin Zheng et al. Viking, 1984, 36 pp. (Gr. 4–6)

4

Understanding Physical and
Emotional Problems

THE middle years that precede adolescence are usually free from physical growth and seem quiescent, but it is a deceptively quiet time of fluid
and fertile preparation for what is to come. Although many youngsters
who are ages 8–12 (grades 3–6) have a calm exterior, practically all have
a vigorous internal emotional life as they become increasingly aware of
the complex variety of life around them. It is a time when acceptance
and approval by others is sought, and when differences, be they in
physical appearance and skills or in emotional states, become more noticeable to the youngster. It is a particularly difficult time for children
who are disabled. Awareness and understanding can help youngsters
through this period, during which excessive conformity can provide a
safe harbor of approval for them.

Youngsters who are passing through their seemingly safe time need to
assess, accept, and appreciate their own physical abilities, as well as those
of children who have fewer or greater abilities. They have to do the same
with their burgeoning emotional life. This basis for understanding themselves in physical and emotional terms will stand them in good stead for
the fast-approaching sexual feelings of puberty, some of which may start
in the late middle years of childhood. It will also help them become
responsible adults who are able to aid and succor those who may have
less of an endowment in one area, as well as to admire those who have
more.

The books included in the following chapter show how youngsters
deal with a variety of physical and emotional problems, or a combination
of both, from the common frustrations of obesity to misplaced guilt.
Furthermore, the stories effectively show characters who are able to
overcome their situations courageously and realistically.

94

Bauer, Marion Dane. *On My Honor*
Clarion, 1986, 90 pp.

The author who is known for her ability to capture completely the interior feelings of the young hero is the winner of the 1984 Jane Addams Children's Book Award for *Rain of Fire*. Her other books are *Like Mother, Like Daughter*; *Tangled Butterfly*; *Foster Child*; and *Shelter from the Wind* (all Clarion; see *Introducing More Books*, Bowker, 1978, pp. 168–171). In this, yet another gripping novel suitable for youngsters age 10–11 (grades 5–6), Marion Dane Bauer writes sparingly and powerfully about an incident that is both traumatic and enlightening, as crucial events often are. It is an emotionally intricate, yet simple dramatic tale about a young boy who learns the power behind making choices when he defers to his daredevil friend who loses his life swimming. The front jacket portrays a young boy holding his head with a look of sorrow and confusion on his face with the offending river flowing serenely in the background. The drawing is in rosy muted shades of brown, red, and peach.

Joel Bates, 12 and out of sixth grade for the summer, reluctantly agrees to go to Starved Rock Park with his friend and classmate, Tony Zabrinsky. He prefers swimming at the Illinois town pool or continuing to build their tree house, but he goes anyway because he doesn't want Tony to think he's "chicken." Tony always comes up with daredevil ideas; this time it's climbing the bluffs about nine miles away. Joel tries to get his Dad to say "No," but after Tony falsely tells Joel's father that Mrs. Zabrinsky gave her permission, Dad only puts him "on his honor" not to go anywhere else. Silently Joel feels let down; he thought his Dad would know automatically (didn't he see the rope on his bike for the climb?)

Mrs. Zabrinsky now takes care of Joel's four-year-old brother, Bobby, and other little children—just the way she used to take care of Joel—while Joel's mother works. Joel practically grew up across the street in Tony's house so he feels closer to Tony than even to Bobby (probably also because Bobby is going through a four-year-old whining stage right now). But Tony is much more than a friend; he represents a zenith of bravery. He is a reckless youngster who wants to try everything regardless of whether he can accomplish it. Joel is more cautious; he often recalls his Mom saying that he was like a little old grandma when he was

small. Because Joel doesn't admire this part of his nature, Tony's reckless-
ness is even more attractive to him. This conflict causes Joel tremendous
emotional conflict, and none more than this situation, which is like so
many others—Tony always gets his own way.

So they set off on each other's bikes. Joel rides Tony's old one, handed
down through three older brothers, and Tony rides Joel's new Schwinn
ten-speed. (Providing he survives climbing the bluffs, Joel hopes to ride
back faster on his bike.) On the long ride, Joel thinks plaintively about
the cool tree house and the pool where he and Tony used to slide into
the water at the shallow end and splash. Determined to be courageous,
he picks up speed on the decrepit old bike to make as much of the next
hill as possible. When he gets halfway up, he turns around to look for
Tony and sees him standing on the bridge over the Vermillion River
gesticulating wildly.

Used to Tony's insensitive actions, Joel begrudgingly goes back. Although he sees his carelessly placed bike—another of Tony's expected
mannerisms—Joel is nevertheless surprised by Tony's desire to go swimming in the foul river. Caught between climbing the bluffs and swimming
in the dirty, treacherous river, Joel doesn't know what to do. He tries to
convince Tony to go back to the pool, even telling him that his Dad told
him never to swim in that river. But much as he tries, Tony tries harder.

Then Tony throws off his clothes and enters the muddy water splashing up a storm, and Joel reluctantly follows. Although the smell of dead
fish is nauseating, Joel nevertheless suggests that they swim out to a
sandbar a few yards away. Tony starts to swim there but buffeted by a
strong current gets pulled under into a deep hole. Joel is stunned by the
realization that Tony really can't swim; now he understands why they
had always stayed in the shallow end of the pool. A million things run
through his mind: it was his idea to swim to the sandbar; Joel's Dad put
him "on his honor" not to go anywhere but Starved Rock; Tony might
drown. Despite repeated dives, Joel fails to find him. Exhausted and
vomiting water, he runs to the bridge and tries to hail a car. Finally an
18-year-old and his gum-chewing girlfriend stop. Although the fellow
tries hard to find Tony, after a few dives he gives up. Quietly panic
stricken, Joel turns down the fellow's offer to drive him to the police,
promising to go to the police by himself.

Instead Joel returns home and withdraws to his bedroom. The enor-
mity of what has happened spins through his mind, and he feels very
guilty. The logical story he concocts to tell his Dad comes out disjointed,

and he starts to smell the bad river odor on his skin. In a daze he takes Bobby on his daily newspaper delivery rounds, something he never does, trying not to face the terrible situation.

Then the police arrive at the Zabrinsky house. Joel's Dad insists that they go over because Joel is the last person to have seen Tony. Everyone knows that, even Bobby, who spreads the rumor that the two spent the day in Joel's room. Joel breaks down and tells the police and the distraught Zabrinskys what happened. Mr. Zabrinsky, who used to hit Tony with a belt, now breaks down and cries, and Mrs. Zabrinsky dazed by the shocking news comments that Tony was more of a handful than his other brothers.

Joel is fully convinced that Tony's death was his fault, but his Dad tries to convince him that he did all he could. When Joel comments about the terrible stink of the river coming from his skin, his Dad says he can't smell it. When Joel asks his Dad to make the smell go away, he simply responds, "I can't." Joel tells his Dad that he feels responsible because he dared Tony to swim to the sandbar. When his Dad says that everyone has to live with the choices they have made, all except Tony, tears come to Joel's eyes. Then Dad suggests that if there is a heaven, Tony is there: "I can't imagine a heaven closed to charming, reckless boys," he says. Joel hopes for something more certain, but finally understands that making his own choices—not hoping for others to make them for him—is the essence of becoming a whole person.

Thematic Analysis

The theme of this highly dramatic slice-of-life story covers the emotional turmoil that many young people experience in their development toward being able to make truly independent choices. The book stresses the necessity of assuming responsibility for decisions, rather than relying on others and thereby being absolved of responsibility for the consequences. It also gently emphasizes the fragile nature of coping with the consequences of choices throughout life. Other themes deal with grief, guilt, punishment, and character evaluation. All are handled sensitively in the development of the story, and as a middle-grader might experience them.

Discussion Materials

To book talk this slim 12-chapter book requires only a slight paraphrasing of the following: the boys' trip (pp. 10–24); Tony's death (pp. 25–

30); Joel's rescue attempts (pp. 31–45); and Joel's turmoil (pp. 46–61). Or one can introduce the first step in the drama—Joel's expectation that his Dad will stop them (pp. 1–9). Other incidents can be highlighted: the bike trip (pp. 10–13); swimming in the river (pp. 17–29); the dirty river (pp. 14–16); the smell from Joel's skin (pp. 59, 86–87).

Related Materials

A nice touch here would be Ted Hughes's poetry *Under the North Star* (Viking, 1981) illustrated strikingly by Leonard Baskin. A story popular with middle-graders, *Battle of Bubble and Squeak* (Dutton, 1979) by Philippa Pearce is also a two-cassette recording from G. K. Hall (1986). Two cassettes of *Going Home* by K. M. Peyton are also available from G. K. Hall (1986). Two films or videos from the National Film Board of Canada are *The Sound Collector* (1983) and *The Plant* (1985).

A host of titles can be useful here: *M. E. and Morton* (Crowell, 1986) by Sylvia Cassedy; *Summer of the Monkeys* (Doubleday, 1976) by Wilson Rawls; *Barefoot a Thousand Miles* (Walker, 1984) by Patsey Gray; *Gorilla* (Morrow, 1984) by Robert McClung; *An Insect's Body* (Morrow, 1984) by Joanna Cole; *Wasps* (Lerner, 1984) by Sylvia A. Johnson; and *Break-through—The True Story of Penicillin* (Dodd, 1985) by Francine Jacobs.

Bottner, Barbara. *Dumb Old Casey Is a Fat Tree*
Illus. by the author. Harper, 1979, 42 pp.

This author-illustrator has produced some excellent titles for middle-graders, including *The World's Greatest Expert on Absolutely Everything—Is Crying* (Harper, 1984). In the title under consideration, Barbara Bottner writes knowingly about young females and ballet. The story is simple enough, true to the heroine and many like her, a rotund second-grader named Casey who wants nothing more than to be a ballet dancer. Unfortunately, she isn't even in serious consideration for a main part in her recital because of her plumpness and lack of grace. Rather than give up, however, she works harder in her lowly part and becomes much better. She also stops eating continually and gains the respect and admiration of her family and friends in the bargain. The story of young grit will be appreciated by 7–9-year-olds (grades 2–4), especially females. Some reluctant readers in grade 5 will also enjoy it.

The black-and-white line drawings done in pen with pencil shadings by Barbara Bottner are numerous pictures of little girls in leotards dancing, leaping, sitting, holding their heads in their hands, and showing all the familiar mannerisms of this age group in dance class with facial expressions that map their underlying feelings. Overall, they are reminiscent of the wonderful sketches of the famous character "Eloise." Besides the five full-page illustrations, two of which run over onto the facing page, every page has a half-page or smaller sketch that extends the text. In one half-page illustration, for example, Casey is doing a round-robin of warm-up exercises that are difficult for a fat little girl. The title page contains a portrait of four ballet dancers, who are playing the part of a tree, goggling at Casey's round tummy. The end piece shows a triumphant Casey with her "tree" arms (dripping with leaves) raised in response to the accolade at the end of the recital.

Casey, plump and about eight years of age, has always wanted to be a ballet dancer. When her second-grade teacher, Mr. Halleck, asks everybody to write what they want to be, Casey doesn't hesitate. She responds the same way she did in kindergarten and first grade. Even her classmate Patrick's comment that she is too fat doesn't deter her. She continues to practice the five ballet positions (albeit with difficulty) and to look at her treasured book, *Famous Dancers of the World*. Finally, she convinces her mother to send her to Mrs. Bellanova's class. There she is the worst in the class; her friends—Marion, Evelyn, and Betsy—are the best.

As recital time approaches, Casey's three friends are confident that each will play the princess. Casey certainly thinks that one will, and that the other two will play the king and queen, leaving the part of the evil prince, mustache and all, for her. Casey decides to practice hard and try out for that part. She works so hard that she forgets to eat her jellied apples—she even gives her brother Derek permission to eat them—and at night falls asleep exhausted without her usual hot chocolate. Then Elizabeth appears at the next ballet class. She is not only "the new girl" but more lacking in grace than even Casey and skinny to boot. Casey knows how she must feel and they become friends.

As Casey skips home with her other three friends, she is consumed by her desire to play the evil prince. She dances all the way home even after she bumps into Patrick who once again tells her that she's too fat to be a dancer. She tells Patrick that by the time she's old enough for the ballet she'll be skinny as a "song," and twirls away.

On the following Tuesday, Mrs. Bellanova announces that Marion will be the princess, Evelyn, the queen, Betsy, the king, and Marybeth will be the evil prince! Casey, Debbie, Rachel, Ronnie, and Elizabeth will be individual trees. The four girls with the main parts pose and giggle with pleasure; the other five just stand motionless. Walking home with her three friends and Marybeth, who tells Casey not to feel bad because she was a "tree" in last year's recital, Casey resolves to do her darndest, even though she blurts out that maybe she won't be there.

Casey works furiously, eats less, and soars like the pigeons she sees in the sky. Mrs. Bellanova notices the improvement at the next rehearsal, and Patrick no longer calls her a fatty. She and her new friend Elizabeth keep looking through her favorite book for plump and skinny dancers who became great, and they keep practicing. When the stage (dress) rehearsal is held and Mrs. Bellanova makes Casey the lead "tree," even Marion's jibe that if she couldn't be the princess she'd like to be the lead "tree" doesn't dampen Casey's spirit.

Finally, recital day arrives. Mr. Halleck and all her classmates, including Patrick, are there along with her mother, father, and brother, Derek. When the hurricane music starts, Casey leads the resplendent trees out on the stage in their leaf costumes. She knows at that moment why she has practiced so hard. She loves to dance; it is more rewarding than anything she has ever done. Taking bows is fun, too. Everybody on stage gets a rose from Marion's bouquet, and Mrs. Bellanova looks proud and happy. Casey's family is delighted, especially Derek who asks if he can have two desserts now that she's a dancer. The best compliment comes from Patrick, who says that she was the best "tree," and that she doesn't "look so fat anymore either." She decides then and there that she's neither dumb, nor fat, nor anything like that any more.

Thematic Analysis

The old maxim "Practice makes perfect" is one of the basic themes of this story, as shown by this spunky youngster's ability to work through difficulties to achieve a desirable outcome. That through determination one can overcome one's problems with hard, sometimes painful work in spite of constant rebukes is stressed. A concomitant though oversimplified theme is the more energy one expands on the task at hand the less one eats. The condition of being overweight is related to easy access to fattening foods and the sedentary life-style of the heroine before a strong desire to achieve in a physical activity takes hold. This story may show middle-graders what it takes to start to change. Current findings on overweight youngsters show the problem to be endemic in America.

Discussion Materials

The story can be summarized up to the recital by introducing the main characters (pp. 1–5, 9), while displaying the cover illustration of "trees" with Casey in the foreground. Many other episodes can be highlighted: the four friends (title p., pp. 5, 10–11, 18–21, 33); Elizabeth (pp. 9, 27–29, 31, 34–35); Patrick (pp. 2, 12–14, 26, 39, 42); Mrs. Bellanova and the ballet class (pp. 3–4, 9, 14–16, 25); practicing (half-title p., pp. 7, 19, 24, 29); the "natural diet" (pp. 4, 7–8, 10, 22, 27, 42); the essence of the cure (pp. 22–23); the ballet is cast (pp. 16–18); Casey's improvement is noted (p. 25); the stage rehearsal (pp. 30–33); and preparations for the recital (pp. 3, 6–41).

Related Materials

Frederick's Alligator (Scholastic, 1980) by Esther Allen Peterson, about a young boy who cries "alligator" too often, is suggested. The nonfiction title *Alligator* (Putnam, 1984) by Jack Denton Scott will intrigue many readers and viewers of the photographs. A suitable title for middle-graders is Richard Kennedy's *Song of the Horse* (Dutton, 1981), about a young girl who likes riding. Robin McKinley's adaptation of *Black Beauty* (Random, 1986), beautifully illustrated by Susan Jeffers, is a good follow-up. McKinley's *Beauty: A Retelling of the Story of Beauty and the Beast* (Harper, 1978) is suggested for better readers. Three titles about dogs and a fourth about a cat are recommended for those in grades 3–5: *Moonshadow of Cherry Mountain* (Four Winds/Macmillan, 1982) by Doris Smith Buchanan; *Cindy: A Hearing Ear Dog* (Dutton, 1981) by Patricia Curtis; *Mystery of the Stubborn Old Man* (Garrard, 1980) by Lynn Hall; and *Wishing Tree* (Hastings, 1980) by Ruth Chew.

Two appropriate films are *Curtain Up* (International Film Bureau, 27 min., also in video) and *Dance Squared* (National Film Board of Canada, or International Film Bureau, 4 min., also in video), which is animated. In the former, children express their opinions of the Sadler Wells Royal Ballet field trip. The Mikhail Baryshnikov poster (5MI) from the American Library Association makes a fine background for this book. Two filmstrips will also be enjoyed by the middle-grade audience: *Fir Tree* (Live Oak Media, 1979) by Hans Christian Andersen and *Blubber* (Pied

Piper, 1984) from Judy Blume's book (see *Introducing More Books,* Bowker, 1978, p. 78).

Bridgers, Sue Ellen. *All Together Now*
Knopf, 1979, 238 pp.

As shown by the author's other three fine novels, *Home before Dark, Notes for Another Life* (both Knopf, 1976; 1981), and *Permanent Connections* (Harper, 1987), Sue Ellen Bridgers has a flair for complex story lines that gently yet dramatically explicate the turmoil that youngsters may undergo. In this title, a 12-year-old sixth-grader spends her last summer as a child visiting her grandparents while her father is a flier in the Korean War and her mother works two jobs. Surrounded by many faces of love and commitment—from the North Carolina townspeople to a brain-damaged 33-year-old man who used to be her father's childhood friend, but is still mentally her age—she becomes aware of the complexities of the human condition which, in turn, helps her to understand her own. Children ages 10–12 (grades 5–7), especially females who are sensitive readers, will find much to appreciate here. An attractive cover displays a photograph of a comfortable old house surrounded by colorful drawings of the North Carolina townspeople and the heroine, as well as a pen-and-ink sketch of the brain-damaged boy-man.

Casey Flanagan gets off the bus from Columbia, South Carolina, where her mother is singing at a night club, to spend the summer with her grandparents, Jane and Ben. Although she is happy when her paternal Grandma, whom she saw last Christmas, meets her, she is unhappy to be away from her friends and familiar surroundings for so long. On her way to her father's old room, she hears Dwayne Pickens, the 33-year-old next-door neighbor, contentedly playing baseball just like a 12-year-old boy would. Even though Grandma says he doesn't like girls—just like many 12-year-old males—Casey is intrigued by him and introduces herself. When Dwayne thinks she's a boy named K. C., Casey keeps up the subterfuge even if Grandma thinks it's wrong, because she wants Dwayne as a playmate.

Soon afterward Casey meets Hazard Whitaker, a 52-year-old who has been a family friend and visitor for the past 25 years, ever since Grandpa Ben brought him home. Hazard, who breaks out in a dance at a moment's notice, reversed his checkered job record by being a waiter at Tutoni's Restaurant for many years; that is until just recently when old man Tutoni had a heart attack. Ever since he began visiting the Flanagan home 25 years ago, Hazard has been courting Pansy, Jane's "girlfriend." Pansy used to be her father's receptionist-bookkeeper when he was alive and now works for Dr. Kemble. Although Hazard and Pansy both want to get married, neither has had the courage to ask over the years. Meanwhile they continue to share a weekly meal with Jane and Ben.

While K. C. plays outfielder in the pitcher Dwayne's solo baseball game, her young Uncle Taylor, who works at the lumberyard with his Father, Ben, invites them to go to the racetrack. At the stock car track, she meets his "girlfriend," Gwen, who works in the five-and-ten-cents store and has bleached blond hair. Although she is not without grace, as Grandma decides over dinner one evening, she refers to Dwayne as Mr. Pickens, which strikes them all as peculiar—especially him. Casey becomes very protective of Dwayne who, in turn, relishes her companionship—he even buys her a baseball mitt with his allowance, which she wears in spite of blisters and pain. Dwayne slowly understands that K. C. is David's boy— the David who used to be his friend, but he can't quite untangle the puzzle.

Meanwhile, the activities continue. Dwayne is delighted when Taylor teaches them both to drive his car. He and K. C. play arcade games and go fishing with Uncle Taylor, and they even go swimming with him. Dwayne vaguely recaptures the fleeting memory of the swimming accident that he had with David when he was 12 and all memories stopped for him. As the summer continues, Hazard and Pansy get married, but the problems in a 25-year romance cannot be readily solved. Hazard has to take siege in a pup tent outside Pansy's house before they can have a conventional start.

Then Dwayne helps Uncle Taylor when he gets in a fight at the racetrack and gets so excited afterward that he drives off in Taylor's car. Because of this, his older brother, Alva, attempts to institutionalize him. Everyone knows that Dwayne doesn't ever want to go to the mental hospital again. Nevertheless Dwayne spends the night in jail. At the hearing the next day the Flanagans and other townspeople swear that they will be responsible for a free Dwayne. Although Alva points out that when his mother can no longer be with Dwayne, the situation may change, everyone convinces him to let Dwayne stay free as long as he can. No one is more relieved than Dwayne.

The good news, however, is short-lived. Casey gets polio and is very ill for days. Luckily, she recovers, but then it is time for her to go home. The Flanagans, who have shown her their steady, stable love, host a party to celebrate her recovery, and everyone celebrates: Taylor and Gwen attend, Pansy and Hazard dance, and Casey, who has a beautiful voice, sings "It Had to Be You." Casey learned a lot over the summer—from little things, like her grandparents' loving looks, Hazard's pleasant ways and Pansy's quiet glow, Taylor's sharing nature and Gwen's practical feelings of love for him, and, above all, Dwayne's acceptance of her both as a friend and as a girl.

At the bus station, they all wave goodbye. Dwayne still calls her, "Hey boy," but then he mumbles, "next summer," and finally, "I love you, Casey," and hugs her. She replies, "I love you, too." The many faces of love and commitment have started to carve out a place in Casey's heart and mind.

Thematic Analysis

The most basic of the many themes in this complex story is the awakening of a sensitive person to the varieties of love and the nature of commitment. The author skillfully arranged several subplots to forward the basic theme: the Flanagans; Pansy and Hazard; and Taylor and Gwen. The "growing-up" stage of the young heroine's life serves as counterpoint to the arrested mental development of the person who was also her father's playmate and brilliantly shows the acceptance and love that can exist between the brain-damaged or retarded and their friends and neighbors. Youngsters will find echoes of their own perceptions and experiences in this fulfilling novel.

Discussion Materials

The one-page summary that precedes the half-title page can be read for an overview. To introduce the main character use pages 3–10, 15–20. The other characters can be introduced in the subplots as they unfold to Casey: Hazard and Pansy (pp. 11–15, 21–32, 33–37); Taylor and Gwen (pp. 40–42, 54–63); the wedding (pp. 78–82, 96–105). Episodes involving Dwayne will be interesting: cutting grass (pp. 48–52); the racetrack (pp. 53–63); the present (pp. 83–86); the arcade (pp. 86–92); driving (pp. 93–95); the movies (pp. 117+); mowing and driving (pp. 119–129); the fight (pp. 156–163); swimming and fishing (pp. 165–177); the court order (pp. 186–190); and the neighborhood rally (pp. 197–208). A description of a mild attack of polio will be informative (pp.

209–220). Two incidents that highlight a theme are: Dwayne yells "Casey," not "K. C." (pp. 221–222) and (p. 229).

Related Materials

Several films useful in this presentation are: *Welcome Home, Jellybean* (Coronet, 1986), about a brain-damaged girl who comes home to stay; *Boys and Girls* (Beacon Films, 1985); and *Good Hearted Ant* (International Film Bureau, 9½ min.), an animated film about ants who celebrate when Cricket is found. Two good filmstrips are *Johnny Tremain* and *From the Mixed Up Files of Mrs. Basil E. Frankweiler* (both Random, 1970). A recording of *Shen of the Sea* (Random, 1970) will serve as a good complement to F. N. Monjo's *Prisoners of the Scrambling Dragon* (Holt, 1980). The nonfiction title *Exploring with Lasers* (Messner, 1984) by Brent Filson tells about present and future technology, while *Children of the Wild West* (Clarion, 1983) by Russell Freedman looks backward at childhood.

Brown, Tricia. *Someone Special, Just Like You*
Illus. by Fran Ortiz. Holt, 1984, 64 pp.

The author comes laden with experience as a journalist, writer of articles, and mother to this, her first, book for young people. According to her preface, this title springs from her realization that there was no suitable title to help her preschool youngster accept the disabled youngster in his nursery school. Hence, the genesis of this book, which has a wide readership and will appeal to ages 5 and up, or those in grades K–4, depending on the way in which it is used. Simply, it fills a need that is always with us. (Tricia Brown's *Hello Amigos* [Holt, 1986], with the same illustrator, is also recommended.) The author and photographer acknowledge the help of many teachers, administrators, parents, and consultants. The photographs were taken at four nursery schools in the San Francisco Bay area, each of which deals mainly with children disabled in one of four large categories: visual impairments; hearing impairments; physical handicaps; and mental handicaps. Twenty-four disabled youngsters were involved—special youngsters, just like the reader.

The six-page bibliography by Effie Lee Morris is worth its weight in gold. It is divided into two parts: Books for Adults and Books for Children, with the children's books separated into five groups: General;

Hearing-Impaired; Mentally Handicapped; Physically Disabled; and Visually Disabled. The annotations are descriptive.

Award-winning photojournalist Fran Ortiz took the pictures: 42 black-and-white photos of appealing children, not counting the cover. Most are full page, a few bleed onto facing pages, and several are smaller photos. The book, including the cover, has been designed by Amy Hill. The simple text is set in large block type and is surrounded by appropriate photographs. The front jacket shows three youngsters sitting on the ground in front of a wheelchair; the back jacket has five smaller versions of photos in the book showing youngsters drawing, counting, playing the piano, sliding, and patting Big Bird's feathers. Small photos also decorate the title page, its verso, and the preface.

The organization of the book is simple and effective for any age. The author defines the term "someone special" by comparisons, emphasizing the similarities between normalcy and disablement—that otherwise "someone special" is just like you or me—while pointing out the various categories: walking; hearing; seeing. Twenty pages stress the similar likes of normal and disabled children: blowing bubbles; eating ice cream; smelling flowers; sliding down slides; playing with toys; swimming and splashing; attending school; constructing art; learning signing; reading braille; going on school trips to science museums and aquariums; going home; eating lunch; washing; resting; waiting for Dad; and yelling when it hurts. Fourteen pages describe the differences among the physically disabled: falling and picking themselves up; brushing their teeth; petting a rabbit; walking a balance beam; playing the piano; talking on the telephone; listening to bedtime stories; dancing; swinging; and helping a friend. Six pages tell just what makes a person special: a beautiful smile; kisses; and hugs. The final double spread of a gaggle of children sitting in wheelchairs or on the grass sums up everything.

Thematic Analysis

The theme that the disabled person belongs to the family of man regardless of his or her condition stresses the similarities of human feelings and needs and accords each young person a place in the ring of friendship. The Golden Rule also includes the disabled: Charity and sensitivity to others' feelings are important in each person's view of himself and his brother. It has been said that civilization is ultimately recognized by its treatment of the elderly and children. The disabled can be added to these criteria, and this book plays a valuable role in extending this awareness to youngsters.

Discussion Materials

This book literally begs for sharing between an older care giver and the young, as well as for small group discussion with those who are older. It can be presented as a picture book emphasizing the parts: introducing disabled youngsters (pp. 6–11); shared activities (pp. 12–29); home activities that are similar (pp. 30–37); things the disabled can do just like you (pp. 35–51); and what makes anyone special (pp. 52–57). The bibliography can also be suggested. Have all the children's books available; some of them can be book talked.

Related Materials

Five titles are excellent for a young audience: *Tallyho, Pinkerton!* (Dial, 1982) by Steven Kellogg, about a Great Dane who takes off in a hot-air balloon; *Dog That Sold Football Plays* (Little, 1980) by Matt Christopher, about young Mike's football team and a mind-reading Airedale; *Jim's Dog Muffins* (Greenwillow, 1984) by Miriam Cohen, about Jim's reaction to his dog's death; *Nadia the Willful* (Pantheon, 1983) by Sue Alexander, about a bedouin girl who grieves over her brother's death; and *There's an Elephant in the Garage* (Dutton, 1980) by Douglas F. Davis, about April who decides to leave home with the banished cat to hunt wild animals. For those in grades 4–6 suggest: Harold Keith's fictional *Susy's Scoundrel* (Crowell, 1974), about a pet coyote; David Taylor's *Next Panda, Please!* (Stein & Day, 1983), about a vet's experiences with unusual animals; Sylvia A. Johnson's *Wolf Pack: Tracking Wolves in the Wild* (Lerner, 1985), a nonfictional account of a subject well liked by middle-graders; and Russell Freedman's *Sharks* (Holiday, 1985), a nonfictional explanation that can also be read aloud to the younger crowd. *The Wilder Summer* (Coronet, 1985) and *Sound of Sunshine, Sound of Rain* (FilmFair, 1985) are good films for middle-graders. The filmstrip *Steadfast Tin Soldier* (Live Oak Media, 1979) by Hans Christian Andersen is useful here. Two noteworthy records are *Hello Everybody! Playsongs and Rhymes from a Toddler's World* (A Gentle Wind, 1986) by Rachel Buchman and *Family Album* (Silo/Alcazar, 1986) by Rick Avery and Judy Avery.

Cassedy, Sylvia.   *M. E. and Morton*
Crowell, 1987, 312 pp.

The author of a number of books for children, Sylvia Cassedy became well known after the publication of *Behind the Attic Wall* (Crowell, 1983), which was chosen as an ALA Notable Children's Book, a best book by *School Library Journal,* and a 1984 International Reading Association/ Children's Book Council Children's Choice. The title also was judged a "masterpiece" by the *Reading Teacher* and received accolades from other reviewing sources. It demonstrates the author's ability to draw on the interior thoughts of children and to make these thoughts explicit in her characters' behavior. Cassedy has polished her craft to a high gloss as a writer and teacher of creative writing.

This story follows in the author's successful tradition of sensitivity portraying a young girl's frustrations and hurts. The climax occurs when she recognizes not only that she is loved, but also that she loves her learning disabled brother. The young heroine discovers something about herself when a strange new friend demonstrates that the heroine and her older brother can be a mixture of dumb and smart and also be imperfect like her friend and, for that matter, all human beings. The full-color front jacket painting by Michael Garland portrays the three friends on the apartment roof, which is the location of the story's climax. It serves as a good introduction to the main characters.

Interestingly, the story is told in brief chapters, each describing an incident which cumulatively reflect the heroine's newly acquired understanding. The book is divided into four parts—June, July, August, and September—with 20 chapters in June, 10 in July, 10 in August, and 2 in September, which serve as an epilogue. It also has a brief prologue. Youngsters age 9–12 (grades 4–7), especially sensitive readers, will be spellbound by each denouement. For example, toward the end the author reveals that the heroine attends a private school on an annual scholarship because she is intellectually talented.

Eleven-year-old Mary Ella (M.E.) Briggs lives with her mom and pop, Mr. and Mrs. Wilson F. Briggs, and her older brother, 14-year-old Morton, in the Jefferson Place Apartments at 275 Coolidge Street. Mom works in a small hospital, Pop owns a bookstore, and Morton, who is learning disabled, is unable to complete seventh grade this June. M.E. has finished sixth grade and is ashamed of Morton; in fact, she has a private joke that his real name is Morton without the "t." She attends the private Agnes Daly School where she has skipped grades three times.

According to Morton's final report card, which she sees inadvertently, Morton must attend seventh grade again in the public school after he spends his usual vacation at summer school patiently trying to catch up. Mom also tries to teach him at home, but nothing seems to help. This worries M.E. First of all, she feels guilty. She thinks that her mother, who often seems angry at Morton, likes her better only because she is smarter. Also, she has no friends, either among her classmates at Agnes Daly or among the neighborhood girls who daily troupe home ahead of slow-moving Morton.

M.E. can only remember having one real friend, Aunt Sophia, who when she visited brought her a magic Easter egg. On it was the sentimental saying that believing in good things makes them come true. (But no matter how hard M.E. tries to believe it, Morton doesn't get smarter.) Her classmates at Agnes Daly are rich and live in a remote neighborhood on Calvin Boulevard. The neighborhood girls—Deirdre, Justine, and Ina—seem removed, too, giving M.E. much to ponder. Early in June, before the workmen finish installing the awning on her apartment entrance, M.E. somersaults on the metal rods. While she is upside down, she sees a new girl, but when she rights herself, the girl is gone.

M.E. continues to fester from her situation. M.E. knows that Morton is able to "mainstream" well, that he loves her, and that he enjoys her companionship. But she is starved for a compliment. Her mom, whom she has always tried to please, seems to accept her nice Mother's Day presents with the same thank-you that she gives Morton for his well meant but poorly made gifts. What is more, Mom, who works each day, and Pop, who had to sell his store and go to work for someone else, seem to have little time for her. Yet she often hears Mom talking to the "listener" (wall) in desperation and is convinced that Mom secretly wishes that Morton were disobedient instead of dumb.

Suddenly in June, Polly, the new girl whom she first saw upside down, shows up at M.E.'s apartment to play. They spend the afternoon painting with M.E.'s pretend "orphan girl" dolls (a set of paint bottles that M.E. received from Mom and kept unopened on her windowsill). M.E. is distressed at first that Polly opened the bottles, but she learns that playing with her friend Polly is fun and decides it was worth the sacrifice. Besides, M.E. knows from watching Polly, who always carries a piece of chalk, that she loves to draw and paint.

But this is just the first of many adventures M.E. has with Polly. She soon discovers that Polly is also Morton's friend and that they play together at her grandma's, where she lives. (Her mother can't take care of both Polly and her sister.) At first, M.E. is surprised and upset, but on a subsequent June visit, Polly and the Briggs children play together with Morton's train set. M.E. assembles the tracks and runs the transformer. Then Morton, much to M.E.'s disgust, playfully runs one of the cars down his sleeve, smiling and saying "Rum-tum-tum." When Polly does the same and they both laugh—Morton in his special way—Polly's attitude of acceptance and willingness to play with Morton are a revelation to M.E. Next, the trio decides to go up to the forbidden roof. Despite Polly's assurance that the brick wall will protect them from falling, the small train car falls on an adjacent, lower roof, and they can't quite figure out how to retrieve it before they leave.

Trying desperately to get some attention and to be like her peers, M.E. takes some tar and deliberately streaks her clean blouse, making it rumpled and dirty, just like Morton and Polly's clothes. When Mom doesn't seem to notice, nothing seems right. Aunt Sophia is dead, Pop has closed his bookstore, Mom has not yet confided in her that Morton will be in seventh grade again in the fall, Polly is a friend both to her and to Morton, and now Polly and Morton are both missing. When M.E. finally finds Polly, she says that Morton is at the movies, but that she didn't go because she already saw the picture.

About then, M.E. decides that Polly is just crazy, not dumb. Nevertheless, when M.E. visits Polly in the one room that she shares with her grandma in July, she is attracted to Polly's flamboyant style of wearing her grandma's clothes and drawing graffiti on everything. They play a ceiling bug race game lying on the floor, which M.E. enjoys losing—one of many adventures she shares with Polly. M.E. even performs a dangerous balancing feat on her apartment house awning to become a "gang" member because Polly tells her that Morton became one by retrieving a glove from the forbidden cellar, though she just barely manages to succeed. Later, however, when Morton shows her Pop's mismatched glove— he really showed Polly—and then laughs in his own funny way, M.E. winds up punching him. As she watches him cry for the first time, she recognizes (also for the first time) that there are various ways of being smart.

Still desperate for attention, M.E. adopts a full-time regime of sloppy eating, spilling milk, and wearing dirty clothes and finally succeeds in gaining her mom's attention. At first, Mom asks why she wants to make herself ugly, but after more of this behavior, Mom tells her that they are ready to send Morton to live on a farm because the situation is so unfair to M.E. Mom's announcement shocks M.E.; she didn't really mean to send Morton away.

Just before Morton is to leave in late August, he tries to retrieve the train car from the roof and falls. As M.E. looks down from the roof, she sees him lying unconscious on the roof below her. For weeks Morton lies in a coma at a large hospital, visited regularly by his frantic family. At first, they all think that he fell while trying to get the car for himself. But Polly tells M.E. that Morton was trying to get the car for her (Polly), and that she told him to do it. M.E. can hardly believe what she hears. When they were looking for Morton, Polly said that she didn't know where he was. Now she says that she thought he was waiting somewhere to surprise M.E. with the car.

M.E. finally realizes that both she and Morton did something dangerous because their friend Polly told them to. She is so angry at Polly that she yells at her loudly in the hospital corridor and begs her mom to be angry at her, too. But when Mom says that she is not angry at either of them and that she loves them both, M.E. finally recognizes how much she really loves her brother and wants him to come home.

As school opens in September, several significant things happen. M.E. receives many sympathetic notes from her classmates; they ask her to be their friend; and Polly announces that she is going home to her mother. Just before she leaves, she goes to the hospital to give the still unconscious Morton the car that she refused to give to M.E., and the two girls meet. At that moment, Morton miraculously opens his eyes and mumbles, "Rum-tum-tum." Then, as Polly is leaving, at Morton's urging M.E. does a neat somersault, just like she did when she first saw Polly.

Thematic Analysis

This complex story has a few themes. Family love, with the attendant generational misunderstandings, is one. Another is a middle-grader's strong need for friends. The most prominent theme, however, is a young person's personal adjustment to a sibling who has learning difficulties. In this story, the large difference in learning abilities between the siblings increases their normal jealous feelings. An awareness and understanding of the deep love that the heroine and her brother share may enable readers not only to help the learning disabled but to participate in their lives as well.

Discussion Materials

The book can be presented by showing the jacket portraits of the three protagonists and describing them: Mary Ella (M.E.) (pp. 27–28); Polly (pp. 20–22); and Morton (pp. 29–32, 62–64, 125–129, 201–202). The plot can be succinctly stated by reading the first four lines (p. 173) and a description of M.E.'s two problems (pp. 132–133). Several of the following excerpts can be paraphrased to deepen the readings: the Briggs family (pp. 53–60); Mother's Day gifts (pp. 48–52); Mother's attempt at friendship for Morton (pp. 132–133); M.E.'s need for friendship (17–19, 178–179); and the three protagonists (pp. 35–40, 134–144, 145–156, 184–187). Any of the following will make interesting book-talk anecdotes: playing "orphan" dolls (pp. 66–72, 73–81), more doll games (83–91), ceiling bug game (pp. 188–189), a dangerous awning balance game (pp. 211–227), trains (pp. 93–109, 116–124); M.E. becomes sloppy (pp. 204–210, 231–234); and Morton is missing (pp. 162–170, 251–252).

Related Materials

Several fiction titles are suggested: *Tallahassee Higgins* (Clarion, 1987) by Mary Downing Hahn; *But, I'm Ready to Go* (Bradbury, 1976) by Louise Albert; *At the Back of the North Wind* (Schocken, 1978) by George MacDonald; *Jacob Two-Two Meets the Hooded Fang* (Bantam, 1977) by Ellen Raskin; *Outside Over There* (Harper, 1981) by Maurice Sendak; *The Very Busy Spider* (Putnam, 1985) by Eric Carle; and *Flossie the Fox* (Dial, 1986) by Patricia McKissack, illustrated by Rachel Isadora. Two nonfiction books are recommended: a book of poetry, *A Light in the Attic* (Harper, 1981) by Shel Silverstein, and an informational title, *Puffin* (Lothrop, 1984) by Naomi Lewis.

A record, a filmstrip, and a film are also suggested: *Little Women* (Caedmon, 1975); *Friends: How They Help . . . How They Hurt* (Sunburst, 1986, 2 fs, also available on video); and *Portraits of Courage* (Filmedia, 1983, 33 min.).

Gates, Doris. *Morgan for Melinda*
Viking, 1980, 189 pp.

This well-known author of novels for young people wrote two earlier books, *Little Vic* and *Blue Willow*, that received the William Allen White Award and the Newbery Honor Book, respectively (see also *Introducing Books*, Bowker, 1970, p. 163). This title, which was succeeded by *A Filly for Melinda* (Viking, 1984), is the story of a ten-year-old girl who conquers her fear of horses and riding with the help of an elderly writer friend. She not only pleases her father and gains an understanding of her own linguistic abilities, but also finally frees herself of hidden guilt over her brother's death. The book bears the stamp of remembered events in the horsewoman-author's life and is filled with interesting facts about Morgan horses and riding in general. The colorful jacket painting by Arthur Thompson shows Melinda in full face superimposed on the Morgan horse, Aranaway Ethan, which is standing in a flower-filled California meadow under low, rolling hills. Youngsters, especially 8–11 year olds (grades 3–6), will find the book enlightening and enjoyable.

Melinda Ross, who is ten and entering sixth grade, has been living in the old ranch house of a new development, Toro Estates, in Carmel Valley, California, for the past few months. Her father, Calvin, is a rural mail carrier, and her mother, Lynn, works to help pay for their new house. Her brother, Martin, who was five years older than her, died of leukemia five years ago. Although her parents rarely speak of him, Melinda has known for a long time that her father, an accomplished horseman, wants to get the rural route so that he can buy one of the last things he promised Martin, a horse. So, after her father gets the rural route and then finds an old barn, she is not surprised when he announces that he wants to get a horse for her, but she is scared to death! She doesn't want to disappoint her father, but she really doesn't want to learn to ride, either.

On the big day, after she stalls with her chores, they finally head down the estate road. As they pass the Morton place, Melinda secretly hopes that Dwight Morton, who is 16, will notice her. Dwight's sister, Diana, is Melinda's classmate and friend. They soon arrive at Dodge Rayburn's red barn, where they are shown a 12-year-old Palomino, Sam, that they can purchase for $400. Cal is tempted because he can only spend $750 and he thinks Melinda can tolerate the gentle Sam. But Melinda is despondent. She doesn't feel any better when her father tells her she has a "natural seat" and deserves one of the $3,000 Morgan horses that are for sale there. Nor does she feel better when he tells her that she needs a horse with more spirit.

The following Sunday the Ross family goes to another horse farm, Morgan Manor, where Mrs. Tower shows them a foal named Mantic Peter Frost that they can buy for $750. Melinda is delighted to learn that she can't ride him for a long time, but then Mrs. Towers tells them that Granite Ranch is selling their seven-year-old chestnut stallion, Aranaway Ethan, which is also a Morgan, for $300, and her father decides to drive them the next day to see the horse. When after a wild jeep ride out to the far pasture, Chuck Railey, the foreman, explains that the Granite Ranch wants to sell the Morgan because it now has enough foals (Ethan's "gets"), the Ross family decides to purchase Ethan, even though Cal will have to train him to be a riding horse. Cal and Melinda fix up the barn and arrange for the vet, Dr. Vance, to geld Ethan. Melinda is relieved to hear him say that it will take about two months before anyone can ride him and willingly adds mucking out the stall and feeding hay to her regular chores. Meanwhile, Father and Dwight dig potholes, preparing to set up a riding ring.

Two weeks later, Missy (Ms. Muriel Zinn), a famous 70-year-old writer of mysteries who lives nearby in a house overlooking the Pacific, asks Father to give her riding lessons and to board the Morgan she plans to lease. Then she asks the Ross family to accompany her to the Morgan show on Sunday, and Melinda is convinced she's a meddler. (Dwight is supposed to come on Sunday to help her father.) But after a chat with her mother, Melinda loses her sullenness and they all go to the show in Missy's little red sports car. There Missy leases Oakhill's Merry Jo, another Morgan.

Missy convinces Melinda to start reading everything and to keep writing. She becomes just like an energetic and beloved grandmother. She gives good advice about writing, brings books to read, takes them to horse shows, and Diana and Melinda to lunch. When Melinda confides to Missy that she really doesn't want to ride, but does so for her father, Missy tells her that the ancient Chinese had a wise saying, "That which you fear will come to pass." Soon both Melinda's writing and her riding improve. She even finds that she really likes Ethan and that he is a fine horse. Missy also explains to Melinda that her parents don't talk about Martin because life is for the living.

In July Missy takes first prize in the Jack Benny (over 39) at the championship Morgan horse show in Monterey. To celebrate she buys a truck, a horse trailer, and her Morgan, Merry Jo. The summer passes with Melinda's parents' spending their three-week vacation around their home and Melinda's working at Rayburn's riding day camp for youngsters. Melinda gets to ride Sam again, and she also plays Scrabble with Missy. She also learns that Cal told Missy how lucky he is to have such a wonderful daughter. Autumn comes and Melinda enters sixth grade.

Around Christmas they take Merry Jo to Dr. Vance hoping to impregnate her. Then Missy goes to visit her brother in San Diego, but before she leaves, she gives Melinda her overhauled typewriter. Soon after Missy returns, she has a heart attack. When Melinda visits Missy, she tells her that the past year with Melinda, her family, and the horses has been the happiest she remembers. Then Missy dies. At the reading of the will, Missy leaves the truck and trailer to Cal, a mink jacket to Lynn, and her horse and dog to Melinda. Melinda is touched; now she will have a little foal, too. Diana's birthday is upon them and Dwight is taking them both to a movie. For a moment, she wishes she were 16, but then she realizes that Dwight would be 21. More realistically she thinks about her manuscript and what she'll do about it in the future.

Thematic Analysis

Among the many themes apparent in the book are valuing oneself, determining one's interests, assessing skills, learning how to deal with awakening sexual feelings, evaluating guilt feelings, and emphasizing life during a time of grief. All are well presented, especially the main theme of feeling responsible because of guilt instead of feeling confident because of your own importance. Wish fulfillment, as expressed in the Chinese axiom (p. 132), can help put things in the proper perspective.

Discussion Materials

The background can be set while displaying the cover drawing of Melinda; the main characters (pp. 3–8, 23); buying a horse (pp. 9–22, 25–47); the barn (pp. 48–70); Missy (pp. 75–88); looking for a horse for Missy (pp. 86–92, 95–104); Father on a horse (pp. 105–110); Melinda rides (pp. 114–123); Missy rides (pp. 125+); the Golden West, Jack Benny prize (pp. 138–152); and mostly Missy (pp. 71–74, 93–94, 135–137, 161–164, 165–186).

Related Materials

The sequel, *A Filly for Melinda* (Viking, 1984), with the filly Little Missy, is recommended. Many titles that highlight youngsters and horses are suggested: For the youngest in the group, *Suho and the White Horse: A Legend of Mongolia* (Viking, 1981), retold by Yuzo Otsuka; *Wild Apaloosa* (Holiday, 1983) by Glen Rounds; and *Horse in the Attic* (Bradbury, 1983) by Eleanor Clymer; for the better readers in the group, *Girl Called Bob and a Horse Called Yoki* (Dial, 1982) by Barbara Campbell; *Valley of the Ponies* (Macmillan, 1982), *Dark Horse* (Morrow, 1983), and *Yesterday's Horses* (Macmillan, 1985), all by Jean Slaughter Doty; *War Horse* (Greenwillow, 1983) by Michael Morpurgo; *Somebody's Horse* (Atheneum, 1986) by Dorothy Nafus Morrison; and *Under the Shadow* (Harper, 1983) by Anne Knowles. Also suggested are the film *Miracle of Life* (Time-Life Video, 1985) and a recording of Frances Hodgson Burnett's wonderful *Secret Garden* (Argo, 1976) read by Glenda Jackson. For those interested in writing and words, a book and a film are suggested: *Words: A Book about the Origins of Everyday Words and Phrases* (Scribner, 1981) and *Writing Says It All* (Barr Films, 1983, 24 min.).

Mazer, Harry. *The Island Keeper*
Delacorte, 1981, 165 pp.

This author has a clear understanding of youngsters: Three of his books have been recognized by the ALA Notable Book Committee, and another appears in *Introducing More Books* (Bowker, 1978, pp. 17–19). The title under discussion is about Cleo, who lives in Chicago with her aloof father and grandmother and severely mourns the recent loss of her beloved younger sister. Her grief propels her to her wealthy father's Canadian island, where through a series of survival adventures she learns to be truly independent and shed the weight that has always plagued her. The story will be read avidly because of its subject and ease of readability, especially by females from 10 to 12 (grades 5–7). The front jacket illustration, which shows the slim blue-jean clad Cleo standing on Duck Island at summer's end, was painted by Peter Caras in the pensive shades of blue and green.

As Cleo Murphy flies to New York and another summer at the New Hampshire White Mountain Riding Camp, she plans to carry out the

"Eight Steps to Freedom" that she has listed. She is coming east after the funeral of her sister, Jam (Jessica), who was four years younger than Cleo and the only bright spot in her life for 12 years. Cleo lost her mother in a senseless car accident nine years ago, and now Jam, her only confidante and friend. Her wealthy father is distant, his mother with whom they live, formal and precise in her expectations.

Ever since Cleo can remember, she and Jam were sent to different boarding schools and summer camps. In between and during holidays, they flew back to their Chicago home for formal contact with their quiet father and demanding grandmother. Grandmother doesn't have any tolerance for Cleo's overweight appearance and lack of poise, which she occasionally blames on the latest boarding school—most recently St. Ives, so Cleo is used to changing camps and schools. Until now she was able to survive because of her love for Jam, but now Jam is gone!

Cleo plans to retreat to Duck Island near the Canadian border where she and Jam spent some time together and wanted to return. She struggles with her flagging courage to telephone the owner of the summer camp, Mitzie Stoner, to inform her, using her grandmother's voice, that Cleo will not be returning to camp that summer. Then she takes a bus to Toronto, where she purchases camping equipment from a helpful young clerk, Glenn. After another bus ride with a heavy knapsack in tow, she arrives in North Adams, about seven miles from Dundee, their family home on Big Clear Lake. The eight steps are almost complete.

Cleo walks painfully, but with determination as she recalls her grandmother's comments about her excessive weight. Making sure that caretaker Frank Garrity doesn't see her, Cleo takes a canoe, fairly confident that she can reach Duck Island. In a short while it appears by chance. She steps ashore and ties up her canoe, feeling successful yet uncertain that she can withstand the loneliness of her new life. She is buoyed by the spirit of Jam, however, and the good times they had together.

It immediately starts to rain, and reality enters her summer idyll, as she rouses stiff from her hiding place. She finds a low-lying tree to hide the canoe from Frank's vision and a cave to shelter herself. After that, everyday tasks of arranging her shelter and gathering food, tasks previously taken care of by others, fill her days, and she learns to take care of herself. Luckily, she read the book Glenn suggested on gathering wild foods before she left it on the bus. She constructs a broom to sweep her cave, builds a fireplace, and allocates the food packages she bought. She also starts a stew pot for each natural food that she collects. With good sense, she only eats a tiny amount of whatever she collects, then waits 24 hours to see the results before she puts any in the pot. She also fishes and swims, and makes friends with the small animals, like her favorite chipmunk, Al Capone, and an owl. The early part of the summer is healing, and though Garrity scans the island with his boat, he doesn't see her.

Before long, however, a bothersome raccoon eats almost all the provisions in her knapsack. She becomes worried, but decides to live off the land as best she can. With the stew pot as her main source of food, she puts everything she can find in it, including fish, berries, and grasses, and starts to eat much less. It is hard, but with each passing day she toughens up and loses a lot of fat. Toward the end of August, Garrity searches the land carefully, calling to her, but she doesn't answer. She isn't quite ready to leave yet. Soon after, however, she becomes violently ill from her usual tiny portion of greens, and after her recovery, a bad storm hits the island. Now she knows she must leave. The summer is over, and she feels that she can return now. The problem is that the storm has smashed the tree and canoe, her only escape.

In desperation, Cleo tries to swim to Dundee, but she doesn't get far. The water makes her feel numb, so she stops swimming and tries to build a raft. After she works on it for days, it quickly breaks up on the rocks, and Cleo is face to face with physical survival without frills. She projects that she can walk across the lake ice five months from now in January, but until then she has no choice but to stay on the island.

Cleo hurriedly makes the cave as winterproof as possible. The hardest part is finding food. As time passes and she finds no plants, and increasingly fewer fish, she is forced to learn to kill to eat—first, a porcupine, then the troublesome raccoon, and finally one of the deer she enjoyed looking at last summer. She becomes toughened in spirit as well as body. Cold and hunger are constant companions, snow and storms continual opponents. Then one day the rest of the deer are nowhere to be found, and Cleo reasons that they have gone across the ice. With mittens, leggings, and snowshoes she fashioned from deer hide, Cleo makes it to Dundee. Almost seven months had elapsed since she escaped to the island.

Back in Dundee, Garrity doesn't recognize her, but after talking to her father on the phone, she and Garrity fly to Chicago. Cleo has changed; she is self-confident now, ready to go on with her life. Her father who has tried to track her down and her grandmother who sees a changed Cleo are glad to have her home. When she announces that she wants to return to St. Ives, everyone knows Cleo is now able to face anything courageously.

Thematic Analysis

Dealing with an unflattering image is difficult enough, but in times of crisis it may become overwhelming. In this story about a young person full of self-doubts and terribly wounded emotionally who is able to face hardships courageously, the theme of gaining independence of thought and action is paramount. The story touches on the loss of a loved one, prepubescent doubts, and misdirected anger, as well. The story effectively details the idea of eating to live, rather than the reverse, albeit under extreme conditions, and the intimate connection between thought and action, or the physical-emotional nature of being overweight. The pain involved in facing situations bravely is also well shown.

Discussion Materials

Although this is a book best savored individually, it should be easy to intrigue an audience with the cover illustration, slim size, and large-point typeface. A reading of the dedication and a summary of Cleo's background will set the story line (dedication, chapter 1 and chapter 2 to p. 15). Many other episodes can be highlighted: Jam's death (pp. 16–18); "Eight Steps to Freedom" (pp. 5, 21–24, 24–25, 26, 38–41); the island connection to Jam (p. 15); Cleo's thoughts regarding her overweight condition (pp. 11–13, 19–21, 25, 29–30, 35, 47–49, 62–63, 75–77, 83); Cleo is forced to eat frugally (pp. 84–95); Cleo imitates her grandmother (pp. 21–24); the camping equipment store (pp. 26–32); finding the cave (pp. 53–58); the chipmunk (pp. 59–60); memories of Jam (pp. 70–71); Garrity searches for her (pp. 75, 97–99); the lost knapsack (pp. 78–83); scavenging (pp. 84–85); illness strikes (pp. 93–95); gathering food (pp. 101–102); time to leave (pp. 103–109); the raft (pp. 95–112); winter arrives (pp. 113–130); killing the deer (pp. 131–138); and the escape (pp. 141–147).

Related Materials

An excellent nonfiction title to suggest is *Foodworks: Over 100 Science Activities and Fascinating Facts That Explore the Magic of Food* (Addison-Wesley, 1986) by the Ontario Science Centre. Two fiction titles are *Green Book* (Farrar, 1982) by Jill Paton Walsh, a short science fiction novella about a girl and her father, and *Foxglove Tales: Chosen by Lucy Meredith*

(Harper, 1984) by Alison Uttley, a collection of humorous short stories about animals. Three other highly recommended nonfiction titles are *Where the Bald Eagles Gather* (Clarion, 1984) by Dorothy H. Patent; *National Geographic Book of Mammals* (National Geographic Society, 1981), edited by Donald J. Crump et al.; and *Are Those Animals Real? How Museums Prepare Wildlife Exhibits* (Morrow, 1984) by Judy Cutchins and Ginny Johnson. For the sensitive reader, suggest Shelley Bruce's autobiography, *Tomorrow Is Today* (Bobbs-Merrill, 1983), her story of her portrayal of "Annie" on Broadway and her battle against leukemia. The recording *Incident at Hawk's Hill* (Random, 1974), about the survival of a little boy, is recommended. Two filmstrips are also available: *Rapunzel* (Spoken Arts) by Barbara Rogasky and *Survival Skills* (Random, 3f). Two suggested films are *Girl Stuff* (Churchill Films, 1982) and *Summer's End* (Direct Cinema, 1986).

Riskind, Mary.   *Apple Is My Sign*
Houghton, 1981, 146 pp.

This author brings a background in English literature and social psychology to this, her first, children's book. A second title, *Wildcat Summer* (Houghton, 1985), has since been published. Obeying the cardinal rule of writing on a familiar subject, Mary Riskind is the daughter of deaf parents. (The word "deaf" is used in the book instead of the current term "hearing-impaired.") She and her siblings—all of whom are hearing— grew up signing and sharing the memories of their deaf parents. Understandably, she has always had an interest in extending a better understanding of the deaf.

This title, which is partially indebted to her father's childhood, tells about a deaf 10-year-old who attends a boarding school because his deaf father is convinced that no trust can exist between the deaf and the hearing. When he returns to school for the spring semester, however— after spending the Christmas holidays with his family, all of whom are deaf, on their apple farm—Harry has shown his father that the deaf and hearing can be friends. Youngsters age 9–11 (grades 4–6), will enjoy the book. They will also be interested in the world of the deaf as it was around the turn of the century, and still may be in many aspects.

The book reinforces the system of signing and finger spelling used by many deaf people. Because word order in sign language is different from the English translation, to eliminate confusion, the author retained the normal English word order, except in the dialogue. There the finger spelled words are printed with hyphens between the letters, and the signs retain the scrambled word order that the deaf translate automatically to normal English word order. In her author's note, Mary Riskind writes that although sign language has changed, and is more fulsome with new signs today, she has limited herself to the signs available to Harry. As it becomes simple for deaf people to automatically translate normal word order to their reordered form, so it is for readers of this book, which has brief examples of deaf word order. Further, the small amount shows some of the difficulties that face the deaf.

Ten-year-old Harry Berger is the second son in a deaf family of six. His rigid father, spunky mom, older brother, Ray, younger sister, Veve, and Anna, the baby, live in an apple orchard in Muncie, Pennsylvania. Mr. Berger is convinced that the deaf and the hearing are separated by an impenetrable nontrusting gulf. So he is receptive when Preacher Ervin, who has traveled among the parsonages in the state, suggests that bookish Harry attend the Bertie School for the Deaf in Philadelphia. Harry not only doesn't think the same way as his father, but he doesn't want to leave his family and his friends at the hearing school, especially Freckles. He knows that he is more "serious" than Ray (even Ray thinks so), but he would like to stay and help his father on the farm.

During his first two weeks at the new school, he makes friends with Spectacles, Cowlick, and Mighty, whose name is Landis. (Their nicknames are signed.) He also encounters Mrs. Slack, the matron, and learns that the master, Mr. Thomas, earned the sign language name "Rapid Heart" when the school boys found him kissing Miss Bertie, the headmaster's sister. Nonetheless, Harry hasn't received any mail and is very homesick. Landis, who became deaf from scarlet fever at age 3 and is at school because his hearing parents don't like to sign, tells him that he doesn't know what it is to be lonely. Finally he receives a caring letter from his father, who inscribes it, "Your loving father," and some of Harry's insecurities and anger flee.

Now that he is working in the print shop at school, it is easy for Harry to honor his father's written request that he draw a picture of the school for Ray. Mr. Bertie, the headmaster, sees the drawing and suggests that he use his creative abilities in the tailoring shop. When a curly-haired girl named Agnes, from the separate girls' school, helps him use the treadle-operated sewing machine, he wonders why they have a "Singer" in a school for the deaf. Then he feels the vibrations in his feet and he understands. On a ride around the big city in a "horseless carriage"—his first ride in a motorcar—he sees the Liberty Bell, which has a crack in it, a defect, just like the deaf. He climbs a nearby wall with some friends, sees a blind man walking with his cane, then stumbles into a large library, but the librarian is closing and asks him to come back.

Back at school, Mr. Bertie personally instructs Harry in vocalizing. After many tiring and frustrating attempts to blow out a candle and stimulate throat muscles, Harry manages to call out the name of the family wagon horse, "Whoa." He is delighted with his hard-won achievement.

The boys at the school practice continually for the traditional Thanksgiving Day football game; they even survive Cowlick's experimental play. On the big day, the hearing school, Harding, wins one, then Harry hands off the football to Cowlick, and the Bertie school wins one, too. As the red captain, Le Roy, shakes Harry's hand, Harry knows that the deaf and the hearing can "play" together. Then the three-week Christmas holiday arrives, and Harry rides home on the train with Agnes, who puts up a good front in spite of her motion sickness. Two stops after she gets off, Harry's entire family is waiting to meet him in the horse-drawn wagon.

Harry is so happy to be home with his family and friends. But when neither Ray nor his father believe his first attempts to call out, "Whoa," to stop the horse, Harry is unwilling to accept their denials. He climbs a tree and once again calls out. When the horse stops—this time in an emergency—his father gratefully insists that Harry climb back in the wagon. He tousles Harry's hair and tells him that he's stubborn just like his father. Later Harry has the opportunity to teach signing to his hearing friend Freckles. Harry's success and Freckles's friendship spur him to contemplate teaching as a career. Although Preacher Ervin, who adamantly believes that the deaf cannot teach, tries to squash Harry's ambition to be a teacher of the deaf at the local school, later that night Harry's mom tells him that anything is possible if you want it enough.

Soon it is fair time at the local grange hall where all the rural townsfolk gather to show their produce and share in the magic and games, and Harry is excited! The family's relish and cider win prizes, but then Freckles is caught using the signs that Harry taught him to coach the hearing boys in the spelling bee. Father blames Harry for teaching him—just as he has always said, the deaf can't trust the hearing. Crushed by the deceipt, Harry nurses his frustration and anger as he runs along the railroad tracks, something the deaf especially shouldn't do. Freckles, who has already apologized to Harry's father, not only saves him from an approaching train, but also tells him how very sorry he is. Both Harry's life and his belief that the deaf and the hearing can understand one another and be friends are saved. At the celebration back in the hall, even his mom dances.

Then it is time to return to Philadelphia. Before Harry leaves, Freckles gives him a yellow cat's eye marble. As they play marbles, Freckles tells Harry that he wants to be his friend and that he is very sorry for cheating. As the train rolls away, Harry fingers the cat's eye and thinks of the stories he will tell at school. This time he isn't lonely, scared, or angry.

Thematic Analysis

Because the main characters are disabled, the main theme is mutual consideration between the deaf and the hearing. The informative story accomplishes its purpose; the reader will easily understand that the deaf need appreciation and acceptance. It is also a poignant family story, as well as one of making friends under difficult conditions. The historical and geographical references also are interesting.

Discussion Materials

The full-color jacket illustration by Tony Howell shows a pensive Harry sitting in a bare-branched tree with a four-seater motor car (circa 1910) and the red brick school buildings in the background. It can be used along with a summary of the story and the main characters: school friends (pp. 1–16); father's letter (p. 7, read aloud); home (pp. 81–90). The author's note (pp. ix–xii) should definitely be read aloud and carefully explained. Other incidents to use are: Agnes, the "Singer," and on the train (pp. 17–23, 70–80); school (pp. 24–30); the motor car and Liberty Bell (pp. 31–38); vocalizing (pp. 51–57); football (pp. 58–69); the Christmas holidays (pp. 81–90); Harry's joke (pp. 91–100); and the events at the grange (pp. 120–130). Harry's rescue from the railroad tracks with its healing effect (pp. 131–139) can be paraphrased.

Related Materials

Two titles from Gaullaudet University Press, which is devoted to the deaf, are recommended: *My First Book of Sign* by Pamela J. Baker and *I Can Sign My Name* (both Kendall Green, 1986) by Susan Chaplin. Another nonfiction title, *How to Really Fool Yourself* (Lippincott, 1981) by Vicki Cobb is a lively book of puzzles and games that is unsettling to the senses. The following books have significant similarities: *Gathering Room* (Farrar, 1981) by Colby Rodowsky; *Circle of Fire* (Atheneum, 1982) by William H. Hooks; *The Sea Witch* (Four Winds, 1981) by Beverly Keller; *Come Sing, Jimmy Jo* (Dutton, 1985) by Katherine Paterson; and *"Who, Sir? Me, Sir?"* (Oxford, 1983) by K. M. Peyton. Three animated films will also be popular: *I Was a Thanksgiving Turkey* (Direct Cinema, 1986) presents the bird's view; *Sound of Sunshine, Sound of Rain* (FilmFair, 1983) is about a seven-year-old blind boy's daily excursions; and *I'm Not Oscar's Friend Anymore* (Churchill Films, 1983) tells how two children can be angry and still be friends. A microcomputer program for the Apple II, *Talking Hands* (Opportunities for Learning, 1987), introduces sign language. The poster "Key into the Library" (ALA, 1986, No. 236), which shows a modern library with a computer catalog, will make an interesting background to Harry's discovery of libraries.

Slepian, Jan. *Lester's Turn*
Macmillan, 1981, 139 pp.

For her first fiction book for children, *The Alfred Summer* (Macmillan, 1980), the author received glowing reviews, the 1980 Boston-Globe-Horn Book Honor Book Award and a place on *School Library Journal's* list of best books for 1980. The sequel, *Lester's Turn,* another tour de force, can be read and enjoyed independently by youngsters age 10 and up (grades 5 and up), but its enjoyment will be enhanced by reading the predecessor. The story deals with Lester's concern over his now hospitalized friend, Alfie, who like Lester is disabled. Lester has cerebral palsy; Alfie has epilepsy and is mentally retarded. In the earlier title, they and two friends were "the walking wounded." Now Lester is the main character; Myron has moved far away; Claire has moved a short distance away; and Alfie is hospitalized. The quad squad is now a trio (read duo), Lester and Claire, with Alfie confined. Jan Slepian writes with humor and a perception that comes from her study of psychology and her field experience in speech pathology with cerebral palsy children.

The front jacket, adapted from a drawing by Tom Allen, shows a pencil sketch of a young male magnified twice—as though in a rear-view mirror—in a gentle shade of green. The portrait reflects the seemingly calm exterior of a youngster who, encased in a body he can't control, undergoes the difficulties and inner turmoil of "growing up."

During Roosevelt's presidency in 1939, Lester Klopper, 16 and a victim of cerebral palsy, lives with his working parents in an apartment in Brighton Beach, New York. Until recently he had three friends to pal around with: Alfie, Claire, and Myron. (Having pals is difficult, if not next to impossible, when you have cerebral palsy. But to Claire and Myron it doesn't matter that he and Alfie are physically handicapped.) Then Alfie's mother died, and Mr. Burt, who travels on business, decided to put Alfie in a mental hospital and to board his younger son with a relative. After that, Myron moved away and Claire moved to a private house close by.

Now Lester visits Alfie regularly, but finds him overweight and dulled by his medication. He seems to eat constantly. Disgusted, Lester decides to kidnap him. He tries to interest Claire Ellingez in the plot, but she is too busy with her new life. At a party in the hospital chapel, Lester meets a volunteer, Tillie-Rose Bloom. When he tries to get away from her in order to take Alfie home with him, she sticks like glue and inadvertently causes the outdoor guard to stop the traveling pair. As he is trying to get past everyone in the hospital, Lester is repelled by all the patients, especially the man who sits at the door in a wheelchair trying to sell raffle tickets to passersby.

Lester plays dumb when the director, tiny Mrs. Brenner, tries patiently to explain to him that Alfie needs his medication and that he would be a tremendous responsibility for him, but he realizes that she might be right. Lester's mother, who continues to hope that he will have normal friends, can't tolerate Alfie for long and doesn't want him around. What will he do to support Alfie? He'll have to leave school and get a job, but where? Finally, Mrs. Brenner suggests that he take Alfie for a day or a weekend to try it out. Meanwhile, Les—as Alfie and Claire call him—is impressed by all the people in the hospital who speak warmly about Alfie.

The following Sunday while both his parents are busy with other things, Les takes the elevated train to Claire's new house to talk about Alfie. There Les meets the upstairs tenant, Lena Lensky, and her son, Alex, a reluctant violinist. Lester thinks that Alex is everything he is not, normal and good-looking, in spite of his constant need to practice, but tiny, foreign-looking Lena is the strangest, most eccentric person he ever met. Lena agrees with Claire that it would be ridiculous for Les to bring Alfie home permanently.

When he gets off the train on his way home, Lester meets Tillie-Rose, who turns out to be a neighbor, near the beach. When she invites him to a barbeque that some of the kids are having on the beach, he reluctantly agrees to go, thinking of his mother's desire for him to have normal friends. During the blanket bundling occasioned by the cold March weather, Tillie-Rose, who is pudgy and much younger than Lester, but is attracted to him, kisses him. At that moment, Lester realizes that he really loves Claire, the tall, skinny child-woman. He tells her so, and she accepts his confession calmly.

Lester then tries out a job at kindly Mr. Apatow's drugstore, but it turns out to be a disastrous experience when he knocks over some bottles because of his spasticity. Still careening from his bad experience, Lester runs into Tillie-Rose outside her father's butcher shop. When she, the motherless, only child of the butcher, offers him a job, he refuses thinking of all the dangerous knives. Then she takes him to the secret basement room she has creatively decorated and offers to board Alfie there, but cautious Lester declines.

The next day Claire arrives as promised to take him to meet her new friend, Jean Persico. But when they arrive Mrs. Persico makes a horrible scene, intimating that Claire is a lesbian because she stroked her friend Blanchie's hair during her last visit. Claire, whose only handicap is her slow rate of sexual development, is confused, and Les, who has begun to recognize sexual feelings but feels thwarted by his spastic body, is outraged by what he witnesses.

Les then introduces Claire to Tillie-Rose and her secret room, slightly against Tillie-Rose's wishes. The two get along famously, however, and the three friends plan to bring Alfie to live in the room. Lena, meanwhile, has an idea to establish the Alfred Fund for which she and Alex will have a concert. They convince the reluctant Alex to participate. Lester's next visit to Alfie further convinces him how popular Alfie is around his fellow patients.

The concert day arrives. Les legally signs Alfie out of the hospital for a weekend. He takes him around Brighton Beach trying to relive the "old days," but Alfie takes seriously ill and because of his disability is unable to report his symptoms. When Les notices how ill he looks, he takes him back to the hospital, instead of going to the concert. They operate for appendicitis, but his appendix bursts and the poisons kill him. Les only wanted to help Alfie not kill him, and now he feels guilty. Mrs. Brenner tells him to stop blaming himself. She suggests that he is using his feeling of guilt the same way he tried to use Alfie as an excuse for not doing anything with his life. When she tells him that Charlie, the man in the wheelchair selling raffle tickets, was just his age when he first arrived, she hits home.

Determined to stay in school and make the best of his life, Lester speaks to Charlie as he leaves the hospital. The patient's friendly question, "You on your way?" receives Les's answer, "Yes I am." When Claire teams up with Alex, Les begins to see Tillie-Rose in a new way.

Thematic Analysis

This astute story about the feelings of the physically disabled, particularly those with cerebral palsy, shows the importance of self-acceptance for all children whether normal or disabled, and that a knowledge of the inner thoughts of the disabled is helpful in understanding them. The main theme, however, is the astoundingly simple truth that regardless of their physical condition, youngsters progress through similar stages at vastly different rates, many times to the consternation of insensitive adults.

Discussion Materials

To establish the tight friendship among the four youngsters, a summation of the earlier title will make a good introduction to this sequel. Or entice the audience by simply introducing the main characters here (pp. 1–2, 8–9, plus the story line p. 4). Several incidents describe the nature of cerebral palsy: going down steps (pp. 1–2); the hospital (pp. 17–19, 26–29); the horseback ride (pp. 32–33); and explanations to Tillie-Rose (pp. 50–51). Other episodes also can be book talked: Lena and Alex (pp. 37–45); Lester's hope (pp. 46–48); looking for a job (pp. 58–63); Tillie-Rose's secret room (pp. 67–71); the Alfred Fund (pp. 91–99); and checking out Alfie (pp. 112–114).

Related Materials

Two autobiographies are accounts of disablement: *Geri* (Morrow, 1984) by Geri Jewell, a cerebral palsy victim, and *I'll Never Walk Alone* (Continuum, 1983) by Carol Simonides, who developed bone cancer at 14. Two suggested titles by Betsy Byars are *Animal, Vegetable, and John D. Jones* (Delacorte, 1982) and *Computer Nut* (Viking, 1984). *Where Are You,*

Angela Von Hauptmann: Now That I Need You? (Holt, 1980) by Barbara Williams, set in 1939, is about seventh graders in the Walt Whitman Elementary School. *Samantha on Stage* (Farrar, 1980), illustrated by Ruth Sanderson, shows the problems of friendship among 11-year-olds. Two titles by Mary Downing Hahn, *Wait till Helen Comes* (Clarion, 1986) and *Daphne's Book* (Clarion, 1983), are especially for females. Complementary films are: *Feeling Good, Feeling Proud* (Direct Cinema, 1982); *Child Sexual Abuse* (Indiana Univ. Center, 1985); and *Backwards: The Riddle of Dyslexia* (Coronet, 1985). A recording of *Summer of the Swans* is also available from Live Oak Media.

Understanding Physical and Emotional Problems: Additional Titles

Ames, Mildred. *Cassandra-Jamie*. Scribner, 1985, 135 pp. (Gr. 5–7)

Anna and Bella. Film, 8 min., also available on video. Cilia Van Dijk/Animated People, 1986. (Gr. 5–up)

Anne of Green Gables. Eight cassettes, 10½ hrs. Audio Book Contractors, 1986. (Gr. 5–8)

Bond, Nancy. *A Place to Come Back To*. Atheneum, 1984, 204 pp. (Gr. 6–8)

Branley, Franklyn M. *Shivers and Goose Bumps: How We Keep Warm*. Crowell, 1984, 96 pp. (Gr. 5–8)

Chambers, Aidan. *Seal Secret*. Harper, 1981, 122 pp. (Gr. 5–6)

Chiefari, Janet. *Kids Are Baby Goats*. Dodd, 1984, 56 pp. (Gr. 3–5)

Corcoran, Barbara. *A Horse Called Sky*. Atheneum, 1986, 204 pp. (Gr. 6–8)

Digby, Anne. *The Quicksilver Horse*. St. Martin's, 1982, 96 pp. (Gr. 6–8)

Goor, Ron, and Goor, Nancy. *All Kinds of Feet*. Photographs by Ron Goor. Crowell, 1984, 48 pp. (Gr. 2–4)

Hall, Lynn. *Danza!* Scribner, 1985, 192 pp. (Gr. 5–8)

Hanson, June Andrea. *Summer of the Stallion*. Illus. by Gloria Singer. Macmillan, 1979, 108 pp. (Gr. 3–5)

Healthy Feelings. Four filmstrips. Random, 1985. (Gr. 4–8)

Herbert, Marie. *Winter of the White Seal*. Morrow, 1982, o.p. (Gr. 6–9)

Lane, Margaret. *The Squirrel*. Illus. by Kenneth Lilly. Dial, 1981, 32 pp. (Gr. 2–4)

Lavine, Sigmund A. *Wonders of Woodchucks*. Dodd, 1984, 80 pp. (Gr. 4–up)

Meyers, Susan. *Pearson, a Harbor Seal Pup*. Illus. by Ilka Hartmann. Dutton, 1980, 64 pp. (Gr. 4–8)

Morey, Walt. *Lemon Meringue Dog*. Dutton, 1980, 165 pp. (Gr. 5–6)

Simon, Hilda. *Sight and Seeing: A World of Light and Color*. Philomel, 1983, 96 pp. (Gr. 6–9)

Spoil the Child. Film, 23 min., also available on video. Direct Cinema, 1985. (Gr. 5–up)

Stolz, Mary. *Cat Walk.* Illus. by Erik Blegvad. Harper, 1983, 120 pp. (Gr. 4–6)

Strieber, Whitley. *Wolf of Shadows.* Knopf, 1985, 128 pp. (Gr. 5–up)

Ten Carrot Diamond. Recording or cassette, 40 min. The Linden Tree, 1986. (Gr. 3–up)

Towne, Mary. *Boxed In.* Harper, 1982, 160 pp. (Gr. 4–6)

The Velveteen Rabbit. Video, 26½ min. Random, 1986. (Gr. 3–up)

Williams, Terry Tempest, and Major, Ted. *The Secret Language of Snow.* Illus. by Jennifer Dewey. Sierra Club/Pantheon, 1984, 136 pp. (Gr. 4–up)

5

Forming a View of the World

DURING the middle years, youngsters from 8 to 12 years of age continue to expand their horizons. They deepen their awareness of the community around them, learn more about their nation, and explore their interest in other peoples and places. Children respond with loyalty and allegiance to people and events in their American culture, and with pride in their own cultural heritage. They begin to develop an understanding of the human condition and of the importance of historical forces. With an incompletely developed sense of historical time—not a completed abstraction until a later age—a child's acceptance of historical personages and events is based on his or her immediate experience. The heroes youngsters have now help them appreciate the history of their country and the planet. What better time to present a view of the world and its peoples!

An inquiring attitude about democratic values and the historical trends in which they flourish is paramount now. So is an interest in other lands and people. In today's increasingly internationally oriented world, youngsters must successfully traverse the stages of learning about their country and other countries of the world. Reading about the lives of youngsters past and present is fascinating for this age group and helpful in forming a view of the world. These book experiences will serve as guideposts.

The books that appear in this chapter fulfill many of the requirements of young people in this area. They are an admixture of current, recent, and ancient history for many differing reading abilities and tastes. A conscious attempt was made to include titles that not only will serve children living in all different geographical locations, but also ones that will stress some of the values that helped form America, as well as others that indicate the cyclical nature of history.

Costabel, Eva Deutsch. *The Pennsylvania Dutch: Craftsmen and Farmers*
Illus. by the author. Atheneum, 1986, 48 pp.

The author-illustrator of this title has a substantial history as a designer of fabrics, wallpaper, greeting cards, china, and many other items, and is also the author of books about needlework. Her education and training in art history and painting and her work experience have combined felicitously with her middle name toward the publication of this book. [In the introduction (p. 8) she explains that "Deutsch" was mistakenly translated to "Dutch."] This nonfiction title briefly describes the life of a typical early Pennsylvania Dutch farm family and introduces the many crafts that were produced by these settlers. The table of contents lists 13 chapters, the majority of which deal with crafts, for example, Quilting and Stiegel Glass, but it also lists four typical home areas, for example, Kitchen and Bedchamber, and three well-known artifacts originated by the Pennsylvania Dutch, for example, the Kentucky rifle and the Conestoga wagon. The informative title will appeal to children 8–11 years of age (grades 3–6), both as a reading experience and as an excellent reference source for an ethnic group of long ago, some of whom still survive.

Eva Deutsch Costabel conducted scrupulous research. She acknowledges the president of the Lancaster Historical Society for checking the manuscript and artwork, and she also includes a valuable brief bibliography (for adults and interested youngsters), an index, and a partial listing of 12 museums that contain American folk art collections. One museum supplied the original prints that appear as seven reproduced decorations (see page 48 for the page references) and an engraving of German farm buildings in Bethlehem, Pennsylvania, in 1757 that was used as the artist's model for the full-color double-spread painting that appears on the title page.

The artist placed full-color gouache paintings—or decorations—on practically every page: 15 full-page paintings and as many decorative ones. The overall effect is one of color and easily identifiable Pennsylvania Dutch artwork. The illustrator reflects the creativity and symmetry of the settlers' crafts. Her style of American primitivism suggests the spirit of the time and place.

The bright jacket drawings are also appealing. The front jacket portrays two settlers standing stiffly like dolls beside their decorated chest and various necessaries. Everything has an appealing pattern that labels it a representation of the Pennsylvania Dutch. The back jacket displays a red heart enclosing two stylized birds bordered by a white rectangle on the warm pumpkin color of the jacket. Although the jacket loudly proclaims "Pennsylvania Dutch," the terra-cotta-and-white endpapers silhouetted with a flag, human figures, and flora and fauna definitely confirm it. Mary Ahern, who designed the jacket and chose the interesting typeface, a combination of florid, bold heads and straightforward text print, added a definite flair to the book.

The Pennsylvania Dutch were actually German settlers who acquired the sobriquet permanently when English speakers mispronounced and misunderstood the diversity behind the word "Deutsch." The settlers spoke German, but they came from many countries: Germany; Alsace-Lorraine; Switzerland; Silesia; Moravia; and Scandinavia. They also represented many different religious sects—Quakers (Society of Friends), Mennonite, Moravian, and Amish. Although most were farmers, many were skilled craftsmen, and the difference in their education was great, from little to university degrees. Most were hardworking, however, treasuring their language and crafts, and most of all their family, community, and church, for they had been forced to leave Central Europe in the seventeenth century because of religious turmoil.

The *Family* portrait opposite the table of contents shows a young family having their picture taken with the chickens in front of their red-roofed house. It is a small family of eight children. The *Family and Home* were important to the hard-working German settlers, who had an intense pride in their possessions and were noted for their cleanliness. Everything was kept clean—even the barns were swept. The *Kitchen* was known for its large fireplace, from which hung all the cooking utensils, while the mantel held some of the necessaries. The cupboard and sawbuck table were also part of the typical farm home (p. 13). The *Bedchamber* generally had a bare wooden floor and was furnished with a quilted poster bed, a painted chest, a wardrobe, and a cradle. A child's toy might also be seen there (p. 15).

The settlers invented linsey-woolsey cloth, a coarse homespun of *Linen and Wool* (p. 16). They are also known for their *Weaving*, especially the double-woven coverlet and beautiful patterns, mainly patriotic themes or birds and flowers, until the invention of the jacquard loom permitted more complex patterns (pp. 18–19). The Pennsylvania Dutch women are recognized for their *Quilts*; making quilts with interesting patterns was a specialty. The women sewed them together with the younger girls who then put them in their dowry chests. Among the many motifs are the star, basket of flowers, and fruit (p. 20). The German settlers' *Barns* were large, larger even than the house, and brightly colored. The hex symbols of the Pennsylvania Dutch were originally used in Central Europe to ward off evil spirits (p. 22). *Fraktur,* or decorative calligraphy taken from a sixteenth-century German typeface, was used by the German settlers in America as an artform. They took their motifs from daily life (pp. 24–25). *Scissor Cutting* was an artistic craft among the Pennsylvania Dutch. They adorned birth and baptismal certificates, as well as other important papers, with intricate designs (pp. 27–28). Making punched and painted *Tinware* was also an indigenous Pennsylvania Dutch craft. The items had practical purposes, for example, "pie safes" or large cupboards for storing baked goods (pp. 30–31). *Pottery Making,* primarily a family industry, was only dependent on local resources, and therefore was easily conducted by the Pennsylvania Dutch. They used red clay from the region and a "scratched on glazed clay" design called sgraffito (p. 33).

Stiegel Glass was named after the baron from Manheim, Pennsylvania. A good businessman, but not a craftsman, Henry William Stiegel employed more than 130 people in the late 1700s (p. 35). The *Woodenware* seen today in the small butter molds that are still in vogue was carved. Decorative squares of carved hardwood also served to bake decorative cookies (p. 37). The penchant of the Pennsylvania Dutch for *Decorated Woodenware* combined their creativity in carving and their skill at decorative painting. Even an Amish bishop decorated small trinket boxes that carry his little red schoolhouse mark (p. 39).

Tombstone Art further extended the Pennsylvania Dutch penchant for embellishment. Some examples are remarkable. Perhaps the rarest are whitewashed ceramic tombstones cast in the shape of a lamb (pp. 40–41). *Clocks* were imported from Europe until the German settlers arrived; after that they made them (p. 42). The *Blacksmith* made many practical and distinguished iron forgings. The *Kentucky Rifle* and the *Conestoga Wagon* are claimed as distinctly Pennsylvania Dutch (pp. 44–45). The rifle was made in small shops in the 1700s, and the wagon carried produce to Philadelphia over the Conestoga Creek (p. 45).

Thematic Analysis

A brief look at flourishing contentment achieved through hard work and the nurturing of natural talents will widen youngsters' view of the way things were in the past in America. A perspective of a diverse people made into one group with a collective name by a pronunciation error whose style of life with their talent for arts and crafts and their love of family and community remain unchanged will increase awareness. The idea of an extended family can be explored, as well as the many activities that may come readily to a youngster's mind upon exposure to the crafts.

Discussion Materials

Four drawings can be displayed to interest the group (the family picture opposite the table of contents, the front jacket, the decoration on the back jacket, and the endpapers). The introduction can then be paraphrased or read aloud, depending on the audience (pp. 8–9). The table of contents can then be summarized and one household area and one craft book talked, for example, the kitchen (pp. 12–13) and scissor cutting (pp. 26–28). The book is so striking and filled with the embellishment beloved by the Pennsylvania Dutch that care should be used not to present too much at once. The book will be especially good as a read-aloud, however, with a follow-up activity (use the appropriate craft; each is cited in the preceding text analysis).

Related Materials

Some suitable nonfiction titles are: *Going to School in 1876* (Atheneum, 1984) by John J. Loeper; *George Washington and the Birth of the Nation* (Watts, 1986) by Milton Meltzer; *Seeds: Pop* Stick* Glide* (Crown, 1981) by Patricia Lauber; *Computer Talk* (Messner, 1984) by Melvin Berger. Four fictional titles are suggested: Sybil Hancock's *Esteban and the Ghost* (Dial, 1983); Valentine Davies's *Miracle on 34th Street* (Harcourt, 1984); Joan Tate's *Luke's Garden and Gramp* (Harper, 1981), two novels; and Cecilia Holland's *The Sea Beggars* (Knopf, 1982).

William Penn: Founder of Pennsylvania, a filmstrip from the Forerunners of Equality series (Random, 1986), is suggested. Two films are also recommended: *Quilts in Women's Lives* (New Day Films, 1981) and *Asante Market Women* (Filmmakers Library, 1983). The "Curious George" poster (ALA, 1986, No. 159) will strike a good background note.

Gibbons, Gail. *From Path to Highway: The Story of the Boston Post Road*
Illus. by the author. Crowell, 1986, 32 pp.

This author-illustrator has produced almost three dozen titles for children in only a decade of publishing. Many are nonfiction picture and board books for the very young; some are nonfiction picture books for middle-graders about how things work, for example, *Lights! Camera! Action! How a Movie Is Made* (Crowell, 1985). They exemplify Gail Gibbons's talent for researching and condensing facts into an appealing and understandable format for youngsters.

In this title, the prolific author-illustrator applies these same talents to a historical subject, which she explains to young people in both words and pictures. She developed the story of the famous Boston Post Road chronologically by highlighting well-known individuals and significant changes from its genesis as an Indian trail to its current status as a modern highway. The book's brief text is clearly written. Youngsters age 6–9 (grades 1–4), will find it intriguing. It can be used as a supplementary text in social studies or read simply for pleasure. Gibbons acknowledges individuals and historical societes in the Bronx, Massachusetts, and Vermont, as well as the Rand McNally Company of Chicago, underscoring her emphasis on reliable research. The last page pictures and briefly describes eight famous travelers of the road from Paul Revere to Mark Twain.

Gail Gibbons illustrated the book in watercolors; her drawings show a verve and primitivism well liked by youngsters. Her paint outlines are varied, some broken and tentative, others heavy and bold. The overall impression of a road bustling with people and animals surrounded by a landscape dotted with trees is eye-catching. Each page has a full-color drawing, 28 in all, 2 of which are double spreads.

The watercolor paintings on the jacket are elliptical in shape and have an attractive white background. The front jacket describes the road during the era of the stagecoach and horse-drawn carriage. It shows a coach pausing at a tollgate while the gatekeeper turns the pike to release it. The smaller drawing on the back jacket shows a brief pictorial history of the road through the ordinary things mentioned in the book—saddlebags, mileposts, boots, moccasins, and a wagon wheel.

An elliptical insert decorates the title and half-title pages, the latter surrounded by four red stars. Each carries an important statement that sets the historical background: "The Boston Post Road was one of the first roads in America" and although we know it as one, it was "three separate roads" connecting New York City and Boston, Massachusetts. They are identified on the title-page maplike drawing as the Upper Post Road, the Middle Post Road, and the Lower Post Road. Each traversed Connecticut; the Upper also ran across Massachusetts, the Middle passed through Hartford, Connecticut, and the Lower followed the Connecticut shore line of Long Island Sound.

When Indians walked on the road 500 years ago, it was only a narrow path. Three moccasin-shod Indians with a bow and arrow and clubs are shown walking the path through the woodland, just as their ancestors did before them. Then in 1640, the colonists also began trodding the trails in their boots. They are depicted shouldering muskets and bartering with the Indians in one scene, and walking along the path beside their humble log homes in another. Following the advent of horseback riding on the trail, which is pictured next, in 1673, the first post rider, pictured on his dappled grey horse, carried the mail over the Upper trail, spotting river crossings and resting places for future postriders. In those days carrying the mail round trip between Boston and New York City took four weeks.

By the time Sarah Knight, who was Ben Franklin's teacher, traveled on the Lower route from Boston to New York City, she must have passed small villages—the path had been widened and could be called a road. Thankful for her safe return to Boston, she happily scratched her feelings on a pane of glass. Some years later, in the middle of the eighteenth century, when Ben Franklin became deputy postmaster for the colonies, he instituted paid postage measured by the mile, and milestones on the road to mark them. By 1770 stagecoach service was inaugurated between the two cities. It helped the postal service, but the road was still rutted and bumpy.

Soon, however, the Revolutionary War intervened. The road was used to move soldiers and equipment, and by the end of the century, it was strengthened with logs and planks to make it more passable. After that, changes came more rapidly. Bridges replaced old river crossings, money was paid at the tollgate to the gatekeeper, who turned the pike so that the journey might continue, taverns and inns dotted the wayside providing some rest and comfort, and stagecoach traffic increased. By the mid-1800s an iron horse, or train, followed the Lower or southern roadbed, and the road was moved parallel to it. Horses and wagons then ran side by side with the trains.

By 1920 the road had been paved and automobiles appeared with more frequency. Soon houses and buses appeared along the road. Today, the Boston Post Road is a four-lane modern highway, humming with traffic, billboards, and flashing lights. Cars, trucks, and buses travel through countryside, suburban areas, and bustling towns, past ever-increasing numbers of stores, motels, restaurants, and fast-food shops. And it takes less than a day to travel by automobile from Boston to New York City.

Thematic Analysis

This historic view of an early American road clearly demonstrates the development of transportation by foot, horse, carriage, train, and automobile over the road through the centuries, as well as the changing ways of the people and the appearance of the countryside. Some adults in the metropolitan New York–Boston area may be surprised to learn that the Boston Post Road was actually three separate paths, but children will absorb this information as a matter of course.

Discussion Materials

From Path to Highway . . . is excellent for a picture-book demonstration, but it can also be prepared in sections highlighting the changes in the road: the Indians on the path about 500 years ago (pp. 4–6); Indians and colonists on the path (pp. 7–8); horses on the path (p. 9); the postrider (pp. 10–12); wagons (pp. 15–16); stagecoach and other traffic (pp. 17–20); inns (pp. 21–23); trains, cars, and trucks (pp. 24–29); and a comparative look at the way it was and is today (pp. 30–31). Some pages to read aloud are: Sarah Knight (pp. 13–14) and famous travelers (p. 32).

Related Materials

Some other nonfiction titles are suggested: Beatrice Siegel's *The Basket Maker and the Spinner* (Walker, 1987), which is gently fictionalized; Jack Prelutsky's *The Random House Book of Poetry for Children* (Random, 1983); Seymour Simon's series *Stars* and *Sun* (Morrow, 1986) and *Jupiter* and *Saturn* (Morrow, 1985); and Roy A. Gallant's *101 Questions and Answers about the Universe* (Macmillan, 1984). Several fiction titles are suitable: *Anno's Flea Market* (Philomel, 1984) by Mitsumasa Anno; *Complete Adven-*

tures of Olga da Polga (Delacorte, 1983) by Michael Bond; and *Adam's Common* (Houghton, 1984) by David Wiseman.

Two recordings are appropriate: *Around the World in Eighty Days* (Caedmon, 1980), read by Christopher Plummer, and Alfred Slote's *My Trip to Alpha* (Listening Library, 1982). Two films that can also be used are *Paddington Goes to the Movies* (FilmFair, 1983) and *Frog Goes to Dinner* (Phoenix/BFA, 1985). The "Pinocchio Knows" poster (ALA, 1986) makes a good visual display.

Goor, Ron, and Goor, Nancy. *Pompeii: Exploring a Roman Ghost Town*
Crowell, 1986, 118 pp.

The authors have five books in print, all published in this decade. *Shadows: Here, There, and Everywhere* (Crowell, 1981) was cited as an ALA Notable Book for children, *In the Driver's Seat* (Crowell, 1982) as a best book by *School Library Journal*, and *All Kinds of Feet* (Crowell, 1984) received many favorable reviews. Ron Goor also coauthored a science title, *Backyard Insects* (Four Winds, 1983), with Millicent E. Selsam. His background in biochemistry and public health attest to his competence in scientific research, and Nancy Goor has a graduate degree in fine arts. Their combined talent produced this thoroughly researched account of the excavated city of Pompeii with numerous black-and-white photographs that amplify the text. The front jacket photograph by Ron Goor is a dramatic view of a stone street in Pompeii. An enlarged photograph of a plaster cast of a Pompeian muleteer, holding a cloth to his mouth to keep out the ashes and poison gases, appears on the back jacket (also on page 12). Youngsters age 10–11 (grades 5–6) will be intrigued and enlightened by this informative and attractive book, designed by Barbara Fitzsimmons.

The book is divided into five chapters, which are further subdivided into pertinent topics. An epilogue serves as a summary, and an index facilitates using the book for reference. The introduction contains a verbatim account of the volcanic eruption of Mount Vesuvius in Italy in A.D. 79. Pliny the Younger describes in a letter to the historian Tacitus what happened to Pliny the Elder (his uncle), who died that day in the eruption. The true-life event sets the dramatic scene for the description of Pompeian life that follows.

The first chapter describes the volcanic disaster, the death of Pompeii at 6:30 A.M., August 25, A.D. 79, its subsequent discovery and excavation, and the archaeological restorations. The second chapter describes how Pompeii looked in A.D. 79, that is, its major features, for example, walls and public areas, by conducting a walk through the streets according to a street plan, which is graphically presented. Some mention is made of the Roman genius in engineering, particularly in constructing water systems.

The public life of the citizens is told through the places they used and the things they did: the Forum, or heart of the city; the general use of graffiti (something like road signs); the extensive religious worship at home; and the great emphasis on popular entertainment. Highlighted here are the theater, amphitheater (for larger crowds), physical fitness and exercise, and the public baths. A brief mention and a photograph of central heating are a fascinating tidbit.

The fourth chapter treats private life in some detail. The rooms in the homes are examined for purpose and probable use, including the slave quarters and the discomforts of the unheated homes. Dining etiquette is quoted from *Cities of Vesuvius: Pompeii and Herculaneum* by Michael Grant (an adult work), and the customary foods that accompanied either a three- or seven-course feast are described. The discussion of childhood in Pompeii shows a remarkable similarity with some of today's toys and games.

The fifth and final chapter deals with the commercial life of the city in four areas: taverns; fulliers (cleaning establishments); bakeries; and farming. Crops, consisting of grapes, olives, and flowers, were the chief trading produce. The large marketplace ("marcellum" in Latin) is mentioned together with an ancient recipe for Garum—a spicy fish sauce for which Pompeii was famous. Because only business and public service were esteemed, other professions are just briefly mentioned. Doctoring is listed, but it bears little resemblance to today's medical practice.

The profusion of photographs—hardly a page does not have several or a full-page photo elucidating the text on the opposite page—nobly augments the brief and pithy yet adequate text, summing up what has been learned to date about this famous long-buried Italian town. Many facts become inescapably clear. For example, in 1864 the archeologist

Giuseppe Fiorelli poured plaster into the cavities inside the hardened lava to expose the original shapes of the enclosed bodies (p. 10); the previous eruption, 17 years earlier, from which most homes and areas had not yet been completely restored (p. 47); the central heating (pp. 62–63); and the elaborately restored (after the first volcanic eruption) house of the wealthy wine merchants, the Vetii brothers.

Thematic Analysis

The facts, reinforced by the dramatic use of photographs, of the volcanically destroyed city of Pompeii, give youngsters a glimpse into the cyclical forces of nature and the fragility of mankind, both of which help to form a view of the world. Of the many subjects that are touched in this truly multidisciplinary adventure, including science, geology, social studies, ancient history, archeology, art, religion, and philosophy, perhaps archeology and historical sleuthing are primary. But because of the many interesting threads that exist here for youngsters, their view of the world cannot but be enhanced!

Discussion Materials

After displaying the jacket, read the introduction aloud, then show the Nucerian Gate with Mount Vesuvius in the background on the opposite page. Also show another picture of Mount Vesuvius (p. 7). To set the scene further, a map of Europe and Italy locating Pompeii can be enlarged and projected (p. 3). Finally, a line map can be identified initially while reading the text by using the index (pp. 115–118). Why Pompeii and Herculaneum are important dead cities should be read aloud (pp. 17–18). To extend this an appropriate picture(s) and corresponding textual explanation can be used from any of the remaining chapters, such as a walk through Pompeii (pp. 28–29); graffiti on the walls (pp. 42–43); art and practical culinary arts (pp. 74–83); or taverns, fulleries, and bakeries, including fast-food counters (pp. 98–103).

Related Materials

Some excellent nonfiction titles are good here: *The Roman Empire and the Dark Ages* (Harper, 1985) from the series History of Everyday Things by Giovanni Caselli extends the historical perspective; *How Did We Find Out about Computers* (Walker, 1984) by Isaac Asimov documents a history of the home computer from the time of the ancient abacus; *Greenland* (Dodd, 1983) by Madelyn Klein Anderson gives an informational account of the world's largest island; *Great Painters* (Putnam, 1984) by Pietro Ventura is a lively art history for grades 4–7; and *Holding Up the Sky* (Dutton, 1983) by Margaret Rau is an account of Chinese youth intermingled with sociological and historical glimpses. Four appealing fiction titles are: *Miracle on 34th St.* (Harcourt, 1984) by Valentine Davies, which expands the classic story and is illustrated with 19 of Tomie dePaola's illustrations; *Cranes at Dusk* (Dial, 1985) by Hisake Matsubara, about a Japanese ten-year-old's conversion to Christianity at the end of World War II; and two horse stories, *Four Horses for Tishtray* (Harper, 1985) by Chelsea Yarbro and *Healer* (Delacorte, 1985) by Peter Dickinson.

Significant audiovisual titles include two films: *The Sun Dagger* (Bullfrog Films, 1982), about archeology in New Mexico, and *The Flower* (International Film Bureau, 1981), a philosophic statement in Zagreb animation about seeing flowers in your own meadow. The blue-ribbon series of two filmstrips *The Italian Romans and the Imperial Romans* (SVE, 1986) will be helpful with this title.

Harvey, Brett.   *My Prairie Year: Based on the Diary of Elenore Plaisted*
Illus. by Deborah Kogan Ray. Holiday, 1986, 40 pp.

This is Brett Harvey's first book for children. A free-lance journalist, book critic, and mother of two grown children, the author knows childhood from the perspectives of both adult and child. Drawing on her own cherished childhood memories of reading and rereading her grandmother's vividly written journal, which described her own childhood "Dakota adventure," Harvey fictionalized her grandmother's account for youngsters. The story is the true-life account of the ordinary life of a young "homesteader" and her family in the Dakota territory of 1889. (In keeping with the aphorism "Truth is stranger than fiction," the grandmother immortalized for youngsters here became a children's book illustrator.) The young, especially girls age 8–10 (grades 3–5), will be fascinated.

The 23 charcoal drawings by Deborah Kogan Ray are breathtaking in their sweeping mimicry of the prairie. Thirteen are double spreads, including the title page, but most pages include text as well. Ten are two-thirds to full-page visual descriptions of the written text. A character sketch of the girl and her father also appears on the half-title page and another of the girl appears on the foreword page. Two smaller decorations include one of Father, dimly seen through blinding snow, trudging to the barn in deep winter, and a single stalk of prairie grass lyrically placed on the verso. The full-color jacket painting, reminiscent of Andrew Wyeth's famous painting "Christina's World," portrays the young, pigtailed "homesteader" carrying a bucket through the tall prairie grass, while a house, barn, and a billowing wash line define the far horizon. The picture in the book of rippling sheets being folded by the two sisters and hung on the line by the mother is eloquent. Such pictures enhance the evocative text immeasurably. As the author says in her foreword, ". . . Deborah Kogan Ray's pictures truly capture that Dakota experience."

As nine-year-old Elenore Plaisted gets off the train in 1889 at a place called Andover in the Dakota territory, she sees a huge figure in rain gear streaming water and hears him call, "Hallo." She recognizes her Daddy behind the greeting. Her Mother, Em, holding the baby, Billy, follows Elenore and her younger sister, Marjorie, who is about six. Elenore hasn't seen her Daddy for awhile because he was out "homesteading"—getting land and building a house. When he sent for them to come, Mother made the long journey with her three children from Lincoln, Maine, to join her husband.

Elenore spends the first night of this strange adventure in a new house made of roughly hewed pine boards. Even though Daddy put horse blankets over the walls, she can see right through them. Sleeping on canvas cots is something new, too, and she can't help wondering what tomorrow will bring. When she sees their house in the daytime on the immense grass prairie that reminds her of the sea, she can't help but think of it as a tiny ship. Daddy tells her that the house is safely hunkered down into a bank of earth for protection against blowing storms.

However, daily chores on the prairie are not so different. On Monday they do the wash: They carry water from the "moat" surrounding the house, build a fire to heat it, and after washing and rinsing the clothes hang them outside to dry. Tuesdays are reserved for ironing and mending. Elenore does the handkerchiefs and towels, Mother the rest. In the afternoons, Mother instructs Elenore in how to use a "darning egg" while they sew. Marjorie and Billy being younger are still playing outdoors, but on Wednesday morning they help tend the garden, first planted with seeds Mother brought from New England. Because plants grow fast on the prairie, Elenore and her sister and brother soon play in the shade of the plant rows.

In the afternoons, Elenore and Marjorie attend to the lessons that Mother—their own teacher—gives them. On Thursday, Daddy drives two miles to Brittons' in the small village for supplies. Elenore likes this trip because she can play paper dolls with the hotel owner's daughter, Jennie, who is her age. On Friday when cleaning is done, everyone has a job, even Billy. Saturday is reserved for cooking and baking—bread, cookies, pies—and the canning of fruit and vegetables from the garden. The finished canning jars made a wonderful sight. But the best day of all is Sunday! No work, except Sunday school lessons. Elenore goes "straddle" horseback riding, that is, until Mother says she is too old and must ride sidesaddle.

The seasons, however, rule, and the chores are arranged accordingly. In the spring, the great (main) plowing is done; each man helps his neighbor. Meanwhile, the children play in the tall grass and even go on picnics to the coulees, or streams. The summer brings different demands and a phenomenon that Elenore finds most interesting, the mirage from the intense heat and flat space. After scorching days tornadoes are commonplace, and for all their beautiful incipient colors, terrifying. Harvesting takes over in the autumn. Once more the men help each other, while the women feed all the thrashers. Everyone works! Elenore celebrates her tenth birthday driving a wagon between the thrashers and the granary, an important and memorable occasion.

Then a fall prairie fire stretches across their land destroying almost everything. Elenore and her Mother try desperately to smother the sparks outside their house with pieces of carpet, while Marjorie and Billy are in the cellar and Daddy is out on the prairie with the other "homesteaders" fighting the fire, but the wall of flames sweeps by them. The morning after, the devastated family realizes that the houses and barn though scorched are still standing because the land around the buildings had been plowed early in the summer.

The winter is even colder than it was in Maine. A parcel containing jars of real fruit and other luxuries like clothes, toys, and books arrives from Mother's sister, Aunt Addie. Aunt Addie also enclosed a special collection of paint and canvases for Mother, whose first painting of hopeful pink apple blossoms heralds the change of the seasonal cycle.

Spring comes, and with it playtime in the meadow. On Monday after the washing is finished and rest and playtime have begun, Elenore asks her mother a question. Mother's firmly stated answer is "We are home."

Thematic Analysis

Seeing homesteading activities through the eyes of a nine-year-old is a broadening experience for the reader. The book's description of ordinary daily tasks and seasonal differences, dictated by the weather, provides an accurate view of what life was like for a youngster in the Dakota territory in the 1890s. The theme of survival within a strong, supportive family is muted, but there. A backward look by a young girl is helpful for youngsters who are forming a view of their heritage.

Discussion Materials

After displaying the full jacket drawing and reading aloud the author's foreword (p. 5), simply introduce the main characters and set the scene (pp. 6–9). The picture of the two girls helping their mother hang the wash can also be shown (pp. 10–11). Or a more elaborate "book talk" can be constructed: the weekly schedule (pp. 10–19 and the corresponding pictures); the seasons, save winter (pp. 20–27); a prairie fire (pp. 28–33); winter, relieved by a "treat" (pp. 34–37); and it's spring again (pp. 38–40). The dramatic tornado episode can also be highlighted (pp. 24–29).

Related Materials

Some titles that will work well are: *Seasons of the Tallgrass* (Morrow, 1980) by Carol Lerner; *Grasslands* (Dial, 1984) by Clive Catchpole; *Tree Flowers* (Morrow, 1984) by Millicent E. Selsam; *Tractors: From Yesterday's Steam Wagons to Today's Turbocharged Giants* (Lippincott, 1984) by Jim Murphy; and *The Pueblo* (Houghton, 1986) by Charlotte Yue and David Yue. Two other appealing titles are *Peter Spier's Christmas,* a visual delight by Peter Spier, and Joan Anderson's *Christmas on the Prairie* (Clarion, 1985), with photographs by George Ancona.

Two recordings and a filmstrip are recommended: *Gathering of Days: A New England Girl's Journal* (Miller-Brody/Random, 1980) from the book by Joan W. Blos; *Wheel on the School* (Random, 1969) from Meindert DeJong's book; and *Brighty of the Grand Canyon* (Pied Piper, 1974) from the book by Marguerite Henry.

Isadora, Rachel. *City Seen from A to Z*
Illus. by the author. Greenwillow, 1983, 26 pp.

This author-illustrator published her first picture book for children, *Willaby* (Macmillan, 1977), in the late seventies. Since then this former ballet dancer has regularly written and illustrated wonderful books for children—about a dozen of her titles are in print—including one she illustrated and coauthored with Robert Maiorano, *Backstage* (Greenwillow, 1978). *Ben's Dream* (Greenwillow, 1979) was chosen as an honor book by the ALA Caldecott Committee and also received the Boston Globe-Horn Book Award.

Rachel Isadora is a marvelous illustrator. Her lush drawings, displaying her enviable talent, and her competent texts have carved a solid niche in the world of children's books. This title is further proof. Ostensibly a simple alphabet book, it is much more sophisticated—one that can be used with reluctant readers, as well as readers in the middle grades. Although recommended ideally for ages 5–8 (grades K–3), the book can be used admirably with youngsters 7–9 years of age (grades 2–4). A native New Yorker, Rachel Isadora uses familiar New York scenery in her illustrations. Youngsters from a big city like San Francisco, Detroit, Los Angeles, Chicago, Dallas, or Atlanta will appreciate the urban scenery in the same way as young New Yorkers. Youngsters from smaller cities and rural locations will find both commonalities and thought-provoking differences in the scenes. But regardless of where they live youngsters will easily identify with the 7–9-year-old characters in the pictures.

This book for all ages uses very small, block print for the 26 alphabet letters and a multiethnic cast of characters in the drawings that bring the city to life. Both words (concepts) and names (labels) describe the ideas that are used to illustrate the alphabet. For example, the word "zoo" describes the letter "Z" and is illustrated by two boys, one white, one black, drawing animal pictures in chalk on the sidewalk. Each letter of the alphabet is opposed by a full-page drawing that is easily identifiable as Isadora's full, lush style. The letter "A" establishes multiethnicity with four portraits emblazoned on the front of a brick tenement (a Caucasian, blond-haired girl; an Oriental girl in traditional costume; a black youngster wearing a white shirt and tie; and a brown-haired Caucasian boy wearing a T-shirt). On the sidewalk in the foreground two young boys play marbles while a young girl stands idly by and an old man saunters past.

The pictures also show the many ages in the neighborhood. For example, the letter "B," illustrated by the familiar beach ball, shows a beach scene with the New York City skyline far in the background. (The skyline is curved like a photograph of a distant object taken with a fish-eye lens.) A fat white woman in a bikini is thigh high in the water surrounded by a multitude of splashing people of all colors and ages. A large beach ball bounces in their midst. Isadora's full-page pen-and-ink drawings with their ink washes use the familiar to denote city life. The almost pointillistic architectural renderings and the body and facial expressions of the characters are engaging.

The illustration of a car wash for the letter "C" shows a street scene with a hilly sidewalk and neighborhood buildings that could be in San Francisco or many other hilly cities. The black and white youngsters who use the fire hydrant to splash a passing car could live in New York, or Philadelphia, or any other city. Youngsters will see similarities with where they live. The sidewalk and buildings are also used as background in several other ways. A detail of the same buildings decorates both the title page and the end note, except that they are photographically reversed. The compelling full-cover jacket illustration uses an enlarged but sparer drawing of the same reversed sidewalk scene, now populated by a little pigtailed black girl and three 7–9-year-old boys of black, white, and Hispanic descent. Their expressions—a smile and two sets of pursed lips—are enticing.

Both boys and girls are an integral part of this book. Highlighted for girls are dolls, hats, tutus, and Christmas store window displays. But both girls and boys will enjoy the familiarity of a subway entrance, friends playing musical instruments, a kitten, black youngsters playing games with a lion mask, a "boombox" playing music carried by a youngster, roller skates, a snowman, a pensive youngster looking out over a window box; a black youngster playing with his yo-yo; and a sidewalk with a zoo chalked on it. Older people will appreciate these pictures, too, but will relate more directly to others: a woman viewing pictures in a gallery; a grandma eating ice cream with her granddaughter; a breathtaking picture of the city aglow at night; grandpa and granddaughter at the ocean; an Oriental grandpa and granddaughter walking (in silhouette); a quiet ride in the park in a horse and carriage; a pushcart food vendor under his umbrella; and a Jewish grandpa with a yarmulke showing his grandchild a valentine. The scenes are familiar and poignant.

Thematic Analysis

Depending on the age of the child who is viewing the pictures and reading the letters, the themes may vary widely. Basically, a child looking at this book will sense the vivacity and diversity of a city populated by ethnic minorities and will realize that many colors describe humanity's shades. Accord among the races is heralded, an idea as important for youngsters who do not reside in cosmopolitan areas as for those who do. An extra bonus is the theme of family love through the generations. This awareness of heritage, although idealized, is real and important in the human condition. The viewer is certain to identify with more than one theme like sharing or making friends. The artwork alone ultimately merits a look.

Discussion Materials

This title lends itself to a lingering display of the pictures, as well as to a typical picture-book presentation. A verbal statement about photographic processes and the reversed architectural drawings (car wash, title page, end note, and jacket drawings) will elicit interest, especially among those 7–9 years old and older. The book can also be book talked based on the gender of the characters in the illustrations: boys (friends, jazz, lion, music, roller skates, yo-yo, zoo); girls (dolls, hats, tutu, Christmas); both sexes (art, beach ball, car wash, subway entrance, kitten, night, snowman, umbrella, window box); and all ages of both sexes (gallery, ice cream, ocean, pigeon, quiet, valentine). Merely mentioning the alphabet should suffice as an introduction for the grade 2–4 audience. Those who know the alphabet will be appreciative, and those who are hesitant may find this title helpful. The book will, of course, be useful in remedial classes.

Related Materials

Some of the many titles that may be suggested are: *The Trek* (Greenwillow, 1985) by Ann Jonas, which illustrates a girl's daily walk as she imagines it; *How My Parents Learned to Eat* (Houghton, 1984) by Ina R. Friedman, the humorous story of a Japanese-American couple's courtship through their daughter's eyes; *Read-Aloud Rhymes for the Very Young* (Knopf, 1986), joyous rhythmic verses by Jack Prelutsky; and *Shadows: Here, There and Everywhere* (Crowell, 1981) by Ron Goor and Nancy Goor, which explains with photographs what shadows are and how they are formed. Four titles about traditional holidays are: *Thanksgiving Poem* (Holiday, 1985) by Myra Cohn Livingston; *We Wish You a Merry Christmas* (Dial, 1983) by Tracey Campbell Pearson, the humorous story of children carolers in a frenzied search for pudding; *Merry Christmas! Children at Christmastime Around the World* (Philomel, 1983) by Robina Beckles Wilson; and *The Truth about Santa Claus* (Crowell, 1985) by James Cross Giblin, a thoroughly researched look at the legends.

Three recordings are helpful here: *What's under My Bed?* (Weston Woods, 1985) by James Stevenson; *The Most Wonderful Egg in the World* (Weston Woods, 1985) by Helme Heine; and *Kim & Jerry Brodey—Family Pie* (Kids Records, 1986), an upbeat rock and roll to reggae tunes of the city. Two films will also be popular: *Curious George Goes to the Hospital* (Churchill Films, 1985) and *In Search of Father Christmas* (Wombat Productions, 1985). The poster of Bill Cosby sharing a book with four multiethnic youngsters (ALA, 1986, No. 6BI) is suggested for an extra visual treat.

Lasky, Kathryn.   *Jem's Island*
Pictures by Ronald Himler. Scribner, 1982, 64 pp.

Between the titles *I Have Four Names for My Grandfather* (Little, 1976) and *Pageant* (Four Winds, 1986), the author has written almost a dozen books for children. Kathryn Lasky's *The Weaver's Gift* (Warne, 1981) was the winner of the 1981 Boston Globe-Horn Book Award for nonfiction. All her titles are noteworthy, and each new one is eagerly sought. *Jem's Island* is an eloquent tale of an overnight kayak trip taken by a young boy and his Dad to an island near their summer vacation home in Maine. It tells about the youngster's anticipation throughout the winter and spring to the afterglow of a well-accomplished experience and fond dreams of adventures to come that rest easily on his mind. Youngsters ages 8–11 (grades 3–6), will like the story. Some of them will also be excited by the practical lessons of "boxing the compass," understanding "the compass rose," and "plotting a course."

Ronald Himler's appealing jacket drawing done in pen and ink on brownish rose paper shows the hero and his Dad disembarking from their kayak at their island destination. On the front jacket, above their figures, is a small pen insert of a small, round island. The illustrator also did 15 magnificent pen-and-ink drawings to enhance the text. Twelve are striking full-page illustrations, some of which extend on the facing page, and three are half-page double spreads set on top of the text. All are worth viewing. Youngsters will be intrigued by two full-page charts that amplify the text and navigation lesson. The endpapers, which show some of the islands in Penobscot Bay, Maine, in an artful pseudotopograpical style, allow the interested reader to follow the travel experiences, imagined and actual.

Jem Gray, about 11, spends his spare time during the winter in his Cleveland, Ohio, home dreaming of paddling the family's mahogany kayak. He spends part of his time rereading the faded, loose-leaf notebook and journal of the 1,000-mile trip in the kayak that his Dad, Ben Gray, and Uncle Peter took about 25 years ago, from Skagway, Alaska, to Seattle, Washington. The names of places and people in the journal, for example, Taku Harbor and Halibut Pete, are magical. This summer, Dad and Jem finally are going to take an overnight kayak trip when they get to their vacation place on Deer Island, Maine. Unlike Alaska, there are no killer whales in Penobscot Bay, but there are dolphins.

When spring turns to summer and they are once again on Deer Island, Jem is closer to his trip. His younger brother, Michael, around 9, who is presently only interested in intergalactic space, is a bit jealous, so he tries to play down the trip by telling Jem that it's only for overnight. Jem's Mom, Liza, tries to lighten things by taking Jem blueberry picking. Jem spends most of the time, however, trying to choose an island in Penobscot Bay that will be within their projected 25-mile round-trip category. Isle au Haut or Kimball Island seem perfect choices, but others—Chatto, Hog, Pickering—are tempting, too. Jem's sister Jessica, about seven years old, and his Dad watch him gather and check the gear. Finally, Dad and Jem check the food and equipment lists that Jem printed in preparation for the journey. Things like hardtack, peanut butter, oranges, and chocolate bars are on the food list; fishing tackle and clam spades (to catch the fish they plan to eat), a spare paddle, a compass, and rain gear are on the other. They are almost ready.

The night before they leave, Dad gives Jem a navigation lesson to Duck Harbor on the chart for Isle au Haut, and Jem draws a course with two straight-edged transparent rulers. He finds it so exciting that he stays up late and charts many others. Early the next morning while everyone sleeps, Jem and Dad stow their gear in the Swedish-made kayak the Wasso. (One of Stockholm's favorite tourist sights is the restored wooden ship, the *Wasso*.) Silently they put on the spray skirts that seal in the paddlers making them a part of the kayak. Jem sits in the stern's cockpit, with Dad leading in the bow, as the kayak quietly glides into the water. The first strokes are thrilling for Jem and make him feel part of the boat and water.

Immediately enshrouded by fog, they have to use Jem's plottings until they reach the tip of Deer Island, arriving right on the projected time schedule. Then the fog lifts, and by lunchtime they are eating hardtack and cheese on a beach on South Porcupine Island. After digging some clams, they paddle on to an uncharted cove that Jem wants to explore off No Name Island. Dad agrees to camp here instead of on their original choice, remembering that self-discovery always seems superior to explorers and the young. They eat their clams, fish for mackerel, and watch the sunset. Jem wonders briefly what his Mom, Michael, and Jessica are doing, then asks his Dad to tell him another Alaskan story. Instead, Ben Gray tells him a Maine story about his own father who lived on Deer Island before a bridge was constructed to the mainland. Although his grandfather had warned the boy that it looked like a northeaster was coming, Ben's father crossed the bay in his boat anyway. He arrived safely, but coming back was almost caught in the storm. At first, Jem can't understand how his great-grandfather could have let his grandfather go, but he slowly realizes that just as his own father and uncle went exploring, now he has to, as well. Afterward they take a "nightglide" in the kayak to see the phosphorescent display of the stars in the water, and Jem thinks of himself briefly as a star paddler. To cap a deliriously happy experience, he sees a pair of dolphins diving just off the bow.

The next morning after a breakfast of freshly caught fish, they take a self-timed picture of themselves as explorers, dismantle their tent, stoke out the fire, clean up, and skirt up for the return trip. As Jem paddles away from the peace of the island past the other islands in Penobscot Bay, he thinks of a future time when he and Michael will be able to make trips, maybe even one of a thousand miles.

Thematic Analysis

Foremost among the several themes in this serene tale of an August kayak trip made by a boy and his Dad is that the view of the world becomes clearer for a youngster who experiences exploits similar to those his grandparent and parent had on both sides of the North American continent. Through the Swedish boat builders, for example, a youngster's sense of geographical place and personal heritage is broadened.

Youngsters' love of exploration at this age is treated with objectivity. Being able to use maps and charts, learning to chart a course, and being able to carry out the necessary tasks independently—albeit with comforting support—all contribute to a feeling of accomplishment.

Discussion Materials

Display the jacket painting, then introduce the main characters and focus of the story (pp. 7–11, 13–14, 18–21). For those who would like to learn some fundamentals of exploring, suggest finding the islands (the endpapers) and plotting a course (pp. 22–26). Also good to read aloud or book talk are: starting out in the kayak (pp. 27–33); eating lunch on South Porcupine Island and finding No Name Island (pp. 35–39); the island sojourn (pp. 40–43); and a "nightglide" (pp. 48–51). The exciting story of Jem's grandfather can also be told (pp. 44–47).

Related Materials

Many titles are complementary: *Beyond the Divide* (Macmillan, 1983) also by Kathryn Lasky tells about the westward journey of an Amish girl and her father; *Millie Cooper, 3B* (Dutton, 1985) by Charlotte Herman tells the story of a third-grader's experiences during the forties; *Fat Gopal* (Harcourt, 1984) by Jacquelin Singh is a story based on an Indian folktale about a poor man outsmarting a rich and powerful one; *Jed's Junior Space Patrol: A Science Fiction Easy-to-Read* (Dial, 1982) by Claudio Marzollo; and *The Long Way to a New Land* (Harper, 1981) by Joan Sandlin is the story of a Swedish family's journey to New York in the 1860s. Several nonfiction titles are also good here: Franklyn M. Branley's *Comets* (Crowell, 1984); Margery Facklam and Howard Facklam's *Changes in the Wind: Earth's Shifting Climate* (Harcourt, 1986); and Sylvia Johnson's *Potatoes* (Lerner, 1984).

A series of outdoor videos from L. L. Bean are excellent. One of them, *Guide to Canoeing*, is a natural here. Two recordings are also suggested: *Carl Sandburg Soundbook for Children* (Caedmon), which contains his Rootabaga stories and other poetry, and Scott O'Dell's *King's Fifth* (Random, 1985), about another young explorer at the time of the conquistadores. The quarterly *Dolphin Log*, available from the Cousteau Society, Inc., attempts to show the interrelatedness of living organisms. Articles, photos, such regular columns as "Nature News," puzzles, and humorous bits enliven a youngster's reading.

Moeri, Louise. *Save Queen of Sheba*
Dutton, 1981, 116 pp.

This author writes compact, readable novels for young people. She is recognized both for dramatic stories and believable young heroes. Louise Moeri has written eight titles that are currently in print. In her longer works she demonstrates an ability to compose highly adventurous tales inhabited by characters, with whom youngsters can easily identify. The titles *The Girl Who Lived on the Ferris Wheel* (Dutton, 1979) and *Downwind* (Dutton, 1984), together with this one, also illustrate the author's versatility in choosing topics of current interest (child abuse and nuclear energy). Their realistic characters struggle successfully with the vicissitudes that prevail. In this pioneer story a 12-year-old boy who is almost scalped in a sudden Indian raid on his wagon train saves himself and his six-year-old sister in a harrowing survival story. Youngsters ages 9–11 (grades 4–6) will be spellbound by this quietly intense story. Boys will especially appreciate the hero's feelings and travails.

As 12-year-old King David struggles to regain consciousness, he can tell from the clots of blood in his hair and a loose flap of skin hanging from a ragged cut on his forehead that he is half-scalped. Slowly he remembers that he had been walking ahead of the wagon train with Mr. Skinner, the guide, when a Sioux raiding party swooped down on them. As he weaves around the seven forward wagons—now toppled with dead occupants inside—he realizes that Pa and Ma were in the wagons that got away, probably to Fort Laramie. He remembers that the long wagon train had separated into two columns after King and his family had joined the trek in St. Louis. The wagons pulled by horses were supposed to follow the north fork of the trail west along the Platte River. By now, of course, the wagons in the rear of their column, including Pa and Ma, had left the trail as quickly as they could. He knows that they will come back for him unless they are seriously hurt, but that doesn't make him feel better, especially when he sees dead bodies and tumbled wreckage everywhere.

Suddenly as he looks at a feather bed near the far wagon (the wagons didn't even have time to form a circle), he sees a child's foot sticking out of the quilt. His six-year-old sister, Queen of Sheba, is alive. She had been riding with 22-year-old Letty Harmon who was telling her wonderful stories. Now Letty lies dead, but she had miraculously saved his sister's life by stuffing her in the bed. Queen of Sheba looks up at him and quietly asks, "Are the Indians gone?" Weakened by a terrible wound and barely able to walk, let alone think, King David realizes that not only does he have to find the rest of the wagons, but now he has the added responsibility of his fragile young sister. Although finding her does compound his problems, King David does not hesitate to include her in his plans, however.

Having given up hope that Mr. Skinner may still be alive, King David finally realizes that they are alone. In spite of the horror of the scene, he tries to find some provisions, but only turns up some apples and cornmeal. He also finds a Sharps rifle with bullets and caps lying under the guide's body. With a bundle of quilts, matches, pots, a little water, a small sack of cornmeal and a bit of bacon that he can barely manage, and a sack of apples that Queen of Sheba reluctantly carries, they start out to find the wagon tracks. It can't be soon enough for King David, who wants to leave that place of desolation, but before he leaves, he memorizes the names of the fallen, for he knows he is their only witness.

Queen of Sheba, meanwhile, cries for her Ma. After quieting her, King David convinces her to wear a pair of shoes that he finds. But she pulls them off, just as she had always done with her shoes in the past. This time is no different. When she recognizes the shoes, she screams that she won't wear uppity Margaret Anne Beecham's shoes. King David manages to calm her, but when she refuses to eat the cornmeal, he has to remind himself that she is only six. Barely able to sustain himself, he doesn't need this.

Their luck improves, however, when he decides to stop on a bank with a clump of willows in which one of the still-harnessed wagon horses, Maggie, had become tangled. After he releases and feeds her with some grass that he painfully collects, he crawls back to his sister to offer her some cornmeal, then falls into a stupor. As he sleeps Queen of Sheba watches pus ooze from his head and tries unsuccessfully to wake him. Finally, she gathers some grass for Maggie and lays down to sleep.

When King David awakens at the following sunset, Queen of Sheba tells him about the pus. As she watches, he cuts open his infected wound with his knife, which ends up saving his life. As the wound drains, he washes it out repeatedly in the stream, remembering how his Ma treated infections, and continues to sleep intermittently. Meanwhile, Queen of Sheba wanders upstream to engage in her favorite activity, making mud pies in the water. Following her tracks, King David finds her holding a piece of wood in her arms, which she calls "dolly." The recuperating boy is fortunate enough to shoot a large rabbit, and after a satisfying meal, he comforts his sister with familiar stories about their biblical namesakes, a great soldier and a great lady. King David thinks to himself that Queen of Sheba will also be a great lady, provided he can keep her alive.

King David now feels confident that he will pick up the tracks and catch the wagons. With his sister riding the horse, he leads them through a field of buffalo bones left behind by white hunters. When a sudden storm arises, he finds a cave underneath an overhang in an outcrop to shelter them. King David wishes he could track in the rain like his Pa, but he can only wait out the storm. By its conclusion, he has figured out that they are about four days away from the wagons, and he is sure that the rest of the wagon train, which must be at or near Fort Laramie by now, will send back a search party.

Meanwhile, King David can't erase the mental image of the terrible carnage. Queen of Sheba, much to her brother's surprise, first tries to scalp her dolly, then bury it, pretending it is Miz Farrier's dead baby, which they had seen her father help bury. That night, before she goes to sleep, Queen of Sheba tells her brother that she is afraid that soldiers will come the next day and kill dolly because she is an Indian. Once the last of their food is gone, King David decides to move from the cave and try to find the wagon tracks.

After riding a few miles on the horse, Queen of Sheba complains about her sore bony legs, so King David decides to let her walk for a while. At sunset he has the good fortune to find the tracks again, but when he turns to tell his sister, she is gone. He backtracks until late at night when he falls asleep with the horse tied to his foot. The next day, just as he is about to give up and ride away, he remembers that her favorite place to play is near water. In an about face he retraces their route until he finds some water in the distance and the shoes that Queen of Sheba has discarded. He finds her crouching over a small pool making mud pies, with an Indian boy and woman watching her. When King David appears, the woman grabs Queen of Sheba. As King David raises his rifle toward the Indian boy, his sister screams, "Kill them!" But instead he lowers his gun; the woman releases Queen of Sheba, takes her child, and runs.

After a hasty departure from the scene, King David and Queen of Sheba head back to the wagon tracks. As they come to a rise, the horse suddenly rears, signaling that other horses are nearby. When King David investigates, he sees three men on the other side of the hillcrest, one of them Pa with his arm in a sling, but Pa nevertheless. He now understands why he went back to save Queen of Sheba. In the background, Queen of Sheba croons softly to her dolly and tells her that she wants to show her to Margaret Anne Beecham.

Thematic Analysis

Survival—and consequently independence—is an important part of the book, but the major theme is the human characteristic of loving and taking care of the young and helpless. In addition, the reality and adventure of the westward trek to the Willamette Valley in Oregon, plus the excellent characterization of King David, bring the long ago to life. The geographical and cultural aspects of this movement, although peripheral to the plot, are so vividly portrayed that a youngster cannot fail to understand their significance. This perspective is another jigsaw piece in a youngster's view of the world.

Discussion Materials

Although this story is best read individually, at least two parts can be read aloud, the biblical names (pp. 51–53) and the Valley of the Dry Bones (pp. 59–65). To introduce the book, display the two characters on the cover and relate the plot (pp. 1–7); the hat on the jacket cover (pp. 23–24); and the adopted shoes (pp. 19–20). You may wish to stress King David's problems with his six-year-old sister (pp. 9–10, 12–13, 16–20, 22–28, 33–38, 41–43, 45–50, 56, 65–66, 71–72, 78–80, 83–85, 87–88, 99, 103, 106–114).

Related Materials

In addition to the author's other titles, *The Naked Bear: Folktales of the Iroquois* (Morrow, 1986), a book of Indian legends edited by John Bierhorst, is recommended. Also suggest David Wiseman's *Jeremy Visick* (Houghton, 1981); Margaret Mahy's *The Changeover: A Supernatural Romance* (Atheneum, 1984); and William Horwood's *The Stonor Eagles* (Watts, 1982). Four suggested recordings are: *My Brother Sam Is Dead* (Random, 1976); *Loner* (Random, 1973); *Legendary Tales of Mighty Men* (Caedmon, 1982), read by Ian Richardson; and *Scary Stories to Tell in the Dark* (Caedmon, 1986). Also suggested are three filmstrips: *Growing Up on the Way West, 1850* (Spoken Arts, 1986); *Settling the West* (Random, 1986, 6 fs); and *First Trails into the West* (SVE, 1986) from the Pathfinders Westward series.

Porte, Barbara Ann. *The Kidnapping of Aunt Elizabeth*
Greenwillow, 1985, 145 pp.

The author, formerly the children's services specialist in the Nassau County (Long Island) Library System, is well acquainted with the reading interests of children, both as a mother and as a librarian. Although she was a writer of magazine articles for adults for some time, she has published five books for children since 1983. *Harry's Visit* (Greenwillow, 1983) was chosen as an ALA Notable Book, and all her books have been favorably reviewed. Her style has been called "subtle and thought-provoking."

Barbara Ann Porte has a sure touch in combining rapierlike wit with comic timing. The result is spontaneous laughter. Her ability to do this reaches a pinnacle in this very serious tale. A school assignment to investigate and write her family history quickly turns into a confusing exercise for the heroine when each family member releases a story that differs (a little or a lot) from another's recollection. The young student can only agree with her cousin's verdict that "the family is peculiar." The author prefaces the book with Isaac Bashevis Singer's statement "that there were really no lies" and adds, "The ones who are last get to make up the stories." Youngsters, especially those ages 10–12 (grades 5–7), will enjoy the book and identify with many of the experiences.

The author includes notes and sources to document two stories, "The Mandrake Root" and "The Sandbox" (both in chapter 4), as well as other literary allusions, and the etiology of folklore, for example, magic pots (chapter 7). The small full-color drawing by Douglas Florian duplicated on both sides of the jacket illustrates "The Dancing Bear and the Chimpanzee" (pp. 81–92), a warm and appealing story for children, reflective of the heroine's family origin in Central Europe and Russia. "The Kidnapping of Aunt Elizabeth," a story told by the heroine's mother (pp. 5–18)—as well as the title of the book—together with the jacket drawing suggest strange high adventure.

A family tree is penned between the table of contents and the opening sentence. The 13 chapters relate the stories told by family members between the school assignment and the preliminary classroom check on the work. Luckily, the reader can always expect the author to describe women's roles well, even historically. Grandma, for example, is a retired lawyer, Mother a biochemist.

When Ms. Baxter, the ninth-grade social studies teacher assigns a family history project, Ashley (Ash) Rush knows she's in trouble. She recalls her embarrassment when she was called to the principal's office in fourth grade because her drawing of her family tree was so interesting. She had had to make it up because of her father's shifting exaggerations and her mother's reservations about spreading family information. Nevertheless, she determines to try again.

When her biochemist parents (Martin and Sonya) come home from their laboratory work, Ash pleads with her mother to tell about her identical twin, Aunt Elizabeth, and the time she was kidnapped. It started as an April Fool's joke, but Elizabeth, who hid in a neighbor's closet, wasn't found until the next day. Meanwhile, the twins' mother, Rebecca, a lawyer, and their father, William, were distraught. The red-haired twins, who were very different, were brought up as "only" children. When they grew up, they, too, had "only" children. Alexandra (Alex) Cohen (Elizabeth's daughter) was three months older than her cousin Ash. As she finishes her story, Mother asks Ash to change the names in the story.

Sylvia Lee, Ash's classmate, can't believe that Ash wants her father to tell her a story, after what happened in fourth grade. It starts out to be about her great-great-grandfather as a small boy in Russia. His older brother, Leo, told him that if he practiced he could lift a bull. But chicken pox intervened in his regime with a young bull, and he spent the rest of his life regretting that he was not the only child in Russia to lift a bull. According to her mother, the story, though interesting, is fraught with inaccuracies, the correct ancestor being one. But her father insists that he always tells the truth, though he also likes to tell interesting stories.

Undaunted, Ash goes to the public library where she learns many things from the librarian and the books: That mothers of social studies students have a habit of rushing to sign out the few library books on family history, and that one can find information in other places in a library, for example, for "family history," under "folklore" ("The Mandrake Root" and "The Sandbox"). Ash concludes that all stories should be left the way one hears them, "embellished."

Ash's mother tries to help by getting her brother-in-law, Max (Alex's father), to tell a family story. Max explains that his sister recorded it from her husband's 80-year-old mother. It tells of women and children escaping from Russia who were denied entrance to a synagogue by a rabbi who claimed they would wreck it. They did. Surprisingly, he asks that the woman's name, Eva Feldman, appear in Ash's report.

About a week before the preliminary work is due, Alex confesses that she had the same project last year when she was in ninth grade, but because she is an only child and didn't have anyone to pass it on to, she didn't save it. In recompense she tells about hitting her playmate Harry with a toy shovel when they were both five. The memory is vivid because he had stitches and she was forced to apologize and help his mother dig in the garden. Ash thinks that this will go well with the library "Sandbox" tale.

In a last flurry Ash finds many tales, including her own, about cooking kasha—a grain native to Eastern Europe—which she contributes to Sylvia's project, and her maternal grandmother's long-distance contribution about why she and Grandpa were married on a holiday (come to think of it, many other relatives who worked were also married on holidays). Grandpa Rush tells her in detail via long-distance telephone about how he flew when he was six (forgetting that Ash asked for a short story), and Aunt Elizabeth tells why Grandma Hofstaeter never has locks (Sonya was always getting stuck). But when Mother looks over Ash's notes, she comments about Aunt Elizabeth's version, "I don't remember it that way at all." Alex then asks Uncle Martin to tell one of his Russian stories, and he responds with the tale of a dancing bear and a white chimpanzee that his father, Sol, told him. But Alex says the story is made up, so Martin demurs, and Ash becomes thoughtful. After a visit and a conversation with her sister, Aunt Elizabeth tells a poignant tale about how as children they used to connect a string between their fingers across the room before they went to sleep.

At preliminary report time Ash listens to her classmates' stories: Horace's grandmother's story of foot washing in a Virginia Baptist church; Irina's Estonian story about her mother's velvet dog; and Sylvia's story about her now-proud Chinese heritage. When Ash tells her mother about the day's events, she learns that her maternal grandmother not only was the youngest in her family but also was special because she was born in America. As Ash tries to understand, she remembers once when Grandma still believed that it wouldn't hurt Chinese persons if you pulled their hair.

More stories from her parents fill Ash's report and her head. She is surprised to learn from her mother that her maternal great-grandma, Katia, who came from Poland, was a poor card shark with a parrot that spoke Yiddish. Ash is pleased because she is responsible for the "neat" Polish story her mother tells. She is also pleased to get a story from her father's visiting cousin, Esther, about a rooster outwitting the czar. She learns that her father, who used to live in the Bronx and work in Coney Island, comes from a musical family. But when Ash finally writes the family history and shows it to her father, he says that it could have been that way, except that his mother died in Russia just before they packed the fiddles.

Although Ash is unhappy with only a check on her work, she learned a lot and there are family postscripts. Grandpa Rush writes special delivery from Florida that Jascha, her father's oldest brother, died of influenza about the same time as his mother did. The letter adds that Martin is secretive just like his mother and her family. Ash concludes, "It isn't so bad being last. The ones who are last get to make up the stories."

Thematic Analysis

The slow awareness of the small knowns that adults take for granted is demonstrated cleverly in the labyrinthic details of this carefully crafted story. The theme of forming a personal view of heritage is developed with wit and humor, by tracing a Russian-Jewish family history. Beyond this, the fragile nature of truth, and its sometimes destructive potential, is a subtle but important theme. A wonderful burst of diverse themes includes scholarly practices, mannerisms of identical twins, classroom practices, and the transmission of prejudice. The awareness that information can be found in tangentially related subjects will be very helpful to youngsters.

Discussion Materials

This book can be book talked in several ways. Read fragments aloud: project an enlarged family tree and read "The Kidnapping of Aunt Elizabeth" (pp. 8–18) and "The Mandrake Root" (pp. 38–40), or "The Dancing Bear and the Chimpanzee" (pp. 83–91) and "The Sandbox" (pp. 41–44). Or re-create the family history project: Father's Russian tale (pp. 21–29); Uncle Max's contribution (pp. 47–50); hitting Harry (pp. 55–64); kasha (pp. 68–71); holidays (p. 73); flying (pp. 75–76); Aunt Elizabeth's story (pp. 79–80); and the connecting string (p. 103). Or concentrate on the exchange of personal information: Ash's problem (pp. 2–4); family exchanges (pp. 6–10); secrecy (p. 18); Father's stories (pp. 26–30); the library experience (p. 36); the cousins (pp. 52–55); the classmate, Sylvia (pp. 66–72); being twins (p. 80); Sonya and Elizabeth reminisce (pp. 93–102); musical talent (p. 118); and Father's reaction to

Ash's report (pp. 133–135). For an especially humorous story, paraphrase or read the episode where Aunt Elizabeth tells how Sonya repeatedly got stuck as a child (pp. 78–79).

Related Materials

Several exciting stories are suggested: *Shadow Guests* (Delacorte, 1980) by Joan Aiken is a suspenseful ghost story; *Grounded* (Knopf, 1982) by Todd Domke is a humorous tale of two boys who are "into" gliding; *Escape to Witch Mountain* (Westminster, 1968) by Alexander Key is a science fiction mystery tale about two orphans; *Serpent's Children* (Harper, 1984) by Laurence Yep is about nineteenth-century Chinese village life; and *Oh, You Dundalk Girls, Can't You Dance the Polka?* (Morrow, 1984) by Barbara Wernecke Durkin is historical fiction set in the fifties. Two other appropriate titles are *Here Come the Purim Players* (Lothrop, 1984) by Barbara Cohen, about a medieval Prague ghetto, and *Ellsworth and the Cats* (Houghton, 1981) by Patience Brewster, a science fiction story about a cat.

The bright "Red" poster (ALA, 1986, No. 35R) makes a striking background. Also recommended for background is the recording *Sing Children Sing: Songs of Israel* (Caedmon, 1979). Two suggested films are *Images for the Imagination* (Kodak, 1980), a 100-year-old history of Eastman-Kodak and photography, and *Ben's Dream* (Made-to-Order Library, 1984), adapted from the book by Chris Van Allsburgh, which portrays a boy's dream of traveling around the world. *Where in the World* (Aristoplay, 1986) is a 2–6 player geography game that will appeal to those in grade 3 and up interested in trivia games.

Sewall, Marcia. *The Pilgrims of Plimoth*
Illus. by the author. Atheneum, 1986, 48 pp.

Marcia Sewall, who recently entered the children's book scene, is noted for her luminous paintings. Her books have appeared on the New York Times Best Book and ALA Notable Book lists and have been selected for exhibition by the American Institute of Graphic Arts and the Bratislava International Biennale. Her three other titles in print are *The Cobbler's Song* (Dutton, 1982); *Riding That Strawberry Roan* (Viking, 1985); and *The World Turned Upside Down* (Atlantic Monthly Pr., 1986). This title not only shows her light-filled paintings, but also is an example of her thorough topical research and felicitous expression. Her admiration for her native New England shines through this exposition of the life of the Pilgrims from the time they left Plymouth, England, and settled on the shore of New England, which covers the highlights of their first few years in America at Plimoth. In the afterthought (ten years later) that closes the book, their plantation and others are growing. Youngsters ages 8–11 (grades 3–6) will find this book delightful and an invaluable opportunity to see and read about the few who came early to America.

The author-illustrator provides a visual feast to help youngsters understand the daily hard work and tragedies faced by the Plimoth Pilgrims that contributed to their sense of celebration at their first harvest—which we know as Thanksgiving. Sewall painted almost 40 full-color pictures in acrylic of the scenes she describes in print: 16 are full-page; 6 are half-page—two of which are double spreads; and 6 are quarter-page. From the paintings on the title and dedication pages to the attractive jacket pictures—not duplicated in the book—the book is well designed. The cheerful front jacket painting shows a busy plantation village scene, with houses and happy Pilgrim folk busily attending to the chores in the bright fall weather, obviously preparing for the harvest feast. It is a warm and welcoming scene just ten years after they crossed the ocean, which is in the background. The back jacket has a small picture of their original ship, the *Mayflower*, sailing on the navy blue water against a rosy-hued sky reflecting a feeling of completion—one of success.

The book is dedicated to the Pilgrim Village Interpreters. Special thanks are also extended to some members of the Pilgrim Society and the Plimoth Plantation. The very readable, straight typeface reflects the spirit of the Pilgrim's fortitude. In that same spirit the language they used is included, for example, the word "Aye" for "Yes." When appropriate, quotes are used in the text from William Bradford's *Of Plymouth Plantation, 1620–1647* and *A Journal of the Pilgrims at Plymouth*, originally printed in 1622, and also the words of the contemporary group the Pilgrim Village Interpreters, with page references given on the verso. The title page illustration shows the men haying and the women bringing them baskets of food with the omnipresent musket bearers mounted on the coastal fortress tower. The small painting on the dedication page depicts a young girl shouldering a wooden yoke with two pails of milk from two goats in the midst of a meadow enclosed by a stockade fence.

The two front matter illustrations smoothly transport the reader into the five sections of the book. The Pilgrims; Menfolk; Womenfolk; Children and Youngfolk; and The Plantation. The glossary of almost 50 words in common use includes two types of words: those not explained textually, for example, pipkins (saucepans, p. 30) and those not in common use today, for example, trencher (plate, p. 28). The book has more of the latter, but they can be easily identified and located (p. 48). The use of gender and role reflects the author's dedication to explain the way things were. Historical research does not judge the mores of another age, but simply reports as accurately as possible, as this author-illustrator has done.

The first section follows the Pilgrims as they sail from Plymouth, England, some to form a Godly community and some, the "Strangers," to gain wealth. After a harrowing trip on the *Mayflower*, the 70 adults and 12 children, together with their possessions and provisions, landed on the coast of New England, instead of Virginia, their planned destination. One baby boy was born at sea and another right after they landed. Having decided to stay because of the fast approaching winter, they started to build a common house on Christmas Day. During the winter their ranks were so decimated by illness that by spring only half their numbers remained.

The next two sections, Menfolk and Womenfolk, describe the everyday life of the community over the next few years. Basic food, clothing, and shelter are described in terms of the division of labor that existed among the struggling community. The men tilled the fields and built the plantation, as time permitted. They inaugurated a strict behavior code and enforced it with the use of stockades. A combination of religious views and community necessity for each person to work productively toward the Pilgrims' purpose mandated their use. The men also took the protection of their womenfolk and children seriously. Aided by Squanto, the only survivor of the Patuxet tribe, which had populated the region, the Pilgrims were able to sign a peace treaty with Massasoit, the great sachem of the area. Their celebration at harvest time was the first Thanksgiving feast. The womenfolk were in charge of cooking and light farming, for example, churning butter and growing garden vegetables. They also sewed and knitted, at first mending what they had brought with them.

In the fourth section, the author-illustrator explains that the children and youngfolk tended the cows, planted and helped with the light gardening, and assisted with the cooking. Only the youngest was permitted to play. Religion naturally took a large share of the Pilgrims' daily life.

All day Sunday was spent in the common house praying and praising the Lord for the bounty. The final section, an epilogue, reports that after ten years the members of the Plimoth Plantation could begin to move outside their enclosure and extend their boundaries. They were prospering. Not only had their plantation grown, but another new, fast-growing community existed at the head of Massachusetts Bay.

Thematic Analysis

The book's manifold themes for all readers include survival, family love, inner discipline, and faith, but certainly foremost is a broader view of the world. Youngsters clearly can see the early Americans, who settled for religious freedom, or in the case of some to gain a fortune, face the challenge of fundamental survival during their first few years in America. A comparison of where we were as a nation then and where we are now will prove edifying, if not astounding.

Discussion Materials

This title can be book talked in picture-book fashion by paraphrasing the main points on each page while showing the corresponding illustration, but it can be introduced in at least two other ways. Both require an initial display of the back jacket illustration of the *Mayflower,* followed by the front jacket painting of the bustling Plimoth Plantation ten years later. In the first or longer presentation, the five section headings can be introduced through the use of an illustration and corresponding readings: Plymouth, England (p. 5 and the second par. on p. 4); the building of the common house (p. 13 and the fourth sentence on p. 12); the first winter (pp. 14–15, both pictures and text); menfolk (pp. 16–17); the first harvest celebration (pp. 6 and 27); the womenfolk (pp. 30, 31, 34 and first par. on p. 35); children and youngfolk (pp. 38–39); and religion (pp. 44–45). For the plantation ten years later, show the street scene (p. 47). For the quicker second talk, show just one picture and paraphrase the corresponding text.

Related Materials

Several books can be used here: *Way Home* (Crown, 1982) by Ann Turner is about a young girl in fourteenth-century England who survives the black plague; *Sea Glass* (Harper, 1979) by Laurence Yep is about an eighth-grade boy caught between the heritage of his American homeland and his Chinese heritage; *Building Blocks* (Atheneum, 1984) by

Cynthia Voight is about Brann who learns to appreciate and respect his father after witnessing his father's childhood through a time warp; *Friends Are Like That* (Harcourt, 1984) by Patricia Hermes is about 13-year-old Tracy who has to choose between loyalty and friendship; and *Zed* (Faber, 1984) by Rosemary Harris is about a now-confident teen-ager's memories of himself at eight, the scared captive of terrorists. Two suggested nonfiction titles are *Strange Footprints on the Land* (Harper, 1980) by Constance Irwin and *How It Feels When a Parent Dies* (Knopf, 1981) by Jill Krementz. Two zany stories by Joan Aiken are also recommended: *Arabel and Mortimer* (Doubleday, 1981) and its sequel, *Mortimer's Cross* (Harper, 1984).

Two films for lighthearted humor and comparison are *Burt Dow: Deep Water Man* (Weston Woods, 1983) and *Good Hearted Ant* (International Film Bureau, 1984). Several filmstrips are suggested: *Growing Up in a New Land* (Spoken Arts, 1986), from the Growing Up with America series, about a young boy growing up in the Plymouth Colony; *English Colonies in America* (SVE, 1986) from the series Europeans Discover America; and *American Indians of the Northeast* (Random, 1986, 6 fs). Outstanding recordings of Shakespeare's plays are available from Spoken Arts.

Forming a View of the World: Additional Titles

Aliki. *Mummies Made in Egypt.* Illus. by the author. Crowell, 1980, 32 pp. (Gr. 4–6)

"American Girls Collection" 3 series (1854, 1904, 1944) of 3 vols. each. Pleasant Co., 1986. (Gr. 3–5)

Barton, Byron. *Building a House.* Greenwillow, 1981, 32 pp. (Gr. K–3)

Baylor, Byrd. *The Best Town in the World.* Illus. by Ronald Himmler. Scribner, 1983, 32 pp. (Gr. 2–4)

Coerr, Eleanor. *The Josefina Story Quilt.* Illus. by Bruce Degen. Harper, 1986, 64 pp. (Gr. 1–3)

Cole, Joanna. *The Magic Schoolbus at the Waterworks.* Illus. by Bruce Degen. Scholastic, 1986, 39 pp. (Gr. 2–4)

Fisher, Leonard Everett. *The Great Wall of China.* Illus. by the author. Macmillan, 1986. (Gr. 3–5)

Hot Bagels: The Hole Story. Film, 11 min. Burma Road Productions, 1983. (Gr. 5–up)

Irvine, Mat. *TV and Video.* Illus. with drawings and photos. Watts, 1984, 32 pp. (Gr. 4–6)

The Juggling Movie. Film, 10 min. Little Red Filmhouse, 1982. (Gr. 5–up)

King, Clive. *Ninny's Boat.* Macmillan, 1980, 246 pp. (Gr. 5–6)

Krantz, Hazel. *100 Pounds of Popcorn.* Illus. by Charles Geer. Vanguard, 1961, 126 pp. (Gr. 4–6)

Lasker, Joe. *A Tournament of Knights.* Illus. by the author. Harper/Crowell, 1986, 32 pp. (Gr. 3–6)

Lunn, Janet. *Shadow in Hawthorn Bay.* Lester & Orpen Dennys, 1986. (Gr. 5–up)

Macaulay, David. *Mill.* Illus. by the author. Houghton, 1983, 128 pp. (Gr. 4–7)

McGinnis, Lila S. *Ghost Upstairs.* Illus. by Amy Rowen. Hastings House, 1982, 119 pp. (Gr. 4–6)

Mainly Mother Goose. Recording, also available on cassette. Elephant Records, 1985. (Gr. K–3)

Markle, Sandra. *Exploring Winter.* Illus. by the author. Atheneum, 1984, 160 pp. (Gr. 4–6)

Merry Ever After: The Story of Two Medieval Weddings, by Joe Lasker. Filmstrip. Live Oak Media, 1979. (Gr. 5–6)

Pellowski, Anne. *The Story Vine: A Source Book of Unusual and Easy-to-Tell Stories from Around the World.* Illus. by Lynn Sweat. Macmillan, 1984, 128 pp. (Gr. 5–up)

The Punctuation Wizard. Film, 24 min., also available on video. Barr Films, 1985. (Gr. 2–6)

Simon, Seymour. *Einstein Anderson: Science Sleuth.* Illus. by Fred Winkowski. Viking, 1980, 73 pp. (Gr. 3–5)

Singer, Isaac Bashevis. *Stories for Children.* Farrar, 1984, 337 pp. (Gr. 5–6)

Splint Basketry Weaving. Film, 79 min. Victorian Video, 1986. (Gr. 5–up)

Stanley, Diane. *Peter the Great.* Illus. by the author. Macmillan, 1986, 32 pp. (Gr. 4–6)

Tales from the Odyssey. Seven filmstrips. Troll, 1986. (Gr. 4–7)

Wartski, Maureen Crane. *Boat to Nowhere.* Illus. by Dick Teicher. Westminster, 1980, 191 pp. (Gr. 4–6)

Yep, Laurence. *Mark Twain Murders.* Macmillan, 1982, 152 pp. (Gr. 4–6)

6

Respecting Living Creatures

FROM their earliest days, children are delighted by other creatures, usually small domesticated animals. Many youngsters are exposed to small animals vicariously through books or actually at "petting" zoos. They also like to look at exotic and larger animals whether in books or from a safe distance in life. They generally have a healthy respect for all species, which continues to develop during the middle years, helping to build a foundation for their future capacity to give and receive affection. The value of youngsters being able to relate well to pets is widely recognized. The caring attitude and comforting behavior that this implies deepens during the middle years as the child begins to understand and appreciate his or her own crucial place among all living creatures on this planet. This can contribute to a positive attitude on the youngster's part based on a sound philosophy of life.

The books in this chapter give youngsters an opportunity to learn to deal with some of the world's creatures, familiar and foreign. They can also learn respect for other creatures and, ultimately, themselves. Some of the books build on youngsters' ability to relate to small animals, encouraging them to think about them in a spiritual, philosophic, and realistic way. Others treat contemporary youngsters who live intimately with their heritage within a different culture. One deals with a youngster's first experience with a large animal from the wild. A couple of books introduce middle-graders to creatures of the sea and air. All of the books are entertaining and full of fascinating information.

Arnold, Caroline.   *Saving the Peregrine Falcon*
Photographs by Richard R. Hewett. Carolrhoda, 1985, 48 pp.

The author has published more than two dozen books for children in this decade under several publishers' imprints. Primarily nonfiction, they

166

are practical and science titles for middle-graders with useful information for this age. Caroline Arnold immerses herself in the book's topic, conducts thorough research, condenses the information, and presents it for interested youngsters in an easy-to-read fashion. This title, a Nature Watch Book, describes the efforts of a group of California ornithologists to save the peregrine falcon. It provides information about the birds and the incidence of fragile eggshells that almost led to their extinction. The fascinating coverage—an example of good reporting—and the photographs will appeal to youngsters age 8–11 (grades 3–6). The book can be read both for curiosity or for science projects. A glossary is included.

Richard R. Hewett is responsible for the numerous color photographs that appear on almost every page. Six of the photographs are credited to the Peregrine Fund and to Jim Jennings. The author and the illustrator both thank the many people who helped in the preparation of this book, for example, one photograph shows Brian Walton, head of the Santa Cruz Predatory Bird Research Group (SCPBRG), holding a chick in his palm, with his staff, Sam Sumida of the Western Foundation of Vertebrate Zoology, and Mark Robertson of the Peregrine Fund. The colorful cover displays two pictures. The front shows a yipping falcon chick being "imprinted" by an adult peregrine hand puppet, the back an adult peregrine silhouetted in the sun.

Although people do not normally think of peregrine falcons as living in big cities, they are increasingly adapting to city life. Chiefly predators of other birds in their natural wild habitat, the "duck hawks" (as they are colloquially called) can find plenty of pigeons, sparrows, and starlings to feed upon, and high places in which to nest on the tall city buildings. The closest most of us get to falcons today is when we see the bird displayed on a perch in the opening segment of the TV series "Falconcrest." For centuries they were treasured by royalty and falconers for their hunting prowess and speed, but by 1940 none were left on the East Coast of America and by 1970 only two nesting pairs were known in California. The insecticide DDT had decimated their numbers by causing a drastic thinning of their eggshells.

Falcons are found all over the world, but only four types are common in the United States—gyrfalcon, prairie falcon, the merlin, and the kestrel. Although these too have been reduced in number, only the peregrine falcon was endangered, largely because the birds that they ate spent the winter in Central and South America where the poisonous DDT was being used on the grain. Adult peregrines appear to have a mustache, and although both sexes have the same color, the female is usually about one-third larger, hence the French word "tiercel" (a third) for the male (defined in the book's glossary). A falcon's feet, beak, keen eyesight (comparable to a person being able to read a newspaper a mile away), and diving speed are designed for catching prey in flight.

Peregrines nest high on rocky cliffs (called aeries) in the wild and generally lay three eggs a year. They will, however, lay a second brood if something happens to the first, and ornithologists use this knowledge to try to increase the peregrine population. The baby peregrines are called chicks, or eyas in the wild. Scientists monitor the broods along the rocky California coast. After leaving all the eggs in the nest for five days, they take the eggs most in jeopardy to the laboratory. Three laboratories that hatch peregrine eggs to try to reestablish the variety are in Ithaca, New York; Boise, Idaho; and Santa Cruz, California. The book describes the work at the Santa Cruz laboratory.

In the hatching station, the eggs are continually weighed, candled, and turned in the incubators for 31½ days. Everything is done to strengthen the eggs and to keep them from losing moisture. Sometimes the tiny cracks in the shells are glued together, sometimes the shells are waxed. Preferably two or more eggs are placed together in the hatcher because the peeps from the emerging chicks seem to provide encouragement. After 24–48 hours of working to crack the shell with its egg tooth, which will soon drop off, the chick emerges wet, matted, and exhausted. After further ministrations, it is put in a brooder to keep it warm, just as the female sits on the brood to keep it warm in the wild. In 8–12 hours it is fed with a tweezer and then with a plastic bag with a nozzle. At this stage, imprinting is begun with peregrine hand puppets. Three days to one week later, an adult bird—sometimes a prairie falcon—that has been imprinted by people is substituted as the care giver. One or two weeks later another falcon that has been imprinted by birds is put in charge. After three weeks the young bird is banded, implanted with a radio transmitter, and carefully replaced in the eyrie nest (to the surprise of the adults that have been tending dummy eggs). Meanwhile, the hatching station also serves as a breeding center. Several pairs of peregrine falcons are sheltered from people and noise by peepholes and distracting sounds from a radio.

At six weeks the juvenile will be the size of its parents with mottled, brown feathers. (Not until it starts its second year will it have adult feathers.) It also begins to fly and hunt for food, although sometimes a released juvenile needs and receives help in getting its food ration. Hopefully this wild bird will stay in its native habitat and procreate, however, some birds are released in cities. As readers look skyward, they will be able to distinguish a falcon from a hawk by its wing spread—pointed for faster diving speed or spread wide for soaring.

Thematic Analysis

The informative description of the effort being extended to preserve the peregrine falcon has the straightforward theme of human respect for other living creatures. The awe-inspiring dedication of those involved in the scientific work serves as a fine role model for children.

Discussion Materials

This book can be easily "book talked." Display both the front and back book covers; show the title page photograph of the peregrine falcon; and read aloud the last page (p. 46). Explain that in between these two are more pages chock full of information and photographs about the peregrine falcon and how scientists are trying to save this endangered species. Tempting snatches of information can be dispensed, for example, the difference between the feathers of a falcon and a hawk (p. 6). One can also highlight the fragile shells (pp. 10–13); the laboratory hatching (pp. 15–39); and setting falcons free (pp. 41–43).

Related Materials

Three other nonfiction titles to suggest are: *A Penguin Year* (Delacorte, 1981) by Susan Bonner, which describes the life-style of these Antarctica birds; *Biology* (Watts, 1984) by Ifor Evans, which introduces a reader to the dynamics of living plants and animals in communities; and *Gorillas in the Mist* (Houghton, 1983) by Dian Fossey, which treats the long-standing observation of this endangered species. Three fiction titles are also suggested: *Last Monster* (Harcourt, 1980) by June Annixter and Paul Annixter, the story of a boy who comes to an understanding of the symbiosis between human beings and other creatures; *Midnight Is a Place* (Viking, 1974) by Joan Aiken, an exciting mystery and adventure story about two English orphans; *Warday: And the Journey Onward* (Holt, 1984) by Whitley Strieber and James W. Kuneta, which describes a trans-American journey by two journalists after a nuclear blast.

Some filmstrips and a recording will be useful: *Will They Survive. . .* (Centre Prods., 1983, 2 fs) with good photographs concentrates on many species from eagles to ferrets; *Birds of North America* (Clearvue, 1986) combines photographs of Roger Tory Peterson's paintings with bird calls and information; and *Mr. Popper's Penguins* (Random, 1975), which is from the comic story of a house painter turned vaudeville trainer.

Baylor, Byrd.   *I'm in Charge of Celebrations*
Pictures by Peter Parnall. Scribner, 1986, 29 pp.

In her many books, the author is recognized for her lyrical celebrations of the Southwest, which she calls home, and the traditions and creatures that inhabit it. Presently Byrd Baylor has more than a dozen books in print in hard- and softcover. For almost a decade, she has been known for her eloquent expression of the spiritual in life as seen through the desert landscape. She is also known for her writings that especially appeal to sensitive young readers. This tone poem, for example, expresses the inner feelings of a young native American who delights in the freedom she finds in the desert and the animals and birds there. The plot involves a young female Indian who celebrates official holidays on the desert and chooses others to commemorate sudden surprises. Youngsters aged 8–11 (grades 3–6), will find the idea interesting and the drawings of the desert landscape fascinating.

Peter Parnall, the illustrator, has been cited by the ALA. Caldecott Committee for three honor titles on which he collaborated with the author: *The Desert Is Theirs; The Way to Start a Day;* and *Hawk, I'm Your Brother* (*Introducing More Books*, Bowker, 1978, pp. 121–123). Once again, the illustrator drew exciting pictures in color and pen that reinforce the author's meaning. The 14 double-spread pictures emphasize the horizontal spaciousness of the desert, as well as the warm orange red colors of the desert earth. The bright terra-cotta sun in some drawings signifies heavy stillness. The large area of white background in the drawings provides visual relief and a sense of spaciousness in the desert (inherent in the text as spirituality). A small color sketch of the Southwest country serves as the frontispiece and welcomes the reader to the desert.

Chance encounters in her desert homeland are a young native American's reason for celebrating. She is accustomed to people asking if she is lonely living in the desert. She laughs and replies, "How could I be lonely? I'm the one in charge of celebrations." Last year she jotted down

108 celebrations in her notebook besides the normal school closings. She writes down the date of her wonderful feelings at chance encounters and celebrates it. Although she insists that she is very choosy, she reflects on six that she experienced the previous year.

Her first real celebration was last March 11, when the dust devils (whirlwinds) suddenly arose, picking up everything around the pickup truck she was riding in, including sand and tumbleweed. She stopped, jumped out, and joined in a happy, whirling dance, counting seven dust devils as she celebrated. Somehow she knows that she will be surprised each time it occurs again.

On August 9, she sees a triple rainbow. At the same moment, she also sees a jackrabbit standing on its hind legs looking at the rainbows, too. This makes the experience even more special, for she thinks that she must be the only person to have seen a triple rainbow and a jackrabbit looking at it, too.

Green Cloud Day happens quickly; it only takes clouds a minute to change shape. It is strange enough to see a green cloud, but late one afternoon on February 6, she not only sees it, but is astounded to see it take the shape of a large parrot, an experience certainly worth celebrating!

One day as she is tracking some deer prints on the rocky ledges, she sees a young coyote. The coyote sees her, too. They stare briefly at each other. The coyote recognizes her as just another creature following along the rocky ledge and travels on. That occurrence makes September 28 a special day, Coyote Day. She celebrates by leaving a feast of apples, pumpkin seeds, an ear of corn, and some ginger cookies on the rocks for the coyote. When she investigates the following day, she finds the food gone. The young Indian girl decides to bring more food next year when she celebrates.

Early in August her nighttime sightings of meteor showers (falling stars), and the fact that she meets someone who saw the same thing 500 miles away, coincide and reinforce her wonderous feeling of speaking the language of the universe. There is no doubt that this calls for a celebration!

But best of all, perhaps, is her New Year's celebration. It isn't the celebration most people think of, and it isn't based on the January 1 calendar date. It occurs for her when the "morning light comes earlier," and the "white-winged doves are back from Mexico." The wildflowers that cover the hills and her favorite cactus in bloom are further signs that herald the date. When everything is right—air and dirt warm on bare feet—she can celebrate. This holiday generally comes around the end of April, usually on a Saturday. Following ancestral traditions and customs, she beats a small drum intermittently and spends the day admiring her favorite places and trails. She celebrates with the desert creatures—the desert tortoise, horned toads, ravens, lizards, and quail. "And Friend, it's not a bad party."

As she returns to her home in the desert, humming to herself as she often does, she wonders why people ask if she's lonely. Surrounded by the living creatures with whom she celebrates and with the white-winged dove flying overhead she thinks, "I have to laugh out loud."

Thematic Analysis

A serene sense of knowing oneself and one's pivotal place in the natural scheme of things is the powerful message in this book. A respect for and celebration of life and other living creatures can give a youngster an inner sense of confidence. Other themes such as celebrating life in nature's cyclical way rather than in the arbitrary and perhaps sterile ways of technology are subtlely forwarded.

Discussion Materials

This book with its striking drawings and elegantly placed vertical stanzas will be easy to "book talk." Display the full jacket drawing of the young native American raising her arms on the desert in homage to the white-winged dove flying in front of the reddish orange sun. Follow by showing the pictures on the title and dedication pages. Read the first page of text aloud while showing an enlarged transparency of it. Then relate the plot and tell about some of the young girl's special celebrations: Dust Devil Day (pp. 10–13); Triple Rainbow Day and the jackrabbit (pp. 14–16); Green Cloud Day (pp. 16–17); Coyote Day (pp. 18–21); meteor showers (pp. 22–23); and the New Year's celebration (pp. 24–28).

Related Materials

A book by the author and illustrator that corresponds well here is *Your Own Best Secret Place* (Scribner, 1979), about a girl who finds a message from William Cottonwood signifying that he will return someday to the desert country. Peter Parnall's *The Day Watchers* (Macmillan, 1985), which he also illustrated, is an interesting account of his own hobby of bird-watching. Two nonfiction explanations of flight are suggested: *Flight: A*

Panorama of Aviation (Pantheon, 1981) by Melvin B. Zisfein and *Air and Flight* (Watts, 1984) by Neil Ardley. Scott Corbett's fictional *Deadly Hoax* (Dutton, 1981) is a fast-paced science fiction story, especially for horror fans.

Two films are recommended: *Corn Is Life* (Univ. of California Pr./ EMC, 1983), about the Hopi Indians of the Southwest, and *Symmetry: A First Film* (Phoenix/BFA, 1983), which explains artistic balance in our environment and its technical representations. Four filmstrips are suggested: *Annie and the Old One* (Random, 1986, 2 fs), from the book by Miska Miles about a Navajo girl and her grandmother; *The Four Seasons in Lenápe Indian Life* (Spoken Arts, 1985, 4 fs), about the historical life of this tribe as it moved through Delaware, Ohio, and Oklahoma; *Understanding Poetry* (SVE, 1985, 4 fs), which explains poetry; and *Holidays Around the World* (SVE, 1986, 5 fs), which introduces holiday practices in Mexico, Sweden, Sierra Leone, China, and the United States.

George, Jean Craighead.   *The Talking Earth*
Harper, 1983, 151 pp.

Jean Craighead George won the 1973 Newbery Award for *Julie of the Wolves.* Her great respect for nature and excellent writing combine in wonderful stories for youngsters (see *Introducing Books,* Bowker, 1970, pp. 144–147 and *Introducing More Books,* Bowker, 1978, pp. 89, 131). Athough she started her career writing well-researched nature articles, she later turned her hand to children's books. Perhaps the leading exponent of excellent nature stories for children today, with more than 15 in print, the author has created a fascinating account of a young Seminole Indian girl who rediscovers her heritage and the intricate balance of life when she is sent alone into the Everglades by her tribe to listen to the animals. She spends three months traveling through the swamp trying to find a way out, learning wonderful things along the way. Youngsters, especially those interested in nature, ages 9–11 (grades 4–6), will find the journey alive with interesting facts and adventures. The front jacket shows the young Indian in her blue jeans poling the dugout canoe as she glides through the Everglades. Petang, her small otter friend, sits up front. A decorative Indian motif border sets the tone.

Thirteen-year-old Billie Wind lives uncertainly between two cultures.

She has spent a summer working with her father and brother, Iron Wind, at NASA in Cape Kennedy, Florida. She does not believe the teachings of her tribe that the animals speak and the little underground people play tricks on human beings. As she tells her sister, 15-year-old Mary, she thinks they are antiquated and foolish, yet she agrees willingly to travel from the Big Cypress Reservation where she lives with her sister and mother, Mamau Whispering Wind, to Panther Paw, their tribal island for the annual Green Corn Dance. This three-week festival is important, especially because her mother is the matriarchal head of the Wind clan and her Uncle Charlie is the medicine man.

Once there, Uncle Charlie questions her about what she told her sister. He decides to send the curious youngster into the Everglades ("pa hay okee") to Lost Dog Island for three weeks to reestablish her beliefs and relearn Seminole ways. At first Billie Wind is not disturbed. Although she still can't understand why Mary told him, she knows he has always been her friend. When he tells her to bring back two lightning bolts, she surmises that the spider lilies that she sees growing close by will be easy to gather and they look like lightning bolts. She also ceases to disdain his old medicine bundle when he informs her that only 8 remain of the 40 medicines that existed in ancient days. But when Uncle Charlie asks Mary to wave white heron feathers over the dugout that awaits Billie Wind at the edge of the island to ensure her safe return, Billie Wind will have none of that. She regards Mamau Whispering Wind's pouch, deposited in the dugout with food, a machete, and a magnifying glass with which to start a fire, far more practical. Calmly expecting that only the facts she has learned will prevail, Billie Wind pushes off into the grass-filled swamp before Mary can wave the feathers.

Little does Billie Wind realize that her three-week punishment will turn into a 13-week odyssey. As the dugout slowly drifts through the Everglades, she sees snakes, alligators, mud turtles, bass, all curiously moving to the west. Instead of heading south to Lost Dog Island, she also heads west. Seeing a hardwood hammock, she decides to spend the night there, rather than in the slough toward which she is headed.

Soon she realizes that the grasses in the Everglades are on fire, that she is caught in the scorching seasonal fire, and from the panic of the animals that the fire is on the island, too. The island becomes a raging tinderbox, but luckily Billie Wind finds a large cave under a sink hole. Every conceivable creature is trying to get in, too, not just Billie Wind. Snakes, armadillos, and turtles drop into the water hole at the bottom of the cave. Billy Wind now realizes, just as Uncle Charlie said, that a serpent (fire) does exist and that animals do talk (give signals).

Later she discovers that the hammock is an old burial ground. When she finds an ancient Calusa pot, she remembers that her height comes from those ancestors, just as her high cheekbones come from the Hitchiti. She also discovers a suckling otter ("petang" in northern Indian dialect) and manages to feed both herself and the other with fish. Petang swims in the bottom pool and leads her to the underground pools beneath the fiery Everglades where the fish live while waiting for the rains to come. Billie Wind also waits, then surfaces with Petang. Before she leaves the cave, however, she finds one of the ancient medicine pouches.

On the hammock surface, she finds the dugout burned beyond repair. By wading through the shallow water amid snakes and alligators she is able to find a cypress tree on a nearby island from which she can make another canoe. While she is fashioning it with her machete, Billie Wind sees bulldozers on the hammock she just left. She recalls that an airport is to be built near Panther Paw. She realizes that the last Calusa traces are doomed and is glad that she at least took the Calusa pot. Meanwhile, the men working the bulldozers see her, barely giving her time to push off. She almost has to leave without Petang but at the last moment he shows up. Laughingly, she accuses him of playing tricks on her now that he is full grown. The festival is long over by now, but she is determined to get back to the reservation even though she doesn't know where she is. Billie Wind already has learned that the animals talk and that the little men underground can play tricks, but her odyssey continues. She makes a houseboat out of her dugout and adopts a baby panther (Coootchobee) whose mother died, even though Petang is jealous at first. Later, when the panther cub breaks her treasured Calusa pot, Billie Wind cries and tells it that it is too curious for its own good. She doesn't have it too long because its father carries it right off the boat.

Then Billie Wind catches a gopher turtle, Burden, and carries it aboard. As the houseboat slides down the Fahkahatchee Slough heading toward the sea, Billie Wind thinks they surely must be traveling in a circle. She does know, however, that she must pay strict attention to the tides, and to the pulls and pushes now. Soon she hears sounds from automobiles, which according to her calculations means she must be close to home. But she is not quite ready. She knows now that the animals talk, but she doesn't understand what they say. She decides that when Burden says something to her, it will be time to go home.

As Billie Wind heads homeward, she continues to listen to and live among the animals. Petang finds a mate and leaves, leaving Billy Wind alone with Burden to face a threatening storm. She realizes that the animals and birds, including Burden, all sensed the low pressure preceding the hurricane. Deserting her houseboat, she heads inland for a place 13 feet above sea level to protect herself from the tidal wave that will come after the hurricane. As she builds a shelter to wait out the storm, she comes upon Oats, a stranded 12-year-old Indian boy, who is on a name quest because he doesn't like his name. He joins her, and while the storm rages her former friend, the panther, visits them. Billie Wind learns that they are near Naples, Florida, and the boy's village on the Chobee River. Oats, newly named Hurricane Tiger, knows that her tribe has been looking for her. Billie Wind finally realizes that Charlie Wind sent her on a mission, not on a journey to punish her. At last she understands the delicate balance in nature among all living creatures.

Thematic Analysis

Respecting living creatures is the main thread in this story. The importance of understanding the delicate balance among all the species on the planet is stressed in the young Seminole's forced quest. An understanding of the balance between nature's rules and the rationality of physical laws is also fundamental. The name quest tribal ritual may be of special interest to the young who often rail inwardly against their given names. The book also contains a staggering amount of information about snakes, alligators, turtles, manatees, the endangered species of panthers, and other animals.

Discussion Materials

This slim volume designed by Trish Parcell will be appealing as individual reading to nature lovers, adventure fans, and reluctant readers. Its nine chapters, averaging 16 pages each, also nominate it for serial reading aloud. Displaying the front jacket illustration of Billie Wind standing in the dugout is an attractive way to begin a book talk. Introduce the main characters and setting (use the chapter heads on the contents page and pp. 1–16). For those who may require more, many episodes can be highlighted: underground fish habitats (pp. 45–49); an Everglades fire (p. 27); a Calusa cave (pp. 30–31); Petang (pp. 32–44); foraging (pp. 62–73); Burden (pp. 109–111); Billie Wind and Burden leave (pp. 126–127); Oats arrives with the hurricane (pp. 128–143); and how the animals talk (pp. 146–147). The second half of the hurricane and how Burden speaks is best left to the reader. The chapter "Coootchobee" is good for reading aloud or paraphrasing (pp. 74–87, 98–99, 101–103).

Related Materials

Two nonfiction titles that relate well are *Rattlesnakes* (Holiday, 1984) by Russell Freedman and *The Tipi: A Center of Native American Life* (Knopf, 1984). Two fiction titles will also be of interest: *Cave Beyond Time* (Crowell, 1980) by Malcolm J. Bosse and *Reina the Galgo* (Dutton, 1985) by Nicole De Messiers.

Several audiovisual titles will also be useful. Three recordings are suggested: *Bambi,* read by Glynis Johns; *A Gathering of Great Poetry for Children, 4th Grade and Up,* edited by Richard Lewis (both Caedmon); and *Oh, Kojo! How Could You!* (Random) read by Pearl Primus. Two filmstrips are suggested: *The Life of a Seminole Family* (SVE, 1986), from the series Six Native American Families, and *Hiawatha's Childhood* (Random, 1986), narrated by Jamake Highwater. Two films are appropriate: *Medoonak the Stormmaker* (Encyclopaedia Britannica) and *A Swamp Ecosystem* (National Geographic Society, 1983). The "Information Jungle" poster from ALA (No. 125) will reinforce the spirit of search in this book talk.

Haley, Gail E.   *Birdsong*
Pictures by the author. Crown, 1984, 32 pp.

Gail E. Haley is the acclaimed author-illustrator of more than eight picture books for children. She won the Caldecott Medal for the well-known title *A Story, a Story* and a few years later, the British Kate Greenaway Award for *The Post Office Cat.* In 1986, Haley's *Jack and the Bean Tree,* a retelling of the Appalachian version of "Jack and the Bean Stalk," appeared. She is a top-notch illustrator as well as an excellent author. This unusual story is especially good with ages 6–9 (grades 1–4), but its many levels of meaning will appeal to all ages.

Haley's illustrations are bold, elongated, and full of detail. This title has 18 full-color paintings, each outlined with a dark brown color that reinforces the notion that this tale is rooted in the countryside and deals with humanity. Two of the paintings are double spreads; 12 full-page illustrations extend onto one-third of the opposite page; and three are single-page illustrations, including the first and last pages of the book and page 13. A one-third page illustration shows a peacock's feather (the magic feather). The colorful painting of Jorinella bedecked in a cloak festooned with bright bird feathers is arresting (pp. 8 and 9).

Jorinella, the elderly bird catcher, sits surrounded by cages, which she handcrafts while a black crow watches. In her medieval cloak and plumed hat Jorinella sets off in her horse cart for the village marketplace to sell her trapped birds. She arranges her stall outside the bustling village, surrounded by clowns, children, noblemen, and others looking for blackbirds for their pies, and is soon sold out. A disappointed clientele tells her that her produce seems to get slimmer and slimmer. They wonder aloud if she is getting too old.

On her way to the village green, Jorinella sees a young orphan girl sitting alone playing her pipes oblivious to the money in her begging bowl. Jorinella asks the girl, whom she names Birdsong because she is surrounded by flocks of birds, to come home and help her around the house. Although Birdsong is somewhat frightened, she agrees.

After Birdsong bathes, Jorinella untangles and arranges her hair and gives her an outfit. She also gives her a magic feather to help her understand the birds. Birdsong discovers that it works when she begins to understand their songs. She is content—she has food, a bed, and the birds of the forest as friends—and her skill on the pipes grows.

Soon, however, Jorinella takes her to a clearing in the forest where she has built a wicker hut covered with leaves. She asks Birdsong to sit inside and play the pipes on the pretext that the sound will help her find her way back from berrying. When Birdsong leaves the hut at the end of the day, she finds that the many birds who were attracted by her playing are caged. Jorinella tells Birdsong to stay the night and guard the birds, until she returns in the morning with the cart. As Jorinella departs, a twisted ugly feather drops from her cloak. Through its magic, Birdsong learns that Jorinella, like her, once played the dry old cracked pipes that Birdsong found in the cottage, but because of greed decided to sell the birds. Horrified, Birdsong releases the birds before Jorinella returns.

When Jorinella comes back, she accuses Birdsong of betrayal, but Birdsong responds by telling her that she knows the story of her heart growing hard. Enraged, Jorinella starts to thrash Birdsong with a whip. The freed birds return and chase Jorinella to the edge of the forest. The eagles and other strong birds lift Birdsong in one of the bird nets and carry her to a secret kingdom that still exists far away from "prying eyes and unfriendly hearts." The birds know where the kingdom is and sing of it.

Thematic Analysis

Although the main theme is a declaration that good will toward all in human nature has a place in this world, that is, a kingdom whose inhabitants are of pure heart, live in harmony, and understand one another, this story has many thematic levels. A corollary theme shows how a young person can be easily deceived, especially under extenuating circumstances, that is, an orphan or a child who feels alone. Whether this feeling of aloneness is a physical reality or a mental state, that occurs developmentally in many children, this story reinforces the positive attitude that one is never alone in nature—lonely perhaps, but not alone. Among the many other themes that are stressed are the disastrous effect of greed and the necessity for youngsters carefully to evaluate proffered kindness.

Discussion Materials

This title is excellent for reading aloud to the young or for presenting as a picture book. Or briefly tell the story line, then display and introduce the book. For independent readers or those older than the suggested grade levels or ages, the book can be read individually. The story works well in grades 3–6 language arts as the basis for a comparison of native bird tales of North and South America. It will also be useful for highlighting the medieval period in social studies and for a study of the story's Appalachian influences. To display some of the illustrations, use the cloak (p. 8) and the medieval village market (pp. 4–5). A reading of the poetry also is recommended (pp. 1, 7, 12, 14, 22).

Related Materials

Recommended for the younger crowd are: *A Medieval Feast* (Harper, 1983) by Aliki, a sumptuous picture book; *Francis, the Poor Man of Assisi* (Holiday, 1982) by Tomie dePaola; and *Mary Had a Little Lamb* (Holiday, 1984) by Sara J. Hale, illustrated by Tomie dePaola. Masayuki Yabuuchi's nonfictional *Whose Baby?* (Philomel, 1985), about the animal kingdom, is suggested for all youngsters. Three other nonfiction titles apply: *Koko's Kitten* (Scholastic, 1985) by Francine Patterson; *Peeping in the Shell: A Whooping Crane Is Hatched* (Harper, 1986) by Faith McNulty; and *Raccoon Baby* (Putnam, 1984) by Berniece Freschet. Three titles that are useful in grades 3–6 are: *Ringo, The Robber Raccoon: The True Story of a Northwoods Rogue* (Dodd, 1984) by Robert Franklin Leslie; *Cully Cully and the Bear* (Greenwillow, 1983) by Wilson Gage, a humorous story illustrated by James Stevenson; and *Andy Bear: A Polar Cub Grows Up at the Zoo* (Morrow, 1985) by Ginny Johnston and Judy Cutchins.

Some audiovisual titles are useful here: *Old Dry Frye* (Film Ideas, 1986), a film and video of an Appalachian folktale; *Practical Self-Defense for Children* (VETS, 1986), a film that gives step-by-step instructions for children in Tae Kwon Do; and *Please Take Care of Your Teeth* (Pyramid, 1985). Two filmstrips are also applicable: *Hansel and Gretel* (Random, 1986) and *The Legend of the Bluebonnet: An Old Tale of Texas* (Random, 1985) by Tomie dePaola, about the courageous spirit of a little girl, She Who Is Alone, who saves her tribe, the Comanche people.

Isenbart, Hans-Heinrich. *A Duckling Is Born*
Translated by Catherine Edwards Sadler. Photographs by Othmar Baumli. Putnam, 1981, 36 pp.

The author first published this nonfiction title in Europe in 1979. It was then translated and published in the United States in 1981. Hans-Heinrich Isenbart followed this book with two other titles: *Baby Animals on the Farm* (Putnam, 1984) and *Birth of a Foal* (Carolrhoda, 1986). All are recommended for young and middle-graders to age 10. The reviews have been favorable and the latter title received an honorable mention in the prestigious New York Academy of Science Children's Science Book Award competition.

A Duckling Is Born is the story of the birth and early life of baby ducklings. With marvelous photographs taken one spring and summer, it shows the courtship, mating, and common behavior of the drake and duck before, during, and after the birth of the ducklings. Youngsters of any age will enjoy the pictures, but those 7–9 years of age (grades 2–4) will find the presentation especially appealing. Together with Joanna Cole's *How You Were Born* (Morrow, 1984), this title will help youngsters discover the fundamental differences in the two birth processes— hatching from eggs and live births.

The photographs by Othmar Baumli are beautiful full-color representations of the familiar mallard—a drake, a female consort, and their ducklings—flying and in and around the water. They are splendid bird pictures, enlarged and especially sharp and clear. Special thanks is extended to the University of Fribourg for the marvelous windowlike eggshell pictures that trace the embryological development from day two to birth. Baumli is responsible for a plethora of photographs; 11 full pages, some extending onto the facing page, and 2 or 3 on other pages along with block-type text. The attractive front jacket highlights a picture from the text of a newly hatched duckling (the first of seven in this brood) 24 hours after the sun has dried its feathers. The back jacket duplicates a cropped photograph that extends onto the last page, portraying the female duck paddling in the blue water surrounded by the summer ducklings.

The book can be divided into three parts for analysis: the identification by gender of the drake and the consort, and their courtship; the nesting, brooding, and hatching; and the summer training—swimming and feeding—before flying away in the fall. The male drakes are easily identifiable early in the fall by their bright colors and ring of green around their neck. The courtship and mating of the drake with a willing female are shown in the illustrations. Feeding, flying, grooming, and contented swimming practices precede their late winter mating, nesting, and brooding.

The appealing pictures of the female duck sitting on the seven eggs are followed by four pages of exceptional photographs of the eggs, exposing the embryos from day two to hatching. The camera catches the first wet, bedraggled duckling as it struggles out of its shell, and 24 hours later a cuddly duckling that has dried out in the sun. After the seven eggs hatch, the mother duck leads the brood to the water. They swim and learn to feed and groom instinctively, just like their parents before them. One photograph shows the drake swimming "wing" at a distance from the duck and her brood. (Ducks mate for life.) This same photograph, sans "Papa" drake, appears cropped on the back jacket.

Thematic Analysis

The birth of animals, including birds, generally elicits warm feelings among observers; youngsters are no exception. They are intrigued with the continuity of animal and avian species and ultimately their own. The factual information is an added bonus for youngsters. This title speaks directly to the birth process of egg-laying species—here the common mallard duck—and imparts intriguing information that helps youngsters to respect living creatures. This book with its photographs is the next best thing to petting a new duckling or watching it hatch. Youngsters up to age 11, or older if they have never seen this type of reproduction, can enjoy this book. Even some toddlers will be able to look at the photographs with appreciation.

Discussion Materials

This title can be presented with the front jacket illustration of the 24-hour-old duckling and a display of the photographs on pages 19–25, which visually describe the development in the egg and the eruption of the duckling from the eggshell. Follow with a brief statement that the preceding pages show how the drake and duck parents prepare for the ducklings' arrival by contentedly swimming, feeding, flying, and grooming over the summer. The following pictures also can be shown: the drake and duck flying and swimming (pp. 11–12); the nest (pp. 15–16); and the summer ducklings (p. 34).

Related Materials

Four titles can be suggested: *How to Dig a Hole to the Other Side of the World* (Harper, 1980) by Faith McNulty is a funny, yet accurate description of a young boy's journey—an extra bonus are Marc Simont's humorous and delightful illustrations; *Moonsong Lullaby* (Lothrop, 1981) by Jamake Highwater is a tale inspired by old native American legends; *Mother Crocodile* (Delacorte, 1981) by Birago Diop, adapted by Rosa Guy, is a story based on a cautionary Senegalese tale; and *Tiny Tim: Verses for Children* (Delacorte, 1982) by Helen Oxenbury is a book with a wide variety of poems. Patricia Lauber's *Volcano: The Eruption and Healing of Mount St. Helens* (Bradbury, 1986) is a mesmerizing nonfictional account, which youngsters will find fascinating.

In a series of six filmstrips, *Wild Life Families* (Random, 1986) shows how baby animals from other species are raised by their parents. The 16mm film *Money Business* (Barr Films, 1985) uses hand puppets to illustrate a young bear's adventures while earning money. The recording *For Kids Only, 2* (Howard Hanger, Jazz Fantasy, 1986) is also useful as background here.

McGovern, Ann. *Night Dive*
Photographs by Martin Scheiner and James B. Scheiner. Macmillan, 1984, 56 pp.

Well known over the three decades during which her books have appeared, this author is respected for her voluminous output of mainly nonfictional science-related titles. Eighteen of her popular titles are in print, among them several that will relate well in this book talk. This science story is about a young girl who goes night diving for the first time after a week of daily scuba diving with her marine biologist mother. The acknowledgments suggest that the locale is Tortola in the British Virgin Islands. The appealing story that surrounds the procedures and adventures during the dives is sure to be fascinating to youngsters ages 9–11 (grades 4–6). It will also be tempting to youngsters ages 8–12 (grades 3–7) who are interested in underwater diving procedures, as well as in seeing the exotic underwater creatures in the photographs.

The book is illustrated by the author's husband and son, but Ann McGovern also contributed pictures of an arrow crab (p. 12) and the eye of a squid (the last page). A scuba diving teacher in the Caribbean who has contributed underwater photographs to many national magazines, James B. Scheiner, her son, is responsible for the colorful photo of an orange ball anemone (an animal that resides in the warm sea waters) on the half-title page (also p. 49). Martin Scheiner, her husband, who used to work in medical electronics but now dives and shoots underwater pictures, contributed the majority of the photographs in the book. He is responsible for shots of such underwater life as spiny sea urchins (p. 12) and the spotted goatfish taken during the day. In addition, he took the various photographs of the young girl—dressed in her diving gear (p. 4); sitting on the boat preparing to dive (p. 9); escaping from the sea wasps and on the wreck (p. 24)—and of Jim, the diving instructor, playing with an octopus (p. 49). The photographs lend an indefinable quality to the clear, poetic text, creating an altogether wondrous experience expressive of a night dive, itself.

Scared to death before her first night dive, a 12-year-old female stands all geared up with her mother and the other divers before Jim, the diving director. Although she has been scuba diving all week off this Caribbean island with her marine biologist mother, the girl is very nervous to be out on a boat on a pitch black night all dressed and ready to dive, even though she has her "C" card, which certifies her as having proper training in diving. It was the first thing Jim had asked to see before he would even consider taking her on a night dive. The fact that she is also the required age is important, too. Paramount, however, is her mother's desire to see a certain kind of parrot fish that spins a protective cocoon around itself so that it can sleep at night.

She is all suited up in her wet suit, with her mask, air tank, regulator, buoyancy compensator, weight belt, pressure and weight gauge, underwater watch, gloves, and diving light. Her Mom also has a compass and special light sticks—that glow green—which she puts on their oxygen tanks. Jim checks the divers. They are a cosmopolitan group: grandparents Randy and Sally who have dived all over the world; Don and his friend, Jenny, a teacher; and Joe, an underwater photographer, who also carries a big strobe light. With Jim's extra light, her Mom's light sticks, and Joe's strobe, she decides maybe she'll be able to see.

Then Jim tells them to turn off the lights and get wet. As she rolls over backward from a sitting position on the side of the boat, she decides to keep her light on. She is definitely unnerved, and with good reason. It is pitch black, and she can't orient herself until she sees a light stick on her Mom's tank. She relieves the pressure on her ears by blowing out, then descends 30 feet in a minute along with the other divers.

Her first surprise is seeing the moon shining on the top of the water from her viewpoint deep underwater, and many more surprises follow. She sees sea creatures everywhere—spiny sea urchins, arrow crabs, brittle stars, and orange cup coral sponges. Then the divers turn off their lights so that they can see the tiny stars (bioluminescence) surrounding them. The fish she sees at night are different from those that she is used to during the day, like the red squirrel fish, which hides under coral ledges during the day and the slow-moving trumpet fish. Some like the blue Tang sport different day and night colors. (All appear in photographs that accompany and amplify the text.) Although she and her Mom see some parrot fish, they do not find the variety they are looking for. After an hour has elapsed, their air is almost depleted and it's time to go topside. Her fear has evaporated in this gorgeous sea world.

Just as she nears the top, however, blobs of stinging sea wasps appear. As Jim helps her get out of the water, he receives a couple of stings, but everyone else is all right. Undaunted, Jim tells everyone to be at the boat the next day at 5:00 P.M. for a special treat—a twi-night dive because dusk is such an active time on a reef. That's also when predators like shark and barracuda hunt their prey (p. 37), but in these waters one does not have to worry about them. Jim announces to universal delight that they are also going to explore the *Rhona*, one of the first iron boats and a shipwreck (1867). Most of the others already have explored the *Rhona* and are thrilled about returning.

On the first dusk dive, the girl sees many fish in the wreck, including a large sea bass that almost traps her in an enclosed space (p. 36). But during refreshments and an hour's wait topside before they go down again, she feels unsure about the next dive. Eventually her bravery returns, however, and she volunteers to be the first in the water. Once on the bottom she quickly feels like a comfortable visitor to this watery planet. One can feel very much alone here, but she knows that she is not. She looks at the unusual fish swimming around her—flamingo tongues, lizard fish, and even the parrot fish in its cocoon (pp. 44–45). When she spots the parrot fish, she signals her Mom with her light, and together they investigate the oddity. Meanwhile, Jim finds an octopus, an eel, and a squid (pp. 49–51).

Delighted with her exciting dives, the young girl finally feels relaxed. She has learned much about the changing reef and herself.

Thematic Analysis

The themes of respecting the living creatures of the sea and overcoming normal fears coexist in this simple and straightforward science story. Brief glimpses also are given of other themes, for example, the family strength in the mother-daughter relationship, diving with another person to fulfill his or her desire, and the mother's occupation, but the main themes are paramount. The healthy respect that the young girl has and develops further toward underwater creatures is interestingly presented in text and photos.

Discussion Materials

Read aloud the brief and intriguing acknowledgment on the rear jacket from a lady famous for her studies on sharks, Eugenia Clark. Follow by displaying the front cover photograph by Martin Scheiner with a brief explanation of the story line and an introduction of the heroine (pp. 1–2). The first four chapters describe the first night-dive adventures; and chapters 4–8 cover the exploration of the shipwreck and second twi-night dives. Pages to highlight are: sea wasps on the topside (pp. 23–27); the parrot fish in its cocoon (p. 47); and the shipwreck (pp. 28–39).

Related Materials

Ann McGovern's *Shark Lady: True Adventures of Eugenia Clark* (Four Winds, 1979) and Elizabeth Tayntor's *Dive to the Coral Reef: A New England Aquarium Book* (Crown, 1986) are especially useful. Other appropriate nonfiction titles are *Wonders of Sharks* (Dodd, 1984) by Wyatt Blassingame and *Digging Up Dinosaurs* (Harper, 1981) by Aliki. Three humorous and exciting fiction titles to suggest are *Isabelle Shows Her Stuff* (Viking, 1973) by Constance Greene; *Do Bananas Chew Gum?* (Lothrop, 1980) by Jamie Gilson; and *Cast a Single Shadow* (Atheneum, 1986) by Kristi D. Holl.

A video of Scott O'Dell's *The Black Pearl* (Random, 1986) can be used for the diving enthusiasts. The filmstrip *Alike and Different* (National Geographic Society, 1985), which demonstrates observational and thinking exercises in nature study, can also be used here. Two suitable films are *City of Coral* (Nova/WNET, 1982) and *Caribbean—Picture Treasures* (Kodak, 1981). The microcomputer software program (for Apple) *Science* (Opportunities for Learning, 1986) can help to develop reading skills in this content area.

Parnall, Peter. *Winter Barn*
Illus. by the author. Macmillan, 1986, 32 pp.

The author-illustrator, a prolific illustrator of more than 60 books, many of them award-winners, is deservedly famous (see *Introducing More Books*, Bowker, 1978, pp. 121–123). Three of his books were named Caldecott honor titles, and several have been cited by the *New York Times* as best illustrated books of the year for children. Parnall has also won awards from both the American Institute of Graphic Arts and the Society of Illustrators, and he has exhibited in fine art museums.

In 1984, in his debut as an author, Parnall wrote and illustrated *The Daywatchers* (Macmillan, 1984). He then published this title, a story of winter hibernation in a country barn both by the regular inhabitants and those that come inside from the woods to use it as a shelter against the cold weather. Parnall's lyrical writing both dramatizes his drawings and clearly explains many secrets about winter in a barn and the small animals that congregate there among the regular occupants. Youngsters ages 7–9 (grades 2–4), will discover many interesting facts and deepen their knowledge of seasonal changes and animal response.

The magnificent charcoal drawings are highlighted with a bit of color in wash. The large proportion of white page to charcoal sketch emphasizes the stark winter season and highlights the animals camouflaged in their crevices. The 15 double-page drawings, including the title page, chiefly portray the interior of a barn. (The text printed in 14-point Baskerville is placed variously on the top or bottom of alternate pages.) The detail sketch of a cat sitting guard at the latched barn door just above the outside drifts of snow provides an inviting welcome on the half-title page. In the title-page double spread, the same cat looks outside from the interior of the barn, changing the viewer's perspective. The reader enters the barn along with two of the animals whose tails can be seen extending from their hiding places. The last picture announces the arrival of spring with a recently hatched chick being surveyed by two lethargic, sanguine-looking animal visitors, while the text states, "New sounds come from the boards." The jacket illustration with the red barn firmly blanketed by drifting snow is breathtaking. A baby-blue sun hangs against the white winter sky over snow-covered fields that are bare except for some rocks on the stone wall and the split-rail fence.

As a warmly wrapped person enters the barn, a few animals are visible—a cat, a horse, a bobcat, sheep, and an owl. While a field mouse scurries over a beam, the many places that animals can hide from the cold become visible in an architectural-like rendering of the barn with its several levels. Chickens and more cats, even an old wasp's nest, become visible. "To most of its creatures, the barn is the world. . . . " Under the massive stones in the floor—laid by a Hessian soldier—there are many niches into which almost anything small can fit. Here, a snake and moles have found a warm place to sleep, along with the ants in the crevices, and field mice have secured a place in the underparts of the barn. Under the grain-room floor, a treasure of food, from alfalfa meal to the salty seaweed vitamins for horses or dogs, is stored.

As winter deepens, the barn becomes home to many different animals. Woodchucks sleep under the barn secured by a stone that keeps dogs from entering the space. Porcupines join the barn's inhabitants settling under rotten hay. A skunk sleeps between the floor boards during the day and goes upstairs at night to eat the food of the regular barn inhabitants—horses, sheep, chickens, and 14 cats. The skunks also eat the cat food. The cats that regularly amble around know that they can drink twice daily when the ice is chopped from the horses' trough. The barn mice are joined by some field mice chased inside by the frigid weather.

As the field mice are joined by other wild animals—bobcats, the fisher, and the great-horned owl, all fugitives from the cold—cooperation becomes a necessity. The terrible cold is a great leveler, and each animal finds its own hiding place without interference. High in the beams toward the roof, the bats that fly insect-control patrols in the summer roost and hibernate in the winter. Carpenter ants also crowd together in their wood holes waiting for the cold to abate. The coon sleeps deep in the hay unheralded to practically all. The lucky chickens keep their feet warm on the backs of the sheep, but then they are regulars. The sheep eat hay and wait for spring when it will be warm enough for shearing.

At last the icicles on the outdoor drainpipes start to melt, and chickadees sip the first drops of water. The icy cold is leaving, and spring is on the way. As the wild animals start to depart and the chicken eggs begin to hatch, a new cycle begins. The winter barn can now resume its more familiar life.

Thematic Analysis

A fundamental awareness of the slowed tempo of animal life in winter is the theme behind this unique view of northern barn life. Cooperation between the regular occupants and the wild animals that enter for protection against the frigid cold is a normal phenomenon among living creatures under harsh conditions. Aside from the book's informational content and the puzzlelike quality of the pictures—just the ticket for young nature lovers—youngsters are sure to appreciate the living creatures in this and every barn.

Discussion Materials

This title lends itself to a picture-book display, but it can also be introduced by showing certain pictures and reading aloud fragments. For example, show the full jacket illustration; introduce the 14 cats (half-title and title pages, pp. 18–19, 20–21, 22–23), reading the text with the last two pictures; and show the barn's interior (pp. 6–7), also reading the text aloud. A rebuslike identification game can be played by displaying a picture, then asking the youngsters to name the animals, for example, the most difficult ones (p. 32).

Related Materials

All of the following titles are suggested: Julia Cunningham's *Mouse Called Junction* (Pantheon, 1980), about a mouse that leaves its safe life to venture into the wild; Eva Bunting's *The Man Who Could Call Down Owls* (Macmillan, 1984), an allegorical tale about a jealous person who tries unsuccessfully to penetrate the world of owls; Priscilla Jaquith's *Bo Rabbit Smart for True: Folktales from the Gullah*, four seriocomic stories about the clever hero, with pictures by Ed Young; Llywelyn Morgan's *The Horse Goddess* (Houghton, 1982), about the self-imposed exile of the daughter of a Celtic chief; and the same author's *Grania: She-King of the Irish Seas* (Crown, 1986), a fictionalized biographical account of a famous Irish queen who tried to preserve her lands from Queen Elizabeth.

The following are suitable videos: *Meet Your Animal Friends* (Video Learning Systems, 1983, 4 vols., ea. 20 min.) contains 23 live-action animal segments with captions and a voice-over narration by Lynn Redgrave; *The Beaver* (Phoenix/BFA, 1985, 25 min.) treats the characteristic behavior of these animals noted for their building skills; and *One's a Heifer* (Beacon Films, 1986, 26 min.) is a live-action search for two lost calves by a young boy. Two 16mm films are also suggested: *Pigbird* (National Film Board of Canada, 1985) and *Katura and the Cat* (Perspective Films, 1983). *Faces: The Magazine about People* (Cobblestone Publ., 1986) is a natural history magazine for children launched with the cooperation of the American Museum of Natural History (New York) that concentrates on many topics in anthropology and natural history.

Paulsen, Gary. *Dogsong*
Bradbury, 1985, 177 pp.

This title by Gary Paulsen was named a Newbery Honor Book in 1986. The author, who lives with his family in Minnesota, is a sports enthusiast. He has written 11 nonfiction books for middle-graders that are currently in print on various sports, for example, *Pummeling, Falling, and Getting Up—Sometimes* (Raintree, 1979) with photographs by Heinz Kletmeier and Joe DiMaggio, which is recommended for ages 9–11 (grades 4–6).

Many of the titles were written in the seventies. In the eighties, Paulsen published the fiction titles *Dancing Carl; Tracker;* and *Sentries* (all Bradbury, 1983, 1984, 1986).

This title mirrors the author's interest in and knowledge of dogsledding and Eskimo ways, both historical and current. In a unique poetic story, an Eskimo youngster recaptures many of his people's ancient ways, as well as his own song, on a trek through northern Alaska. It is a gritty "rite of passage" story, suffused with the beauty of its poetic writing and a dreamlike quality. Youngsters ages 10–12 (grades 5–7) will find the strange survival techniques fascinating and the dream sequences and other glimpses into ancient ways gripping.

The book is separated into three parts: The Trance; The Dreamrun; and Dogsong. Russel's own seven-stanza Eskimo poem—earned through his trek—concludes the final pages. The old Eskimo way of assigning a song is similar to "naming" or finding one's identity. The book is dedicated to an Eskimo to honor her song. The first part covers Russel's discovery at the hands of the elder, Oogruk, of what he must do to assuage his discontent with the new ways. Each of the five chapters in this part begins with a restatement of an old Eskimo saying.

The Dreamrun, or Part 2, consists of chapters 6–14, of which chapter 14 is also entitled "The Dreamrun." Alternating chapters, beginning with chapter 7 and ending with chapter 13, are "time slips" that foreordain for Russel events similar to those his ancient-self ancestor underwent. Carefully constructed and poetically written, the words mimic the quality of ancient Eskimo legends and lore. "Dogsong," Russel's song, is the short poem that concludes the book. The striking and strong full-color front jacket painting by Neil Waldman portrays a stylized young Eskimo in his hooded parka with a small silhouetted image of a dogsled pulled by five running dogs.

Russel Susskit lives in an Alaskan village with his father in a standard government house during the winter. In the summer they move to the fishcamps. (His mother left with a white trapper years ago.) Russel who is 14 is unhappy with everything. He detests the cigarettes that his father constantly smokes (and his coughing), the holy pictures that his religious father has hung everywhere, the rose-patterned oilcloth on the table, and most of all the snow machines that all Eskimos use nowadays instead of traditional dogs. Only old Oogruk has any dogs left, but they haven't run for a long time because of Oogruk's advanced age.

As father and son eat—Russel eats old style (the meat is raw or partially cooked), but both still use an ulu (short curved knife) to cut the seal meat extending from their lips—they talk about Russel's discontent. Father explains that part of the discontent comes because of Russel's age and the rest from their heritage—something he doesn't understand. He tells his son that Russel's grandfather died walrus hunting on the ice when he was very young. He suggests that Russel talk to Oogruk, who is old and sometimes wise and tells him that Oogruk's words are sometimes shaky, but his songs are always true. Father also suggests that Russel take seals' heads as a treat for Oogruk because he loves the eyes.

Oogruk lives the old way: his five dogs and sleds just outside; seal-oil lamps for light; caribou skins on the floors; and a small breechclout for indoor clothing. Russel enters in the usual Eskimo way without knocking. The home reflects old Eskimo style: walls decorated with harpoons, lances, arrowbags and bows, squirrel-skin undergarments, caribou-skin parkas thick with smoke, and everything oiled and in good condition. The old milk-blind man enjoys his feast of seal eyes, which most Eskimos discard these days. Afterward, in a relaxed state from the warmth and food, Russel sinks into a trancelike state, while Oogruk drones on about how things were in the old days.

Soon Russel moves in with Oogruk and learns many things. He makes practice runs with the dogsled; he follows Oogruk's advice on shooting, "Look 'inside' the center"; and he understands the old Eskimo belief on killing animals for food, "It is because the animal wishes to be taken then." Russel hunts caribou, deer, and seal (and is trapped temporarily on the ice). He begins to hear his song starting spontaneously.

Finally Oogruk leaves with him on a seal hunt to await his imminent death on the ice in the old Eskimo way. He tells Russel to run long with the dogs to find himself and his song. Reluctantly Russel leaves Oogruk, and when he returns he finds the old man sitting with legs outstretched on the ice in the old Eskimo way and smiling in death.

As Russel heads north across the ice, he eventually turns east toward the land feeling confident, because he has weapons, dogs, a sled, and the land. He travels hard trying to establish a rhythm. Finally, after eating, Russel makes a tent shelter where he and the dogs all sleep together comfortably, for the first time since leaving Oogruk. During this sleep, Russel has a series of dreams in which he sees himself as an early ancestor. (Eventually Russel finds himself in a similar situation with only the animals changed over the eons of time.) In the first dream, a woman and two children, fat and sleek, are left in a skin tent by a hunter who sets off with his wolves (dogs) to hunt a woolly mammoth for food for his family. When Russel sees the hunter's face, it is himself. The next day on the tundra in his camp, Russel digs up an old stone lamp, much older than Oogruk's. As he falls asleep, he continues dreaming. The hunter returns to his ancient Eskimo village with his kill, the woolly mammoth, and the celebration lasts for many days as they sing of kayaks and walrus, and dance until exhausted.

Russel rides out a two-day storm in his tent, then continues his trek, for as Oogruk taught, "It isn't the destination that counts. It is the journey." The dogs pick up and follow the tracks of a snow machine. They run long and hard. Russel is so tired that he hallucinates. He sees his dream man trying to get home while the woman and children lay starving. The woman fingers a strangulation cord as she wipes the children's lips with the last drop of rancid lamp oil. In full consciousness, Russel finds a half-frozen pregnant girl, Nancy, near the snow machine she had taken to come out on the tundra to die. Waiting for her to regain consciousness in the tent he makes, Russel sleeps and dreams for the fourth and final time on this trek. He dreams that there is no settlement; only two human bones remain and a stone lamp, which a fox carries off and buries. Only the hunter and sled stand where the tent had been. Russel is now sure that he is an extension of that hunter.

When he awakens, Russel discovers that the young woman is awake and going to survive. Although Nancy loses her still-born baby, she eats some meat from the polar bear that Russel is able to kill. Then they head for a coastal settlement to get her medical attention. Russel is satisfied. He has completed a journey of discovery and now has a working knowledge of running a dogsled, living off the harsh Arctic land, discovering old Eskimo ways, saving Nancy, and himself.

Thematic Analysis

The important themes here are self-discovery, surviving under extreme conditions, and an understanding of traditional ways. The poetic expression of an old culture makes exciting reading, with the traditional Eskimo respect for living creatures shining throughout brilliantly. The respect for the tight web of the Arctic ecosystem is well shown in this eloquently expressed story of a boy caught within the mechanisms of change within an ancient culture (pp. 43–44).

Discussion Materials

The book can be introduced by using its three parts as natural divisions. First introduce the main character, then paraphrase the setting and the preparation for the journey (pp. 1–75, read aloud pp. 30–32). Next, paraphrase the "dream" (chapters 7, 9, 11 ,13) and suggest that Russel's journey parallels it. Finally, read aloud the "Dogsong" poetry (pp. 175–177). Another interesting "book talk" would be a concentration on the "old ways" (some examples are pp. 9, 11, 13–18, 19–29, 31, 32–35, 42, 43–44, and 47); Russel's training in running a dogsled (pp. 34–39); and killing a large polar bear for food (pp. 156–161).

Related Materials

Five titles to suggest are: *Wind Is Not a River* (Crowell, 1978) by Arnold Griese, which tells about two Eskimo children who report their Aleutian Island capture by the Japanese in 1942; *A Time to Keep Silent* (Putnam, 1980) by Gloria Whelan, about a girl and her father who move to Upper Michigan after her mother's death; *Tales Mummies Tell* (Crowell, 1985) by Patricia Lauber, which relates information about mummies, including a woolly mammoth; *Secret in the Stlalakum Wild* (Atheneum, 1972) by Christie Harris, which explores a young girl's discovery of the Indian "wisdom of the wild" in British Columbia; and *Goodbye, My Island* (Greenwillow, 1983) by Jean Rogers, which tells about an Eskimo's last winter on King Island in the Bering Strait before she and her people are relocated to the mainland.

Both a cassette and two filmstrips of *Dogsong* are available (Random, 1986). Another recommended recording, *Julie of the Wolves* (Caedmon, 1978), is a good counterpart to this title with its female main character. A kit of Jack London's *Call of the Wild* (Listening Library, 1971) can be used; a recording of the title is also available from Caedmon. The video *Solitudes* (Phoenix, 1986) is suggested from the series Profiles of Nature. Four filmstrips are especially useful: *Eskimo Legends* (Spoken Arts, 1986); *The Arctic Through Eskimo Eyes* (Random, 1986, 4 fs); *Matthew Aliuk: Eskimo in Two Worlds* (SVE, 1979) from The Many Americans series; and *Me Power: Building Self Confidence* (Sunburst, 1985), winner of the National Education Association festival. The latter is also available in video.

Rogers, Jean. *The Secret Moose*
Illus. by Jim Fowler. Greenwillow, 1985, 64 pp.

Jean Rogers, who lives in Juneau, Alaska, wrote three children's books for Greenwillow in 1983 and 1985, including *Goodbye My Island* and *King Island Christmas*. The former title, which received the Alaska State Reading Association Award, is recommended for grades 5–7, the latter for grades 3–5. The highlighted title is for children ages 8–11 (grades 3–5). The story treats a few weeks in the life of a boy who finds a wounded moose in his Alaskan backyard. He cares for the cow until she gives birth to a calf and they move on. The book dispenses a great deal of information about moose in a satisfying story that young people will like. The author's writing is crisp and clear, resulting in an easy book for youngsters to read. They will also be aided by the large type size.

Jim Fowler, who also lives in Juneau, Alaska, has always been interested in wildlife. He drew many soft pencil sketches for this title, including a detail of the moose's face and a decoration of birds on a leafing willow branch. The 17 appealing drawings of the main characters and the moose include four full-page drawings; two of the moose and two of the other central characters, one of which extends onto the facing page. Two of them are three-fourths of a page; the majority of the main characters are full page. Two unusual drawings are half-page double spreads that lend an extended view of the horizon. A full-color drawing on both sides of the jacket shows the young hero on his hands and knees in the snow staring at a large, sanguine-looking moose that is lying in a clump of early leafing willows. The appealing drawing states the book's mood perfectly, and youngsters ages 8–11 (grades 3–5) will be enchanted by it.

As Gerald Perry, about ten, sits at the breakfast table with his parents and older sister, Anita, eating his oatmeal, he sees a moose loping through his snow-covered yard. Although not an uncommon sight in Gold Stream Valley where he lives in Fairbanks, Alaska, Gerald is quietly excited. He keeps the sighting his own private secret, not believing his good luck in hiding it from Anita, about 13, who always seems to know or find out everything. His Dad leaves for work, as does his Mom, who works at the Fairbanks Public Library. Anita feeds and waters her pony, Charcoal, in the barn down by the stream. Then she and Gerald go off to school on the bus.

After school on this early May day, Gerald can hardly wait to go out and investigate, never expecting to find the moose, but delighted that it can be kept a secret. Gulping down his gingersnaps, while Anita has her daily ride on Charcoal for the brief time the seasonal light will permit, Gerald sets out to follow the moose. He starts tracking where he saw the moose disappear near the wide, shallow stream behind the barn. Losing the tracks, he almost gives up, but then decides to try one of the islands in the middle of the stream that he and his friend used as a camp last summer. Getting to the high island is difficult through the slushy snow and melting ice. In a thicket among the budding willows lays the huge moose. Although the moose doesn't move, it does open an eye to survey Gerald, then closes it. Gerald notices an ugly blood-encrusted gash on the moose's flank, and he becomes very concerned: First, about hunters, even though it isn't fall, and also about how to help the animal.

Gerald goes home and calls his Mom and asks her to bring home a couple of books about moose from the library. She does, and as he spends the evening reading about the species he learns that this moose is a female cow—she has no antlers—how moose respond when angry or annoyed, and their feeding habits. He watches the moose eat the surrounding willow stems, but the books say that they need to eat a large quantity. On Wednesday, Anita's late afternoon at 4-H, when Gerald usually rides Charcoal for her, he gives the moose the carrot and apple he usually brings to Charcoal, at least the core. Getting the apple core to the moose without getting too near her is difficult, but Gerald is correctly cautious. He extends the apple core on a willow branch, but when she eats the branch Gerald gives up and decides to feed her willow branches instead.

Each day Gerald spends all his free time cutting willow branches and piling them on a rake to deliver them to the seated moose. At first he gets tangled in the bushes, but after determined effort he manages to feed her each day for four days. Because he smells so strongly of willow, his mother suggests that he scrub down well. Between reading his favorite book, *Deneki* (Indian for "moose"), cutting willow branches, and getting them to the moose, Gerald devotes every spare moment to the moose for four days. Meanwhile, he asks his Mom if he can have the book *Deneki*.

The next day he returns to find the moose standing, foraging further along the stream, followed by her new calf. Gerald knows at a glance that if he had been minutes earlier he would have seen the birth. He watches for as long as he can, as the calf suckles and the moose moves slowly

196 · INTRODUCING BOOKPLOTS 3

along the stream. Then he picks up his shears, rake, and log carrier and splashes home across the melted snow. That evening Gerald's Mom informs him that his book is out of print, but that her friend Margaret thinks she has a copy for him.

The next day Gerald goes back to the island after school hoping to say "goodbye" to the moose and her calf, but knowing deep down that they have gone upstream foraging, as traveling moose do. (His book has a map that charts their foraging range, of which the Perry property is a part.) Disappointed, yet refreshed at having had a wondrous experience he is pleased that evening to receive Margaret's present of *Deneki*, dually inscribed "To Bobby from Aunt Helen, Christmas 1967" and "A good book never dies, just gets passed on. For Gerald from Margaret, 1985."

Thematic Material

This title, which will appeal to young nature lovers, has a dual theme: One theme is a healthy respect for living creatures and the second is the self-worth that helping another species on the planet can bring. Along the way it is full of practical information about moose that is fascinating for all, but especially for youngsters in the Northwest and Alaska. A youngster's love of tracking at this age is also important here. The strong connection between learning from books and carrying out the activity is essential.

Discussion Materials

Displaying the full jacket painting showing the two main characters, Gerald and the moose, should be sufficient to arouse interest, followed by a brief retelling of the story line (pp. 7–15; picture pp. 8–9). Or the book can be presented through the drawings: the moose (frontispiece, pp. 14, 39, 51–52); Gerald (pp. 12, 20, 22, 26–27, 32, 35, 36–37, 40, 42); with Anita (pp. 46, 56); with Mom (pp. 60–61, 64); and *Deneki* (p. 63). A special episode that deserves book talking is feeding the moose (pp. 31, 45; picture p. 23).

Related Materials

Here are some good titles: *Buffalo: The American Bison Today* (Clarion, 1986) by Dorothy Hinshaw Patent, a nonfictional account; *Every Living Thing* (Bradbury, 1985) by Cynthia Rylant, short stories about the changed lives of people through relationships with animals; and *Cowboys of the Wild West* (Clarion, 1985) by Russell Freedman, a nonfictional account of nineteenth-century cowboys. Three appealing stories are: Mary A. Whitely's *A Circle of Light* (Walker, 1983); Isabelle Holland's *A Horse Named Peaceable* (Lothrop, 1982); and Charlotte Graeber's *Grey Cloud* (Four Winds, 1979).

Four 16mm films to use are: *Animal Populations: Nature's Checks and Balances* (Encyclopaedia Britannica, 1984); *The Day the Universe Changed: A Personal View by James Burke* (Churchill Films, 1986); *Critter the Raccoon* (International Film Bureau, 1982); and *I'm a Mammal and So Are You* (Benchmark, 1981). The video *The Vancouver Island Marmot* (Phoenix/ BFA, 1986) is also suggested. A recording of *Animal Stories* (Caedmon, 1982) by Walter de la Mare is available, as is Jean Craighead George's filmstrip *Snow Tracks* from the Random Nature series. The ALA poster "Curious George" (No. 159) is a great one to use with this title.

Respecting Living Creatures: Additional Titles

Ancona, George. *Sheep Dog.* Illus. by the author. Lothrop, 1985, 64 pp. (Gr. 4–6)
Anderson, Norman D., and Brown, Walter R. *Lemurs.* Illus. with photographs. Dodd, 1984, 64 pp. (Gr. 3–6)
Branscum, Robbie. *Murder of Hound Dog Bates.* Viking, 1982, 90 pp. (Gr. 5–6)
Calvert, Patricia. *Hour of the Wolf.* Scribner, 1983, 147 pp. (Gr. 5–6)
Cobb, Vicki. *More Science Experiments You Can Eat.* Illus. by Giulio Maestro. Lippincott, 1980, 126 pp. (Gr. 3–5)
Crystals: Flowers of the Mineral Kingdom. Film, 13 min. Stanton Films, 1983. (Gr. 4–6)
Dixon, Paige. *Walk My Way.* Atheneum, 1980, 139 pp. (Gr. 5–6)
Freddy the Detective by Walter R. Brooks, read by Pat Carroll. Recording, 2s. Caedmon, 1982. (Gr. 3–6)
Haas, Dorothy. *The Secret Life of Dilly McBean.* Bradbury, 1986, 224 pp. (Gr. 5–7)
Heide, Florence Parry. *Treehorn's Treasure.* Drawings by Edward Gorey. Holiday, 1981, 64 pp. (Gr. 3–6)
Hermes, Patricia. *Who Will Take Care of Me?* Harcourt, 1983, 99 pp. (Gr. 3–6)
King, Clive. *Me and My Million.* Crowell, 1979, 180 pp. (Gr. 4–6)
King of the Wind by Marguerite Henry. Recording, 2s. Random, 1971. (Gr. 4–6)
Klass, David. *The Atami Dragons.* Scribner, 1984, 144 pp. (Gr. 4–6)
Kulkin, Susan. *Mine for a Year.* Photos by the author. Coward, 1984, 80 pp. (Gr. 4–6)
Lassie Come Home by Eric Knight. Recording, 2s. Caedmon, 1973. (Gr. 4–6)
Le Guin, Ursula K. *Leese Webster.* Illus. by James Brunsman. Atheneum, 1979, o.p. (Gr. 3–5)
Lights, Action, Africa! Film, 55 min. Benchmark Films, 1983. (Gr. 5–up)

Michel, Anna. *The Story of Nim: The Chimp Who Learned Language.* Photos by Susan Kulkin and Herbert S. Terrace. Knopf, 1980, 72 pp. (Gr. 4–6)

Nixon, Joan Lowery. *Magnolia's Mixed-Up Magic.* Illus. by Linda Bucholtz-Ross. Putnam, 1983, 43 pp. (Gr. 2–4)

Noguere, Suzanne, and Chen, Tony. *Little Koala.* Illus. by Tony Chen. Holt, 1980, 32 pp. (Gr. 2–4)

Rabbit Hill by Robert Lawson. Recording, 2s. Live Oak Media, 1972. (Gr. 4–6)

Rikki-Tikki-Tavi and Wee Willie Winkie read by Anthony Quayle. Recording, 2s. Caedmon, 1980. (Gr. 4–6)

Rodowsky, Colby. *Evy-Ivy-Over.* Watts, 1978, 153 pp. (Gr. 4–6)

Rounds, Glen. *Blind Outlaw.* Illus. by the author. Holiday, 1980, 94 pp. (Gr. 4–7)

Taylor, Theodore. *Trouble with Tuck.* Doubleday, 1981, 110 pp. (Gr. 4–6)

Yates, Elizabeth. *Seventh One.* Illus. by Diana Charles. Walker, 1978, 148 pp. (Gr. 5–6)

7

Understanding Social Problems

IN spite of continuing adult controversy over the advisability of children confronting social concerns at ever earlier ages, youngsters do it. They are not immune to the world's tremendous amount and transfer of information, and with it the increased visibility of social issues. A youngster's ability to deal with urgent social topics depends on age, experience, mental organization, and other factors. For those who are just learning to think abstractly—after finally feeling comfortable with concrete thinking—the introduction to social issues can be an intriguing yet difficult stretch—easier for some than for others. Although they may be somewhat confused by the seeming contradictions between adults' words and actions, middle-graders are generally able to respond by modifying their plans and making their own decisions. A vicarious introduction to some of society's problems can extend these capabilities and help middle-graders evaluate their own beliefs and behavior.

The books in this chapter treat social, economic, and political issues in contemporary society. Some highlight more than one important concern of a social issue illustrating their complexity; others stress interpersonal relationships within these issues. Two books deal with an ethnic group; two with social injustices as old as humanity. Four books treat issues that are receiving increasing societal attention; one offers a historically recurring solution to political concerns. There are no new social concerns, only those that seem new to today's society.

Adler, C. S.   *Fly Free*
Coward, 1984, 159 pp.

Since 1979 the author has published 18 books, the latest for middle-graders, *Split Sisters* (Macmillan, 1986). Her first title, *The Magic of the Glits* (Macmillan, 1979), received both the Golden Kite and the William

Allen White awards. In her latest novels she uses her full name, Carole S. Adler. This prolific author is popular with youngsters; she writes about their reaction to current topics. A former middle-school teacher and mother of three sons, she interprets the thoughts and actions of the young person knowingly and with compassion. She simplifies and highlights the important points that are recognizably familiar to the reader. Her easy prose appeals to reluctant readers, while dealing with topics that are highly interesting to older youngsters as well as middle-graders.

In *Fly Free,* a withdrawn, abused heroine who hopes to fly away like the birds learns that the one adult she loves is not her natural father. Although this at first leads to a confrontation, the story ends with a hopeful solution. Youngsters age 9–12 (grades 4–7) will find the story compelling. The full-color jacket painting by Troy Howell portraying the heroine and her young brother walking solemnly through the Vermont woods will appeal to female readers.

Tall and skinny for 13, Shari, who lives in Vermont, is the only girl in the Lally family. Twelve-year-old Doug, an entrepreneur, and 11-year-old Walter, an inveterate reader, although different are inseparable. Their parents, Zeke, a long-distance truck driver, and Charlotte, a neurotic housewife, are another pair, at least when Zeke is home. That leaves six-year-old Peter (Petey) who is Shari's constant companion. Shari is expected to take constant care of Petey, but the quiet girl does not mind, both because she loves him and because she can also feel like they, too, are a pair.

When Zeke is home, the family has some semblance of normalcy. He calms Charlotte, and she responds well to his catering. Zeke also makes Shari feel good; and she looks forward to his coming home. Unfortunately, he isn't home often. When he is away, Shari lives in a perpetual state of apprehension, waiting for her mother to slap, pinch, or hit her, or abuse her verbally. Shari has always been shy, but Charlotte's cruel name calling has made her even quieter. She speaks softly trying to be invisible.

During one of Zeke's summer hauling trips, Shari takes Petey into the woods on one of her favorite bird-watching trips. Shari finds solace in watching the birds fly. They make her feel free. (Last summer Shari had a parakeet, but Charlotte, who hates all animals, deliberately released it.) As Shari climbs the steep embankment, Petey so admires his sister's climbing agility that he tells a stranger that she can jump and fly. (She can at least jump!) When they reach their favorite spot in the ravine,

Petey starts to "pan gold," a favorite game. Shari finds a beautiful little crystal bird and also sees a lady release a sparrow hawk into the wild. (She knows from local gossip that it must be Mrs. (Eve) Wallace, the new neighbor.) To Petey's surprise, the last thing she says as they prepare to leave is that she would like to be a pilot.

When they return home, like a typical six-year-old Petey tells Charlotte about the crystal bird. Charlotte thinks that Mrs. Wallace must have lost it and tells Shari to ask her for a reward. But Shari can't do it. Instead, she leaves it at Mrs. Wallace's cabin door. Meanwhile, Charlotte's girlfriend, Bee Jay, the beauty parlor co-owner, takes them for a swim—everyone, that is, but Shari and Petey, who won't get in the car because he is afraid of Bee Jay's dog. When the car pulls off without them, Shari feels sorry for the wailing Petey. Although the house is locked, she pacifies him by telling him they'll "pan gold" and ask Mrs. Wallace for food. Mrs. Wallace who is pleased by the return of her sentimental treasure welcomes them.

Then Zeke comes home, and Charlotte prepares a belated birthday party for him. Unpredictably, Charlotte doesn't follow her usual pattern of leaving Shari alone. Zeke doesn't protect her, as usual, so Shari runs to the woods. There she finds Mrs. Wallace bird-watching. Shari shows the older woman an eagle's nest and they spend some pleasant time together. When they encounter Sue Ellen Braverman and her sisters trying to release their stuck cow, it brings back bitter memories to Shari. Although their mothers were childhood enemies, Sue Ellen and Shari decided to be friends in first grade. The friendship lasted until third grade when Sue Ellen guessed that the bruises on Shari's arm were caused by her mother and told everyone in class. Since then, they have been distant. Happily, Mrs. Wallace agrees that Sue Ellen is "prickly."

Soon after, Mabel, the owner of the country store, delivers a parakeet to Shari from their mutual friend Eve Wallace and arranges with Charlotte to let Shari keep it. Shari names the parakeet Blue Boy and checks the window screen carefully. On repeated visits with Eve Wallace, Shari discusses her family circumstances and her interest in learning to be a pilot. Mrs. Wallace tells Shari about volunteering in the bird-banding census. She also visits Charlotte to tell her about bird-banding and to leave pamphlets for Shari.

A few days later Charlotte tells Shari that Mrs. Wallace came visiting. Soon afterward Shari, with Charlotte's permission (Petey wants to stay home), has a satisfying three-hour visit with Eve Wallace. On her way home from Mrs Wallace's, Shari finds Petey lying unconscious in the ravine. After making sure he is alive, she runs home to tell Charlotte and to get help. Although Charlotte tells her to stay and wait for Doug and Walter, Shari runs back to try to help him. The emergency team arrives and takes the unconscious boy to the hospital in an ambulance accompanied by Charlotte.

When Charlotte returns home hours later, she accuses Shari of leaving Petey and won't let the distraught girl go to the hospital. Shari retorts by saying that at least Zeke loves her. Then Charlotte yells back that Zeke is not her father and pushes Shari so hard that she hits her head against a kitchen cabinet. Although her daughter is bleeding Charlotte hurriedly leaves to go to the hospital. Shari goes to Mabel's store for some milk and faints. As Mabel drives her home, she tells Shari that Charlotte was a "goody-goody" when she was a child growing up in her grandparents' home, but became "wild" in her early teens.

Although Shari is in need of attention, she is too proud to accept it from Mabel. Later, however, she stumbles to Eve Wallace's home. The older woman listens as she washes away the blood and tries to comfort Shari by imparting some wisdom. She offers Shari a bedroom—just like her granddaughters'—and the crystal bird to keep. Mabel can scarcely believe that Shari is abused, but Eve assures her it's true.

Feeling contrite, Charlotte later tells Shari about her strict upbringing, about Shari's pilot father who died skydiving before Shari was born; and that Zeke married her knowing about her pregnancy. But most important to Shari, Zeke explains that she is his daughter and he loves her. Shari is willing to try again! Best of all, Petey comes home safe and sound.

Thematic Analysis

Child abuse is complex. To the victim, the physical and emotional pain can be overwhelming. One of the many manifestations of this prevalent social problem is well described here. The heroine's need for parental love and approbation is further complicated when she finds out that the one adult whose approval sustains her is not her biological father. The bond of love between the two "outsiders," Shari and Petey, is also an affecting theme. Overall, the story holds out hope for the heroine and the reader.

Discussion Materials

After displaying the jacket, introduce the Lally family from Vermont—Shari, 13; Doug, 12; Walter, 11; Peter (Petey), 6; Charlotte, 32;

and Zeke, the eldest. Paraphrase the story line to Shari's first knowledge that Zeke is not her father (pp. 9–18). Introduce the friends, Mabel and Eve Wallace, and Charlotte's girlfriends, Bee Jay and Lina, through the episodes, highlighting: Shari's love of birds and flying (pp. 11–14, 19, 25, 48–54, 71–79, 90–94, 97–99, 116–120, 149–151); panning for gold (pp. 20–27); Charlotte and her girlfriend Lina converse (pp. 28–33); Bee Jay and the swimming trip (pp. 44–48); the old and new parakeet (pp. 39–41, 84–88, 96–98, 115–117, 134, 158); when Zeke is home (pp. 58–59); Eve Wallace (pp. 76–79); Mabel's store (pp. 82–84); the crystal bird (pp. 34–37, 40–44, 56, 64–65, 122–123, 134, 138); and finding the unconscious Petey (pp. 101–105).

Related Materials

Some other titles are: *It Must've Been the Fish Sticks* (Holiday, 1982) by Betty Bates; *Boy Who Wanted a Family* (Harper, 1980) by Shirley Gordon; *In the Circle of Time* (Knopf, 1980) by Margaret J. Anderson; *An Orphan for Nebraska* (Atheneum, 1980) by Joy Talbot; *That's One Ornery Orphan* (Morrow, 1980) by Patricia Beatty; and *Anna to the Infinite Power* (Scribner, 1981) by Mildred Ames. For sophisticated readers suggest: *Poisoned Web* (St. Martin's, 1982) by Anna Clarke and *Clan of the Cave Bear* (Crown, 1980) by Jean Auel. Two nonfiction books are also suggested: *The Children We Remember* (Greenwillow, 1986) by Chana Byers Abells and *The Handbook for Latch-key Children and Their Parents* (Arbor, 1983) by Lynette Long and Thomas Long.

Two suitable recordings are: *Christmas Carol*, available from Caedmon, and *Blue Willow*, from Live Oak Media. Two are suggested films: *Home, Sweet Homes: Kids Talk about Joint Custody* (Filmakers Library, 1983, 20 min.) and *All Summer in a Day* (Learning Corp., 1983, 25 min.).

Avi.   *The Fighting Ground*
Lippincott, 1984, 157 pp.

This prolific, award-winning author has written more than a dozen books; 14 are in print. Avi is also a librarian and the father of two sons, to whom he dedicated this story about two harrowing days in the life of a young lad during the American Revolution. Although the youngster initially wants to fight like his older brother and his father (before he was lamed), his first skirmish and subsequent capture by three Hessian soldiers convince him that fighting is a complex adult political solution, and that it is more important to make informed choices. Youngsters ages 10–12 (grades 5–7) will enjoy this taut adventure story and be stirred by the emotional struggle about fighting that ensues within the hero, as happens with many youngsters.

Ellen Thompson's arresting jacket illustration portrays the hero held with an arm lock around the neck by the oldest Hessian outside the open cabin door. On either side stands another Hessian ready to raise his bayonet against the band of American volunteers. The bright colors of the military costumes are striking against the nighttime background and suggest the adventure within. The artist also drew a full-page frontispiece in pen and ink with ink wash showing the young hero carrying his younger sister through the field.

The story's tightly organized structure adds to its suspense and fast pace. The book is divided into two parts representing the two days that circumscribe the story: April 3, 1778 (pp. 3–123) and April 4, 1778 (pp. 125–152). Each part is further subdivided by chronology (time heads which monitor the events): April 3, 1778 from 9:58 A.M. to 11:50 P.M. and April 4, 1778 from 12:30 P.M. to 10:30 A.M. The glossary, "The German Translated," which is referenced chronologically by the time heads, translates the German speech of the Hessian soldiers from the time they capture the hero until they are killed: April 3 (3:47 P.M.) to April 4 (5:50 A.M.).

Thirteen-year-old Jonathan lives on a New Jersey farm with his parents and younger brother and sister. His older brother is soldiering under General Washington in Pennsylvania in this second year of the American Revolution. His Pa, who fought during the winter near Philadelphia, returned home lame to do the spring planting. Jonathan is surrounded by war and its ferment on the family farm 20 miles north of Trenton, a city that General Washington won two years ago.

From local talk Jonathan well knows the fear of the German-speaking Hessian mercenaries, as well as the anger toward those Loyalists who side with the British. He daydreams constantly of taking up a gun and fighting just like his brother and father. He also sees himself in the fancy New Jersey uniform sporting a blue jacket with red facing, wearing white leggings, and carrying a beautiful new gun. Meanwhile, he has to content himself with helping his father with the farm labor and listening for the warning bell that calls men to arms from the tavern where the volunteers drill 1½ miles away.

When the bell tolls at mid-morning on April 3, 1778, Jonathan and Pa are hoeing the field. After a moment, Pa sends Jonathan to the house to see if anyone has come with news. As Jonathan turns to go, Pa in a severe tone of voice tells him not to go any further. Father and son lock eyes briefly, and Jonathan is dismayed to see fear in his father's glance. Jonathan quickly goes to the house and gets permission from his perplexed mother to go to the tavern. As he rushes off toward the tavern, he scarcely hears his mother's admonition to come right back.

When Jonathan arrives at the tavern, he finds the corporal sitting on his horse, trying to gather some men to head off the rebels who are coming up the road from Pennington seven miles south. Only 15 volunteers have appeared by the time the corporal says they have to be off, so the corporal conscripts the willing Jonathan who borrows the tavern keeper's musket, promising to return it. Some of the men wonder what happened to the Snydertown men that the corporal said were coming and what brought out the Snydertown Committee for Public Safety, but they set out to face the enemy—now estimated at 25 by the corporal.

As the volunteers march to Rocktown, where the corporal plans to engage the enemy, Jonathan struggles to hoist the large musket, which he can't carry on his shoulder like the others. He meets a man who served with his father in Philadelphia and discovers that some of the men consider the corporal too eager to fight. Jonathan, however, thinks he is strong and forceful. By mid-afternoon the Hessians come marching along the road heralded by military music. Ordered to load their muskets and fire in alternate rows at 250 yards, the volunteers do their level best, but utter confusion ensues. After struggling clumsily to load his gun, Jonathan fires and starts to reload. In the smoke and confusion, Jonathan suddenly finds himself alone with the Hessians' bayonets pointed directly at him.

Jonathan spins about and runs. He hides in the woods in terror, but by 4:00 P.M. he is captured by three German-speaking Hessians. By 6:00 P.M. they are back on the road where the skirmish took place. After waiting out a rainstorm, they bring him to an empty log house. Thoughts of escape enter Jonathan's mind, but he feels helpless—a failure to the volunteers and dependent on the Hessians. Jonathan discovers a silent little boy in the house and when he milks the cow he finds the boy's dead parents outside. He tries to bury the parents while the little boy sleeps nearby, but makes little headway until he convinces the oldest Hessian to send the youngest soldier out to help. When they all go to sleep after the burial, the old Hessian ties himself to Jonathan with a rope, but Jonathan observes calmly that he can untie the knot.

By 8:45 P.M. Jonathan has his musket aimed at the Hessians to kill them, but he can't do it. In despair over his failure, he flees carrying the sleeping boy. By midnight he sees a fire and finds eight of his former companions, including the corporal. He tells them everything. When the little boy answers the Frenchman among them in his native tongue, he promises to take the child and find his older brother in the army. Jonathan also learns from the corporal that the volunteers had held off the Hessians, except for the three who pursued Jonathan. The corporal wants him to take them back to the house to see if the Hessians are still sleeping. Not wanting to kill the Hessians, and suspecting that the corporal and the Snydertown Committee for Public Safety are probably responsible for the French couple's deaths, Jonathan feels confused. Nevertheless, he goes with them.

At midnight the volunteers wait outside, while Jonathan looks inside the log house, not expecting that Jonathan will rouse the Hessians. When he does, the old Hessian frantically grabs him around the throat. As the four emerge amid a volley of shots, Jonathan miraculously dives into the cabin. The Hessians die outside the door, their uniforms torn and dirty now. The corporal sends Jonathan back into the house for the musket he borrowed, but Jonathan, in a rage, splinters the gun against the fireplace.

By the time they get back to the tavern Jonathan, who continues to walk homeward, is sadder and wiser. Although the corporal, whom Jonathan considers a brave man, calls Jonathan brave, Jonathan knows now about complexities that he never dreamed existed. In two short days, he knows a little more about the Loyalists, the Hessians, and the volunteers. Jonathan also knows now that the fear he saw in Pa's eyes was not for Pa, but for him. He is grateful to be home "and alive."

Thematic Analysis

The complexities involved in what at first seems a simple solution is the primary theme of this subtle adventure story. The youngster's strong urge to be patriotic and to settle things by fighting, though natural at this age, denies the differences among people and the complexity of their values, let alone those of society as a whole. Understanding these differences and complexities is the primary theme. Only after understanding these differences and complexities can a person deal with the ultimate question of allegiance, which is a difficult concept for any age. Understanding that a willingness to fight for democratic values means an acceptance of dissimilar values is fundamental.

Discussion Materials

This adventure tale lends itself to a book talk that highlights the following episodes: Jonathan at the tavern (pp. 10–15); Jonathan struggles to carry the gun (pp. 16–27); the volunteers wait (pp. 32–37); loading the musket (pp. 38–45); the skirmish (pp. 46–51); running away (pp. 52–58); captured (pp. 58–75, 153–155); the log house (pp. 76–79, 156); the little boy and the burial (pp. 80–99, 156+); the escape (pp. 100–112); reunion and understanding (pp. 113–131); the finale (pp. 132–145, 157); afterthoughts (pp. 145–148); and home (pp. 149–152). Be sure to show the jacket and frontispiece and give the setting (pp. 3–10). Add that a skirmish took place, followed by a capture by three Hessians, an escape, and a return to capture them.

Related Materials

Some stories are: *Night Journeys* (Pantheon, 1979) by Avi, the story of a young orphan in colonial America, which is continued in *Encounter at Easton* (Pantheon, 1980); *Captives in a Foreign Land* (Houghton, 1984) by Susan Lowry Rardin, the tale of terrorists' capture of six children; *Jump Ship to Freedom* and *War Comes to Willy Freeman* (Delacorte, 1981; 1983) by James Lincoln Collier and Christopher Collier; *Child of War* (Holiday, 1984) by Mary Ann Sullivan, about the war in northern Ireland as related through the eyes of the young heroine; and *Caribou* (Greenwillow, 1984) by Meg Wolitzer, the story of a young woman whose brother goes to Canada rather than fight in Vietnam. The powerful nonfiction title *Ain't Gonna Study War No More: The Story of America's Peace Seekers* (Harper, 1985) is also suggested.

Four useful films are: *Bravery in the Field* (National Film Board of Canada, 1980, 28 min.); *Two Soldiers* (Pyramid Films, 1985, 30 min.); *Washington, D.C.* (National Geographic Society, 1983, 20 min.); and *Fourteen Rats and a Rat-catcher* (Weston Woods, 1982, 10 min.). Also suggested is the commended video *You and Your Parents: Making It Through the Tough Years* (Sunburst, 1984). The recording *Trumpeter of Krakow* from Random is also suggested.

Byars, Betsy. *Cracker Jackson*
Viking, 1985, 146 pp.

This well-known author has received the ALA Newbery Award and several ALA Notable Book citations for children. For the past two decades, Betsy Byars has written popular titles for youngsters; presently 28 hardcover titles are in print with more in softcover (see *Introducing Books*, Bowker, 1970, pp. 23, 207; and *Introducing More Books*, Bowker, 1978, pp. 144–147). Betsy Byars's books are exceptionally well written and easy to read. She constructs her plots carefully and develops her characters in fine detail. Her use of brief flashbacks in this title helps to clarify the hero's motivation and development. The title could be used as an exemplar of this literary device. Yet, the short episodic chapters together with the book's socially significant topic commend it as an interesting, easy read. When the young hero confirms that his favorite former babysitter is being physically abused by her husband, he tries to help. Although he personally is unsuccessful, his mother is able finally to resolve the situation satisfactorily. Youngsters ages 9–12 (grades 4–7) will find the title about the topical social issue of wife beating reassuring from a youngster's point of view.

The delightful jacket drawing by Diane de Groat strikes the proper mood. It presents a young boy crouched beside his bicycle, which glows from Day Glo paint, searching the bushes around a slightly tattered-looking old house. Standing in the background on the wraparound porch is a young woman holding a baby.

Eleven-year-old Jackson Hunter (Cracker to Alma, his former babysitter; Jackie to his best friend, Goat) lives with his mom, Kay, a stewardess, in an apartment 1,000 miles from Los Angeles where his thrice-divorced dad dwells. His dad telephones him every Thursday night at 9:00 P.M. because he sincerely loves his only child. The truth is, however, that Jackson is now barely able to tolerate his dad's joking nature. Jackson is tired of the Bela Lugosi imitations that are part of each telephone visit. In fact, Jackson can almost understand why his parents are divorced.

Three years after the divorce, Jackson is almost used to living in a single-parent family. Mom often works for several days at a time, but a neighbor, Kim, helps out. Mom's emphasis on good manners sometimes bugs him, but he figures it's not only part of her personality, but also because of her training as a stewardess. Only three things really distress Jackson: a continually runny nose, kissing girls, and listening to opera. He has a good friend, Goat (Ralph) McMillan, who may be mischievous and a master of the joke—according to the school principal—but is nonetheless a long time, close companion.

As Jackson opens a letter that is obviously written by a female and says simply, "Keep away, Cracker, he'll hurt you," he knows it's from Alma, his former babysitter. She is the only person who calls him Cracker, even though his Mom asked her not to. Alma is now married to Billy Ray Alton and has a baby girl named Nicole after a soap opera heroine. Cracker remembers fondly how he and Alma used to visit Billy Ray's garage before they got married, and he still occasionally visits Alma and six-month-old Nicole in the Alton house next to the garage. Recently Alma, who worships and delights in her baby, made him feel Nicole's first tooth, much against his better judgment.

But, Billy Ray doesn't want Cracker to visit anymore. For some time now, he has suspected from Alma's bruises that Billy Ray beats her, and this letter confirms it. It reminds him of another letter that he received in third grade, saying "You stink," which he found out Bubba Riley had deposited in his desk and answered, "You do, too." Cracker wants to resolve this letter quickly, too, especially because it confirms his worst fears—that Alma is being hit.

Jackson telephones Goat to ask him for help, but Goat is grounded. After Mom goes out, Jackson calls Billy Ray's garage and hears him say, "It's that kid again. I'm going to kill that kid if he—." Cracker is scared. He remembers the impressive python tatooed on Billy Ray's arm. Alma's protestations that Billy Ray is a fighter with his father's temper do nothing to placate Cracker's fears. But he decides to bike over to Alma's by himself to check on her, anyway. Alma tries to assure Cracker that she is fine, but she cannot deny her visible bruises. When she asks him to leave as quickly as possible without being seen, he is sure that she needs help. As he leaves he is very careful. He knows that his glowing bike is visible to the nearby garage. (Goat kids him that some bikes have a touch of Day Glo, but Jackson's has it all over.) Cracker is scared! He remembers coming home from wading with Alma covered with leeches when he was five. He was unconcerned until Mom tried to get them off. He was scared then, too.

Safely home, Jackson finds out from Mom that Avondale, 26 miles away, is the nearest shelter for battered wives. He and Goat try to think of a way to check on Alma, and Goat comes up with the idea of using his older sister, Rachel's, official paraphernalia for collecting for UNICEF. On the way to visit Alma, Goat collects twenty-nine cents. But Rachel insists he took $5, so the two boys rake leaves at $1 an hour to raise the money. Unfortunately, their work efforts end disastrously when Mrs. Martino, their first customer, doesn't accept their reason for jumping on the leaf pile. A week later Mom reports that while she was downtown she saw a radiant Alma on her way to buy clothes for Nicole's coming photography appointment. Cracker recalls when he and Alma visited the palmist, Sister Rose, and her smelly cats and learned that Alma would marry Billy Ray. Alma was radiant then, too.

Soon after Cracker gets a telephone call from a tearful Alma in which she finally admits that Billy Ray not only hits her, but is now hitting Nicole as well and threatens to kill them both. Cracker doesn't know what to do. Mom is in Chicago, but she left their big car in the basement garage, and he thinks he can drive it. At 7:30 P.M. bolstered with pillows and accompanied by Goat who is going to share the driving, Cracker picks up Alma and Nicole and sets out for Avondale. They travel 15 tortuous miles, then Alma insists on returning. Reluctantly, he agrees to take Alma home, but he can't understand why she wants to return. During the long drive many thoughts go through Cracker's mind, but none stronger than the memory of Alma's affection for her Barbie doll collection. Jackson knows that she still has it. When he finally gets home, he wearily goes to bed feeling that he has failed.

A week later, Jackson is still upset and hangs up on his joking dad. When he calls back, Mom who knows the problem by now tells him about it. Mom also calls Alma to try to persuade her to leave her husband. She arranges to drive Alma to Avondale, but Alma doesn't appear. Cracker is despondent but thankful that his competent mom is now in charge. Suddenly he sees his mom drive off toward Alma's house. By the time Cracker bikes there, he finds the house a wreck with Barbie dolls scattered everywhere. Alma and Nicole are in the hospital, battered but alive. Nicole is comatose and does not regain consciousness for four days.

Alma now agrees to go to Avondale. She tells Cracker that Sister Rose told her she'd be sorry, but she isn't because she has Nicole. When Dad arrives acting seriously, he and Cracker drive Alma and Nicole to the shelter. Cracker doesn't feel any differently really, but he knows that this experience is his first step in "growing up." Alma sends two short letters to him and Mom. In Jackson's letter she tells him that she'll always love him.

Thematic Analysis

Wife beating, an old social problem that has finally become prominent among society's concerns, is the primary theme of this book. Youngsters' limited ability to help seriously with this weighty matter does not mean that they do not have deep feelings about the victims, particularly when they are friends. The author allows the adults to effect a realistic resolution without denying the youngster's depth of feeling. Ordinary boyhood escapades provide comic relief from the story's tension. The single-parent home and friendship are corollary themes.

Discussion Materials

First display the jacket painting, then introduce the plot and characters—Cracker, Alma, and Mom—by paraphrasing the anonymous letter (pp. 3–8, 13). Add other characters: Billy Ray (pp. 10–11); Goat (pp. 11–13); and Dad (pp. 15, 38, 102–106). Several threads can be developed in the book talk: remembrances of Alma (pp. 16–17, 18–23, 28–32, 65–70, 129–131); the first bike visit (pp. 17–23, 24–27); UNICEF, Goat, and leaf raking (pp. 46–64); Cracker's drive to Avondale (pp. 77–95).

Related Materials

The following books are suggested: *How I Put My Mother Through College* (Atheneum, 1981) by Corinne Gerson tells about a single-parent family with a 13-year-old girl and her younger brother; *When Sirens Scream* (Dodd, 1981) by Robert E. Rubenstein describes a family's involvement with a nearby nuclear plant leak; *The South African Quirt* (Little, 1985) by Walter D. Edmonds relates a boy's rebellion occasioned by an unfair and cruel beating from his father; and *Always, Always* (Macmillan, 1984) by Crescent Dragonwater tells the life of a girl whose parents are divorced. Three other books can be used: *Ask Me No Questions* (Holt, 1982) by Ann Schlee based on actual circumstances of starvation and sickness among asylum children in Victorian England; *In the Year of the Boar and Jackie Robinson* (Harper, 1984) by Bette Bao Lord, about a young Chinese girl's adjustment to America in 1947; and *Gavriel and Jemal: Two Boys of Jerusalem* (Dodd, 1984) by Brent Ashbranner, which describes the tension-filled life of two boys—one Jewish, one Palestinian—who live on opposite sides of the city.

The following audiovisual titles are recommended: *Values: Making Choices* (Random, 1986, 4 fs); two recordings, *The Adventures of Robin Hood* (Listen for Pleasure, 1986) and *Bert Breen's Barn* (Random, 1977); the video *Katherine Hepburn's Tales of Beauty and Magic* (SVE, 1986); and the 16mm film *Spouse Abuse* (KUTV News, 1982, 10 min.).

Cameron, Ann. *More Stories Julian Tells*
Illus. by Ann Strugnell. Knopf, 1986, 82 pp.

This author has three books in print, including this title. The earliest, *The Seed,* appeared in 1975; the predecessor to this title, *The Stories Julian Tells,* was an ALA Notable Book for children in 1981. *Harry (the Monster),* now out of print, was published in between. All her titles are recommended for middle-graders and advanced lower-grade readers.

Ann Cameron writes about ordinary childhood activities in an exciting and humerous fashion. This title, chosen as a 1986 best book by *School Library Journal,* includes five short stories involving a young black boy, his younger brother Huey, friend, Gloria, and his Dad, Ralph: "A Day When Frogs Wear Shoes"; "The Bet"; "I Learn Firefighting" (divided into three episodes); "The Box"; and "A Curve in the River." They range from a tall tale told by Julian's Dad to relieve the youngster's boredom to stories about Gloria's bet that she can move the sun, Julian's discovery of how to be a helpful older brother, Dad's present of rabbits, and Julian's realization that he belongs to the family of mankind as he watches message bottles flow into the fast-moving water under the bridge. Youngsters ages 7–9 (grades 2–4) will relate to these tales and find them comfortable to read.

With her customary verve, the illustrator of *The Stories Julian Tells,* Ann Strugnell, drew numerous, detailed black-and-white sketches for this book. A double-spread illustration portrays the climax of each of the five stories. The typical double spread for "The Box" shows Julian and his brother, Huey, on the sofa staring at the present Dad brought home. In the background are the huge alligators, snakes, and sea monsters that fill their imaginations. Six full-page drawings interpret the text—one for each story, except "The Box," which has two. The first illustration, for

"The Box," shows the two brothers looking at Dad on the front steps holding a large present; the second shows a brown-and-white rabbit. Five or more decorations in the story "I Learn Firefighting" highlight the firefighting metaphor, for example, the author employs Smokey the Bear for the older brother's realization that he has caused an unfortunate incident. The title page of each story is decorated with drawings—one depicts a line of frogs in sneakers—and each story concludes with an end-note drawing, such as a message bottle bobbing in the water. The full-cover drawing in color portrays the three youngsters raising delighted faces to look at the jumping frogs wearing shoes overhead.

In "A Day When Frogs Wear Shoes," Julian, seven, his little brother, Huey, and his friend, Gloria, are sitting on the front steps complaining about the slow summer day. They decide to visit Dad's garage. After they help Dad for awhile, he decides to close early and take them to the river to show them that on hot days like this "frogs wear shoes." They have fun playing in the water and examining the frogs, while Dad snoozes under a tree. When they are satisfied that frogs don't wear shoes, they return to tell Dad. Imagine their surprise when he tells them to put on their shoes and socks and they find a frog in each shoe!

In "The Bet," after Julian beats Gloria jumping, she bets him that she can move the sun. Julian immediately takes the bet and agrees the winner will be treated to a movie. Using a mirror, Gloria wins by reflecting the sun's rays from her bedroom window, which is directly opposite Julian's window, on the west wall of Julian's bedroom. Julian accepts the defeat nobly, even though he never expected to pay a girl's way to a movie.

As the three children in "I Learn Firefighting" play in the backyard, Julian jumps off the swing and lands in the sand pile. Gloria follows, but Huey, who keeps postponing his turn because he's scared, loses it. When he protests, Julian calls him "a scaredy-cat." The next day Huey stays in his bedroom practicing jumping from the top bunk, except at mealtime when to Julian's amazement Huey eats three portions of the formerly disdained broccoli. When after a loud crash Huey emerges with a bloodied nose and Mother reassures him, saying that even his hero, "superboy," cries, Huey tells the whole story. Expecting punishment, Julian is pleasantly surprised to hear Dad tell him that he has to learn to be "a good older brother," just the way Dad is "still learning how to be a father, too." With coaching Huey makes the jump, but when asked what did it, Huey quickly responds, "broccoli."

In "The Box," Dad arrives home carrying a large present. Julian and Huey look at the box with anticipation. Then Dad brings out two knives and their anticipation turns to heightened apprehension. Despite visions of dangerous monsters, when Dad tells his sons to open the box with their hands, they do so and find two rabbits inside, which they promptly name Jake and Bean Sprout. Gloria helps them cut up some lettuce and carrots with the knives.

In "A Curve in the River," Julian is intrigued by the fact that the planet earth is mostly water. He secretly puts a note in a bottle with his name and address on it and a plea to the recipient to contact him, and throws it in the river near his home. To his dismay Gloria telephones soon afterward to say that she has the bottle. Disgusted, Julia holds Gloria responsible for subverting his world travel dreams and tells her not to come around anymore. When his dad notices Gloria's absence, he investigates, and Julian tells him what happened. Dad explains to Julian that the bottle got stuck at the nearby curve in the river, and promises to take him to the bridge further down the river. He encourages Julian to write a new message and also talks him into letting his friends do likewise.

Finally Julian and his friends are all ready. Dad drives them in his pickup truck to the bridge where the water flows fast to the sea. They make wishes and toss their bottles in the water. Julian makes four wishes: that the bottles will sail together; that they won't get trapped; that they will help make new worldwide friends; and finally and most important that he can visit his new friends.

Thematic Analysis

Among the many themes in the stories are the importance of family love and support; the benefits of friendship; the joy of discovering old truths (tall tales, aphorisms, and scientific principles) in the serious business of play; learning to be a good older brother (as well as a good father); and learning to accept and relate well to pets. Discovering that one can communicate with others in this world assumes an important place as the poignant conclusion of the final story. Stories that reflect the exercise of good parenting and the concept of internationalism address the specifics and generalities of human concerns.

Discussion Materials

This title can be book talked or read aloud. After displaying the colorful jacket, paraphrase the youngsters' frog escapade (pp. 3–20) and show the illustrations (title page, pp. 8, 9, 16–17, 18, 20). To highlight "The Bet" (p. 31, including the pictures) read it aloud, emphasizing both the scientific principle and the commonplace childhood activity of betting, or the sun on the wall in Julian's room (pp. 28–29). To demonstrate how to be a better sibling read pages 32–39 and ask how the fire was finally extinguished (pp. 50–51). "The Box" can be paraphrased to stress parenting (pp. 53–67), displaying the dramatic picture of the two brothers on the sofa (pp. 60–61) and the lovely picture of the rabbits (p. 66). "A Curve in the River" can also be paraphrased while displaying the illustrations, but be sure to read the ending (pp. 81–82).

Related Materials

Two picture books that this audience will enjoy are Riki Levenson's *Watch the Stars Come Out* and *I Go with My Family to Grandma's* (Dutton, 1985; 1986). Two comic titles will also be of interest: *Marguerite, Go Wash Your Feet* (Houghton, 1985) by Wallace Tripp and *Hornswoggle Magic* (Little, 1981) by Otto Coontz. Three other stories will entertain readers interested in humor, science fiction, and historical fiction: *Fat Men from Space* (Dodd, 1977) by D. Manus Pinkwater; *Invasion of the Brain Sharpeners* (Knopf, 1981) by Philip Curtis; and *Lion to Guard Us* (Crowell, 1981) by Clyde Robert Bulla.

The "Learning Begins at Home" pamphlets (ALA) in English and Spanish and the "Sugar Ray" poster (ALA, No. 118) will be useful. Two recordings also apply: *J. T.* (Random, 1978, 2s), read by Charles Turner, and *Peter Rabbit and Friends* (Weston Woods, 1986), the classic Potter tales read by Pauline Brailsford. Two films are suggested: *Only the Ball Was White* (Films, Inc., 1981) and *Henderson, 7th Avenue Bug Patrol* (Media Projects, Inc., 1983).

Cooper, Susan. *The Selkie Girl*
Illus. by Warwick Hutton. Macmillan, 1986, 32 pp.

Susan Cooper is recognized as an accomplished author by readers of children's books. In two decades she has published almost a dozen books in the United States, many of them in both hardcover and softcover. She is perhaps best known for her fantasy novels for young adults, the fourth book of which, *The Grey King* (Macmillan, 1978), won the 1979 ALA

Newbery Award. Although her earlier books *Over Sea, Under Stone* (Harcourt, 1966) and *Dawn of Fear* (Harcourt, 1970) are for youngsters ages 9–11 (grades 4–6), her recent books *Jethro and the Jumbie* (Atheneum, 1979) and *The Silver Cow: A Welsh Tale* (Macmillan, 1983) are suggested for ages 5–9 (grades K–4).

An exceptional writer of lyric prose, Susan Cooper brings her substantial ability to a zenith in this retelling of a tale told in many versions around the far outer islands—the Orkneys and Shetland—of the author's native Britain, as well as in Scottish and Irish outposts. It is an allegorical story about the capture of one of three seal sisters by a lonesome young man on the one day of the year that the sisters appear on land as maidens. It tells how she marries the young man, bears five children, and after years returns to the sea with the good wishes of her two youngest children, who provide the means for her to do so. Thereafter, the sea seems to protect her land family. Although children ages 5–8 (grades K–3) will enjoy the tale and its illustrations at their simplest level, their powerful message will be appreciated by those ages 9–11 (grades 4–6).

The British illustrator Warwick Hutton is known in the United States for the more than half-dozen books he has illustrated here in the past decade including another title by Susan Cooper, *The Silver Cow: A Welsh Tale.* His light-filled, airy drawings epitomize his belief that illustrations for children "should have depth and distance, space and mood." His repeated use of blue and green, relieved by touches of cheerful yellow sunshine, herald the seaside life; the watercolors defined by broken lines highlight the nearby spaces and stress the distant background; pen shadings suggest depth. The overall effect is pleasing and leaves ample room for those who like to roam in their visual imaginations.

Warwick Hutton's 24 illustrations, besides the title page, end-note, and dedication pictures, sparingly, yet completely, reflect the author's intent in this romantic tale. Eight are full-page illustrations, two of which extend onto the opposite page as half-page illustrations. The remainder of the pictures are half-page illustrations. The artist's informal, borderless style reflects the spacious, rugged landscape. He also did the two jacket illustrations: The back jacket shows three seals swimming underwater; the front jacket shows them swimming on the surface of the water, with two seal heads and a golden-haired maiden visible to the viewer. From the three seals on the green binding to the sand-colored endpapers, this well-designed book communicates the loneliness of the sea.

"The islands rise out of the sea. . ., and strange things may happen there." On the seventh day of the highest tides of the spring, Donallan happens to go to the beach to gather seaweed for his garden. Suddenly he hears music, and when he investigates he sees three beautiful girls sitting on a rock beside the sea. He is instantly smitten by the maiden with the long golden hair, but, when the girls hear his dog growl, they snatch the shapeless, gray bundles lying at their sides and plunge into the sea.

Donallan is forlorn. He lives alone, except for his dog and cat, Angus and Cat, in a croft (farmhouse) on a lonely island. He fishes in his boat and keeps ten sheep grazing on his few acres of land, but he is lonely. His parents are dead, and few people live on this lonely landscape. He often wishes for the sound of a human voice. The more he thinks about the magical girl, the more he wants her, but all he sees is the endless sea.

Picking up his load of seaweed, he starts home. On the way he meets the island's oldest man, lame Old Thomas. Donallan tells him what has happened, and that he is in love. Old Thomas knows immediately that the selkies (seal girls) are the daughters of the King of Lochlann whose kingdom is beyond the sea's rim. Recognizing that he can't influence the young man, he strikes a canny bargain with him. In return for a promise to dig seaweed into his garden every year, the ancient fisherman tells Donallan how to capture the selkie girl.

Old Thomas explains that on a special day the following year Donallan must steal the maiden's gray bundle without which she cannot return to the sea. Old Thomas tells Donallan to hide the sealskin bundle and make sure it is well-kept, or else the girl will die. He adds, however, that she will "go back to the wild in the end." Donallan doesn't pay any attention to the final remark, but goes about his business for a year and then does exactly what he was told.

When the special day arrives, Donallan manages to steal the maiden's gray bundle. Although she jumps into the sea with her two selkie sisters, she returns to beg Donallan for the bundle. Instead of returning the bundle, he asks her to be his wife. As she emerges from the water, he covers her with a soft woolen poncho that belonged to his mother and leads her to his croft.

Donallan hides the sealskin then marries the selkie girl whom he calls Mairi, continually making certain afterward that the sealskin never cracks or dries out. Over the years, they have five beautiful children—Dougal, Margaret, Niall, Kate Annie, and James—and Mairi works patiently, as long and hard as Donallan, on the croft. Often, however, perceptive Kate Annie wonders why her quiet mother turns longingly toward the sea.

One summer day the youngest child, James, who is about nine and very curious, sees his father take a sealskin from behind some stones, oil it, and return it to its hiding place. After his father has gone out with the three older children, he tells his mother and Kate Annie what he saw. Both James and Kate Annie see their mother smile for the first time, as she exclaims, "You have found my skin!" As they retrieve the sealskin, Mairi is able to laugh pleasurably again.

With the gray bundle under her arm, Mairi takes her children down to the sea. She tells them that she was taken from the sea against her will, and that she has five other children in the sea. Although they don't want her to go, Kate Annie states bluntly, "It's their turn." She comforts Mairi and James, adding "I'll look after James." As Mairi enters the sea, she gives the children her love and the sense that she will always be near. The children see three seals swirling and frolicking together before they swim away. Then Kate Annie and James go home.

When Donallan returns, he realizes what Old Thomas said came true. After that, the sea protects Donallan and his children forever, even during storms. Indeed, the sea wind around the croft seems to murmur lovingly. As was said at the start of the tale, "And strange things may happen there."

Thematic Analysis

Folklore is full of wise sayings and beliefs. This retelling of an ancient tale has several themes, depending on the experience and age of the reader or listener. The idea of uprooting unwilling persons and transporting them from one culture to another is heart-wrenching for all concerned. The idea of sexual discrimination, no matter how well intended, can also only lead to sadness for everyone. These ideas emerge as a theme of freedom in this haunting old tale that speaks to the human condition of love and compassion.

Discussion Materials

This picture-book retelling of the selkie tale deserves a thorough reading and rereading to commit the tale to memory for storytelling. The audience will be delighted. The book can then be recommended for further enjoyment. The few hinges of action are simple and can be incorporated with personal embellishments. For a more visual presentation, project several of the pictures with either an opaque or overhead projector (title page, pp. 5, 11, 17, 19, 21, 27, 28). The tale can also be told through the illustrations. An open-ended question (such as "Why did Mairi return to the sea?") will provide a basis for discussion after everyone has read the book. To read aloud, divide the story into its parts: Donallan's discovery (pp. 3–7); the bargain with Old Thomas (pp. 8–13); a selkie wife (pp. 14–19); Mairi's discovery of her sealskin (pp. 20, 25); Mairi's return to the sea (pp. 26–27); and forever after (pp. 30–32).

Related Materials

Many titles can be suggested: *The Thunder God's Son: A Peruvian Folktale* (Greenwillow, 1981) by Ariane Dewey; *Mufaro's Beautiful Daughters: A Tale* (Lothrop, 1987) by John Steptoe; *Robot-Bot-Bot* (Dutton, 1980) by Fernando Krahn; *The Battle Horse* (Bradbury, 1981) by Harry Kullman; *Alanna: The First Adventure* (Atheneum, 1983) by Tamora Pierce; *Magnum Fault* (Houghton, 1984) by Raboo Rodgers; and *Green Island* (Vanguard, 1982) by Michael Schmidt. Three nonfiction titles are: *Take a Trip to Spain* (Watts, 1985) by Jonathan Rutland; *Nature's End: The Consequences of the 20th Century* (Warner, 1986) by Whitley Strieber and James Kunetka; and *Toxic Waste: Cleanup or Cover-up?* (Watts, 1984) by Malcolm E. Weiss.

Two recommended filmstrips are *Canadian Fairy Tales* (SVE, 1986) and *The Silver Cow: A Welsh Tale* (Weston Woods, 1986). The recording *Rebecca of Sunnybrook Farm* (Caedmon, 1980), read by Julie Harris, is also useful. Three suggested films or videos are: *Wee Gillis* (Churchill Films, 1986); *One* (The Little Red Filmhouse, 1984); and *With Babies and Banners* (New Day Films, 1979).

Griffith, Helen V.   *Georgia Music*
Illus. by James Stevenson. Greenwillow, 1986, 24 pp.

Since the early eighties, the author has published a handful of books for children; all are in print, including *Foxy*, a book for youngsters age 10–13 (grades 5–8). Her three titles for younger children in the Alex series are well known. Helen V. Griffith's books generally include animals, and the remembered sounds of birds and other animals assume a large place in this title. A young girl, who spends an idyllic summer with her grandfather, learns to re-create the musical sounds of his rural cabin to cheer him when he comes to live in her home. The bird motif highlighted in the story is appropriate coming from the pen of a writer who is an inveterate bird-watcher. The author writes a poignant story about ageism (a difficult concept for middle-graders) from a child's simple perspective, one that youngsters age 7–9 (grades 2–4), can read independently. Children in grades K–3 will delight in the illustrations.

James Stevenson, a noted illustrator, has been known for years through the pages of the *New Yorker* magazine. He is also well known for his illustrations in children's books—more than three dozen are in print. Stevenson is a marvelous collaborator for this title. Each of his inimitable drawings is distinctive with squiggly, broken lines and the sometimes sardonic humor characteristic of his magazine cartoons. His full-color art, done with pen and watercolor, re-creates the poignant quality of the story. Ten full-page illustrations lovingly portray the reality of the child's vision of her Georgia summer in all its shabbiness and glory and her grandfather's remembrances. The first illustration (p. 3) has two printed lines under it, but the other nine are on the pages opposite the corresponding text. On the print pages the illustrator drew sketches of items that are familiar sights during the girl's summer at her Grandfather's, for example, the clothesline, the porch glider, a cricket, a wheelbarrow, and a vine growing on the wire fence. One sketch shows the little girl's Baltimore home (p. 20), enhancing the text and opposite illustration which shows the girl playing the mouth organ next to her grandfather in her home. The title page is also decorated with the railroad images that are visible from her grandfather's Georgia cabin. The end note is a picture of a mockingbird that echoes a recurring motif, "sassy old bird." The book will be long treasured for its warm and gentle portrayal in both words and pictures of a youngster's devotion and respect for older loved ones.

A young girl lives in Baltimore, Maryland, in a traditional stone row house where, it used to be said, they scrubbed the flat stone step landing every morning. Last summer, when she was eight, she went on the train with her mother to visit Grandfather, who lives all alone in a small cabin near the railroad tracks. Her mother had to return to Baltimore, but she left her delighted daughter there for the summer. Although she was shy and Grandfather was quiet at first, they got along fine.

Grandfather hadn't been doing much lately during the winter, only odd jobs and watching the railroad trains that passed in front of his yard. When spring came along, however, he was rested and ready to put on his straw hat and turn over a patch of earth beside his cabin with the hoe that he kept under the porch. He planted collards, black-eyed peas, and melons. The large and generous patch kept him busy, so he was doubly happy to have his granddaughter's friendly presence. She was not only company, but willing help. Even when she stepped on a few seedlings by mistake, he never mentioned it. She liked her grandfather and enjoyed his habit of watching the passing trains when their garden work was done.

They worked in the garden all morning listening to the mockingbird sings its songs as it flew along the fence from post to post. Grandfather called it "sassy old bird," and they laughed. Then they would have lunch and rest under the tree on the grass where they could hear all the sounds of nature: bumblebees, crickets, grasshoppers, and rustling leaves. As the summer music crooned steadily, they napped. In the evenings, Grandfather would play tunes on his mouth organ (harmonica), then they would sleep to the night sounds of the katydids and tree frogs. Sometimes, they could hear the mockingbird call nearly all night long. So the summer passed, and soon it was September. Grandfather put her on a train bound for Baltimore, and Mother promised she would return the following summer.

However, next summer has come, and it isn't the same. When she and Mother arrived in Georgia, they found weeds all around and Grandfather sitting on the porch slumbering with a cover on his legs and his eyes closed, so they took him back to Baltimore. Now he sits silently in a chair in their home looking out a window, just staring at the city street sadly. His granddaughter tries everything to cheer him up, but nothing works. She even pulls out his mouth organ (harmonica) and asks him to play her a tune, but he just looks at it forlornly. In desperation, she learns to play a little tune on the mouth organ. Although he doesn't say anything, she knows he likes it.

From then on she practices every day and slowly learns all the tunes her grandfather played for her in Georgia. Now she plays them for him. Soon she starts to play different tunes—sounds she remembers from Georgia last summer. They aren't real songs, but they remind her of the "cricket chirps, bee buzzes, and tree frog trills and bird twitters" she recalls. She is surprised to hear her grandfather chuckle and whisper, "sassy old bird," but she immediately realizes that she has re-created the

Georgia music for her grandfather, too. They look at each other and laugh!

Thematic Analysis

The theme of the young wanting to help and in their own way understand the older senior citizen, especially beloved elders, is beautifully expressed in this mutually satisfying story for young and old. The concept of "ageism," while complex even for adults, is difficult, if not impossible, for youngsters at a tender age to understand. Family love and caring is a concomitant theme. Both young and old can readily identify with the sounds of nature, herein called Georgia music. Although music is used here as a literary motif, its essence is based in the feelings of humanity.

Discussion Materials

This book can be presented in typical picture-book fashion by displaying each page and paraphrasing the story, or it can be used as a read aloud by employing these or other divisions: the setting (pp. 1–7); Georgia last summer (pp. 8–15); and this summer in Baltimore (pp. 16–24). For book talk for independent readers, display the front cover (also p. 13), then tell about the girl's first summer in Georgia and the sounds she and her grandfather heard (p. 10). Next show the illustrations on the back cover and pages 8 and 9 (read pp. 8 and 10). Finally, show the illustration on page 19 and talk about the grandfather in Baltimore (paraphrase pp. 16 and 18). In conclusion, pose the question "What did the little girl do to help her grandfather?"

Related Materials

The youngest in your audience will enjoy Jill Bennett's *Teeny Tiny* (Putnam, 1986), a retelling of the classic ghost story of a bone in a cupboard. Independent readers in the middle grades will appreciate the following stories: *Hocus-Pocus Dilemma* (Knopf, 1980) by Pat Kibbe, which explores a youngster's interest and belief in ESP; *Sport* (Delacorte, 1979) by Louise Fitzhugh, an adventure story about an 11-year-old and his extended family; and *Behind the Attic Wall* (Crowell, 1983) by Sylvia Cassedy, which investigates a youngster's discovery of a secret room. *Badger on the Barge and Other Stories* (Greenwillow, 1985) by Janni Howker, five short stories that treat relationships between the young and the elderly, is recommended for sophisticated readers. Three nonfiction titles are also suggested: Carl Sandburg's poetry *Rainbows Are Made,* selected by Lee Bennett Hopkins (Harcourt, 1983); *Life: The First Fifty Years, 1936–1986* (Little, 1986); and Brent Ashabranner's *Dark Harvest: Migrant Farmworkers in America* (Dodd, 1985).

Always In Season (ALA, 1986), a 140-slide set or ten-minute videotape, is useful with this title. *Lullabies Go Jazz: Sweet Sounds for Sweet Dreams* (Jazz Cat, 1986) will be an effective recording. Two suggested filmstrips are: *Tucker's Countryside* (Random), from the book by George Selden, and *Birds, Birds, Everywhere!* (SVE, 1986, 3 fs). Two recommended 16mm films are *Twilight* (Bronnimann/Dorsey, 1983, 7 min.), about an old man whose only link to the world is through his young nephew, and *If You Knew How I Feel: Jana and the Crowing Hen* (Centron, 1983, 36 min.), about the protection of a pet by a young girl and her grandfather.

Hamilton, Virginia, retel. *The People Could Fly: American Black Folktales*
Illus. by Leo Dillon and Diane Dillon. Knopf, 1985, 178 pp.

Virginia Hamilton, a respected author who has been publishing books for children for two decades, has received many honors, including the Newbery Medal and two ALA Honor Book citations, the Boston Globe-Horn Book Award, the National Book Award, the Coretta Scott King Award, and the Edgar Allan Poe Award. More than a dozen of her excellent titles are currently in print (see *Introducing Books,* Bowker, 1970, pp. 66, 115; and *Introducing More Books,* Bowker, 1978, pp. 9–12). This title, chosen one of 1985's best books by both *Booklist* and *School Library Journal,* combines her scholarly, lifetime interest in folklore with her powerful, poetic writing in a collection of 24 folktales retold with spirit for children. Youngsters age 9–12 (grades 4–7), will find the short tales stimulating listening, viewing, and reading.

Leo Dillon and Diane Dillon, the well-known illustrators who did the 40 striking black-and-white pen-and-ink wash drawings for this book, received the ALA Caldecott Medal for two consecutive years in the late seventies. Their distinctive stylized illustrations are easily identifiable. In this title, the Dillons not only applied their customary detailed patterning, for example, of fabrics (p. 168), but also their fondness for formal borders. Each picture is enclosed by a narrow, generally gray, frame.

Their collaboration as illustrators is especially fortuitous here. Their elegant pictures keenly interpret the serious note behind the comic folktale facade and seem to mirror exactly what the author had in mind.

Each tale in this oversize book has at least one full-page illustration. A couple of longer tales have more. Most of the stories also have one half-page illustration; the longer stories have several. Youngsters will find pictures everywhere, both in their minds and on the page. The full-color jacket painting, which illustrates the majestic climactic moment of the concluding title story, portrays Toby, the old slave, and a group of field hands—men, women, and babes—flying in a beautiful sky over the tiny receding plantation. The expressions of hope and contentment, and the patterns on the tattered fabrics worn by the female characters, are exquisite. The illustration will entice readers to look inside.

The bibliography (pp. 175–178) cites, alphabetically by author, the scholarly list of writings that Hamilton used and those that interested adults or youngsters can search to deepen their interest in the tales. The author's preliminary statement heading the bibliography is significant for both the scholar and the uninformed youngster: Other versions of the tales exist; they have been told in "many ways by a number of Storytellers." After each tale, even the briefest, "Bruh Lizard and Bruh Rabbit" (pp. 31–34), several paragraphs explain or document the tale. The documentation generally tells where the tale originated, its derivation or similarities with tales of other countries, and the like. Sometimes certain changes in the text are highlighted. The dialect in which the tale was originally told is also included. Where the dialect used is little understood, for example, in "Bruh Alligator Meets Trouble" (pp. 35–42), a glossary is provided.

In a succinct introduction (pp. ix–xii), the author introduces the American black folktale, which in essence was "a celebration of the human spirit," written in sorrow. They were also survival tales. Virginia Hamilton expresses "the tales in a more realistic, readable fashion." She uses black English, colloquial language, or dialect, such as Gullah, as appropriate, and adds a glossary. The tales are very readable, and the author's beautiful expression flows freely for the young reader.

Virginia Hamilton divides the collection into four sections, each representing a genre: animals; magic; the supernatural; and fantasy escape. Each section is introduced by a section title and a small decorative device designed by Jane Byers Bierhorst. The first section, "The Lion, Bruh Bear, and Bruh Rabbit: And Other Animal Tales," is made up of seven tales, including "The Tar Baby" in one of its more than 300 versions. The second section, "The Beautiful Girl of the Moon Tower: And Other Tales of the Real, Extravagant, and Fanciful," contains six stories, including "A Wolf and Little Daughter" (pp. 60–64) and one of the longest tales in the book, "Wiley, His Mama, and the Hairy Man" (pp. 90–103). The third section, "John and the Devil's Daughter: And Other Tales of the Supernatural," has five scary and moral tales, the first of which carries the same title as the section (pp. 105–137).

The fourth and final section, "Carrying the Running-Aways: And Other Slave Tales of Freedom," includes six tales. "Carrying the Running-Aways" (pp. 141–146), the first story in the section, is a true-life tale of freedom that was told recently to the author by her mother. The documentation following the tale is the only one that bears Virginia Hamilton's signature. The concluding tale, "The People Could Fly" (pp. 106–173), is a moving testament to those under the yoke of slavery—those who could "fly," as well as those who could not escape.

Thematic Analysis

Freedom, liberty, and survival under hopeless conditions, as well as the determination to keep hope alive without the knowledge of oppressors are themes that suffuse the stories. The slaves kept alive their ancestral interest in the animals around them, which is but a short step from representing them as surrogates in their folklore. This relationship with animals is a corollary theme. A few tales, specifically moral tales of behavior for young people, exhibit other themes.

Discussion Materials

This attractive book has many uses, from individual reading, to reading aloud, or as a reference source in social studies or language arts. It can be read aloud in a month or slowly over a semester, or it can be book talked. Display the covers and tell or read the title story (pp. 166–173). The "hinges of action" for telling the story are: long ago in Africa people could fly magically; people forgot how to fly when they suffered the misery of slavery; some, however, did not lose the magic even though they discarded their wings; the old man, Toby, retained the magic, as did Sarah, carrying her babe; the overseer, Driver, cracked his whip on the babe who cried from hunger; when Toby helped Sarah and the babe, he muttered the magic over them: "Kum. . .yali, kum buba tambe"; Sarah and the babe flew away; the next day the nearby slaves who absorbed the magic rose and flew; although the overseer and the master tried to kill Toby, he spread the magic to many in the field and rose, shepherding the group to "free-dom"; but Toby couldn't take everyone; those who couldn't fly told about those who could; and as they became free, they told others, just as I have told you. Or read the introduction (pp. ix–xii), then display the jacket and one picture to illustrate each of the four sections—animals: "Tappin, the Land Turtle (pp. 20–25; picture p. 23); magic: "A Wolf and Little Daughter" (pp. 60–64; picture p. 62); the supernatural: "Little Eight John" (pp. 121–125; picture p. 123); and freedom tales: "The Talking Cooter" (pp. 151–155; picture p. 153).

Related Materials

Charlie's House (Crowell, 1983) by Clyde Robert Bulla tells the story of a 12-year-old who serves for seven years as an indentured servant in eighteenth-century England, and *Return to South Town* (Crowell, 1976) by Lorenz B. Graham describes David's return as a medical doctor, only to find that some old prejudicial attitudes still exist. Other suggested titles are: *This Strange New Feeling* (Dial, 1982) by Julius Lester; *Girl on the Outside* (Lothrop, 1982) by Mildred Pitts Walter; *Let the Circle Be Unbroken* (Dial, 1981) by Mildred D. Taylor; *Come a Stranger* (Atheneum, 1986) by Cynthia Voight; *The Meantime* (Houghton, 1984) by Bernie MacKinnon; and *Upon the Head of the Goat: A Childhood in Hungary, 1939–1944* (Farrar, 1981) by Aranka Siegal. Five useful nonfiction titles are: *Winners and Losers: How Elections Work in America* (Harcourt, 1984) and *The Incredible Sixties: The Stormy Years That Changed America* (Harcourt, 1986), both by Jules Archer; *The House on Spruce Street* (Atheneum, 1982) by John J. Loeper; *Fireworks Tonight!* (Hastings, 1984) by Martha Brenner; and *All God's Children Need Traveling Shoes* (Random, 1986) by Maya Angelou.

A filmstrip to suggest is *Mama Don't Allow* (Random, 1986). Two recordings are *Tailybone and Other Strange Stories* (High Windy Records, 1986) and *A Hundred Dresses* (Random, 1975), read by Lucy Martin. Recommended 16mm films are: *Miles of Smiles, Years of Struggle* (Benchmark, 1983) and *Branches of Government: The Executive Branch; The Judicial Branch; The Legislative Branch* (National Geographic Society, 1982). The large October 1987 poster of old railroad steam engine trains from 1829–1839, part of the continuing Wonderful World of Stamps series, makes a good display for this presentation. For a free copy, write the U.S. Postal Service, Wonderful World of Stamps, Philatelic Sales Division, Washington, DC 20265-9998.

Jukes, Mavis. *Blackberries in the Dark*
Illus. by Thomas B. Allen. Knopf, 1985, 42 pp.

The author has written only three books, but each is noted for its eloquent and thoughtful expression. Mavis Jukes's first book, *No One Is Going to Nashville,* was an Irma Simonton Black Award-winner; the second, *Like Jake and Me,* was on the ALA Notable Books for Children list for 1985 (see *Introducing Bookplots 3,* pp. 18–21). This, the author's third title, was selected a 1985 best book by both *School Library Journal* and *Booklist,* as well as an ALA Notable Book. It is an unsentimental yet touching story about a young boy who spends a ten-day summer vacation with his grandmother after his beloved grandpa's death. The two lonely people share their sorrow and surmount their loss with joy. The story is serene and restorative in its feelings. It will help youngsters acquire a healthy attitude toward a deep sadness in life. Youngsters ages 8–10 (grades 3–5) will find the book both comforting and invigorating.

The illustrator, Thomas B. Allen, drew 22 soft yet detailed pencil sketches to complement and illustrate the events described in the text. Sixteen are full-page illustrations placed traditionally on the page opposite the corresponding text. One serves as the frontispiece, another appears at the end of the story. This arrangement reflects the traditional background of this poignant slice-of-life story. Three of the pictures are horizontal half-page double spreads placed under the text. Three are half-page drawings. The three decorations on the title, dedication, and end-note pages also symbolize the contents: They portray Grandpa's Yankee baseball cap, his fishing knife, and a summer bird on a branch heralding life.

Nine-year-old Austin feels awkward as he gets off the plane to visit his grandmother for ten days. When he left the ranch last summer, Grandpa was there symbolizing all the things Austin could look forward to over the long winter. This summer only his grandmother is there to pick him up. Austin is happy to see her familiar smiling face, but somehow it isn't the same. He misses his deceased grandpa.

Grandmother's neighbor, Wayne McCabe, drives them to the ranch in his pickup truck. Along the way, Grandmother comments on how helpful Wayne has been since Grandpa died. Although Austin replies politely to Grandma's questions about eating the food on the plane, for the most part he is quiet, thinking about his grandpa and the days he was planning to spend with him, learning more about baseball, fishing, driving a tractor, and just plain having a glorious time with a wonderful grandpa. As they drive by the river, the three notice a man fly-fishing with his rubber waders pulled up to his hips. Wayne invites Austin to go fly-fishing at Two Rock Creek on Saturday with him and his boys. Austin just shrugs; Grandmother answers that they'll see.

Everywhere Austin looks on the ranch reminds him of Grandpa. He notices that the grass around the barn needs mowing, the empty swing that Grandpa fixed for him still stands, the coat closet looks so empty without Grandpa's coats and shoes. He sees sadness all around. When Grandmother asks why he doesn't want to go fishing, Austin says that he's never fished with anyone but Grandpa, and besides he doesn't know how to fly-fish. Grandpa was going to teach him this summer. Grandmother replies that Wayne will teach him, but Austin quickly answers that he doesn't want him to.

Austin continues to look around the house. He sees his grandfather's fishing knife in the cupboard and questions Grandmother about the rest of Grandpa's fishing gear. She tells him that it is still in the barn. She hasn't touched it yet. Just straightening the house has been difficult enough for her. She shows Austin her 100-year-old doll with a necklace of coral beads that she found in the attic. Regretfully, she says she has no one to give it to. As she encourages Austin to examine the beads, they break. Austin helps her pick up the beads, then Grandmother puts them in a saucer high in the cupboard together with the doll. She suggests that Austin could restring the beads, but he says that he doesn't know how. Besides, he wants to look at the tractor.

With Grandmother's approval, Austin goes to the barn where the tractor waits for him, cranked and ready, together with Grandpa's fishing gear, his photographs, and his baseball cap hanging on a nail on the wall. When Grandmother appears in the doorway, Austin recounts how he and Grandpa picked blackberries in the dark last summer, then brought them to her to make a pie. He repeats that Grandpa was going to teach him to fly-fish this summer. As Austin recalls his treasured memories and brushes away his tears, the two bereaved relatives hold each other. Grandmother trembles, but recovers and suggests that Austin has time to pick some blackberries before supper.

As Austin goes down to the river, he hears some cracking noises. When he looks up, he sees that Grandmother has been following him. She is all decked out in Grandpa's fishing outfit—vest, waders, pole, and funniest of all the Yankee baseball cap—though somewhat disheveled from stumbling down the enbankment. She tells him that she hasn't been down to the river for years and had almost forgotten how beautiful it is. The two novices find the spinning reel and attach it. They also find Grandpa's handmade, colored flies. Austin attaches a fly—as though he were threading a needle—while Grandmother ties it to the fishing line with a crochet knot. Grandmother says she always told Grandpa that he would make a good seamstress because he was so clever with his handiwork. Austin practices holding the fly in one hand and casting with the rod in the other.

After awhile, Grandmother says that they had better go home for supper, but when Austin wants to stay and eat blackberries instead, she agrees—it's a family tradition to eat blackberries in the dark. They have a wonderful time. Grandmother even catches a brook trout, which they release afterward. Austin, wearing the baseball cap now, tells Grandmother that Grandpa would be happy to know that he was learning to fly-fish at Two Rock Creek. Grandmother agrees and adds that the next day they will learn to drive the tractor, and that Saturday they will go fishing with Wayne.

As they cross the field on the way back to the ranch house, Grandmother says she has saved something for him. Later she enters Austin's bedroom and finds him sitting on the bed stringing the coral beads. The antique doll rests against his pillowcase, which has a cowboy pattern on it. Grandmother sits next to Austin and presses Grandpa's fishing knife into his hand. She comments, "This is yours, too." They both smile.

Thematic Analysis

This simple story with its depth of feeling truly emulates the importance of the theme of death for a child. The strong support and understanding that the young boy receives from an important person in his life expresses the hope and continuity that make such a heart-wrenching loss more bearable for the young. The story emphasizes the youngster's feelings of love and appreciation for his grandmother, who automatically understood him and adopted the grandfather's role, and his willingness to help a dear one in her sorrow.

Discussion Materials

The book can be presented through its pictures or book talked highlighting various episodes. In either case, display the front jacket, which presents Austin wearing the Yankee baseball cap. Point out the tin can for blackberry picking in the background on the fence post, and introduce Grandmother and Austin (frontispiece, pp. 1–3). Then show the pictures to page 23 and ask the question "How did Grandmother and Austin help each other resolve their sorrow?" To book talk, introduce the characters and tell the plot between the frontispiece and pages 24–25. Ask the same question, but as a hint also show Grandmother all gussied up in Grandpa's fishing gear (p. 28). The excellent fly-fishing episode can be read aloud (pp. 30–34), or the antique doll episode can be paraphrased: the doll is presented and ignored (pp. 12–17) and the sharing, including the doll (pp. 41–42+).

Related Materials

Many stories relate well to this story: *Treehorn's Wish* (Holiday, 1984) by Florence Parry Heide tells about the famous youngster's three birthday wishes, with Edward Gorey's illustrations heightening the story's forlorn quality; *Lucky Stone* (Delacorte, 1979) by Lucille Clifton explains how a young girl listens to her great-grandmother's stories, particularly about the lucky stone that is now hers; *Call Me Ruth* (Doubleday, 1982) by Marilyn Sachs relates how an eight-year-old came to America with her mother to join her father, who dies soon after; *Root Cellars* (Scribner, 1981) by Janet Lunn describes the life of an orphan during the American Civil War, after the death of the grandmother with whom she lived; and *Friendstone* (Dial, 1981) by Martha Derman tells about an 11-year-old's summer in the Adirondacks with her beloved great-grandmother.

Several audiovisual materials can also be suggested: a recording of *The Adventures of Tom Sawyer* (Listen for Pleasure, 1986), read by Robby Benson; Meindert DeJong's *House of Sixty Fathers*, available from Random as a kit and video; Miska Mile's *Annie and the Old One*, also available from Random as two filmstrips and a video; and the video and 16mm film *Grant Wood's America* (International Film Bureau, 1986, 29 min.).

Rylant, Cynthia.   *A Fine White Dust*
Bradbury, 1986, 106 pp.

The author is well known for her five honored picture books (see *Introducing Bookplots 3*, pp. 26–28). Since 1985 Cynthia Rylant has also published four distinguished books for middle-graders and older readers that directly touch youngsters' emotions. In *A Fine White Dust* (a 1987 Newbery Honor Book), a youngster learns to reconcile his religious beliefs and the differing ones of his parents and a friend after a traumatic experience with a preacher. He learns to appreciate a personal expression of religion. All readers, and especially sensitive ones, will find the story deeply moving and true-to-life. Youngsters ages 10–12 (grades 5–7) are the primary audience.

The author's economical writing style commends the book for easy reading; however, its content is "rich as a plum pudding" for thoughtful readers. The first 12 chapters allude both to the 12 apostles and the route to Calvary in the Christian tradition; the final chapter, labeled "Amen," suggests that personal salvation can be attained through personal understanding. The strong and appealing jacket painting by Neil Waldman in muted tones of brownish rose portrays the young boy staring out his window, imagining the lean young preacher man hovering over him.

Thirteen-year-old Pete Cassidy realizes that he has spent the past year trying to sort out the events of last summer. As he looks at the crumbled ceramic cross with its fine white dust that he has been unable to throw away, he decides that telling about last summer will free him and let him get on with his life. He has always had a religious nature, one his Pop, a telephone lineman, and his Mother have never shared. They only accompany him to church in their small North Carolina town on special holidays like Christmas and Easter, even though the town is dominated by a Baptist and a Methodist church. Once, when Pete was brave enough to broach the subject of religion, his Pop asked him, "Does what people think bother you?" Pete blurted out that he is mixed up. His Pop said that there may be "More than you can see. . . . Things you might not understand." Pete remembers that Mother gave Pop a look and he didn't continue.

Pete feels desperately that he needs to be saved from hell by someone. His classmate, Rufus, who is practical and very different from his best friend, Pete, who is spiritual, announced in fifth grade that he was a "confirmed atheist." In spite of their religious differences the two became fast friends; Pete knows he can always count on Rufus. Pete also remembers going to Vacation Bible School (VBS) and painting ceramic crosses every summer—the crosses are still on display in Mother's kitchen. Last summer, however, he felt he needed something more, so when Pop suggests the tent revival meeting, Pete decides to go.

Pete attends his first revival meeting the same night. Imagine his surprise when he discovers that the preacher is the hitchhiker he saw on the highway and decided was a pickax murderer. Pete saw him again staring at him in the local drugstore. Figuring everyone in the store was about to be murdered, Pete grabbed a comic book and feigned great interest. Luckily, Rufus appeared and the two boys ran off for chili dogs, while Darlene Cook, the drugstore waitress, served the blue-eyed stranger a hamburger. Pete remembers the day clearly. It was June 11, his last day in seventh grade.

The revival is full of new experiences for Pete, among them the feeling of being trapped by sweating humanity. The assistant pastor, whom he knows, and the hymns are as he expected, but not the preacher man. Pete is transported! He joins the waiting line to the preacher man, and when his turn comes, he says, "Yes, praise God," indicating that he wants to be saved. The preacher man places his hands on Pete's head and tells him that he is reborn. Along with others, Pete faints, awakening in the arms of a fat, tear-stained woman.

When Pete returns home, he tells his Mother that he has been saved, but she simply says, "I'm glad for you." Feeling joyful, he bikes to the drugstore hoping to see the preacher man. He does find him, and they have a long conversation. Although Pete talks mostly about himself, he discovers that the reverend's name is James W. Carson (although he asks Pete to call him Jim); that Jim had many "wild days. . . . Holiness didn't come easy. . . . [His] eyes enjoyed what the Devil could paint"; and that Jim thinks Pete might become a fine preacher. All negative thoughts about Jim vanish!

After Pete's parents retire early the next night, Pete goes to his second revival meeting at which he is mesmerized and finds himself in tears. The following day at the drugstore Rufus forthrightly asks Reverend Carson where he is from. When the reverend gives him a convoluted answer, he is immediately suspicious. While Rufus listens, Jim tells Pete not to be corrupted by anyone. Feeling rejected by his friend, Rufus leaves, but Pete hardly notices.

At the third revival meeting, Pete is once again enchanted and imagines himself as the preacher. He thinks he sees his mother in the tent's back benches, but he is not sure. If she is there, he is certain she can see that he loves the preacher man. After the revival meeting, Pete hangs around until Jim accompanies him to the filling station soda machine. Jim tells Pete about his life, stressing his loneliness and uniqueness. Both are qualities with which Pete identifies. When Jim asks Pete to join him to help save people, an awed Pete agrees. They plan to meet at the filling station about 10:00 P.M. after the final revival meeting the next evening.

As he surveys his home and takes a few mementos the next morning, Pete realizes how much he will miss his Pop and Mother. Rufus drops in as Pete is packing a duffel bag and can't believe what he hears. But nothing Rufus can say seems to make any difference, so he leaves. Pete does chores around the house all day and leaves about 9:30 P.M., after explaining to his folks that he is going to help clean up after the meeting. At the filling station, Pete talks to the last person to come out of the revival meeting, Joanie Fulton, the organist. She says the revival was great. But at 11:00 P.M. the filling station is deserted except for Pete. By 1:00 A.M., Pete realizes that the preacher man isn't coming, but Rufus has been waiting for him, and together they walk back to Pete's house in silence.

The next day at noon Rufus returns and wakes him. Pete retrieves the long letter he had written to his folks. It takes him about four days to get over his rejection. Rufus tells him that Darlene Cook and the preacher took off in her car. The news is all over town. A close-mouthed Darlene comes home three weeks later. By this time Pete has bought a guitar and has his favorite photograph of his parents and himself blown up. On reflection, Pete realizes that he can always count on his parents, who know when to leave him alone, and that he needs to appreciate good friends like Rufus more.

Pete and Rufus have a good time in eighth grade, with football and all. This year Pete has been better able to see that the world is full of different types of people, some religious, some not, some who go to church, some who are religious in other ways. He also realizes that he can throw away the pieces of the ceramic cross now and still possess a fine white dust internally.

Thematic Analysis

This book has several themes: family support and strength; nondemanding and comforting friendship; recognition and acceptance of the many different reactions to organized religion; and understanding that one must have realistic expectations. Understanding that one cannot count on another person for salvation is fundamental.

Discussion Materials

The novel can be introduced easily by showing the jacket and telling something about the main character (pp. 12–17) and the story line (pp. 3–11). Several episodes can be described: the summer tent revival meetings (pp. 17–21, 34–35, 47–51); conversations with the preacher man (pp. 26–30, 40–44, 51–57); parents (pp. 4–5, 14–17, 24–26, 31–35, 46–47, 62–63). Read the letter aloud (pp. 83–85) and introduce Rufus (pp. 10–12).

Related Materials

Four related stories are suggested, three with a heroine and one with a hero: *Melinda Takes a Hand* (Morrow, 1983) by Patricia Beatty tells about Colorado frontier life; *Days of Terror* (Book Society of Canada, 1979) by Barbara Smucker describes the family life of Russian Mennonites in western Canada; *Emily Upham's Revenge Or. . .* (Pantheon, 1978) relates an adventureful historical kidnapping patterned on the nineteenth-century Dime Novels; and *Who Kidnapped the Sheriff? Tales from Tickfaw* (Atlantic Monthly Pr., 1985) by Larry Callen tells adventure tales about Pat O'Leary that are reminiscent of *Tom Sawyer*. Several nonfiction titles are also suggested: *Soda Poppery: The History of Soft Drinks in America* (Scribner, 1986); *Meet the Witches* (Lippincott, 1984) by Georgess McHargue; and *Mountains and Earth Movements* (Watts, 1984) by Ian Bain.

A recording of *Dark Frigate* (Random, 1972) is available, from the book by Charles Boardman Hawes. Three films can also be used: *The Car of Your Dreams* (Pyramid Film and Video, 1985, 18 min.) is an entertaining look at the history of cars through three decades of automobile advertisements; *John Wycliffe: The Morning Star* (Gateway Films, 1983, 75 min.) is about the English translator of the bible; and *The Church of the Russians* (NBC News Archives, 1983, 115 min.), available only in video format, is about the second largest Christian church in the world—the Russian Orthodox church.

Understanding Social Problems: Additional Titles

Avi. *Shadrach's Crossing.* Pantheon, 1983, 178 pp. (Gr. 4–6)
Baron Munchausen, Eighteen Truly Tall Tales, read by Peter Ustinov. Cassette. Caedmon, 1972. (Gr. 4–6)

Beatty, Patricia. *Turn Homeward, Hannalee.* Morrow, 1984, 208 pp. (Gr. 5–6)

Cauley, Lorinda Bryan, retel. *The Town Mouse and the Country Mouse.* Illus. by the author. Putnam, 1984, 32 pp. (Gr. 2–4)

Clark, Margaret Goff. *Latchkey Mystery.* Dodd, 1985, 128 pp. (Gr. 4–7)

The Courage to Care. Filmstrip, 30 min., also available on video. Anti-Defamation League of B'nai B'rith, 1986. (Gr. 5–up)

Cunningham, Julia. *Flight of the Sparrow.* Pantheon, 1980, 130 pp. (Gr. 5–6)

Daly, Niki. *Not So Fast, Songololo.* Illus. by the author. Atheneum, 1986, 32 pp. (Gr. K–4)

Doctorow, E. L. *World's Fair.* Random, 1986, 288 pp. (Gr. 6–up)

Fisher, Leonard Everett. *Ellis Island: Gateway to the New World.* Illus. by the author. Holiday, 1986, 64 pp. (Gr. 3–7)

Gerson, Corinne. *Son for a Day.* Illus. by Velma Ilsley. Atheneum, 1980, 140 pp. (Gr. 4–6)

Hammer, Charles. *Me, the Beef, and the Bum.* Farrar, 1984, 215 pp. (Gr. 4–6)

Hyde, Margaret O. *Sexual Abuse: Let's Talk about It.* Westminster, 1984, 96 pp. (Gr. 5–6)

It's the Truth, by Rosenshontz. Recording. RS Records, 1985. (All ages)

Karp, Naomi J. *Turning Point.* Harcourt, 1976, 154 pp. (Gr. 5–6)

Kaufman, Charles. *Frog and the Beanpole.* Illus. by Troy Howell. Lothrop, 1980, 189 pp. (Gr. 5–6)

Kilgore, Kathleen. *The Wolfman of Beacon Hill.* Little, 1982, 192 pp. (Gr. 6–up)

Kyte, Kathy. *In Charge: A Complete Handbook for Kids with Working Parents.* Knopf, 1983, 96 pp. (Gr. 4–7)

Langton, Jane. *The Fragile Flag.* Harper, 1984, 224 pp. (Gr. 5–6)

Maruki, Toshi. *Hiroshima No Pika.* Illus. by the author. Lothrop, 1982, 48 pp. (Gr. 4–6)

Mason, Bobbie Ann. *In Country.* Harper, 1985, 247 pp. (Gr. 5–up)

Meltzer, Milton. *Poverty in America.* Morrow, 1986, 122 pp. (Gr. 5–up)

Myers, Walter Dean. *Young Landlords.* Viking, 1979, 197 pp. (Gr. 5–6)

Pampe, William R. *Petroleum: How It Is Found and Used.* Enslow, 1984, 64 pp. (Gr. 5–up)

Sebestyn, Ouida. *Words by Heart.* Atlantic-Little, 1980, 162 pp. (Gr. 4–6)

Shoeshine Girl. Film. Learning Corp., 1981. (Gr. 4–6)

The Story of Chaim Rukowski and the Jews of Lodz. Film, 55 min. The Cinema Guild, 1983. (Gr. 5–up)

8

Identifying Adult Roles

WHILE the controversy over whether a child's sexual role is determined before or after birth still continues, it is generally accepted that the middle years of childhood are important in identifying and incorporating adult social roles. It is a crucial time for middle-graders to be exposed both directly and vicariously to the actions of mature individuals. At this age youngsters emulate the behavior of adults, especially those in close proximity. The increasingly independent actions that follow yield satisfaction for youngsters and an enlarged sense of maturity. Reading, viewing, and listening also are invaluable aids in this socialization process. Imaginative youngsters can "try out" many different adult roles within the pages of a book. Although direct exposure to a role can truly heighten a child's experience, vicarious exposure can, nevertheless, augment the child's awareness of social roles that are either different or difficult to explore.

The books in this chapter describe various social roles, from a dentist-father and sports reporter-mother to a black male and a white female astronaut, from the exotic occupation (for many today) of rodeo rider (extended in the book to a young daughter) to the unusual occupation (for a female in the early part of the century) of author. Two titles examine artistic talent, both real and imagined; others explore necessary traditional occupational roles in American society and introduce young readers to the accepted care givers of medical practice. Each book not only gives the middle-grader knowledge about the role, but also provides some nurturing insight into adult behavior.

Greenwald, Sheila.   *Give Us a Great Big Smile, Rosie Cole*
Illus. by the author. Little, 1981, 76 pp.

The author-illustrator Sheila Greenwald is known for her humorous books. She has published about 15 books for children in almost two decades; 8 of them are still in print. The most recent titles in the popular Rosie Series are *Valentine Rosie* (Little, 1984) and *Rosie Cole's Great American Guilt Club* (Little, 1985). The first Rosie title was well reviewed with phrases that highlight the author's skillfulness at humorously describing otherwise traumatic incidents in the heroine's life: "sparklingly funny" (*Kirkus*), "comic misunderstandings" (*Horn*), and "hilarious, incisive and tender" (*St. Louis Dispatch*). They stress the author's ability to transform a child's ordinary problem into a humorous and resolvable incident.

This story involves a youngster whose photojournalist uncle does a book about each of his talented nieces when they reach ten years of age. Unlike her two older talented sisters, however, the heroine has no talent. She takes violin lessons simply to please her mother. But in the end, the plucky heroine gets out of a music recital, the book, and future violin lessons merrily and without any hurt feelings. Youngsters ages 8–11 (grades 3–6) will find this story warm, appealing, and funny.

Sheila Greenwald drew 53 black-and-white pen-and-ink sketches that illustrate the story with humor and vitality. Two full-page illustrations that communicate the central child's feelings in the story show the heroine dejectedly mounting the steps to the school of music and courageously playing her violin in Central Park to try to get signatures to eliminate future lessons. The simple line drawings clearly show the facial expressions and body language. The final page portrays the heroine and her friend Hermione doing what they do best at their age—playing "dress-up" and celebrating their lack of talent. The illustrations add to the laugh-aloud jocularity and make a funny story even funnier. Be prepared to suggest the sequels!

Ten-year-old Rosamond (Rosie) Cole lives on the East Side of New York City with her mom, Sue, her dad, and two older sisters, 13-year-old Anitra and 12-year-old Pippa. Both her sisters attend a professional children's school; Rosie goes to their former school, Read, nearby. Ever since Rosie's tenth birthday dinner with her family and Mom's brother, Uncle Ralph (U.R.), at Gino's in the park six weeks ago, Rosie has been worried about becoming the heroine of her uncle's new book. When Anitra, who attends the American School of Ballet because she is talented and loves ballet dancing, was ten, U.R. wrote *Anitra Dances*. (Rosie thinks the book definitely romanticizes Anitra. The day Anitra lost the part in the *Nutcracker* ballet to Zora Slonim, for example, she called Zora a klutz and said she used pull to get the part.) Then when Pippa was ten, U.R. wrote *Pippa Prances*, describing Pippa's skill and interest in showing, jumping, and riding her horse, Doobie. Now it's Rosie's turn, and the thought terrifies her. When she overhears U.R. ask Mom if Rosie has "pulled her act together," Rosie knows her suspicions are correct. She feels so terrible that she barely hears her horse-betting uncle confide to his sister that he needs "another book real bad."

Rosie has two famous and talented sisters, but Rosie knows she is not talented. For the last three years she has tried diligently but come up with zero talent, perhaps except for taking chances or giving "cockeyed glances." Rosie sees things concretely and has few illusions. She has been taking violin lessons for two years with Theodora Radzinoff (T.R.), her mom's college chum, but Rosie knows she has no musical talent. She only goes twice a week to please her mom. Once a week she has a private lesson; on Tuesdays, she plays chamber music in a quartet with Debbie Prusock (viola), Linda Dildine (piano), and Hermione Wong (cello) at T.R.'s West Side School of Music. Lately, Hermione, who walks with her to school, claims to be her best friend. She knows Rosie is ten and what that means.

When U.R. finally schedules a time to photograph Rosie at T.R.'s school, Rosie fortifies herself with her usual chocolate soda and a danish at a luncheonette counter before she climbs (feeling dumber with each ascending step) the brownstone steps to the school. She has had the same feeling in the past each time she climbed those steps, but today it is more pronounced. T.R. and her friends are dressed up and acting cheerful. But as Uncle Ralph clicks away, Rosie feels increasingly horrible. Meanwhile, T.R. and Uncle Ralph start to call each other Teddy and Ralph. Oblivious to the sound of the camera, they seem to be having a wonderful time, and Ralph tells Teddy that he will be back Thursday. Before U.R. leaves, however, he confides to Rosie that he never thought he'd be able to "get a book out of [her]," and that he needs one because he's broke. As he says to her that book will be called " 'A Very Little Philly,' I mean 'Fiddler,' " Rosie dashes out despondent.

Everyone else responds to the news of the book with great enthusiasm. Girls in class come up to Rosie smiling to announce that they are her best friend. Mrs. Winston, her teacher, comments that she didn't know Rosie was so musical, and T.R. telephones Rosie's Mom a few times each day. Mom even redecorates the living room and Rosie's bedroom, where U.R. is going to photograph Rosie practicing. Even though an apartment neighbor, Didi Rapposo, complains about the terrible sound Rosie makes when she practices and Mom carpets their adjoining wall, U.R. continues to snap away, saying, "Give us a great big smile, Rosie Cole." Rosie gets glummer. Then U.R. arranges to photograph her at her school assembly where Mrs. Winston suggests Rosie play for them, and things seem to be going from bad to worse.

Inadvertently, Rosie meets U.R. at the West Side luncheonette where he is reading his draft manuscript. Rosie feels so nauseous after he reads her a statement from the manuscript saying that she loves to play the violin that she orders a cup of tea. She feels trapped. She hates to play the violin but U.R. needs this book. Family love triumphs, however, and they go together to Rosie's next violin lesson, where T.R. announces that the music school's May 20 recital will feature a solo performance by Rosie, as well as Rosie's "quartet" performance. In the intervening weeks, T.R. will personally give Rosie a lesson every day, including a tape playback. Rosie is depressed.

After shopping with Mom and U.R. for a pink dress with a black bow and white patent leather shoes for the recital, however, Rosie begins to enjoy her new status. On her first Saturday alone without T.R. or U.R., who are out on a date, Rosie becomes restless and goes to visit Hermione. When Hermione wraps herself in a sheet and begins to lip-sync, Rosie tells her that pretending doesn't make her a star. Hermione angrily punches her and yells that Rosie is a dreadful violin player. Later at home Rosie has a tantrum and T.R. and U.R. try to placate her with a visit to a concert at Carnegie Hall. Backstage the violinist laughs when Rosie tells him she hopes to be like him some day, and the adults exchange knowing glances, admitting privately that they have created a monster. Standing beside the tape recorder, T.R. tries to correct this. She explains to Rosie that the bad violin music she hears when she enters the school of music is Rosie's. Rosie feels miserable again, but she and T.R. agree not to burst U.R.'s bubble. T.R. suggests that Rosie smile a lot in the photographs.

After a consoling chat with Anitra, Rosie decides that she can't go through with the recital. Rosie packs her bag to run away and heads across Central Park where she comes across some musicians performing. She looks carefully at their signs asking for donations toward their tuition and gets a courageous idea.

Rosie dashes home, dresses in her recital outfit, and prints a sign asking for signatures on a petition that says she is not musical. She takes her fiddle, races to the park, and sets up. As she plays, she doesn't mind a bit if people laugh, as long as they sign the petition that she intends to give to Mom. Everyone sees her, including Pippa, the building superintendent, and Mrs. Rapposo. Suddenly, Mom arrives and to Rosie's amazement signs the petition while her two sisters applaud.

They all go home happy. Mom telephones T.R. and U.R., who both congratulate Rosie on her stand. Even Rosie's concern about Uncle Ralph's need for a new book is forestalled. Mom tells Rosie that T.R. is helping U.R. on a new book about a young racehorse. Rosie immediately knows that the title is "*A Very Young Filly.*" After a visit from the married couple T.R. and U.R. in June, Rosie goes to Hermione's to celebrate. They both dress up and pretend to be stars. They have a wonderful time.

Thematic Analysis

Unrealistic expectations put unbearable tension on children. Some, like the heroine in this story, can cope; some cannot. This spoof explores the various sides of a serious subject: the importance of recognizing and nurturing talent, when present, and the problems associated with investing mistakenly in talent when it is not present, particularly for the youngster without talent. Middle-graders need role models for their own interests and talents to emulate at their own speed. Identifying these talents and being able to match them with role models are difficult tasks at best. Those with innate talent such as playing a musical instrument, singing, or athletic ability need competent, professional evaluation. (The word talent is used loosely, but in the larger sense each person is talented in something, and the time at which this interest becomes visible varies.)

Discussion Materials

An interesting book talk might begin with a textual reading of the anecdote that explains the title (p. 34, first par.); display the illustration showing Rosie mounting the steps to the school of music (p. 23, read second par.; pp. 22, 25); show the jacket illustration of Rosie dressed in her recital outfit practicing, and tell how Rosie decided to solve her problem (read pp. 68–69). Fill in with the story line. Among the other episodes that can be presented are: family (pp. 4, 5–6, 7, 8, 9, 12, 29, 63); friends (pp. 18, 20, 24, 26, 30, 36, 51, 54, 74, 76); music lessons and T.R. (pp. 16, 21, 23, 25, 42, 59, 60, 61, 62); U.R. (pp. 5, 13, 29, 34, 39, 40, 56, 58); Rosie's lack of musical ability (pp. 3, 10, 11, 13, 14, 21, 30, 31, 32, 44, 47, 49, 55, 59, 60, 61, 62, 67, 68–69, 70).

Related Materials

Many titles can be suggested: *How Lazy Can You Get?* (Atheneum, 1980) by Phyllis Naylor Reynolds; *Big Anthony and the Magic King* (Harcourt, 1980) by Tomie dePaola; *The Toady and Doctor Miracle* (Macmillan, 1985) by Mary Blount Christian; *Cave of the Moving Shadows* (Dial, 1979) by Thomas Milstead; *Nutcracker* (Crown, 1984), translated by Ralph Marheim and illustrated by Maurice Sendak; *Rusty Timmon's First Million* (Lippincott, 1986) by Joan Carris; and *The Dancing Horses* (Holiday, 1982) by Helen Griffiths. Some nonfiction titles are also suggested: *Electronic Musical Instruments: What They Do, How They Work* (Morrow, 1984) by Larry Kettlekamp; *You Can't Be Timid with a Trumpet: Notes from the Orchestra* (Lothrop, 1980) by Betty Lou English; *Dorothea Lange: Life Through the Camera* (Viking, 1985) by Milton Meltzer; *Just Look: A Book about Paintings* (Scribner, 1980) by Robert Cummings; *Breaking Tradition: The Story of Louise Nevelson* (Atheneum, 1984) by Natalie S. Bober; *Louisville Slugger: The Making of a Baseball Bat* (Pantheon, 1984) by Jim Arnow; and *Codebuster!* (Whitman, 1985) by Burton Albert. The ALA "Lemonade Stand" poster (1986, No. 117) makes a suitable background to emphasize the heroine's enterprising nature.

Haskins, Jim, and Benson, Kathleen. *Space Challenger: The Story of Guion Bluford—An Authorized Biography*
Carolrhoda, 1984, 64 pp.

One of the two titles in print by these recognized writers of nonfiction for young people, this title is for grades 3–6. The other, *The Sixties Reader* (Viking, 1986), is for grade 7 and up. Jim Haskins alone is well known for more then a dozen nonfiction titles. Many are biographies of black Americans written in the late seventies, such as *About Michael Jackson* (Enslow, 1985). The combination of writing about people of current popularity and interest for youngsters and of presenting accurate and inspirational content in a readable biography for them is a winning one. The story of the first Afro-American astronaut in America, Guion (Guy) Bluford, is inspiring in its clear presentation of the value of family love and support and personal hard work in attaining one's ambitions. Guy Bluford was guided toward higher vocational education, but through his own determination and his family's support, he became a pilot and a Ph.D., and ultimately an astronaut. Youngsters ages 8–11 (grades 3–6) will find Bluford's story invigorating and well worth emulating.

The book has eight chapters—approximately eight pages each—whose straightforward presentation lends itself to the interested as well as the reluctant reader. The four-page glossary with definitions from "Aerodynamics" to "Zero G" explains any textual terms that may be awkward or unknown. A two-page index makes the work useful for reference about a typical space flight mission. The 20 color and black-and-white photographs that appear in the midsection of the book are courtesy of the National Aeronautics and Space Administration (NASA). Six are full-page color photographs of Guy Bluford and his teammates aboard the simulator or *Challenger* in preparation for the space flight.

The "first Black American in space," 40-year-old Lieutenant Guion (Guy) Stewart Bluford, Jr., was one of the five astronauts who ascended in the 100-ton space shuttle *Challenger* at 2:00 A.M. on August 30, 1983, from Cape Canaveral, Florida. At the time Guy Bluford wasn't just thinking about himself "simply as a lucky human being." He was thinking about his parents who had told him from his earliest years that "if he worked hard and tried hard he could do anything he wanted."

Guion Stewart Bluford, Jr., always had "an interest in things that fly." Born November 22, 1942, in Philadelphia, Pennsylvania, Guy took after his father, who was a mechanical engineer. (Guy's mother was a teacher and he has two younger brothers, Eugene and Kenneth.) Guy, who always wanted to build planes not fly them, wanted to be an aerospace engineer. He was a privileged youngster, whose family encouraged him. He also was a Boy Scout. He lived in an integrated community, and he went to integrated schools, even before "Little Rock," which occurred when Guy was in junior high. (His relatives and friends in the South were surprised because he went to an integrated elementary school.)

When Guy was in high school, the counselors told him that he was "not 'college material.' " The launching of *Sputnik* about that time increased Guy's interest in science, but his marks were weak, especially in reading, and his guidance counselors advised him not to go to college. Neither he nor his parents ever doubted that he and his brothers would attend college, however. After all, he wanted to be an aerospace engineer.

Between 1960 and 1978, Bluford became a pilot and a Ph.D. In 1960, he enrolled at Pennsylvania State University for aerospace engineering and graduated from the Air Force Institute of Technology (AFIT) in

1978. He joined the air force branch of the ROTC and became a "fullbird," or pilot, in his senior year at Pennsylvania State. After serving as a pilot in Vietnam, he enrolled for his master's degree in aerospace engineering at the Air Force Academy (AFA) and went to work as an engineer at Wright-Patterson Air Force Base in Ohio. (He was married to Linda Tull, a fellow student at Pennsylvania State, and had two sons before leaving for Vietnam.)

In 1978, 35-year-old Bluford became "Guy Bluford, astronaut"—one of the almost 9,000 who applied for the astronaut program. Thirty-five individuals were chosen, including Sally Ride, Ph.D., and Bluford. Bluford and his family moved to the Johnson Space Center in Houston, Texas, where he started intensive training that led to his participation in *Challenger*'s third flight, which was the seventh mission for the shuttle program.

Although he was not the first black American in the program (the first left after four years and the second died in a plane crash soon after he was appointed), Bluford was chosen as one of the three mission specialists on *Challenger*'s third flight. Two other black Americans were included among the 78 in the astronaut program. Bluford was in charge of deploying an East Indian satellite and also helped with the experiments. Many famous people watched the *Challenger* orbit from its Florida base, including Bill Cosby, who made a statement expressing his racial pride: "Our race (has been) . . . qualified for a long time. . . . The people who have allowed Guy to make this mission are the ones who have passed the test."

Once in orbit, the astronauts aboard the spaceship *Challenger* had to allow reality and training to take over to perform necessary tasks—even eating and sleeping—in a weightless environment. Experiments also had to be conducted, leaving little time for sightseeing. Fortunately, the three-day mission was routine and successful; even the fire alarm set off by a delicate sensor was a false alarm. President Reagan thanked the team via a special telephone hookup and told Guy that he was "paving the way for others."

A reticent man, Lieutenant Colonel Bluford is humble about his place in history as the first black American in space. He considers himself a fortunate man, one who by working for NASA has been able to do what he most admires and accomplish his desires. He likes the idea of being a role model and says to all youngsters, "(You) may find it difficult at times—I had to struggle through those courses at Penn State—but if you really want to do something and are willing to put in the hard work it takes, then someday—bingo, you've done it!"

Thematic Analysis

The straightforward theme of a hero for youngsters to emulate appears throughout this story about a black American astronaut. The condensed and objectively stated highlights of a 40-year lifetime will attract young readers. Although the occupation of astronaut seemed so elevated for the hero, his complete rejection of unfortunate school guidance let him begin a steady march toward his objectives. His slow and steady climb from early childhood through education to this summit should inspire readers. Strong family support in a black family also is well shown. The hero's willingness to admit that he had "to struggle" in his baccalaureate days to compensate for obvious deficiencies in subjects other than science is a firm secondary theme.

Discussion Material

A family tree clearly showing the events in the hero's life can be constructed and projected from a transparency as the book is presented. First show the jacket and introduce the memorable *Challenger* mission (read pp. 7–10). Project the transparency and talk about the family tree: birth (November 22, 1942) in Philadelphia, Pennsylvania, and family (p. 11); boyhood (pp. 12–13); early wish (p. 14); schooling (pp. 17–18); college, 1960–1964 (pp. 19–20); undergraduate ROTC (p. 21); marriage and sons (p. 21); pilot in Vietnam (p. 22); Ph.D. in computer software (p. 23); astronaut (pp. 37–38); work aboard the *Challenger* (pp. 44, 46–51); and the landing (pp. 52–53). Two episodes deserve mention: the condensed space program in 1983 (pp. 38–42) and working aboard the *Challenger* (pp. 46–51). Accompany this last episode with the photographs (pp. 24–36) and the back jacket picture (read the explanation).

Related Materials

Some suggested titles are: *Rescue Chopper* (Westminster, 1980) by Ruth Hallman; *The Warrior's Apprentice* (Simon & Schuster, 1986) by Lois McMaster Bujold; and *Alexander* (Houghton, 1984) by Scott O'Dell. The following nonfiction titles are also suggested: *Louis Armstrong: An American Success Story* (Macmillan, 1985) by James Lincoln Collier; *Firehouse* (Morrow, 1983) by Bernard Wolf; *Computers in Everyday Life* (Watts, 1984) by Ian Litterick; *More Basic: A Guide to Intermediate Computer Pro-*

gramming (Holt, 1984) by Shelley Lipson; *Cosmic Quest: Searching for Intelligent Life among the Stars* (Atheneum, 1984) by Margaret Poynter and Michael J. Klein; and *To Space and Back* (Lothrop, 1986) by Sally Ride and Susan Okie.

The eye-catching "Locker Room" Poster (ALA, 1986, No. 203) makes a good background statement. Three films are suggested: *Working: Communication and Media* (L.C.A., 1982, 19 min.); *Computer, Tool for the Future* (MGS, 1983, 23 min.); and *Growing Up with Rockets* (Cinema Guide, 1986, 58 min.). The recording *Women of Courage: Sally Ride* (Electric Co., 1985) is also suitable.

Hest, Amy.   *The Purple Coat*
Illus. by Amy Schwartz. Four Winds, 1986, 32pp.

Amy Hest is a comparative newcomer to the field of publishing; her first book for children, *Maybe Next Year,* was published by Clarion in 1982. Since then she has written three more, including this title. The author writes well about remembered childhood incidents and environments. For example, her first book is set in her grandmother's home, and this title takes place in Grampa's city tailor shop. The memories of childhood that the author describes through the eyes of her small heroes are unsentimental and universal experiences to which today's youngsters can relate; the reactions are the same. The author, who is the mother of young children and lives in New York City, the setting of this story, understands and expresses childhood events and feelings in a bright and cheerful text. A little girl convinces her grandfather, a tailor, to make her a purple fall coat instead of the usual navy blue one, when he recalls that her mother also once wanted something different when she was young. Children ages 7–9 (grades 2–4) will be enchanted both by the delightful incident and the charming pictures.

The book is illustrated by Amy Schwartz, who is an author and illustrator of her own work and also illustrated two of Hest's other titles for children. A talented artist, Ms. Hest drew 22 pictures in full color, including three decorations, that are redolent of the thirties and the forties, yet could represent scenes of today. They are familiar to a child's searching eye in a plain and comforting way. The purple endpapers and the triumphant final half-page picture of the heroine standing on the front step of her home wearing the purple coat add a proper note of satisfaction. The jacket illustration showing the heroine standing opposite her grandfather in his high-rise tailor shop hefting a swirling bolt of purple wool concretely and visually condenses the book's plot against a navy blue background. The four full-page illustrations and five three-quarter-page double spreads, each outlined in fine pen line, amplify the text and add a cheerful touch to the reassuring story. The facial expressions sketched on the cartoon-type faces effectively convey the characters' emotions.

As Gabrielle (Gabby) stands on her front steps watching the golden leaves drop into her yard, Mama joins her and says, "Coat time, Gabrielle!" Gabrielle, who is about seven, remembers clearly that once again they are about to pay a fall visit to Grampa in New York City, where he has a tailoring shop, for a winter coat. Gabrielle likes the train ride aboard the Silver Express from their home in suburban Meadowlawn to Pennsylvania (Penn) Station in New York City. She presses her nose against the window for an hour and watches the world whiz by. From Penn Station, they walk through long, crowded tunnels and walkways to the Broadway local subway, which will take them to their destination. The noise is so loud that Gabby shields her ears. When they finally reach the tall office building that houses Grampa's tailor shop, they take the elevator to the twenty-eighth floor. The elevator is so full of people and so fast moving that Gabrielle finds it difficult both to breathe and to hold on. Luckily, the ride only lasts a minute, but as she gets off the elevator, she has to yank up her woolen knee socks.

As Gabby and Mama walk past many office doors down the linoleum-covered corridor, they discuss the impending coat. Mama says that Gabby should have big gold buttons on her new navy blue coat, but Gabby wants a purple coat this year. Mama can't understand why Gabby wants such a difficult color. Besides, Gabby always gets a good navy blue coat.

Discouraged and silent, Gabby slips in and out of her fringed moccasin shoes as she walks down the corridor.

She is only too happy when she opens the door to Grampa's shop. As the three embrace in the center of the shop, Gabby is so happy to see Grampa again that she hugs him delightedly. Grampa's tailor shop has a bare wooden floor and is full of attractive spools, buttons, and bolts of cloth. It also has a desk and a sewing machine, and from its windows one can look up and down at the city. Gabby heads straight for the bolts of cloth lying on the open-faced shelves, and before long she finds the purple bolt she wants. Grampa intervenes, however, by magically producing, as always, a plate of deli sandwiches for lunch. Mama eats one rapidly and hurries off to do her city shopping, leaving Grampa and Gabby sitting on top of his desk eating their sandwiches. This treat is one that Gabby likes and has come to expect. Grampa enjoys his lean pastrami sandwich and tries to get Gabby to try one, but she sticks to her usual, salami. Grampa tells her that occasionally she should "try something new."

When lunch is finished, Grampa announces that he has put out several navy blue bolts for Gabby's selection. But Gabby brings him the purple bolt and says that this year she wants purple. When Grampa bluntly asks what Mama thinks, Gabby says that she didn't say "no," simply that navy was what Gabby always wore. Gabby then describes exactly what she wants: a long purple coat with a hood and a back pleat to make it easier to run. Grampa counters that navy is so traditionally "classic," but Gabby reminds him of what he recently told her—that it is good to try something new once in a while. Grampa rubs his chin thoughtfully and stares out the window. He remembers that Gabby's mother wanted a tangerine dress when she was around the same age as Gabby, and he recalls also that he finally made it. Grampa comes up with a good idea, a reversible purple and navy coat. Gabby is pleased. She knows that her grandfather is an exceptional tailor and that the coat will be perfect but she has just one request—that he make the purple side first. Grampa begins by taking all the measurements. Even though Gabby doesn't like the fittings she goes along with the pesky details. Next Grampa cuts a paper pattern on the large sewing table as Gabby watches. When Gabby asks again about the pleat and hood, Grampa assures her about the pleat, but adds that the coat will have a hood only if enough fabric is left after cutting.

About 4:00 P.M., Mama returns and comments on the beautiful pieces of purple cloth on the table. Grampa explains that Gabby is going to have something different this year—a reversible purple and navy coat. Mama is shocked. Gabby feels like hiding, fully expecting her to explode. But when Grampa quickly reminds her about her own tangerine dress, Mama sits down in the wooden swivel desk chair and kicks off her heels. She remembers how much she wanted the tangerine dress, as well as how unlike her it was. Then she tells Gabby that the purple color is undeniably gorgeous and that her coat is going to be "the best purple coat ever."

Soon Gabby has her hooded purple coat. As she stands bedecked in her reversible double-breasted coat with a contented look on her face and a smile in her heart, the leaves are almost gone.

Thematic Analysis

Developing the ability to make wise choices is a long and arduous task, one that is gravely important for responsible adults in every sphere of life, for example, as citizens of a democracy, and one that is at first best nurtured through a process of gentle love and understanding. This book delightfully shows how a grandfather's understanding and love, plus a mother's remembrance of a similar desire when she was about the same age, permit a youngster to make a decision about the color of her clothing that may aid in future decision making. Another less noticeable but important theme for middle-graders, that of an adult occupational model—in this case a tailor—is well explicated. Choosing a character in such a comparatively obscure occupation in American society today as a role model is beneficial for everyone.

Discussion Materials

An easy book to present, this title may be suggested to independent readers by displaying a few pictures and relating the story line, or it can be read aloud. To present it to independent readers, show the picture and read the text of Gabby and Mama on the step (p. 5); show the picture of their arrival at Grampa's (pp. 12–13); show the jacket and relate the story line. To read aloud, separate the book into five parts: the trip (title page–p. 11); lunch (pp. 12–17); business (pp. 18–25); Mama's return (pp. 26–31); and Gabby in her coat (p. 32). The story can also be paraphrased or told through the pictures.

Related Materials

The following titles are suggested: *I'm in Charge* (Little, 1985) by Joan Drescher depicts a youngster's beginning independence in a working family; *But What about Me?* (Harcourt, 1976) by Sandra Love tells about a youngster whose mother returns to work; *Tony Savala* (Herald, 1972) by Dorothy Hamilton describes a young boy's reacquaintance with his sheepherder grandfather in the Nevada Rockies; *A Place Between* (Viking, 1986) by Suzanne Newton relates a youngster's struggles in a new town in which her father has secured work. Two valuable nonfiction works are *If You Are a Hunter of Fossils* (Scribner, 1980) by Byrd Baylor, with Peter Parnall's drawings, which lyrically describes a geologist's work, and *From the Door of the White House* (Lothrop, 1984) by Bruce Preston, which describes a doorman's personal memories from Eisenhower's to Ford's presidencies.

The poster "Anna Roosevelt" (ALA, 1986, No. 124) serves well as a background note. Three films are suggested: *Teedie: From the Childhood of Theodore Roosevelt* (Films by Edmond Levy, 1985, 25 min.); *Toscanini: The Maestro* (Films for the Humanities, 1986, 60 min.); and *Sandsong* (Wombat Productions, 1981, 20 min.). A charming recording read by Carol Channing, *The Purple Cow Goops, and More Goops* (Caedmon, 1986), from the writing of Gelett Burgess, also fits this presentation.

Howe, James. *The Hospital Book*
Photographs by Mal Warshaw. Crown, 1981, 94 pp.

Since the publication of his first coauthored titles for middle-graders, *Bunnicula: A Rabbit Tale of Mystery* and *Teddy Bear's Scrapbook* (both Macmillan, 1979; 1980), which were well received, James Howe has continued to write as a sole author; 16 of his titles are in print. The number of his titles printed each year has steadily increased; in 1986 alone, six were published. Some of the stories are for primary-graders, but many are for middle-graders. Most of Howe's books are fiction; however, he has also written nonfiction titles suitable for middle-graders and junior high students. James Howe, who is in his early forties, writes clearly and compassionately about the universal concerns of youngsters. He does painstaking research for his nonfiction titles. For example, in this book he acknowledges the institutions and individuals that helped him write it: seven hospitals—several of them New York City hospitals—their staffs, their patients and their families, and a number of social agencies. This book represents a guided tour of a hospital for both child and parent. It introduces and describes the medical treatments, the routine daily care, and the people with whom the child may come into contact. In the process it addresses emotional concerns and reassures a youngster with information. Children ages 9–11 (grades 4–6) will read it independently. Younger children or reluctant readers will find the photographs helpful and intriguing.

Mal Warshaw, who provided 56 black-and-white photographs for the book, his first effort for children, dedicated his work to his wife and grandchildren. The title is profusely illustrated; practically every page signals a different informative and reassuring experience for children. Twenty-five full-page photographs enhance the text (easy-to-read 14-point typeface) and visually express the honesty in the people and the routines shown. The four photographs on the jacket portray youngsters undergoing different routine medical procedures; one youngster playfully conducts a procedure on himself with realistic-looking play equipment.

Seven brief chapters conduct a tour of a hospital for the reader, briefly answer a child's sometimes unasked questions, and end triumphantly with the return home of a child-patient. The first chapter, "The Hospital," acknowledges the new experience in one page with the assurance that you (the reader) will be helped and sent home as soon as possible. The complementary full-page photograph of a young boy, about nine, having his blood pressure and temperature taken is a reassuring way to begin.

In the next chapter, "What Is Going to Happen to Me," the tour continues. Speaking directly to the reader, the text starts at the admissions office, where routine forms are filled out by parents. From there, the child-patient travels in a wheelchair wearing a plastic wristband (identification) to the hospital room. The photograph (p. 15) shows two boys lying in bed with their food trays in front of them. The text next describes the hospital bed and its mobility, television sets, toilets, schoolrooms and playrooms for ambulatory youngsters, and the patients' nightclothes. A treatment room is likened to a clinic or doctor's examination room. A nurses' station is highlighted, together with an explanation of nurses' "shifts." Medical treatment in the hospital room or in the treatment room by doctors or nurses is discussed, as well as pulse, height and weight measurements, and urine samples. Blood samples and "taking blood" also are explained. Accompanying photographs show detailed scenes (omitting faces). The author frankly says that it hurts, but only for a few minutes.

Hospital personnel are identified in chapter 3, "Who Is That Person?" Starting with a doctor, James Howe categorizes doctors simply into interns, residents, and personal physicians. Nurses, lab technicians, "child-life specialists," dietitians, custodians, and parents are also defined.

"What Is That Thing," chapter 4, explains the ordinary objects to which a child-patient may be exposed, such as the washbasin, bedpan, urinal, emesis (throwing-up pan). The author offers some reassurance by stating that not everyone needs the emesis or the stretcher bed and that a patient may be able to get out of the bed or wheelchair. The most common medical tools are described: stethoscope, otoscope (ear), ophthalmoscope (eye), tongue depressor, reflex hammer, sphygmomanometer (blood pressure), thermometer (temperature), x-ray (including the CAT scanner), and electrocardiogram (EKG).

"How Will I Get Better," chapter 5, is an honest and important exposition for children. The text concentrates on many different kinds of treatment, but admits that needles and injections are often used. A full-page photograph of an approximately 11-year-old male grimacing while receiving an injection introduces the chapter. IVs, casts, and oxygen-breathing machines (IPPBs) are also mentioned. Surgery is examined step by step, from not eating beforehand, through transportation to the operating room (OR), to being helped onto the operating table, the anesthesiologist, the type of anesthetic, the recovery room, and postoperative stitch removal.

Chapter 6, "How Will I Feel," represents an overwhelming concern for any child-patient—pain and the right to express it. The book states that some pain should be expected, especially after surgery, until the body has a chance to heal. The author strongly suggests asking if it will hurt to help prepare oneself. Feelings of anger are explored, and such useful ways to discharge them are listed, such as playing with hospital-like equipment or pounding clay. Feeling scared is recognized as common to children and adults alike and asking questions to alleviate this feeling is encouraged. The book shows how one can learn to get through a scary and difficult situation.

The final chapter is satisfying. Parents pick up a young boy, a discharged child-patient. The photograph shows the mother waving goodbye to the child's roommates. Everyone is smiling!

Thematic Material

The straightforward theme mirrors the author's intent—to familiarize children with a strange environment, hopefully to overcome fear and lessen anxiety over a potentially frightening experience. Few experiences are more pressure-laden for middle-graders than a hospital visit. This book provides them with a reliable cushion of honesty and accuracy on which to "practice" gaining confidence.

Discussion Materials

This title is easily introduced. To reassure the youngsters, show the jacket photographs, together with the book's first photograph (p. 12), while paraphrasing the text (p. 13). Follow by reading the five sentences on page 94 while showing the photograph of the youngster going home (p. 95). Next, conduct a tour of the hospital. Display the photograph of the nurses' station and explain the night shift (pp. 20–21) to illustrate chapter 2, "What Is Going to Happen to Me?" To show nurses and interns as explained in chapter 3, "Who Is That Person," use pages 30–31. Chapter 4, "What Is That Thing," can be shown with the pictures on pages 44, 45 or 46, and 47. "How Will I Get Better," chapter 5, can be shown realistically with the picture on page 60. Surgery can be briefly described (pp. 66–81; picture p. 72). "How Will I feel," chapter 6, can be illustrated with the pictures on pages 83 and 92. The coping mechanisms outlined on pages 88–91 can be read (picture p. 91).

Related Materials

Some suggested titles are: Mildred Phillips's *The Sign in Mendel's Window* (Macmillan, 1985), illustrated by Margot Zemach; Helen Oxenbury's *The Queen and Rosie Rat* (Morrow, 1980); Patricia Wrightson's *Night Outside* (Atheneum, 1985); Joan Phipson's *Hit and Run* (Atheneum, 1985); and Steven Callahan's *Adrift: Seventy-six Days Lost at Sea* (Houghton, 1986). The nonfiction titles *Oh Boy! Babies* (Little, 1980) by Alison C. Herzig and *Dr. Wildlife* (Watts, 1985) by Rory C. Foster also are recommended.

The "Curious George" poster (ALA, 1986, No. 159) can be used in this presentation. Three films—also available as videos—are suggested: *Curious George Goes to the Hospital* (Churchill Films, 1983, 15 min.); *Medical Technology* (National Geographic Soc., 1986, 25 min.); and *Cell Wars* (Bullfrog Films, 1986, 11 min.). Two recordings are also suggested: *See and Be* (Caedmon, 1982, also cassette) by Rachel Carr and *You Read to Me, I'll Read to You* (Spoken Arts, 1986) by John Ciardi and his children.

Lasky, Kathryn. *The Night Journey*
Illus. by Trina Schart Hyman. Warne, 1981, 150 pp.

Since the late seventies, Kathryn Lasky has published well-reviewed books for children. This title, for example, was cited for middle-readers on the ALA Notable Book list. She has become a highly regarded author whose new books are eagerly anticipated. More than a dozen of her titles are in print. The author writes in an appropriately simple style for the subject and grade level. For example, *The Night Journey* is a seemingly simple story of the young heroine's interest in her great-grandmother's tale of her childhood and her family's escape from tsarist Russia. (The great-grandmother currently lives in a modern extended family with the heroine.) The heroine's ordinary school experiences serve as counterpoint to this elaborately layered story, which reveals fundamental principles of life. Kathryn Lasky describes the story's episodes both humorously and seriously as they really occurred and in a way that the reader can appreciate. Youngsters ages 10 and up (grades 5 and up) will enjoy the nuances of this exciting yet reflective story.

One of the devices the author uses exceedingly well to maintain interest and lead to a suspenseful and satisfying conclusion, as well as to deliver a strong philosophic statement, is the clever segueing of the great-grandmother's remembered tale of exciting past events with the heroine's own commonplace occurrences. Kathryn Lasky's smooth passage from past to present provides continuity for the reader. The author uses 14 "time slip" passages. The four-page epilogue, which contains the final anticlimax, expands the story from the great-grandmother at age 9, when she escapes from Russia, to the heroine-listener-learner at age 14, to the heroine-writer who starts to write the story at age 18.

Trina Schart Hyman, long recognized as a marvelous illustrator of children's books and lately an author-illustrator of note, contributed her distinctive talents to enhance the text. She drew 20 black-and-white illustrations, two of which are full-page; the rest are mostly half-page. The title-page illustration (which extends onto the facing page) shows the heroine listening to the great-grandmother's tale, while in the foreground the figures of the seven-person extended family file singly behind the father as they flee a Russian town. The end note shows two of the great-grandmother's favorite possessions that span her lifetime: a picture of her in native costume as a nine-year-old in Russia, given to her on the eve of their escape by her old-maid Aunt Ghisa (p. 132), and her tea glass, for use with her beloved samovar, with a lemon opposite it. The heavy black outlines and shadings help to reflect the nighttime escape, and the typical Hyman facial expressions portray the characters well; the piquant expression of the nine-year-old heroine is poignant.

Rachel (Rache) Lewis, a 14-year-old only child who is in ninth grade, is not too happy about losing a lead part in the school play, *Oklahoma.* That her school friend, tall and gangly Amy, who just moved to Minneapolis,

Minnesota, from Brooklyn, New York, was given the "Ado Annie" part despite her Brooklyn accent doesn't make it any sweeter. However, Rache does have the solace of a strong Russian-Jewish family, which includes her dad, Ed, an architect, and her mother, Leah. She also has a great-grandmother, Nana Sashie, whom she loves.

Although Nana Sashie is old—she was born in Russia in 1891—she is fond of telling Rache that she is old-old and that Nana Rose, her daughter and Rache's grandmother who lives nearby and visits often, is merely young-old. Every morning Ed and Leah or Nana Rose carry Nana Sashie from her upstairs room to the downstairs rocking chair. Rache is used to Nana Sashie dozing at the dinner table and also to the things, according to Leah, that Rache mustn't mention for fear of causing a stroke—things like talking about the "old days," playing concert music that reminds Nana Sashie about her deceased husband, Reuven Bloom, a violinist and conductor.

But nothing will deter the two—great-grandmother and heroine—from telling and listening to the historical tale. Rache is so fascinated by Nana Sashie's tale, and Nana Sashie so pleased to tell it, that they are both spellbound. As the old woman tells her clearly remembered harrowing tale, Rache listens intently. Forbidden to have these storytelling rendezvous any longer, Rache resorts to stealing into Nana Sashie's room at night. Nana Sashie's voice takes on the vigor of the youngster she becomes in the tale, and many nights pass until the escape is accomplished.

Nine-year-old Sashie lives in a two-room apartment, number 23, on Kreshchatik Street in Nikolayev, Russia, that is filled with love, problems, and her family of seven. Her mother, Ida, tends to all of them, including the younger children, Louie, 1½, and baby Cecile, only five months old. Sashie's father, Joe, a machinist, works as a lathe operator in a local factory. His maiden sister, Ghisa, who is active in the artists' group in town, is also a talented seamstress. The seventh member of the family is Zadye Sol, the paternal grandfather who lives with them in the Jewish ghetto. Their close quarters ensure that Sashie hears the communications among the adults about the pogroms that have been carried out during Tsar Nicholas's current reign. All the family members feel the need to escape. As Sashie, who has no particular friends in the area, except Moishe (Mismatch) or Zev, listens closely, she realizes that they need to leave immediately, but the ideas she hears are nebulous. After thinking carefully about the proposed amorphous plans, Sashie diplomatically suggests that a piece of each plan is worthwhile and when put together the pieces make a workable plan. At nine, she is wise enough to let each adult suggest the best part of his or her plan to form a workable one.

Meanwhile, Rache's daylight hours are filled with everyday activities. She decides to help coach Amy. She also watches Nana Sashie expertly use her tool chest with cyrillic lettering on it to help Ed fix a pipe. She helps Dad prepare a birthday feast for Leah, while he speaks French and calls her Ra Chelle, and is also present as her mother and grandmother find the top of Nana Sashie's old samovar and don't really know what it is. Luckily, they find out and the samovar is reconstructed, ensuring that it can preside in Nana Sashie's bedroom boiling tea just as it did in Nikolayev. It keeps her company like a silent soldier from her childhood days until the day she dies.

Two days before Purim, Sashie's family leaves Nikolayev in darkness along the Bug (Boog) River, which originates in the Ukraine, in reversible outfits made painstakingly by Ghisa. On the underside are colorful Purim costumes. Each family member chooses a character from the *Book of Esther*. Ida is wearing the samovar top as a crown imitating Queen Esther. They travel in a chicken wagon driven by Wolf Levinson, a haunted specter of a man who works as a furnace man in the same factory as Sashie's father. Zadye Sol, who was convinced that he wouldn't be alive when the family left, nonetheless accompanies them laying under the chickens and saying his prayers. The younger babies complain little (if they did, their mouths would be covered). Each member carries some precious possession smaller than a chicken: Joe, his tool chest; Ghisa, her picture of Sashie; Ida, her samovar; and Sashie, after much thought about her doll Tovah, chose the beautiful counting book Aunt Ghisa sewed for her, which showed beloved remembrances of Nikolayev, especially Sashie's favorite park, where she pleaded with her father "not to speak Yiddish in the park, only Russian."

The ride in the chicken cart driven by the specterlike Wolf Levinson is fraught with terror. Wolf, the embodiment of "someone desperate" who Sashie suggested to her father might get them a horse and wagon, saves them by killing some chickens over them when a patrol of Russian soldiers stops the cart. As Wolf leaves the family in L'Bove, they are sorrowfully overlooking the desolation and human devastation that is a pogrom. Joe then drives the wagon onward toward the guard whom Wolf has arranged for them to bribe. Sashie presents the guard with the samovar filled with Ida's *hamantaschen* cookies. Inside the cookies are the gold pieces that they had received in exchange for their possessions. Sashie also convinces the guard to take some plain cookies for his fellow guards, but the process is so fast that neither Sashie nor the guard knows which cookies are which.

So they pass over to freedom, and soon they are at Ida's relatives in Stepinova. During one memorable meeting along the way, the group meets Reuven Bloom. Although Sashie is only nine, she thinks about this wonderful fiddle player as the journey continues. Ten years later they meet again in America, and she becomes Mrs. Reuven Bloom. The tale is told.

Events move swiftly once Nana Sashie finishes. The doctor tells Leah and Ed that Nana Sashie has decided to die. All the family can do is to stay with her constantly. This woman dies bravely as she lived, from Nikolayev to America, having passed on her story to Rache. Rache often wonders at how closely her three maternal progenitors resemble each other facially, and also why her mother and grandmother did not react to the heritage the way she does. Rache is obviously a wonderful depot for Sashie's story.

Thematic Analysis

This multilayered story has many themes. The universal theme of good and evil is set against the historical background of the pogrom, the "holocaust" and modern religious intolerance. Human frailty and guilt are also explored in the character of Wolf Levinson who cannot erase his own cowardice. The juxtaposition of a historical extended family against a modern one presents another theme. The great-grandmother's appealing revelation to her great-granddaughter who has always seen her as an adult that as a nine-year-old girl she helped formulate an escape plan with her family strengthens the child's concept of her grandmother as a role model. The philosophic idea of the historical continuity of mankind is written large throughout this fascinating story.

Discussion Materials

This book can be presented in many ways. Begin each presentation by showing the jacket painting by Hyman of old Nana Sashie at night with the moon shining through the window telling Rache about her Russian-Jewish family whose members are reflected in the large samovar. The framed photographs on the back jacket further identify the characters from both eras, 1900 and present. Introduce the characters (the jacket and pages 1–14). Describe the settings and read the dedication (one page before the half-title page), which lyrically states the theme of good and evil. The "time shifts" occur on pages 14, 20, 44, 50, 59, 67, 81, 96, 145, and 146. Trina Schart Hyman's pictures also introduce characters and tell the story (pp. 8, 11, 16, 39, 68, 71, 76, 80, 93, 98, 109, 115, 121, 127, 132, 137, 142, 150). Sashie's escape story, as told to her great-granddaughter Rache, can be told or read. Several episodes demand book talking: Nana Sashie uses the toolbox (pp. 22–24); Purim (pp. 24–28, 52–57, 120); the escape plan and its execution (pp. 28–34, 42–43, 76, 96–114, 116, 131–138); Wolf Levinson (pp. 34–42, 114); *hamantaschen* (pp. 50–52, 58, 138–141, 142–144); the samovar (pp. 61–67, 91–95); the family's possessions for the trip (pp. 68–75); Rache and her father cook (pp. 82–90); and Reuven (pp. 118–129). The epilogue is conclusive (pp. 145–150); read the letter (pp. 148–149).

Related Materials

Several titles to suggest are: *Refugee* (Dial, 1977) by Ann Rose; *Daughter of Witches* (Ace, 1983) by Patricia Wrede; *Journey with Grandmother* (Macmillan, 1960) by Edith Unnerstad; *Close Enough to Touch* (Delacorte, 1983) by Richard Peck; and *Pony Problem* (Dutton, 1977) by Barbara Holland. Four nonfiction titles can be used: *Puppeteer* (Macmillan, 1985) by Kathryn Lasky; *The Story of Football* (Morrow, 1985) by Dave Anderson; *Commodore Perry in the Land of the Shogun* (Lothrop, 1985) by Rhoda Blumberg; and *Women of the Four Winds* (Houghton, 1985) by Elizabeth Fagg Olds. Two films are recommended: *Making Overtures: The Story of a Community Orchestra* (Bullfrog Films, 1985, 28 min.) and *It's All Done with Strings* (Encyclopaedia Britannica, 1986).

Martin, Bill, Jr., and Archambault, John. *White Dynamite and Curly Kidd*
Illus. by Ted Rand. Holt, 1986, 32 pp.

Bill Martin, Jr., is a prolific author with many titles in several series: Little Nature Books, Wise Owl Books, and Young Owl Books. In 1983 he also published *Brown Bear, Brown Bear, What Do You See*, illustrated by Eric Carle, followed by two titles illustrated by Ted Rand, *The Ghost-eye Tree* (Holt, 1985) and *Barn Dance* (Holt, 1986). This title, which also was published in 1986, demonstrates the perfect collaboration between the author and the illustrator Ted Rand, whose beautifully expressed, imaginative ideas are reflected in his striking conceptions. The book is skillfully designed, from the stamped cover showing Curly Kidd riding the bull, to the arrangement of the small amount of text on each (sometimes every other) page, to the indention of lines to indicate the dialogue between Curly Kidd and his youngster. The story treats a youngster's anxiety and admiration as she watches her rodeo-circuit father win his latest riding event on a mean, massive bull. In the exciting tale, which captures the excitement of a rodeo stampede, the youngster learns a little trick from her dad to allay her anxiety (think of something else) and realizes that she can grow up to be just like him (a rodeo rider). The discovery on the last page that the youngster who wears a cowboy hat throughout the story and looks like a little cowboy is a girl takes the reader by surprise and makes the message even stronger. Boys and girls 7–9 (grades 2–4) will find the rollicking story both exciting and surprising. Just watch the faces of boys in grades 7 or older!

The illustrator Ted Rand is a well-known artist on his native Pacific Coast and nationally through *Life* magazine and the *New York Times*. His wondrous illustrations are more than eye-catching—they are eye-stopping. In this title they seem larger than life, magically evoking the movement, dust, and splash of bright colors in a rodeo. They include 15 double-spread pictures, one full-page illustration, plus the rodeo announcement poster on the title page. Rand also did the full-color jacket painting. The drawings are a combination of paint washes, colored ink outlines, and spatterings of ink and paint that represent the mayhem in the rodeo ring. Acrylic highlights, especially in the white of the bull and rodeo horses, are also used effectively. The colors are earth tones heightened with splashes of bright blue sky or red clown wig. The rectangular shape of the book gives a long horizontal axis to the borderless illustrations, which together suggest an extension of the activities in boundless space. The large-size figures and objects blare the majesty of a rodeo, and the overall effect is one of energy.

As Curly Kidd (Dad) ties on his chaps in preparation for his imminent rodeo ride, his scared youngster (Lucky), arrayed in a similar cowboy outfit, chats incessantly and asks dad if he isn't scared, too. Dad tells him about his trick of thinking about places he'd like to go to take his mind off his nervousness. Taking the hint, the youngster starts to think about Riverton, Wyoming, where Grandma lives as a good place to go. The youngster glances about and sees the rodeo hands place White Dynamite, the meanest bull in the United States, in the chute. (Curly Kidd won White Dynamite in the luck of the draw.) It is a good thing that Curly Kidd is considered (according to his own admission) the best bull rider in the whole United States and Canada, because White Dynamite sure looks huge and fierce. With every confidence in his dad, the youngster tells him that maybe someday there will be two rodeo riders in the family. Dad says, "Sure, why not?" and agrees that his youngster can be number 13-2, while he'll remain number 13-1. But he doesn't like the youngster's suggested name, Curly Kidd's Little Kid. Instead, he suggests the youngster's own name, Lucky Kidd, be used. In the final few minutes before the ride, the father and the child each chew sticks of gum—well, at least Curly has only two—to ease the tension.

As Curly Kidd mounts the huge bull in the chute, the youngster watches and tries hard to think of places to go. Noted rodeo towns, such as Casper and Cheyenne, Wyoming, fall from the youngster's lips. As the litany continues, the bull explodes from the open chute into the rodeo ring with Curly Kidd hanging on with the required one hand for the necessary time. The red-wigged rodeo clown holding a polka-dot parasol bravely provides an extra thrill for the crowds by frolicking near the main attraction. A rodeo horse rider also comes close to provide what safety he can for the bull rider. The 24-ton bull is so treacherous-looking, however, that it isn't long before they both run for cover to the sidelines.

Meanwhile, the youngster watches intently from the rail, concentrating on noted rodeo states like Alabama, Minnesota, Indiana, and Arizona. As Curly Kidd manages to stay aboard the pitching and heaving bull and the excitement increases, the youngster rapidly starts to combine cities and states, like Omaha, Nebraska. With only four more required seconds left for Dad to hang on, the youngster finally bursts out with Mexico. By then the crowd is standing in the bleachers. In the final moment of excitement as two rodeo horse riders circle the main attraction to help Curly Kidd, the youngster spits out the name of the biggest and best-known rodeo stampede—the Calgary (Canada) Stampede. At the end, the bull, whose middle name is Doomsday, twists and turns tortuously unwilling to surrender. The clown is so amazed by Curly Kidd's skill and bravery that he loses his hat. He is obviously not alone, however, because the youngster also swallows the chewing gum.

Just as the youngster says, "Walla Walla, Washington," the rodeo ride is over with Curly Kidd victorious. A rodeo rider closes in to help him dismount, while the clown tries to distract the bull by rolling a large inflated inner tube into its line of vision within the rodeo ring. The youngster is thrilled. Dad wins 97 out of a possible 100 points for the ride. The youngster, of course, thinks that Dad deserves 100 points, even if he is limping. When Dad says he can't tell how he is yet, because his head is "still ridin' that bull," the youngster's heart is still pounding, too! Dad tells the youngster, "If you're going to be a bull rider, you have to get used to the inner pounding." Then he smiles and pulls off the youngster's cowboy hat exposing her ponytail.

Thematic Material

Aspiring to be perfect like one's parent and to do the same exciting work is natural for a middle-grader. This adult role model theme is vital to the story. The father's satisfying admission that his young daughter might assume his role someday and the attendant anxiety that must constantly be handled and conquered is also important. The climactic denouement recognizes the sexist stereotype and communicates the realistic adult message that being upset in heart and mind must be recognized and handled.

Discussion Material

Young children and reluctant readers will respond to a typical picture-book presentation of this generous, large-figured picture book with an evocative text. Sharpen up a southwestern twang! To stimulate independent readers show the following pictures: Curly on White Dynamite at first (pp. 12–13); the middle of the ride (pp. 18–19, 22–23); and the jacket painting. The last two displays can be merged (they are in scale) by making transparencies to show both the rider and the bull together. An interesting book-talk motif would be the litany of places that the youngster repeats while Dad rides: (pp. 2–3, 11, 12, 15, 16, 18, 22, 24–25). For those interested in facial accuracy, compare the youngster and Dad (pp. 8–9 and the last page, p. 32).

Related Materials

A range of titles can be suggested: *Opening Night* (Greenwillow, 1984) by Rachel Isadora demonstrates with lush illustrations ballet dancing as seen by a young girl; *Does Anybody Care about Lou Emma Miller?* (Crowell, 1980) by Alberta Wilson Constant describes a girl at the turn of the century who campaigns in a mayoralty race; *Seven Daughters and Seven Sons* (Atheneum, 1982) by Barbara Cohen relates the story based on an Iraqi folktale of an enterprising young woman; *The Illyrian Adventure* (Dutton, 1986) by Lloyd Alexander describes a heroine who struggles against political intrigue to carry on her deceased father's archaeological dig; *No-Return Trail* (Harcourt, 1978) by Sonia Levitin tells about the arduous journey in 1841 of the first woman to cross the Rockies to California; and *Megan* (Dodd, 1983) by Kathleen Magill relates the frontier story of a tall, feisty young female. Two nonfiction titles are recommended for further reading: *In Kindling Flame: The Story of Hannah Senesh, 1921–1944* (Lothrop, 1985) by Linda Atkinson and *Takeoff! The Story of America's First Woman Pilot for a Major Airline* (Crown, 1984) by Bonnie Tiburzi.

Three films to use are *Cowgirls* (Direct Cinema, 1986, 29 min.), also available as a video; *Legacy of the American Cowboy* (Kodak, 28 min.); and *Cannonball Simp* (Phoenix/BFA Films and Video, 1983, 27 min.). Two suggested recordings or cassettes are *Southwest Tales* (Spoken Arts, 1986) by J. Frank Dobi and *People, Animals, and Other Monsters* (Caedmon, 1982), read by Jack Prelutsky.

Meltzer, Milton.   *Dorothea Lange: Life Through the Camera*
Illus. by Donna Diamond. Photographs by Dorothea Lange.
Viking, 1985, 58 pp.

Well known and respected, Milton Meltzer is a prolific author. Over several decades he has compiled a listing of excellent titles, primarily nonfiction, for children in grades 2–7 and up; almost two dozen titles are in print. Meltzer does scrupulous research and writes in a vital style. As author Jean Fritz said in a review of the featured title, "It [the title] makes no compromise with either truth or style." Meltzer launched Viking/Kestrel's biography series Women of Our Time, which presents the lives of twentieth-century women, from historical figures to current headliners for children ages 7–11. He had earlier written the book *Dorothea Lange: A Photographer's Life,* and his interviews, the places he visited, as well as the letters and diaries he examined, were a fertile background. Notwithstanding his recognition of the difficulty in capturing the "complicated truth of another human being," his biography of a female photographer and personality both attends to the purpose of the series and attests to Meltzer's skill. Meltzer is recognized as an able social historian, but his affinity to his subject, who also lived and worked throughout the Great Depression (1929), also contributed to the vitality of this title. The life of the famous woman photographer is presented in six chapters, from her early days to her final years, with a brief highlight about the social effects of her photographs. Youngsters ages 8–10 (grades 3–5) will be delighted by the heroine's determination to become a photographer.

Donna Diamond's six illustrations have the look of photographs (see also *Introducing More Books,* Bowker, 1978, pp. 7–9). She used pencil and pen to produce the remarkable clarity of line and shading that is her signature. Five are full-page illustrations with fine pencil outlines; one is a quarter-page picture set horizontally on two pages that portrays a jalopy and a tent city of migrants during the 1930s (chapter 4) and corresponds to Lange's famous photo "Migrant Mother—1936." The eight famous photographs by Lange reproduced in the book undeniably set a mood and enhance Meltzer's text.

Both sets of Dorothea Lange Nutzhorn's grandparents had immigrated from Germany and settled in Hoboken, New Jersey. She was born May 25, 1895, to Henry, a young lawyer, and Joan Lange, a librarian. They lived in a rented row house on Bloomfield Street. Although the family moved frequently to other New Jersey towns, they eventually returned to Hoboken. Dorothea loved her strong and handsome mother, but her mother put a great emphasis on appearance, and Dorothea was very sensitive because she was lame in her right leg from polio. She had been called "limpy" by other children since she was seven. Dorothea also loved her father who laughed a lot with her, read to her, and took her to the theater. She never understood why he left without saying a word to her when his marriage broke up. Dorothea rarely ever mentioned him after that.

Joan had a librarian's job on New York's lower East Side and took Dorothea with her to an elementary school there (P.S. 61). Dorothea was an outsider; she didn't live nearby and had no friends. She learned early to step gingerly around "the bums" in the Bowery. After school she spent her time in the library waiting for her mother to go home. As she looked out the windows, she watched the city's teeming immigrant life. She spent endless hours looking at pictures—in the library collection, in newspapers and magazines at home, and the ones she saw with her eyes outside her windows in the afternoon.

Dorothea entered Wadleigh High School uptown with its population of 3,600 girls, but she was overwhelmed and often skipped classes roaming the crowded streets back to lower New York. She would have failed at school if not for a teacher interested in science and social issues, Martha Bruere, who became a life-long friend. Dorothea thought of the Bruere family—father, a surgeon; brother, interested in reform politics; and sister, an executive in a bank, as her own real family. By comparison her grandmother, a talented seamstress who had a terrible temper, and her great-aunt Caroline, a teacher and the family member with whom Dorothea found the most comfort, did not seem as attractive. Dorothea did form one same-age life-long friendship, however, with a high school classmate, Florence (Fronsie). Together they cut classes and took in free cultural events, or just roamed.

By the end of high school Dorothea knew she wanted to be a photographer. In the early 1900s, however, jobs for women were severely restricted to working in a factory or as a nurse, teacher, librarian, or secretary, never as a photographer. Her mother insisted that Dorothea become a teacher and attend a teacher-training school, but Dorothea was determined to become a photographer, even without a camera. At age 17 she found an after-school job with Arnold Genthe, a well-known portrait photographer. She learned a great deal and never forgot his admonition to catch "the true character of the sitter." Dorothea quit teacher-training school and started a round of photography jobs that taught her the business aspects of the field, as well as the technical ones. She became an official studio camerawoman when she substituted one day and both the boss and customer liked the print. She knew she had reached the first rung toward her goal when she heard her mother say, "My daughter's a photographer."

When Dorothea was 23, she and Fronsie, a Western Union office worker, took one suitcase and about 140 dollars and went to San Francisco where they were robbed. Dorothea shed her last name, officially becoming Dorothea Lange, and opened a portrait studio on Sutter Street, which was her life for many years. Two years later at age 25 she married Maynard Dixon, a painter, and subsequently had two sons, Daniel and John. Often apart, the couple had a stormy marriage. Trying to take landscape pictures high in the Sierra Mountains in 1929, Dorothea decided to concentrate on people of all kinds. Although she still had to make studio portraits to help support her family, Dorothea wanted to work more with her camera among the homeless and hungry people, and in the middle of the Great Depression in 1933, Dorothea exhibited some documentary photos that expressed this wish. Paul Taylor, an economist and professor at the University of California at Berkeley, saw the exhibit and involved Dorothea with the plight of the unemployed. From 1934 to 1935, she worked closely with Taylor illustrating his government studies of California migrant workers. The Taylor-Lange reports became well known in Washington, D.C., and they were married, both for the second time, in December 1935 and went to live in Berkeley.

Dorothea continued to take photographs among the people, and her photo "Migrant Mother" brought her fame, but she now had five children (Paul's children, Ross, Marget, and Katherine, lived with them). Between her photography and her home responsibilities, she had too much to do. She was an imperfect mother, moody and selfish, and everyone suffered. On a photography tour of the South, she finally met her federal boss, Roy Stryker, in Washington, D.C., and forces seemed to be coalescing to help them improve unsavory social conditions at this time: newspapers and magazines started to use photographs to illustrate the printed articles about social conditions and the new 35mm camera appeared (although Dorothea never used it as her primary tool). By 1939 Dorothea's photographs showed the power of the pictures in helping to illuminate the miserable conditions among the poor.

By World War II government projects were redirected to war-time concerns. Fortunately Dorothea had a Guggenheim grant to photograph the religious communities in the West. After December 7, 1941, the Japanese-Americans on the West Coast were interned by the federal government, and strangely the federal government hired her to make a pictorial record. Today Dorothea's photographs remind us of this terrible tragedy.

Around this time Dorothea's ulcer began to bother her seriously. Years of stress dealing with her outside work and her responsibilities at home became oppressive. She did not pick up a camera again for three years. By the time she did, her focus had changed. Her photographs were now about relationships, especially family. She spent lots of time with her children and grandchildren and encouraged their friendships and celebrations—her family called her "the Napolean of holidays." Dorothea had become famous; friends like the photographer Ansel Adams collaborated on a *Life* magazine article, she taught at the California School of Fine Arts, and she traveled with Paul on three long overseas trips. She spent her last days aware of her terminal cancer preparing a photographic essay about American country women for the Museum of

Modern Art (New York). Dorothea died with her family at her bedside three months before the exhibit opened. "She was an artist . . . [who] discovers new truths in the cause of man."

Thematic Analysis

This slim story has many themes—courage, determination, sexism, racial prejudice, social problems, and the power of the media. The one that is most important, however, is the story of the career of a pioneer female photographer. It illustrates the grit, personal sacrifices, and imperfections of the courageous artist-photographer, and also suggests some of the possibilities and personal costs involved. The story clearly identifies a different adult occupational role for women without sugarcoating the determination and personal sacrifice that may be required.

Discussion Materials

To book talk this title, display the cover picture of Dorothea Lange and her camera and read aloud the first paragraph on the back cover. Then set the scene by paraphrasing her life to age 17 (pp. 1–9; picture p. 4), or use the plot summary and read aloud from the second paragraph on page 2 to the first paragraph on page 3. The following episodes can then be paraphrased: apprentice period (pp. 10–17; picture p. 14; read aloud second par. p. 12); early San Francisco years (pp. 18–31; picture p. 21; read aloud second par. p. 20); years of increasing fame as a documentary photographer (pp. 32–38; pictures pp. 34 and 35; photograph p. 36; read aloud pp. 34–35); years with Stryker's group making human documents (pp. 39–46; picture p. 45); and World War II work documenting the internment (pp. 47–57; picture p. 56; read aloud first par. p. 50). Show Dorothea Lange's photographs (frontispiece, pp. 24, 27, 29, 36, 41, 49, 54).

Related Materials

Some books to suggest are: *The Story of American Photography* (Little, 1980) by Martin W. Sandler, illustrated with photographs; *Architecture Is Elementary: Visual Thinking Through Architectural Concepts* (Gibbs M. Smith, 1986) by Nathan B. Winters; *The Skyscraper Book* (Crowell, 1981) by James Cross Giblin, illustrated by Anthony Kramer, photographs by Anthony Kramer; *Leonardo da Vinci: The Artist, Inventor, Scientist in Three Dimensional Movable Pictures* (Viking, 1984) by Alice Provenson and Martin Provenson, paper engineered by John Stejan; *Digging into the Past:*

Excavations in Ancient Lands (Scribner, 1986) by W. John Hackwell; and *Drawing Life in Motion* (Lothrop, 1984) by Jim Arnosky.

The following audiovisual titles are also suggested: *Basic Art by Video I: Beginning in Art and Painting* (MasterVision, 1984), a video; *Meet the Newbery Author: Virginia Hamilton* (Random, 1975), a filmstrip; *Andrew Wyeth* (Films for the Humanities, 1983, 63 min.) and *Strange Occurrence at Elmview Library* (FilmFair Communications, 1983, 17½ min.), both films; and *Nutcracker* (Caedmon, 1972), a recording (2s) read by Claire Bloom from the book adaptation by Janet Schulman.

Porte, Barbara Ann. *Harry's Mom*
Illus. by Yossi Abolafia. Greenwillow, 1985, 55 pp.

This award-winning author started publishing books for children in the early eighties with the first two titles in the Harry Series, *Harry's Visit* and *Harry's Dog* (both Greenwillow, 1983). Her other titles are for older children (see *Introducing Bookplots 3*, Chapter 5, pp. 156–160). This title, the third book in the Harry Series, demonstrates Barbara Ann Porte's keen talent for describing real characters and situations in a nonstereotypical way. In it, the motherless hero continues to learn more wonderful things about his mother from his small circle of relatives and to think about incorporating a little of each of their varied adult roles into his anticipated own. This Greenwillow Read-alone title will be read with interest by children ages 7–9 (grades 2–4).

Yossi Abolafia, who also illustrated the previous titles in the series, painted similar cartoon-style sketches in full color with thin pen outlines for this book. They include 36 pictures, 5 decorations, plus two full pages of the hero's school report printed in pen. Nine of the 36 drawings occupy a full page, and one is a half-page double spread. Practically every page in this profusely illustrated title has a sketch showing Harry, who looks a bit older but as perky and like "everyboy" as usual, and the other characters doing precisely what the author describes in the text. The colorful yet simple sketches illuminate a young boy's body language, with which youngsters can easily relate. The attractive jacket shows Harry in a stuffed chair framed by a red telephone on one side and bright flowers on the other cheerfully looking at a picture. A floor plug and an electric cord are highly visible. The sketch on the back jacket shows Harry sitting with his school desk partner and best friend, Eddie, pointing out the dictionary definition of the word "orphan" (the literary device upon which the story unfolds).

Harry Moskowitz, about nine, lives with his dad, Dr. Sol Moskowitz, who is a dentist. Harry doesn't remember his mother, who died when he was one year old, but sometimes he wonders what she was like. At school, he and his best friend, Eddie, share a two-person desk and work well together. One day, as they are looking up spelling words as a desk assignment, Harry comes across the dictionary definition of the word "orphan" and can't help showing Eddie: "A person without a mother or father, or both, is an orphan." Their teacher, Ms. Smith, tells them to be quieter and to look up the words independently. But Harry is astonished that he is an orphan and can't put it out of his mind.

On their way home from school in their integrated neighborhood, even the customary greeting and proferred bag of freshly baked raisin cookies from Eddie's mom (which Harry gladly accepts) doesn't put this new idea out of his mind. Cookie bag in hand, Harry heads straight for Dad's office. No one is in the waiting room, so Harry knocks on Dad's door. When Dad answers and says that Harry must wait until he finishes working on Ms. Miller's molar, Harry starts to cry. Although he recovers in time to reply "no" when his father asks if he is sick he completely forgets about the cookies while he waits. Ms. Miller soon emerges, however, and says something that Harry can't quite understand because her mouth is stuffed with cotton. It sounds like "You have grown," of course she's incorrect; Harry knows he's the shortest boy in his class.

When Dad joins him, Harry tells him that he just found out he's an orphan. Dad seems surprised and asks Harry how he can be an orphan with all his loved ones around—Aunt Rose who lives nearby, Grandpa and Grandma Moskowitz, and Grandpa and Grandma Murray, his mother's parents who live in Oklahoma. Dad also tells Harry that dictionaries tell how words are used by people, and that not one of Harry's relatives considers him an orphan. Feeling better, Harry offers Dad some cookies and they go into the kitchen to make some hot chocolate to go with the cookies. While they snack, Harry asks Dad to tell him again about his mom.

Dad tells Harry that Mom was very brave, pretty, and smart. She was a sports reporter and died in a racing car accident, one of her avocations.

Dad tells him again of the many exciting things she did: scuba diving, flying a plane, and mountain climbing. After the conversation, Dad suggests that Harry walk over to see Aunt Rose while he calls her to say that Harry is coming. Harry is happy to go. Aunt Rose, who keeps his dog, Girl, for him because Dad is allergic, confirms everything that Dad said and tells him more about his brave mom: about the time she rode an elephant in India and the time she went skydiving. She embraces Harry and tells him that he will always have her. Aunt Rose also tells him how much his mom loved him and that she called him "little Mr. Moskowitz." Harry feels much better now. He decides he is going to be like Mom.

That night Dad and Harry telephone Grandpa and Grandma Murray in Oklahoma. Harry's grandparents, who are pleased to hear from him, tell Harry what his mom was like when she was his age. Grandpa says she was very brave, riding her horse, Blacky, bareback on their farm, just in case she ever joined the circus. When Harry says he's not that brave, Grandpa quickly adds that she really was scared of bees, and that Harry is just like his mom—smart, a reader, and a lover of all animals—except bees. She had a dog, Mulligan, a turtle, Martha, a three-colored cat, Lucky, and a tank full of fish. Grandpa and Grandma Murray tell Harry that they are really lucky to have Harry. Then Dad says goodbye and tells them that on some days he and Harry miss Mom terribly. After a good night kiss, Harry sleeps soundly.

The next day at school Harry responds to Ms. Smith's request to write about someone you know and what you want to be when you grow up by printing two pages. The teacher compliments Harry on the first page about his mom because he put the commas in all the right places and showed imagination. On the second page, about what he hopes to be, Harry incorporated everything. He wants to ride a horse on his farm in Oklahoma, which has a sign on the fence, saying: Dr. Harry Moskowitz, dentist.

Thematic Analysis

This simple story has dual themes: the identification and emulation of adult roles, and the comforting safety web of a loving extended family within a single-parent family. An unusual component, and a welcome one, is the restatement of information about a brave mother who engaged in activities that American society still reserves for males. The middle-grader's tendency to look for and try to identify adult patterns is nicely shown for this developmental age. The youngster's incorporation of what he has heard from his family members and what he has experienced results in a finale that rings true.

Discussion Materials

This title, aimed at independent readers, can be introduced by showing the front jacket illustration of Harry looking at a picture of his mom and the one on the back jacket, showing him pointing out the dictionary definition of "orphan" to Eddie. Paraphrase the plot: Harry, who feels despondent when he finds out he is an orphan, hears from his dad, his Aunt Rose, and his grandparents that his mom was brave and smart and that he is much like her. This reassurance helps him feel better and want to emulate her strengths as well as his father's fine parenting role. Display the following: the illustration on page 5 (the same picture is on the back cover); Harry and Eddie and the cookies (p. 8); going home to Dad (pp. 10–11); the shortest in the class (read p. 14); Harry hears more about his mom from Dad (pp. 24–25), from Aunt Rose (pp. 130–131), and from Grandpa and Grandma Murray (pp. 38–45); and Harry's two school reports (pp. 51 and 53–55).

Related Materials

Three fiction titles are suggested: *Ruby* (Bradbury, 1980) by Amy Aitken, about a young girl who decides to campaign for president; *My Mother Is the Smartest Woman in the World* (Atheneum, 1982) by Eleanor Clymer, about a politically active family whose mother campaigns for mayor; *Garland for Gandhi* (Parnassus, 1968), about a young East Indian girl on whom the Mahatma makes a deep impression. Three nonfiction titles will also serve well: *Our Golda: The Story of Golda Meir* (Viking, 1984) by David A. Adler; *How to Write a Great School Report* (Lothrop, 1983) by Elizabeth James and Carol Barkin; *The Young Writer's Handbook* (Scribner, 1984) by Susan Tchudi and Stephen Tchudi.

The following audiovisual titles are suggested. Two films are *My Mother Was Never a Kid* (L.C.A., 1981) and *Zubin and the IPO* (Anti-Defamation League of B'nai B'rith, 1983). Three recordings are *Twenty-one Balloons* (Live Oak Media, 1978); *Mary Poppins* (Caedmon), read by Maggie Smith; and *Hans Christian Andersen in Central Park* (Weston Woods, 1979). Two filmstrips are *Charlotte Zolotow—The Grower* (Random, 1983) and *Exploring the Writing Process* (Walt Disney Educational Media, 1986, 5 fs). The ALA "Literacy" poster (1986, No. 237) with its dictionary definitions is a perfect accompanying background.

Yates, Elizabeth. *My Diary—My World*
Westminster, 1981, 187 pp.

The author, well known for her title *Amos Fortune, Free Man*, which won the 1951 ALA Newbery Award and the first William Allen White Award in 1953, has written more than two dozen titles for young people; five, spanning three decades, are in print. *My Diary—My World*, the first title of her autobiography, was followed by the sequel *My Widening World: The Continuing Diary of Elizabeth Yates* (Westminster, 1983). This highlighted story, based on the author's 1917–1925 diary, circumscribes the privileged life of a determined young girl from age 12 through 20. The heroine, who strives to be a writer, lives the seemingly idyllic existence of the wealthy at the turn of the century. Although she is faced with strong family objections, the heroine stoically surmounts her obstacles. The story is told as a loving family reminiscence and gives the reader a glance at the way it was early in the century for one small element in society. This historical look into a stratum of society in a different world, where the heroine also attains her goal, will appeal to female readers ages 10 and up (grades 5 and up).

A few old snapshots are reproduced on the jacket and at the chapter headings. The three on the front jacket show the young author and her family; several paragraphs of text stating the heroine's early desire to be a scribe are reproduced on the back jacket. The eight chapters, divided into the years 1918–1925, are preceded by a smattering of appropriate snapshots, which add a certain charm to the book. Each chapter is further subdivided by diary dates, some of which reoccur, including her winter birthday, New Year's Day, and specific dates in spring, summer, and fall. The descriptive entries follow the diary format and build sequentially into the story of a girl growing up. The book is dedicated to the author's parents, "who gave me great gifts—security, discipline, and their love." The preface establishes the format in conformity with the heroine's five-year red-leather diary, "A Line a Day," which Elizabeth received at age 11 from the seamstress, Miss Hyde.

As the mature author looks at her first diary entry, she remembers her past fondly. She is 12 again, December 6, 1917 (St. Nicholas Day). Elizabeth (Betty to her four-year-younger brother Bobby) is the next to youngest in the wealthy Yates family of Buffalo, New York. Her eldest sister, Teresa, is married and living apart from the "big, brown house" on

Delaware Avenue. Walter, her eldest brother, is also away, serving in the World War I army. Jinny (Virginia), an able student, attends Smith College and keeps Elizabeth well supplied with reading lists.

In 1918, Dick, Harry (two years older than Elizabeth), Elizabeth, and Bobby are home with Mother and Father. Father reads the *Wall Street Journal* daily, manages his inherited money in his downtown office, and raises his family strictly and with love. He believes wholeheartedly in the inscription on his Norman English family crest, "Sois Feal," or "Be Thou Faithful," and expects the same of his children. Elizabeth's mother, although strict and also a firm believer in the social niceties of her "place" for herself and her children, tells lyric Irish fairy tales. Then there is Brier, the family dog, who prefers Elizabeth's company.

Life is regulated in this household. Birthdays are always special, starting with the small pillow gift, perhaps a colored hair ribbon, dispensed by Mother. Christmas follows a regular pattern of decorating the house, celebrating the holidays, and burning the tree and other decorations outside in a bonfire on January 12. And in this household each child gets a private bedroom when he or she reaches age 14. Elizabeth, who formerly roomed with Bobby, is delighted to have Teresa's redecorated third-floor room. She also gets to serve table with Lizzie, the maid, at her parents' frequent small dinner parties, just like all the 14-year-old Yate girls. Also special to young Elizabeth are the household help: Maria, the kitchen cook; Andy, the groundskeeper; Lizzie, the maid; Miss Hyde, the seamstress whom Elizabeth helps weekly; and Mrs. Schmidt, from whom Elizabeth learns ironing. Elizabeth is shocked that Mrs. Schmidt wants to change her name to Smith because of the prejudice toward Germans during World War I. Finally, spending time at the family summer residence, Hillhurst Farm in Orchard Park, is a wonderful and regularly expected occurrence. The younger children spend most of their time riding, wading, and picnicking but it is a working farm, and "disciplines" also are a part of the experience, such as making butter for profit and market shopping to help Elizabeth with her weakest school subject.

Certain events also capture Elizabeth's attention at age 13 in sixth grade. As World War I engulfs everyone, she and five friends form Just Us Girls (JUGS), an organization to do war work (knit, make sachets and pincushions) to raise funds. The mutual friends are from the Franklin School (all girls). Elizabeth also spends free moments playing with her dollhouse, sometimes accompanied by Bobby, moving around the doll inhabitants,

Mr. and Mrs. Stockton, and making up stories. The day Mother gives her the book *What Every Young Girl Should Know* is a disturbing one for her, because she doesn't understand the book. She calls her friend Jean to find out what it means. Not long afterward, she tries to comfort Jean, when Alan, Jean's older brother, is killed in France. Then Elizabeth's mother calls Elizabeth selfish and inconsiderate, and the 14-year-old, five-foot six-inch, 115-pound, tall, gangly girl stops eating candy for a year. She also has her portrait painted by Elizabeth MacKinstry and recovers triumphantly from mastoiditis.

Teachers and school occupy a large part of Elizabeth's young existence. (She clearly remembers accompanying her mother to her teacher Miss Kelly's wake. Afterwards came many maiden ladies—the Misses Keyes, Watkins, Clements, and Conway, each of whom contributed in one way or another to the development of this eager wordsmith and reader.) But, try as she does to go to the public school, Hutchinson High, Elizabeth finishes at Franklin because that is what her parents wish. Elizabeth suspects that she was born with a pencil in her hand and likes nothing better than following the sage advice to write at least a line a day. She varies her writing projects among a novel, "Called Coward," poetry, and school themes. She also reads a good deal.

Meanwhile, Elizabeth's parents arrange for her to attend many cultural activities—symphonies, art exhibits, even a trip abroad to Venice and England. Elizabeth knows that she is expected to assume "her place." She knows that Jinny, who graduated summa cum laude from college and was offered an assistant professorship, turned it down because her parents thought she should marry someone suitable (wealthy) and leave the position for someone who needs it. Father buys Elizabeth a show horse, Bluemouse, to replace 22-year-old Old Joe and gives her a generous $25 allowance because she has done so well in the "farming" business.

But Elizabeth is silently determined to achieve her writing ambition without denying her parents' wishes. Although she suffers her first rejection slip for her poems, she continues to ride Bluemouse, tries to please her parents, and grows up rapidly. She even receives an innocent, unexpected kiss and a future marriage proposal from a young man who to add insult to injury is shorter than the then five-foot nine-inch, 125-pound heroine. After a summer at camp and a job in an equestrienne camp the following summer, Elizabeth finally convinces her parents that she must be a writer. With Bobby and her parents, Elizabeth heads for

New York City on a train with the Newark newspaper of her first printed poem firmly in hand.

Thematic Analysis

Several themes are prevalent. On the surface, the way life was for a few between 1917 and 1925 in the northeastern United States is pleasantly drawn. Some young readers will enjoy the journey through time into the past. Youngsters will learn the universality of strong family love and support, even if the family is not in agreement with the child's goal. The well-expressed theme of "growing up" occupationally (recognizing and working against obstacles) clearly shows the young reader that steadfast determination is important in attaining a satisfying conclusion.

Discussion Materials

This book can be book talked in at least two ways: by following the diary format and choosing an important incident for each year, or by highlighting interesting incidents in various categories. To illustrate the latter method, for example, introduce the plot and read pages 7–9, display the front jacket and read the copy on the back jacket; the family crest (p. 114); the household help (p. 61); gossip among the girls (p. 75); a "born" writer (pp. 8, 16–17, 36, 48–49, 82, 84–85, 91–93, 109–110, 131–136, 170, 173, 182–186); auspicious occasions (pp. 42, 71, 94–95); horse stories (pp. 66–67, 70–71, 89); a rejection slip and subsequent publication (pp. 170–173, 182–186); making butter (pp. 67–69, 74); a perspective on Jinny's position (pp. 64–66, 122–125); riding Bluemouse and Old Joe (pp. 66–67, 70–71). An adventure that begs to be book talked is the episode on Bluemouse (pp. 109–111). The book is full of incidents that can be told or read aloud by year and season or school year and vacation.

Related Materials

Some complementary nonfiction titles are: *Homesick: My Own Story* (Putnam, 1982) by Jean Fritz, illustrated by Margot Tomes; *Magazine behind the Scenes at Sports Illustrated* (Little, 1983) by William Jaspersohn; *Dear Diary* (Avon, 1983) by Jeanne Betancourt; *We Are Your Sisters: Black Women in the Nineteenth Century* (Norton, 1984) by Dorothy Sterling; and *Love Strong* (New Amer. Lib., 1985) by Dorothy Greenbaum and Deirdre Laiken. An ample selection of fiction is also available: *Traitor: The Case of Benedict Arnold* and *Make Way for Sam Houston* (both Putnam, 1981; 1986) by Jean Fritz; *Unclaimed Treasures* (Harper, 1984) by Patricia Mac-Lachlan; *Fantasy Summer* (Putnam, 1984) by Susan Beth Pfeffer; *The Sound of Anthems* (St. Martin's, 1983) by Marjory Alyn; *Family Resemblances* (Random, 1986) by Lowry Pei; and *The Refugee Summer* (Delacorte, 1982) by Edward Fenton.

Videos that can be used are: *Writer's Realm* (Agency for Instructional Technology, 1987, 2 programs, 14 min. ea.); *The Indomitable Teddy Roosevelt* (Churchill Films, 1983, 93 min.); *Dear Diary* (New Day Films, 1981, 25 min.); and *Summer's End* (Direct Cinema, 1985, 33 min.). The recording *Our Musical Past, Vol. 2* (OMP-103 Compact Disc, Library of Congress Information Office, Box A, Washington, DC 20540), featuring scores that were popular in 1916, will provide a splendid background.

Identifying Adult Roles: Additional Titles

America's Railroads. Film, 22 min., also available on video. Cypress Films, 1985. (Gr. 5–up)
Arnowsky, Jim. *Flies in the Water, Fish in the Air: A Personal Introduction to Fly Fishing.* Lothrop, 1986. (Gr. 5–up)
Beatrix Potter Has a Pet Named Peter. Filmstrip. Random, 1985. (Gr. 3–6)
Belleville, Cheryl Walsh. *Theater Magic: Behind the Scenes at a Children's Theater.* Carolrhoda, 1986, 48 pp. (Gr. 4–6)
Boslough, John. *Stephen Hawking's Universe.* Morrow, 1984. (Gr. 5–up)
Burleigh, Robert. *A Man Named Thoreau.* Illus. by Lloyd Bloom. Atheneum, 1985. (Gr. 3–5)
Clark, Mary Higgins. *Stillwatch.* Simon & Schuster, 1984. (Gr. 5–up)
Demuth, Patricia. *Joel: Growing Up on a Farm.* Dodd, 1982. (Gr. 5–7)
DeWeese, Gene. *Computers in Entertainment and the Arts.* Watts, 1984, 112 pp. (Gr. 4–6)
Flamenco at 5:15. Film, 30 min., also available on video. Direct Cinema, 1985. (Gr. 5–up)
Hoban, Russell. *La Corona and the Tin Frog, and Other Tales.* Illus. by Nicola Bayley. Merrimack, 1979. (Gr. 4–6)
Hoban, Tana. *Shapes, Shapes, Shapes.* Illus. by the author. Greenwillow, 1986. (Gr. K–5)
Hurd, Thacher. *The Pea Patch Jig.* Illus. by the author. Crown, 1986. (Gr. K–3)
Iooss, Walter, and Jenkins, Dan. *Football.* Abrams, 1986. (Gr. 4–7)
Leisure Time Photography. Film, 18 min. Beacon Films, 1982. (Gr. 5–up)
Levitin, Sonia. *Roanoke: A Novel of the Lost Colony.* Illus. by John Gretzer. Atheneum, 1973, 213 pp. (Gr. 5–6)
Lord, Beman. *Perfect Pitch.* Illus. by Harold Berson. Gregg, 1981, 55 pp. (Gr. 2–4)

Made in China. Film, 30 min., also available on video. Filmakers Library, 1986. (Gr. 5–up)

Myers, Walter Dean. *Black Pearl and the Ghost; Or One Mystery after Another.* Illus. by Robert Quackenbush. Viking, 1980, 36 pp. (Gr. 2–4)

Read Along Super Sports. 6 cassettes. Coronet/Random, 1976. (Gr. 5–6)

Ritter, Lawrence S. *The Story of Baseball.* Morrow, 1983. (Gr. 4–7)

Robbins, Ken. *Building a House.* Macmillan/Four Winds, 1984. (Gr. 3–5)

St. George, Judith. *The Brooklyn Bridge: They Said It Couldn't Be Built.* Putnam, 1982. (Gr. 5–7)

Sherlock Holmes Soundbook, read by Basil Rathbone. Recording, 8s, also available on cassette. Caedmon, 1977. (Gr. 5–up)

*Sherrill Milnes' Homage to Verdi.*Video, 56 min. Kultur, 1986. (Gr. 6–up)

Silverberg, Robert. *The Majipoor Chronicles.* Arbor House, 1982, 314 pp. (Gr. 5–up)

Sun Jingxiu et al. *We Live in China.* Illus. with photos. Watts, 1984, 64 pp. (Gr. 4–6)

A Visit with David Macauley. Video, 25 min. Houghton, 1983. (Gr. 2–7)

What Did You Say? (Oral Communications). Film, 14 min. FilmFair Communications, 1983. (Gr. 4–7)

9

Appreciating Books

IF the United States is to be a nation of readers, our society must continue to expose middle-grade children to the joys of good literature. Because children ages 8–12 generally look at a wide range of materials, they can be introduced quite easily to fine writing and beautifully illustrated, well-designed books. Aside from introducing them to the sheer pleasure of reading, this helps them to form a standard based on superior books and to further their still developing sense of abstract thinking. With their expanding mental acuity 8–12 year olds will readily absorb continuing excursions into learning, comprehension, and appreciation. Encouraging middle-graders to think abstractly by examining hypothetical problems and their solutions is one of the by-products of reading pleasure.

The books in this chapter have been chosen for their literary style, language, and imagery, both in the written word and visual representations. Illustrations and book design add luster to the books for children, giving them more to contemplate, and can help them in this process. Each book contains a superior story that is eloquently expressed, and many are wonderfully illustrated and designed. Collectively they are a paean to the beauty of ideas, written words, and lustrous illustrations. They can rest easily on a child's mind and lead the child to other worthy books.

Baker, Olaf. *Where the Buffaloes Begin*
Illus. by Stephen Gammell. Warne, 1981, 46 pp.

This author was born in England in the 1870s and came to the United States in 1902. Olaf Baker was deeply impressed by the wilderness and recent past of North America. Based on these interests, he wrote some popular novels for youngsters, including *Shasta of the Wolves* and *Thunder*

Boy. Baker spent a great deal of time in the West, especially in the territory of the Blackfoot Indians. His fascination with the West, in general, and the Blackfoot nation, in particular, shines throughout this tale, dedicated to his friend Red Eagle, which is an eloquent retelling for children of one of the legendary Blackfoot tales. It expresses his deep affection for the heritage of the North American continent. Baker published the story in 1910 in the important children's magazine *St. Nicholas*. The young hero witnesses the birth of the buffalo from the center of the lake just as is recounted in the legend told by the Indian campfire. Surrounded by buffalo in an awesome stampede from the lake to his village, the young Indian unexpectedly thwarts a raid by an enemy tribe and becomes part of the legend himself. Youngsters ages 9–11 (grades 4–6) will appreciate the exciting spiritual story, as well as the elegant drawings.

Stephen Gammell is well known as an illustrator; two dozen titles that he illustrated are in print, four of which he also authored were published in the early eighties. For this title, he did 27 pencil drawings, illustrations for the half-title, title, and dedication pages, decorations for the four chapters, and a two-color (blue and sepia) illustration for the jacket. Eight full-page drawings, 7 double-page spreads, and 12 mostly half-page illustrations illuminate the text. The front jacket displays an emblem of a bison (buffalo) enclosed in a circular border; a smaller version of the same drawing appears as the decoration introducing each chapter. The back jacket displays in detail an Indian artifact (pouch) in blue and sepia. Stephen Gammell's art expresses the spaciousness of the landscape of the Great Plains, especially the skies, and the aura of Indian life and culture with strong horizontal lines. His striking portraits of Nawa and Little Wolf have an underlying strength. The bisons are shown in their glory both en masse and individually through exquisite shading. In some pictures fading lines impart a mistiness that heightens the lengendary quality of the story. The spectacular drawings are highly evocative of the dreamlike nature of a campfire legend.

Nawa, the ancient wise man, keeps the legend of the sacred lake to the south where the buffalo begin fresh and vital for the young in the Indian tribe. The story of the buffalo rising out of the middle of the lake and coming to shore at "the right time, on the right night" is told often by the evening campfire. It is an old legend, even older than Nawa.

Ten-year-old Little Wolf lives in a time long ago in a teepee on the prairie with his Blackfoot tribe. He is the fastest runner among his friends, and he is without fear. The wildest pony is fair game to him. Wise for his age, Little Wolf knows all the terrible things that can happen—angry bison, fierce wolves, and scalping by his people's enemy, the Assiniboins. But he also knows that he need not worry unnecessarily because he is cautious. He has heard the legend of the buffalo all his life, and in his fertile imagination he dreams of them. During the winter while the wind howls around the teepee, he dreams of the buffalo, angry and terrifying when he first sees them, but finally after smelling him becoming friendly. Little Wolf dreams of them all winter. As spring approaches, he acts impulsively. He must see the buffalo!

Little Wolf unhobbles his pony from the herd, identifying it by its white forefoot and patch. As he rides his pony through the evergreens south to the large lake, the sun is just rising. Traveling slowly, he searches the prairie horizon carefully. He sees a grayish spot in the distance but decides that it is a herd of antelope. He also sees flowers and birds close by—prairie roses and prairie grouse. In spite of these harmless sights, he keeps a sharp lookout for the Assiniboins, knowing instinctively that it can be especially dangerous when everything seems uncommonly quiet. Toward late afternoon as he approaches the lake he sees many animal traces leading to it. Most numerous are those of the buffalo. Little Wolf dismounts and hobbles his pony. He throws himself down on a hillock above the lake's low bank and waits patiently.

As the night passes and the distinctive orange light of the prairie sky appears, Little Wolf hears an intermittent murmur from the center of the lake. He watches and listens, sometimes hearing the sound in the center of the lake get louder. Nawa's song keeps repeating in his memory, "Do you hear the noise that never ceases? It is the Buffaloes fighting far below. They are fighting to get out upon the prairie. They are born below the Water but are fighting for the Air, In the great lake in the Southland where the Buffaloes begin!"

Rising suddenly whether from sleep or dream, Little Wolf sees a large herd of buffalo coming noisily from the lake, just as he has seen them in his winter dreams. Overcome with delight, Little Wolf leaps to his feet and cries out joyfully. The buffalo hear him and momentarily stand still, but then a roar goes up among them and they stampede onto the prairie toward Little Wolf. He answers their roar with another cry, and together they gallop northward. Little Wolf's pony can normally outrun the herd, but is too tired now even though his young masters' yelps urge him to try. Little Wolf and the buffalo seem to be traveling together on some unknown mission, caught up in the wild excitement of the stampede. As they rush over the prairie, the buffalo sweep aside everything in their way, yet they do not harm Little Wolf. They seem intent on some purpose, unknown to Little Wolf, until he sees the Assiniboins running to regain their mounts and realizes that he and the herd have thwarted a surprise dawn attack on his tribe. The buffalo stampede cuts off the Assiniboin retreat, trampling them. Toward the end, Little Wolf falls down with his pony but by then he is at the rear of the stampede and he is able to jump clear as the last buffalo passes. Little Wolf stands beside his righted pony and watches the last buffalo disappear.

Once again beside the evening campfire up North among the evergreens of the Blackfoot territory, the Indians tell the story of the place where the buffalo begin. Now, however, they add to the legend the name Little Wolf as the boy who saved his tribe.

Thematic Material

This beautiful book both to read and to view is one that youngsters can truly appreciate. An evocative romantic quality emanates from the dreamlike legend and its lush portrayal in pictures that is a combination of courage, excitement, and an affirmation of the powerful connection between the conscious and subconscious levels of the mind. The book presents a thrilling glimpse for youngsters into the generation of a legendary young hero.

Discussion Materials

The book is well suited for reading aloud or simply book talking. To read aloud, five ten-minute sessions will tell the tale thoroughly. First, read the title page and show the drawing. Then display the dedication page drawing and read the inscription (pp. 2–3); show the portrait of Nawa (p. 4); and read the preface, while displaying the picture (p. 4). Next, the short chapters in four sessions: the winter dreams (pp. 6–11); the lake and the emergence of the buffalo (pp. 12–23); the stampede (pp. 24–31); and the surprise Assiniboin raid (pp. 32–46). Finally, display the two jacket drawings. This plan can be compressed into one session. If the group is a self-assured, independent collection of readers, another plan can be used for book talking: Display the jacket and background of prairie grass, buffalo, and Blackfoot Indians, then show the illustrations on the half-title, title, and dedication pages; and read the legend introduction (p. 5) while displaying Nawa's portrait (p. 4). Describe the first scene by showing the drawings and paraphrasing the text (pp. 6–11). Also show the pictures and paraphrase the text on pages 15, 18–19, and 21. Be sure to read aloud page 23 f. and show the pictures on pages 26–27, 31, 36–37, 40–41. Display the final pictures without comment (pp. 42–43).

Related Materials

Three fiction titles are suggested: *Yellow Fur and Little Hawk* (Coward, 1980) by Wilma Pitchford Hays; *Navajo Slave* (Harvey House, 1976) by Lynne Gessner; and *Mysteries of Harris Burdick* (Houghton, 1984) by Chris Van Allsburg. Some nonfiction titles are also suggested: Arlene Hirschfelder's *Happily May I Walk: American Indians and Alaskan Natives Today* (Scribner, 1986); Virginia Haviland's *North American Legends* (Philomel, 1980); and Jamake Highwater's *Ceremony of Innocence* (Harper, 1985).

The film or video *Children of the Long-Beaked Bird* (Bullfrog Films, 1986, 29 min.), about 12-year-old Dominic Old Elk's life today, is recommended. Three filmstrips are also suggested: From *Tales of the Plains Indians* (Random, 1986, 6 fs), "The First Buffalo," (fs 6); *The Girl Who Loved Wild Horses* (Random, 1986) from the striking title by Paul Goble; and highlight *Where the Buffaloes Begin* (Random, 1986), narrated by Jamake Highwater accompanied by native American tribal music.

Bierhorst, John. *Spirit Child: A Story of the Nativity*
Trans. from the Aztec by the author. Illus. by Barbara Cooney. Morrow, 1984, 30 pp.

The author is known and respected for distinguished texts for young people. More than a dozen of John Bierhorst's thoroughly researched and lyrically composed books are in print. Some treat the Indians of North America and their mythology in a scholarly fashion; others explore the author's love of American poetry, stories, and music, such as *In the Trail of the Wind* (Farrar, 1971); *The Sacred Path* (Morrow, 1983); and *The Girl Who Married a Ghost* and *A Cry from the Earth* (both Macmillan, 1978; 1979), which are ALA Notable Books. A few of Bierhorst's titles reflect his interest in and knowledge of the Aztec language and the Mayan and Incan cultures: *Black Rainbow: Legends of the Incas and Myths of*

Ancient Peru (Farrar, 1976) and *The Hungry Woman: Myths and Legends of the Aztecs* and *The Monkey's Haircut: And Other Stories Told by Maya* (both Morrow, 1984; 1986).

In an author's end note, John Bierhorst explains that this title is a translation of the Nativity story from five of the folios of Fray Bernardino de Sahagun's *Psalmodia Christiana* (Mexico, 1583), one of the first books published in the New World. It was written in the Aztec language with the assistance of Aztec poets, combining stories from the bible with touches of medieval legends and Aztec lore. Although gospels of Matthew and Luke provide the basic story, the text adopts typical Aztec construction: short paragraphs, dialogue, and direct address. Addressing the reader directly clearly demonstrates the way in which the Nativity story was used orally with the local population. These same literary devices are useful with middle-graders, as well as older reluctant readers. The expertly translated Aztec tale is a moving interpretation of the Christian story of Jesus's birth. The picture-book format recommends the book visually for any age, but it is especially recommended for independent readers ages 9–11 (grades 4–6).

Jane Byers Bierhorst designed this beautiful book, from the warm red binding and endpapers to the large-size typeface, achieving a stately balance. The famous illustrator Barbara Cooney, a two-time ALA Caldecott Award-winner, for *Chanticleer and the Fox* (Crowell, 1982; orig. 1958) and *Ox-cart man* (Viking, 1979), and recent ABA award-winner for the best picture book, *Miss Rumphius* (Viking, 1982), painted 14 exquisite illustrations for this book. As the two dozen other titles she has in print show, she has always been concerned with capturing the light and quality of a locale. Her pictures with their bright, clear compositions brilliantly reflect this.

Barbara Cooney does "on the spot" research. Her illustrations in this title capture the colors, textures, and landscapes that she saw during her trip to Mexico. Six illustrations are half-page double spreads, set horizontally and headed or followed by the text; four are full-page illustrations. These are framed by native flower borders or by the abrupt color contrast with the ample white space around the text, which also helps give the book its crisp look. Two unbordered double spreads with large freestanding or seated figures surrounding the text are breathtaking in their stark simplicity. There are two decorations: an initialed flower starts the story, and two types of Aztec drums head the author's end note. An elliptical title-page picture of Aztecs celebrates the Nativity, and a rectangular chapter-head picture of an exploding volcano announces the time before Jesus's birth when the devil was king. Cooney's orangish pink-and-purple jacket painting shows Aztecs adoring the baby Jesus, with flowers strewn on the ground, while angels (Aztec children) herald Jesus's birth with garlands. Paint and brush are the media for the artwork in this beautiful book, which reflects the skill and care of the designer, illustrator, and author.

The Nativity story has a special place in Judeo-Christian hearts and memory, wherever it is known. In cultures other than those in North America or Western Europe, the story also has threads of the prevailing culture, which Christian missionaries may have transplanted. As Christian priests spread the gospel or "good news," the story retained its message of hope, while absorbing some of the history and cultural background of the people.

This awesome story, translated from the Aztec, was used by the missionaries in Mexico in the 1500s. It starts long, long ago when the devil ruled the world—5,000 years after the world began. The devil is clever; he seduces people into doing seemingly happy things without explaining that he will force them to work hard and starve in the Dead Land when he closes their eyes. But everyone knows that when Jesus comes to earth, the people will be saved.

Mary and Joseph have been miraculously chosen to be the (Aztec) parents of Jesus—Mary because she is so pure, Joseph because he is so good and wise. The angel Gabriel visits Mary in Galilee in the city of Nazareth to tell her that she will bear a babe, to be named Jesus. The angel Gabriel also announces that "He will rule [and the rule] will never end." On the order of Caesar, the good-hearted Joseph leads his pregnant wife to Bethlehem where she gives birth to the spirit child for whom all wait in hope.

Mary wraps Jesus in a cloth and lays him in a manger where "the cows eat dry grass." The sun rises in the night sky announcing Jesus's birth while Mary holds him and Joseph watches over them under a thatched palm roof surrounded by blooming poinsettias (native to Mexico). Mary kneels and worships the Lord Jesus, and the event is heralded everywhere: a fountain of sweet oil sprouts in Rome (Italy), grapevines blossom in Jerusalem (Judea), and there is peace on the earth. The angel Gabriel visits the shepherds outside Bethlehem and tells them to go to the city to sing the King's praises, Alleluia. Hosts of angels singing "Alleluia" and scattering songs and flowers appear in the sky. The star of David, heralding Jesus, born of Jacob, also appears, as had been foretold.

As everyone watches, three kings come to Bethlehem from the East bearing myrrh, incense, and gold for the infant Jesus. When the ruler of Judea, Herod, hears, out of jealousy he asks where this king of the Jews is. He summons the three kings and asks them to report to him after they have visited Jesus, disingenuously telling them that he wants to go to worship Jesus, too. The three kings follow the new star to the palm-roofed manger in Bethlehem. After they worship and offer their gifts, as they sleep they see the spirit child in their dreams. He sends them straight home, for Jesus, although only a baby in human form, is God and knows everything. "His holiness and mysteriousness are exactly the same as the holiness and mysteriousness of God the father himself." He has come to save the people; it is the long-awaited day of salvation. "It shines on us, it lights our way." As the story ends, wonderfully invigorating rain falls on the dry earth.

Thematic Analysis

In the Christian religion the story of the Nativity is the reaffirmation of hope, the triumph of good over evil. The themes here are at once manifold and as unified as the story. The powerful message in this book, simply delivered and tempered by the exotic translation from the language of the Aztec people who originally received the message, is magnificently expressed in the paintings, beautiful design, and eloquent recounting, definitely making the book one to appreciate.

Discussion Material

This title can be savored in many ways, from an individual reading and viewing, to a picture-book presentation, to a discussion of many subjects (religion, Aztec language, Mexican landscape, and people), depending on the audience and the purpose. For older middle-graders who may be familiar with the Nativity story but are not necessarily of the Christian faith, book talk on the flora and fauna in the pictures might be interesting (jacket, pp. 5–6, 8–9, 10–11, 12–13, 15, 18–19, 21, 24, 26–27, 29), pointing out on page 15 that poinsettias are named for the ambassador who introduced them to the United States; or on the Aztec people (jacket, title page, 5, 6, 8–9, 10–11, 12, 15, 18–19, 21, 22–23, 24–25, 26–27, 29, end note); or on the landscape (jacket, pp. 5, 8–9, 15, 16–17, 29).

Related Materials

The following are suggested: *The Hungry Women: Myths and Legends of the Aztecs* (Morrow, 1984), edited by John Bierhorst; *Children of the Maya: A Guatemalan Indian Odyssey* (Dodd, 1986) by Brent Ashabranner; *Mexico* (Childrens Pr., 1985) by R. Conrad Stein; *The Caribbean and Gulf of Mexico* (Silver Burdett, 1985), edited by Pat Hargreaves; *Cuba* (Watts, 1985) by Edmund Lindop; *Daydreamers* (Dial, 1981) by Eloise Greenfield, illustrated by Tom Feelings; and *Cat's Cradle, Owl's Eyes: A Book of String Games* (Morrow, 1984) by Camilla Gryski.

The "Snoopy" poster in Spanish (ALA, 1986, No. 33S) adds a good background note that extols the Spanish language of today's Mexico. The filmstrip *Sing, Pierrot, Sing* (Random, 1986), based on Tomie dePaola's book, is also suggested. The cassette *Circle Around* (Tickle Tune Typhoon, 1985) is good as an exit device for the group.

Hodges, Margaret. *Saint George and the Dragon: A Golden Legend* Adapted by the author. Illus. by Trina Schart Hyman. Little, 1984, 32 pp.

Well known for this title, which won the 1985 ALA Caldecott Award, this author has written many books for children (see, for example, *Introducing Books*, Bowker, 1970, p. 101). Two other titles in print are *Knight Prisoner: The Tale of Sir Thomas Malory and His King Arthur* (Farrar, 1976) and *The Avenger* (Scribner, 1982). Margaret Hodges, professor emeritus, has long been respected in her field of children's literature, especially in folktales. She is a specialist in tales from the British Isles and has pursued a long-time scholarly interest in the seminal works from which they came. This book developed directly from that interest and study, and Hodges's recognized literary talent guaranteed an eloquent adaptation.

In this excerpt from the famous work *Faerie Queene*, written by Edmund Spenser in the sixteenth century, Una, a courageous princess in a countryside being devastated by a fierce dragon, after a long and stormy voyage, prevails upon the Fairy Queen to send help. George, the Red Cross Knight, agrees to accompany Una and try to slay the dragon. After three fearsome bouts, George kills the dragon and frees the countryside of its terror. Una and George enter the castle where they are happily married before he leaves to finish his knight's service. Youngsters ages

9–12 (grades 4–7) will appreciate the imagery of the lyrically written legend and the dramatic illustrations that accompany it.

Trina Schart Hyman, a noted illustrator, won the Caldecott Award for this title. Since she burst upon the field of illustration in the early seventies, readers have been enjoying her glorious illustrations. She has 31 titles in print and is the author-illustrator of four: *Little Red Riding Hood* (Holiday, 1982); *A Christmas Carol* (Holiday, 1983); *A Child's Christmas in Wales* (Holiday, 1985); and *King Stork* (Little, 1986). For this book, Hyman did 27 illustrations that interpret Hodges's text brilliantly. They are full-color paintings, meticulously crisp, detailed, and more. For example, the journey through the wood (p. 9) is reminiscent of Arthur Rackham; the pastoral scenes of the countryside and ordinary folk are charming (p. 13); and the portrayal of the dragon is imaginative (p. 21). The expressive faces, distinctly Hyman, are appealing (p. 26).

Hyman's illustrations add a definite luster to the beautiful text. The full-color front jacket illustration introduces the tale with a picture of George, the Red Cross Knight, inserted on one side of the border and the dragon on the opposite side. The back jacket shows a young boy scrivening with a quill as an older couple approach his humble cottage ostensibly to get a story transcribed. The half-title page contains the same reddish brown double frame with corner inserts that appears in all of the other illustrations. The *Faerie Queene* genesis of the tale is suggested in a misty grey drawing reminiscent of Aubrey Beardsley's artwork. Two double-spread paintings (title and dedication pages) carry forward this expressive misty idea and commence the journey. Eleven bordered full-page illustrations appear opposite 11 similarly bordered pages of text. Native flora, mythic beasts, and fairies are enclosed in the border inserts. Two other pages (pp. 14, 21) extend the full-page illustrations into the border insert on the opposite page of text. The book is richly illustrated with pictures on every page, and the medieval atmosphere is readily apparent.

Long ago when fairy folk lived on the land, a young princess, Una, set out to find someone who would slay the dragon that was devastating the countryside. Many country people had moved away, others had moved into the fortified castle with Una's father and mother, the king and queen. After much searching, the Queen of the Fairies sends her Red Cross Knight, George, who is untried in battle but willing to go with Una. Una (the supplicant) is thankful.

Una and George travel back to Una's countryside through the wilderness. George rides his draft horse and carries a spear and shield embla-zoned with the sign of the Red Cross. Una, covered with an elegant dark cloak, rides on a white donkey with a white lamb on a leash cavorting beside her and a dwarf carrying food. They rest from the arduous trip at a hermit's hut. The hermit tells George that he must postpone a trip to the golden castle (high city) that he sees on the skyline in favor of con-quering the dragon in the valley below. He also tells George that he was stolen and adopted by the fairy folk, that George is really English, and that he is destined to become the patron saint of Great Britain, Saint George of Merry England.

When Una awakens, she and George go down to her countryside. They see Una's mother, the queen, waving from the castle, and along their path welcoming smiles on the faces of the country folk. Their happiness is short-lived, however, because the dragon suddenly appears, filling the air with terrifying roars and clashing its brassy scales as it rears. The dragon is so enormous even when lying down that it casts a shadow as big as the surrounding rolling hills. The brass-plated tail with its upright armored teeth, which is almost a mile long, turns and twists as the dragon moves, and when the dragon stands on its rear legs the claws dig into the earth. Venomous fighting claws extend from the front arms. The long tongue strikes out from among rows of sharp teeth in its fire-breathing mouth. Huge batlike wings extend from both shoulders.

Even though the dragon is a monster—a combination of the most horrifying parts of many creatures—and a giant before which mortal man seems tiny, the brave knight raises his spear and attacks. His spear glances off the impenetrable scales and the dragon's tail knocks him off his horse, but George quickly remounts and attacks again. The dragon then picks up the horse and rider, and in trying to free itself, the horse throws George to the ground. George picks himself up again and strikes a tremendous blow from which the dragon withdraws bellowing, but not before its fiery breath sears George. Although George sinks to the ground wounded and burned, he falls on an ancient spring of healing water.

When the sun rises, George is ready to fight again. In a fierce struggle George cuts off some of the dragon's tail and a claw that grips his shield. Raging and bellowing, the dragon withdraws, breathing gusts of fire on George. Fortunately, George falls under the healing mist of an apple tree, and when he rises the next morning, he is ready to continue the battle. Una, who tends him throughout the ordeal, trembles with fear during this third encounter. Although the dragon is finally fearful; nevertheless it charges with its mouth open to swallow George. At that instant, George thrusts his sword into the mouth and kills the dragon. As smoke issues from the dead dragon's mouth, everyone celebrates. The country people thank George, gathering flowers to make garlands in his homage, and the ordinary folk in the castle join them. After the king and queen kiss their daughter and also thank George, the king, who has hoped long for a savior, promises George that he will be the next king. George protests, however, because he has promised six more years of knight's service to the Fairy Queen. Nevertheless, the king says that if Una and George love each other they can be married immediately. Una changes into a lovely bright gown that melts George's heart, and they are married. After George serves his promised time, he earns his familiar name, Saint George of Merry England, and becomes the patron saint. They live happily ever after.

Thematic Analysis

This legend can be understood as the personification of subconscious primitive human fears or as a didactic statement regarding the postponement of instant gratification. It can also be interpreted as a mythic statement about the slow and difficult social processes in the development of nations. But the book can best be appreciated for its external literary and artistic qualities. It has so much information, from the adapted sixteenth-century text to the medieval costumes, that the subliminal mythic messages are best subordinated to an appreciation of an exquisite work. The adventures of a courageous young man and woman and the triumphant conclusion are inspiring.

Discussion Materials

The book can be shown in many ways, for example: as a typical picture book, by reading aloud, or by book talking the plot or a subject area. Although paraphrasing does a disservice to the lyric prose, a picture-book presentation can be used for younger children. Reading aloud, however, is probably desirable for most readers, including younger or reluctant readers. Three sessions are suggested. Display the book, and follow this plan in a straightforward manner, from jacket to conclusion: the journey (jacket–13); the fight with the dragon (pp. 14–25); and the celebration (pp. 26–32). To book talk, relate the simple plot and display the front jacket. Follow with these episodes: Una and George on the

288 · INTRODUCING BOOKPLOTS 3

journey (p. 6); the dragon (p. 14); and the celebration (p. 29). Or special subjects can be book talked for serious, better readers: costumes (all pictures); identification of flowers (pp. 7, 8, 11, 12, 15, 16, 19, 20, 22, 23, 27, 28, 31, 32); or a description of a dragon (p. 15).

Related Materials

Some useful nonfiction titles are: Nancy Willard's *A Visit to William Blake's Inn: Poems for Innocent and Experienced Travelers* (Harcourt, 1981), illustrated by Alice Provenson and Martin Provenson, artfully shows various scenes in an eighteenth-century British inn; *Tomie dePaola's Favorite Nursery Tales* (Putnam, 1986) contains poems and fairy tales illustrated in the well-known artist's usual style; and John Keegan's *Soldiers: A History of Men in Battle* (Viking, 1986) gives a pictorial history of warfare for the interested student. Mary Luke's fictional *The Ivy Crown* (Doubleday, 1984) paints an intriguing picture of court life surrounding Henry VIII's sixth wife, Katherine Parr, that will attract female readers.

The filmstrip of this book, *Saint George and the Dragon* (Random, 1986), is recommended. Two recordings are also suggested: *Reluctant Dragon* (Caedmon, 1976, 2s), from the classic title by Kenneth Grahame, read by Boris Karloff and *Kim* (Caedmon, 1976, 1 cassette), excerpts from Rudyard Kipling's adventure tale read by Anthony Quale.

Huynh, Quang Nhuong.　*The Land I Lost: Adventures of a Boy in Vietnam*
Illus. by Vo-Dinh Mai. Harper, 1982, 115 pp.

The author's only published book for children, this popular title, which appeared in paperback in 1986, has been well received by both reviewers and readers. A native Vietnamese who was born in Mytho on the central highlands and graduated from Saigon University, Quang Nhuong Huynh was disabled in the Vietnamese War and came to the United States for medical treatment. Now a U.S. citizen living in Columbia, Missouri, he has earned degrees in French and comparative literature. The book is a collection of his boyhood adventures—the exotic experiences that accompanied his youth—and is exciting to read. Children ages 9–11 (grades 4–6) will be spellbound by the strange landscape and beasts that were commonplace for the youngster.

Vo-Dinh Mai, who was born in Hue, Vietnam, and received artistic training in Paris, is an artist of international note. Besides designing UNICEF greeting cards, he also has illustrated many books. For this title he did 16 full-page black-and-white illustrations with ink washes. The illustrator's delicate style evokes the fragile beauty of remembrance reflected in the author's text. The attractive color painting on the jacket portrays the young boy sitting on his pet water buffalo against a vivid Vietnamese sky with menacing animals watching warily from the nearby jungle.

The author's introduction is invaluable. It explains the setting for his tales (pp. ix–xi). Everything is governed by the two seasons, rain and drought, each of which lasts six months on the central highlands where the boy was born. Depending on the season, the boy's father is either a farmer or a hunter. The family lives in a hamlet with about 50 other families. During the rainy season, they plant and cultivate fields of rice, sweet potatoes, and other foods; even Mother and his seven sisters, who manage the household chores, help in the fields. The boy starts working at age six like all farmers' children. Being male, he looks after the family herd of buffalo, tills the fields, and fishes for the family. At age 12, he joins his father hunting in the jungle during the dry season. He learns to track and identify edible food. The boy also attends school in the lowlands because his father is the village teacher and the boy's family respects education. Like most youngsters, the boy learns about his heritage through his parents and his elders, the neighbors whose bamboo houses with their roofs of coconut leaves are close together, and his own observations.

Looming large in the boy's daily life is the task of protecting against the ever-present danger of thieves and wild animals. Four animals are especially dreaded—the tiger, the lone wild hog, the crocodile, and the horse snake. Although their houses protect them from the deep cold of the winter and a deep trench surrounds each house (the sole entrance is along a "monkey's bridge" bamboo stick that is pulled into the house at night), the villagers constantly have to be on guard against the jungle animals and the dangerous inhabitants of the river, which is the villagers' lifeline to markets and shops. (The frontispiece illustrates the landscape vividly.) The boy fondly recalls a seemingly never-ending round of serious adventures that were not noticeably interrupted by the long war being waged nearby during most of his youth. They can be arbitrarily divided into two categories: animal adventures that involve the boy and those that involve other people or that he hears. However, all of them are an ordinary part of the boy's life.

The boy begins by lovingly describing his pet, Tank, a water buffalo that herds the family's other buffalo because he is the fiercest fighter in the whole region. The boy remembers vividly the day his father released Tank from tilling the soil when he outwitted an infamous neighboring buffalo thief (chapter 1). He also recalls how Tank helped catch prize white catfish from the river with strings tied to his horns (chapter 5). The boy concludes his adventures with the story of Tank's death (with tears in his buffalo eyes) from a gunshot wound received during a sudden nearby battle in the long war (chapter 15).

Tigers are mentioned in many episodes, although no separate incident highlights them. Perhaps that says something about their extreme perilousness. The gripping episode of a crazed lone wild hog that kills a young farmer but is finally killed by the villagers is worthy of reading aloud (chapter 3). After a clever plan to incapacitate a man-eating river crocodile is carried out, "Mister Short" no longer has a tail with which to upend the river boat and poler and presents little threat to the river boats (chapter 4). Another story about the feared crocodiles tells how Lan was rescued by her betrothed after she escaped an old crocodile while bathing in the river (chapter 8).

The boy's reminiscences about snakes are more numerous. His friend and companion, a ten-year-older cousin, demonstrates how to keep a python from fatally squeezing you. Let it twine, then hold the head and tail in separate hands, and "gently" bite its tail (chapter 2). In another dramatic event, the boy watches as the villagers successfully track and kill a wounded horse snake (chapter 6). The boy also recounts the heroic adventure when his cousin kills a horse snake that has become intoxicated by the hogfish oil lamp that the boy carries and follows them at dusk (chapter 10). He also tells about the deadly two-steps snake (that's how far one gets after a venomous bite) that was an "under the house" pet for many years (chapter 14).

Seven adventures highlight relatives and other villagers who pass on cultural heritage to the boy. Many also include domesticated animals and birds, as well as the dangerous river and jungle creatures. Two of the episodes have already been described—the one about the young woman rescued from the crocodile (chapter 8) and the other about taming a python by biting its tail (chapter 2). The boy fondly recalls his resourceful and beautiful grandmother with whom his family lived in the rural

Vietnamese tradition—her love of opera, her expertness at karate, and her courageous acts with bandits (chapter 7). He also remembers the little altar on the road at which he burned incense and prayed for his ancestors whose tombs lined the road. In his religious faith, everyone cares for the tombs, especially on lunar New Year's Day (chapter 9). He learns more about traditional respect for elders from a lonely neighboring old lady who attempts the impossible by trying to make a faithful pet out of a monkey (chapter 11). His father teaches him something about monkeys when he trains one to catch the squirrel thiefs in the banana groves (chapter 12). In a poignant episode, the boy and his younger sister (when he is seven) are temporarily successful in uncaging their pets, "unfaithful birds," when they learn to addict them to an evening drink of water laced with opium residue. Unfortunately, the birds are killed when their addiction forces them to fly in a storm, which they would not ordinarily do, trying to return for their evening drink (chapter 13).

Thematic Analysis

Many themes undergird this story; in fact, all the developmental themes for middle-graders are present, including family love, friendship, and respect for living creatures. This title can be used for many of them—they are strong and suffuse the entire book—but it is better used as a book a middle-grader can appreciate. Middle-graders will find the adventure-filled episodes especially fascinating because of the cultural differences and the universal similarities of boyhood.

Discussion Materials

The book can be introduced to a group of middle-graders by displaying the jacket and setting the scene for the adventures (ix–xi). Several illustrations can also be shown to illuminate the stories: Tank, the pet water buffalo (p. 4); a lone wild hog (p. 19); a horse snake (p. 44 or 83); a crocodile (p. 69); and Grandmother and a sister (p. 60). To place the book into the historical-political context, read and paraphrase the final chapter on the death of Tank when a battle in the ongoing war breaks out in the hamlet's fields (pp. 113–115). The two-steps snake pet story describes home life in the hamlet and makes an exciting collection even more appealing (pp. 104–112). The lone wild hog episode is especially intriguing (pp. 17–26). If you decide to read aloud (the book is perfectly adapted to this presentation), plan 16 sessions, one for each chapter preceded by a reading of the introduction, "The Land I Lost" (pp. ix–xi).

Related Materials

Three titles that combine stories about other cultures and wonderful illustrations by author-illustrators are: *Paper Crane* (Greenwillow, 1985) by Molly Bang; *Jumanji* (Houghton, 1981) by Chris Van Allsburg; and *The Village of Round and Square Houses* (Little, 1986) by Ann Grifalconi. *Desert Voices* (Scribner, 1981) by Byrd Baylor and Peter Parnall is a lyric presentation of ten desert animals. *The Statue of Liberty* (Harcourt, 1985) by Sue Burchard and *Annie John* (Farrar, 1985) by Jamaica Kincaid are nonfiction and fiction titles for good readers.

A few audiovisual titles are useful: the filmstrip *The Story of Ferdinand* (Live Oak Media, 1986); the film and video *The Challenge of the Caucasus* (MTI Film & Video, 1986); and two recordings, *Wind in the Willows* (Pathways of Sound, n.d., 8s) and *Robinson Crusoe* (Caedmon, 1977, 2s). The "Curious George" poster (ALA, 1986, No. 159), makes a suitable background.

Kellogg, Steven, retel. *Pecos Bill*
Illus. by the author. Morrow, 1986, 42 pp.

Steven Kellogg is well known and respected as an author-illustrator of children's books. He has illustrated and authored more than 80 titles (almost two dozen are in print). He has also illustrated 17 titles by other authors. Kellogg's style of writing and illustration is comic yet compassionate. He is also sympathetic to the interests and needs of children, as illustrated in some of his recent titles: *Tallyho, Pinkerton!* (Dial, 1982); *Best Friends* (Dial, 1986); and *The Orchard Cat* (Dial, 1983). His talent has ripened and risen to new heights in the vigorous tales he recently began adapting and illustrating, among them *Paul Bunyan* (Morrow, 1984) and *Chicken Little* (Morrow, 1985). His adaptation of the famous American tale *Pecos Bill* follows in this vein.

This familiar tale describes some of the humorous and exaggerated events in the life of the mythic American cowboy, like when he ingeniously converted a snake into a lasso, conquered the stallion Lightning, and established the Hell's Gulch gang, the rodeo, and the first ranch.

The story takes the active boy baby in a Conestoga wagon from New England to Texas, where he is yanked into the Pecos River by a Texas trout, raised by a family of coyotes, and settled in Texas as a child cowboy. He travels on a tornado with Slewfoot Sue to California, where he is reunited with his family and decides to return to Texas with them. This book can be shown to younger children because the illustrations are full of detail and visual humor. Among independent readers, however, this tall tale adaptation will be appreciated best by children ages 8–10 (grades 3–5).

Steven Kellogg is noted for distinctive illustrations with a humorous flair, never more visible than in this tall tale adaptation, for which he did 36 full-color paintings. The free spirit and hyperbolic quality of the story blend perfectly with this illustrator's style. The illustrations include detailed outlines and shadings, accomplished in a variety of ways, including paint, pen, canvas textures, and highlights (with a subdued use of acrylics). The colors are evocative of time and place, for example, the earth colors of the Southwest. The facial expressions of the characters are broadly comic, with careful application to the numerous characters in some illustrations. They are pictures in which children enjoy roaming visually; and they truly augment the boisterous tale. The action-filled illustrations provide a visual fantasy for which the viewer secretly hopes.

Kellogg also did the enticing title-page picture of the smiling infant Bill spooning honey to three plump bears from the back of the Conestoga wagon while his horrified mother waves her arms, as well as the attractive endpapers, and the two jacket illustrations. The front endpapers show the wagon train leaving a New England village and climbing into the woods where three bears watch from behind some rocks. The back endpapers display a typical (for Kellogg) illustrated map of the United States and Canada (Pecos Bill chases Lightning to the Arctic Circle) with banners and figures showing the locations of the exploits inside the book—a veritable treat for the young explorer-reader. The back jacket shows a rattlesnake in the form of a five-star rose clenching the yellow rose of Texas in its mouth. The front jacket portrays the young cowboy hero lassoing the white stallion Lightning while the snake's head and Bill's cowboy hat fly off in the opposite direction. Slewfoot Sue appears on a tornado cloud above the purple hills. The painting mirrors the explosive action within the pages.

When Bill is just a baby, he and his relatives leave crowded New England and head westward in a wagon train. His feisty ma is soon chasing the bears to which baby Bill, as garrulous as his ma, feeds honey. When they get to eastern Texas, Ma thinks she would like to settle, until she sees a homesteader's shack about 50 miles from the peak on which she stands. Vowing that it is too crowded, they push on. Soon they reach the Pecos River. While trying to catch a huge Texas trout, Bill falls in, and the fast-moving current carries him downstream far away from his family. A coyote pulls him from the river and raises him in the coyote family. Bill becomes an outdoor creature, howling with the coyotes, jumping across cliffs with the big-horn sheep, and generally learning to be "larger than life." He lives like that until a Texan about his own age named Chuck finds him. Chuck gives him a cowboy outfit like his own and tells him all about the outlaws and longhorns in Texas. Pecos Bill, as he is known from then on, decides to try combining the two. He starts the first ranch in Texas, and with his friend Chuck he sets out to find the Hell's Gulch gang, the worst of the outlaws.

Along the way, Pecos Bill struggles with and conquers a giant rattlesnake and a terrifying "critter" that is a mixture of tarantula, puma, and gorilla. With the two creatures in tow, Pecos Bill meets with the gang. He replaces Gun Smith as boss, makes a lasso out of the snake, and with a coyote yell teaches the young cowboys to rope the longhorn cattle that they will ranch. Each cowboy receives a buffalo-hide lasso for cattle roping. They have such a good first day that they hold the first rodeo to celebrate, and Pecos Bill decides to collect every steer in Texas for the ranch.

Around the campfire that night, Chuck tells Pecos Bill, who needs a horse to be a proper cowboy, about Lightning (also called Widowmaker), the fastest and most beautiful horse in the world. With his ever-present lasso (the snake), Pecos Bill chases Lightning across the Arctic Circle, the Grand Canyon, and three states, finally singing to the horse of his admiration and promise of devotion. Pecos Bill offers Lightning freedom, but he chooses instead to be Pecos Bill's steed.

To settle the cowboys' continual complaints about the repetitiveness of driving the herd between the summer and winter ranges, Pecos Bill inaugurates the Perpetual Motion Ranch on Pinnacle Peak, which always has winter at the top and summer at the bottom. He even invents cattle with short legs on one side to enable them to stand securely on the steep pinnacle. Pecos Bill is soon known worldwide as the greatest cowboy.

Cupid's arrow strikes when Pecos Bill sees Slewfoot Sue on the back of a huge Texas catfish as he and his cowboys revel in the lake in their free time. He proposes marriage and Slewfoot Sue agrees to marry him if

Pecos Bill will buy her a wedding dress with a bustle and let her ride Lightning to the ceremony. He accomplishes the first request easily, but has trouble with the second. Although Slewfoot Sue is an accomplished rider, Lightning bucks her up around the moon. She falls to earth, but her bustle bounces her back into the air several times, until Pecos Bill figures out a plan to rescue her. He lassoes a tornado, catches her, and they ride the tornado to California until it dissipates. When they touch ground, they land on Ma and Pa's wagon.

Pecos Bill, now a fine young man, and his betrothed greet the beaming family and friends who are still looking for the missing Bill. They all return in triumph to Pecos Bill's Texas ranch where they live happily. Today, their descendants tend cattle on ranches all over Texas.

Thematic Material

Although the tall tale of a legendary hero, this title represents several themes: family love, survival, understanding nature, persistence, and creativity. Aside from the story's mythic glorification of Texas and its hard-working ranch hands, this adaptation portrays the legendary hero as a youngster from infancy through young manhood. The young reader will easily identify with the themes, and simple enjoyment of the book is indicated.

Discussion Materials

The book can be presented as a typical picture book to younger children or reluctant readers, who may then be encouraged to read it independently. As an alternative, display the front jacket portraying Pecos Bill along with the back jacket showing the rattlesnake forming the five-pointed Texas state star. The illustration on the front endpapers of the Conestoga wagons leaving New England as the bears watch, followed by the title page closeup of baby Bill feeding honey to the bears, can also be shown. The back endpapers should then be shown, tracing the travels and exploits of Pecos Bill. The pictures in the book can be related to the map on the endpapers: Bill and his kinfolk head west (pp. 2–3); the first rodeo (pp. 22–23); Pinnacle Peak (pp. 30–31, 32–33); Bill chases Lightning toward the Arctic Circle (pp. 25–29); and Bill and Slewfoot Sue ride a tornado to California (pp. 40–41). The start of cattle roping (pp. 14–21) is an interesting and informative episode to highlight. Another is the Lightning incident (pp. 24–29). Some youngsters may wish to see the wedding dress and bustle (p. 36).

Related Material

Several titles are suggested: *Alphabatics* (Bradbury, 1986) by Suse Mac-Donald, an unusual gymnastic look at the alphabet; *King Bigood's in the Bathtub* (Harcourt, 1985) by Audrey Wood, with gorgeous illustrations by Don Wood that enliven the hilarious story; *Mr. Yowder, the Peripatetic Sign Painter: Three Tall Tales* (Holiday, 1980) by Glen Rounds presents three stories formerly separately published; *The Seven Days of Creation* (Holiday, 1981) by Leonard Everett Fisher, with spacious-looking paintings that illustrate a powerful story; *Basil in the Wild West* (McGraw-Hill, 1982) by Eve Titus, a humorous mystery story; *The Piney Woods* (Greenwillow, 1981) by George Shannon, a refreshing tale about a peddler; and *There Is a Carrot in My Ear and Other Noodle Tales* (Harper, 1982) by Alvin Schwartz, a collection of six comic tales about silly people.

Two recordings available from Caedmon are *Rip Van Winkle* (1 cassette) and *Queen Zixi of Ix* (1 cassette) by L. Frank Baum, read by Ray Bolger. Three films are also suggested: *Don't Tread on Me* (Sasnett Film, 1983, 25 min.), about the Texas annual rattlesnake hunt; *Lots of Kids Like Us* (Gerald T. Rogers Prods., 1983, 28 min.), an entertaining dramatization; and *A Jury of Her Peers* (Texture Films, 1981, 30 min.), a dramatic presentation about farm women making a silent statement of justice at the turn of the century.

Orlev, Uri. *The Island on Bird Street*
Trans. from the Hebrew by Hillel Halkin. Houghton, 1983 (Jerusalem, 1981), 162 pp.

The Israeli author of short stories and an adult novel, *Lead Soldiers*, Uri Orlev recently began writing for children. He received the 1981 Mordechai Bernstein Award and was cited as a 1982 IBBY Honor Book recipient in Israel for the featured title. It was subsequently translated from the Hebrew by Hillel Halkin and published in the United States, where it won the ALA Batchelder Award, a biennial prize for the most distinguished international children's book published in the United States.

As youngsters, Orlev and his younger brother lived in the Warsaw ghetto until they were sent to the infamous Bergen-Belsen concentration camp. He survived and settled in Israel at the end of World War II.

Orlev wrote a story about a young Jewish boy who dwells alone in a Polish ghetto waiting for the return of his father from whom he was separated in a periodic German "selection" for transport. The boy retains his humanity, instilled by his parents' earlier teachings, through an arduous six-month survival ordeal. He solves basic problems of living—scavenging for food, shelter, and clothing—and even becomes sufficiently confident to circumvent the ghetto wall several times to go to the Polish side, where he finds both taunts and companionship. The boy is reunited with his now partisan-fighter father, just as the emptied ghetto is opened as housing for other Polish people. In this riveting story, each problem is deeply felt by the reader. Youngsters ages 10–12 (grades 5–7) will find the writing stimulating, but they will also find themselves drawn into the story—exploring how to solve the hero's problems and feeling the terror that is the boy's constant companion.

Eleven-and-one-half-year-old Alex lives with his parents in one room that they share with the Gryns and their three children (Tsippora, Avrom, and Yossi) in the Polish ghetto for Jews. His mother recently went to visit friends in ghetto A, the largest ghetto, and never returned. (Ghetto B, the first cleared, is where the richest Jews live; ghetto C houses the forced factory workers like his father.) The Germans, accompanied by Polish (some Jewish) policemen and a few informers ("rats"), systematically empty the ghettos through transports or "selections" by carting the people to extermination camps. During the night many looters from both within and outside the ghettos take anything that is left, causing an escalating paucity of everything from money to food for those whose lives have so far been spared. Until now Alex has been fortunate, although he barely tolerates the Gryns with whom they store emergency food in a hidden place (bunker).

Alex's father works in the nearby rope factory. So far they have been able to survive because of his forced labor. Father, who was a boxer in the army in an earlier war, teaches Alex to shoot his gun, a Beretta, which he has kept and now gives to Alex. Alex also has a pet white mouse, Snow, that comes when he whistles. He misses his mother who was a Zionist and wanted to go to Israel, but he grimly accepts that she is dead.

Old Boruch, the factory storeroom manager, saves Alex when the Germans and the police find him and his father hiding among the rope bales during a "selection." Boruch covers for the boy by telling him to go to the bombed ghetto house at 78 Bird Street and wait there for his father, "no matter if it takes a week, a month, or even a whole year." The house at 78 Bird Street is a falling ruin in which the ghetto youngsters formerly played. Alex knows the house well, even its small cellar entrance. Completely alone there, Alex falls asleep in the cellar on the knapsack Boruch thrust in his hands. The next day, after investigating, Alex decides that the partial third and fourth floors will be a safe hideout, safer than the cellar. It even has a working faucet.

The need for food and to retrieve Snow from his former room gets Alex moving immediately. He watches carefully as he makes his way on his dangerous late night trek down Bird Street. When he reaches his former room, he collects Snow and a meager portion of his hidden food. Pan Gryn doesn't want to give him any, but his wife, Pani, intervenes, while Tsippora, Avrom, and Yossi silently watch the angry exchanges.

Although little Yossi pleads with Alex to stay, he returns to his cellar, confident that his father will return. He spends time gathering treasures (children's books, provisions, and clothes) from the adjacent empty houses, but soon realizes that only the basic necessities and a few children's books are important. After that he concentrates on finding food and fixing his upper-floor location. Before he leaves the cellar again, however, he chalks a cryptic, childlike treasure map on the bricks to tell his father he is there.

As Alex continues to scavenge, traveling through the connected building lofts because the streets are so dangerous, he finds another cache of food, but is interrupted by a couple and their little girl, Martha, who only leave him a slim share. Later, however, he saves Martha by shooting at her captor, a gruff looter, and scaring him away, but Martha returns to her hideout without telling Alex where it is, a vital secret among the ghetto dwellers. Alex gets some rope from the factory and wood to make a ladder to climb to his new abode. On one of his recurrent trips, he meets Bolek, a doorman from a building on the Polish side near number 78. When Bolek tells Alex to come to him for help if he needs it, Alex is surprised and pleased; finding someone trustworthy is rare in the ghetto. Alex continues to work in the cellar on the ladder and live in his unfinished "duplex." Suddenly one morning, cars arrive and there is a loud explosion in the cellar; many people are carted off. Without knowing, Alex has been working over a large and deep bunker. After the explosion, he investigates and takes away the remaining food; he even takes a shower in the well-stocked bunker, planning to return. But by the next night the officials have dynamited the bunker entrance.

Soon it is autumn; Alex has been at number 78 for two months and is fairly settled. Ropes that look like electrical wires hanging outside the old building allow him to draw the ladder up out of sight, and he has a larder filled with provisions. When he isn't searching for food, he spends his time reading and playing with Snow. He discovers that he can watch the Polish side over the ghetto wall that abuts number 78 from the air vent and even finds a pair of opera glasses to help him. He becomes familiar with the habits of the doormen, the grocery and vegetable store owners, the bully Yanek, the doctor who lives across the street, the girl on the floor above the doctor who does her homework daily at the window, and a crazy lady who cleans all day and goes out all night. After he watches for about a month, he sees newcomers enter the doctor's office by saying to the doorman, "To the doctor, governor."

Suddenly, after the Germans have spent three days clearing out ghetto A, just as they had done in ghettos B and C, two young men, one with a gunshot wound, burst into the ruins of number 78, followed by a German officer. Alex kills the officer with his ever-present Beretta. He is so proud of his people's resistance that he is on his way to join the uprising in ghetto A when this happens. Instead, he asks Freddy and Henryk, who is wounded, to hide in his place upstairs. Freddy dresses in the dead German's uniform and goes to Bolek, his liaison. Meanwhile, Henryk needs immediate medical attention. Alex dresses carefully and using a secret passage slips out to get the doctor for Henryk. The doctor returns with him and removes the bullet, promising to come again, but the next day Alex sees him being picked up by the gestapo.

When Henryk finally recovers after three weeks of serious illness, Alex takes some of the money Henryk offers him and goes across the ghetto wall again. He stops for food in the grocery store, plays in the park with some boys, and meets Stashya, the girl about his age who does her homework daily opposite his observation post in number 78. He also visits Bolek and his wife who feed him and urge him to come to live with them. They explain that the officials will soon tear down the wall and open the ghetto to relieve the housing shortage. Nevertheless, Alex demurs, reiterating that he is waiting for his father. Meanwhile, he continues to make a few careful visits to the park outside the ghetto to play ball with some boys and take Stashya ice skating. In the midst of these forays, a nearby doorman collects money from him and other people who use the secret passage, including Henryk who uses it to escape after leaving Alex some money.

Winter sets in, and Alex has to be careful about leaving tracks in the snow. He is also constantly concerned now that the kerosene that keeps him fairly warm will not last. On his last trip to the park to take Stashya ice skating, he falteringly tells her that he is a Jew. To his surprise and pleasure, she replies that she is, too.

Just before Christmas, the ghetto wall is demolished. Bolek comes for Alex, but he still won't leave. As Bolek is leaving, he tells Alex to put a stick in his window if he needs him. Stashya also comes to the ghetto surreptitiously to tell Alex that she is moving to the country. During a blizzard two weeks after she leaves, just as Alex is sure that his kerosene will not last the winter and that he is completely alone, he suddenly recognizes his father's voice coming from underneath his hideout talking to a companion about the son he has lost. The two are reunited amid laughter and tears, and Alex tells his father about some of his experiences during the past six months. Then his father asks him to put a stick in the window to signal Bolek because he is the partisan liaison he is supposed to contact. The year is 1944.

Thematic Material

The theme of this story, which is based on real-life experiences, is elementary survival. In spite of horrifying events under the most extreme conditions, the young hero is able to retain the softening effects of civilized thought in his approach to his desolate environment and its forlorn inhabitants. By example, the book shows the reader what supreme responsibility and devotion are. The hero never once wavers in his decision to wait for his father and never diverges from his optimistic belief that his father will come for him. The book will be appreciated for its realistic description of human strength and sensitivity, as well as for its excellent translation.

Discussion Materials

This is a fine book for individual reading. The graphic description of a ghetto in the introduction should be read aloud in full, or in parts extended with an apt paraphrasing (pp. vii–xi). The pen-and-ink street map of the ghetto, which locates the book's action, can be enlarged and projected. After paraphrasing chapter 3 (pp. 15–22; be sure to read aloud pp. 21–22), present the thread of the plot about Alex: Old Boruch tells Alex to wait for his father at 78 Bird Street; Alex tries to establish himself there; Alex's desperate attempts to get provisions; Alex's encounters with others in the ghetto; Alex maneuvers outside the ghetto; and finally, Alex responds to the opening of the empty ghetto for resettlement. Episodes to illustrate these points in the plot are: the ruined house on Bird Street (pp. 26–29); reunited with Snow and the Gryns (pp. 43 f.); searching for food (pp. 50–55, 82–84); the rope factory (pp. 56–58, 71–74, 75); shooting the Beretta (pp. 60–63); revisiting the Gryns' empty bunker (pp. 66–68); Bolek, the Polish partisan (pp. 68–70, 126–131, 151–152); the large bunker at 78 Bird Street (pp. 79–82); outside the ghetto (pp. 87–95, 120–126, 132–133, 134–136); the uprising in ghetto A and the two young men (pp. 96–105); the doctor (pp. 106–117, 118–119); and Stashya visits 78 Bird Street (pp. 152–154).

Related Materials

Two titles to suggest are *Escape If You Can* (Viking, 1977) by Eva-Lis Wuorio and *They Cage the Animals at Night* (New Amer. Lib., 1984) by Jennings Michael Burch. Three other titles may have appeal: *Running Loose* (Greenwillow, 1983) by Chris Crutcher; *Center Line* (Delacorte, 1984) by Joyce Sweeney; and *Gaffer Samson's Luck* (Farrar, 1984) by Jill Walsh Paton. The nonfiction paperback *Am I Normal?* (Avon, 1985), made from a successful film, treats male concerns during puberty in a dignified manner.

Two award-winning films (also available as videos) that go well with this title are *Bambinger* (Beacon Films, 1986, released 1984, 26 min.) and *The Courage to Care* (Anti-Defamation League of B'nai B'rith, 1985, 30 min.). Two recordings that parallel the reading tastes of the young hero are *Gulliver's Travels* (Spoken Arts, n.d., 2s) and *J. R. R. Tolkien Reads and Sings His the Hobbit and the Fellowship of the Ring* (Caedmon, 1975, 2s). The "Jogging Shoe" poster (ALA, 1986, No. 54JO) is also appropriate as background. The hero-reader deserves a library (chock full of books) poster as a backdrop.

Pinkwater, Daniel.   *The Worms of Kukumlima*
Dutton, 1981, 152 pp.

The prolific writer Daniel Pinkwater (aka Manus, D. Manus, and Daniel M. Pinkwater) has authored more than 26 titles for children (see *Introducing More Books*, Bowker 1978, pp. 217–220). Since the late seventies, he has been tickling funny bones as he continues to write humorous, fantastic plots enjoyed by many young readers. Probably no author captures as he does the popular imagination of youngsters. Nor are many authors as skillful in portraying the farcical adventures in these comic tales. Pinkwater, a fantasist for children, has written primarily fiction: wild, weird, adventure-filled tales beloved by imaginative young people. Three of his more recent titles for middle-graders are *The Moosepire* (Little, 1986); *The Muffin Fiend* (Lothrop, 1986); and *The Frankenbagel Monster* (Dutton, 1986).

Youngsters ages 9–12 (grades 4–7) will appreciate this story about a young hero who travels to Africa with his rich inventor grandfather and his grandfather's explorer friend to find a strange variety of worm that talks and plays chess. The author who also often does his own illustrations and jacket paintings contributed a bright, colorful, stylized, albeit primitive, picture of a giant earthworm in an equatorial landscape with blue mountains in the background. The painting, reversed and repeated on the back jacket, makes an intriguing entrance to the engaging story.

Ronald Donald Almondotter gladly surrenders his summer vacation and typical "kid jobs" like baby-sitting to work for his eccentric grandfather, Seumas Finneganstein, at the World Famous Salami Snap Company. His rich grandfather is the inventor-manufacturer of salami snaps, which are used for salami casings, some kinds of cheese, and plastic-bag closings. Grandpa also receives payments from franchises. As if that isn't enough, Finneganstein also invented the little plastic thing that ties the bag around loaves of bread and is the chief stockholder in the World Famous Little Plastic Thing Company. Nevertheless, he still drives an old car and listens to classical music over the radio daily with his employee Milton X. Mohammedstein. Although Ronald has plenty to do oiling the machines and sealing the boxes, the three eat lunch daily at the nearby Filipino cafeteria (the deli still uses string ties on the salami) and play gin rummy. Fortunately, Grandpa reimburses Ronald for his losses because playing gin is part of the job.

Soon after, Sir Charles Pelicanstein, the world famous explorer, shows up elegantly attired. He convinces his old explorer friend (years before Seumas settled down the two had traveled the Amazon together) to form an expedition with him to find a variety of intelligent worm in Kukumlima, Africa. Sir Charles tells an interesting story about the papers of Gordon Whillikers, assumed dead, who had adopted an earthworm, Raymond, as a pet and played chess with it. Whillikers's papers come from the recently defunct London Earthworm Society. The plan is not without problems, however: Kukumlima is not on the map, and Sir Charles claims that vast areas are still unexplored. But Sir Charles's biggest worry is the difficulty of financing the expedition without the society's funding. Excited by the prospect of becoming an explorer again, Seumas offers to finance the expedition, providing Ronald can come, and Sir Charles agrees.

Grandpa and Ronald receive protective injections from Dr. Stonestein and explorer essentials from Pierre Pierre in his shop, Adventurers Outfitters (Ronald is thrilled with his camping pocketknife). Meanwhile, Sir Charles arranges for African accommodations with Baboon Safaris Limited in Nairobi and contracts for their flight with Air Enterprise, operated by the brothers Roosman and Rassman. Mother, who still can't quite understand, continues to sew name tapes in Ronald's outfits, while Father warms to the idea.

Resplendent in their explorer garb, they are picked up by Captain Rassman, who is their limousine driver (a station wagon), and taken to the VIP lounge (a small room stocked with instant coffee, Hershey bars, and a folding cot). Captain Rassman, now the baggage handler, pushes a wheelbarrow with their gear to the *Flagship*, which the three explorers board on a swinging rope. The rusty propeller-driven cargo plane, flown by the brothers, lands at Embakasi Airport, Nairobi, after many hours of thermos food, chocolates, some sleep for Ronald, and gin rummy for the elders. The two smiling captains say that they will be waiting for their return.

Ethiopian Ali Tabu, the Baboon Safaris Limited driver who meets them, takes them to the office of Mr. Jiwe, the boss, all the while chattering about his bad luck as a driver. Even though Mr. Jiwe assigns them a safer driver, Hassan, a Pakistani, they insist on taking Ali Tabu, too, especially when he explains that he lost Mr. Whillikers somewhere around Lake Manyara in Tanzania, though he still doesn't know where Kukumlima is. The party sets out in a Land Rover and Bedford truck. Hassan, who is a take-charge person, tells the explorers that it is easy to start and takes them to Baba Pambazuka, the only person in Africa who can help them find Kukumlima, especially if they bring him a gift of a pinball machine.

After five or so unsuccessful days at Lake Manyara, they go to a nearby general store. Baba, who is the owner, is delighted with the pinball machine and alternates between playing it and directing them to Kukumlima, a place of magic that is not on any map. "Only at the moment when not one of you is thinking about Kukumlima, or where you are . . . a good sign (is) if you find the Elephant Portal." When Baba adds that Mr. Whillikers asked for the same information, they are overjoyed. They buy a lot of provisions and continue their safari. The euphoric feeling lasts at least a week.

One morning they awake to an elephant stampede. Unlike traveling herds, the elephants surround them in a tight formation and force them on a dangerous climb in their Land Rover to a sheer rock outcrop with an opening. The explorers squeeze through the Elephant Portal and rumble down the interior steps. At the bottom they discover that they are stranded in a crater whose sheer walls crumble when they try to escape. They soon find George Whillikers, however, in command of the robot elephants guarding the entrance. They discover that he also commands the worms that arrive on moonless nights to transport the crater's elephant mice to their planet, Bleeegh. Whillikers is the worms' shepherd, and in return they leave him boxes of crunchy granola. Raymond, the worm that occasionally used to play chess with Whillikers at first, is the spokesworm for the others.

Whillikers, a gemologist, excitedly shows the explorers all the precious gems on the crater's floor and his pet elephant mouse, Ellis, who gathers the other elephant mice. When Whillikers tells them about the worms' visits, Sir Charles and Grandpa exchange knowing glances. Their suspicions are confirmed as they find the worms crawling out of the crater floor for their next visit. They are enslaving the elephant mice underground.

Grandpa effects his escape plan. In preparation he has two big foot blobs and two hand-held balloons made for each person from the strange rubbery tree sap and the plastic containers for transporting the elephant mice. Mr. Whillikers also sees that everyone takes some gems. When everything is ready, Ellis signals the elephant mice in the blind earthworms' entrance hole. As the elephant mice emerge, followed by the worms, the explorers take off. They elevate themselves by foot blob and balloon. As they are ascending, the crater begins to heave in an earthquake, just as Grandpa and Sir Charles predicted, but they finally reach the rim. As they continue to float upward, the explorers realize that no one can see Kukumlima because it is always in cloud cover.

Dismayed when the wind blows them to the great desert, they are heartened when they see a familiar rusty plane in the distance. Disgorging the remains of their baggage, including most of the gems, they land after signaling the captains. They are finally homebound aboard the inglorious but welcome cargo plane.

Thematic Analysis

This book is an irreverent spoof of some social conditions. For the sensitive older reader, some of the comments about the airplane trip and the safari outfitting, for example, will have more than the usual humor. For the majority of children, however, the action-filled adventure story dwells on the special companionship and understanding between grandfathers and grandsons. Two threads also expand the young explorer's interest: the possibility that unexplored spaces may still exist and an imaginative way of looking at problems and coming up with inventive concrete solutions. Baba Pambazuka's manipulative use of "wisdom" to sell his foodstuffs is a good example of the fine mix of reality and imagination. This adventure-filled title will be appreciated by many youngsters.

Discussion Materials

To book talk, introduce the plot and the three main characters (pp. 1–13). Display the stylized jacket picture showing a large earthworm against an equatorial African background. Any of the following episodes can be highlighted: preliminary plans for the African safari (pp. 14–28); traveling on Air Enterprise (pp. 29–38); Ali Tabu (pp. 39–44); Hassan (pp. 45–58); Baba Pambazuka (pp. 59–70); in search of Kukumlima (pp. 71–80); the robot elephants and the Elephant Portal (pp. 81–88); Gordon Whillikers, the crater, and the elephant mice (pp. 81–114); the worms (pp. 115–133); the escape (pp. 115–147); reunited with the captains (pp. 148–151); and the epilogue (p. 152).

Related Materials

Another Daniel Pinkwater title, *The Frankenbagel Monster* (Dutton, 1986), will appeal to the fans of this type of zany humor. Four other titles also can be suggested: *The Devil with the Three Golden Hairs* (Knopf, 1983), retold by Nonny Hogrogian; *Piggybook* (Knopf, 1986) by Anthony Browne; *In a Dark, Dark Room and Other Scary Stories* (Harper, 1984) by Alvin Schwartz; and *The Nova Space Explorer's Guide: Where to Go and What to See* (Potter, 1985) by Richard Maurer.

Some useful audiovisual titles are: *Little Oz Stories* (Caedmon, 1983, 2s); *Peterkin Papers* (Caedmon, 1973, 1 cassette); *Journey to the Center of the*

Earth (Caedmon, 1978, 2s); *20,000 Leagues under the Sea* (Caedmon, 1977 2s); and *The Solar House* (National Film Board of Canada, 1986), a film and video. According to the American Library Association, "The force is with those who hang Yoda." The "Yoda" poster (ALA, No. 36Y) is certainly an appropriate background note for this book.

Sattler, Helen Roney. *Dinosaurs of North America*
Illus. by Anthony Rao. Lothrop, 1981, 151 pp.

A former elementary schoolteacher and children's librarian, the author has written a comprehensive book for youngsters age 8 and up (grades 3 and up) about the dinosaurs of North America. Her knowledge of young people's interest in dinosaurs at around age 8 is based on her own personal experience, and that of a grandson to whom the book is dedicated. (Dinosaurs have been a long-standing, common interest of youngsters.) Mrs. Sattler has been a prominent author of nonfiction since the early 1970s. She is also the author of some picture books with formats for different abilities. Her writing style is lucid, her research detailed, and her organization for this age group exceptionally clear. Her interest in this subject is further demonstrated by the publication in 1983 of *The Illustrated Dinosaur Dictionary*, and in 1984 of *Baby Dinosaurs* (both Lothrop).

The well-known artist Anthony Rao drew numerous greenish cast pencil sketches illustrating each of the 80 different types of dinosaurs reported to have existed. The more than 300 dinosaur fossil remains that had been found and studied by paleontologists by 1981, 80 on the North American continent, are treated by the author and illustrated with careful detail by Anthony Rao. The book has 26 detailed full-page drawings, at least three times as many smaller line drawings—interspersed with the text—of less numerous dinosaurs (according to fossil remains), and four double-page spreads of the better known and more numerous species, such as Triceratops. In the front jacket illustration, which also appears as a full-page illustration on page 136, a drawing of Torosaurus is dramatically set against a white background. The back jacket shows a slightly enlarged detail of the horned head of Styracosaurus, which appears on page 128. The illustrator—perhaps unknowingly—has visually underscored the theory of a weakened magnetic field as a causative factor for the disappearance of the dinosaurs (see p. 144).

APPRECIATING BOOKS · 307

Every word in this book is worth reading and studying, from the acknowledgments to the subject and illustration index. The introduction is
brief, but from a credible source—Dr. John H. Ostrom. The short bibliography includes scholarly titles mainly published in 1970. The reference
charts show where North American dinosaur fossils were found, for example, in Alberta, Canada, and in New Mexico, and how the land and sea
masses on the planet looked during the four geological ages (with the
world as it is today included for comparison). But perhaps most important
for establishing the book's reliability are the first and last chapters, "What
Is a Dinosaur?" and "The Mystery of Dinosaur Extinction."

As Mrs. Sattler states (and as corroborated by Dr. Ostrom and many
other authorities), contrary to stereotypical ideas of dinosaurs, "Some
were fierce, but most were harmless, peaceful animals. . . . And many
were probably not as dumb as people used to think." She also reports that
some of the dinosaurs may have evolved to warm-bloodedness. This is still
a "raging" controversy among paleontologists (as shown on WNET's
broadcast, with Drs. Baker and Ostrom taking extreme and moderate pro
views). In the final chapter, Mrs. Sattler presents more than 12 current
theories to explain the disappearance of the dinosaur.

Chapters 2–5 divide evolutionary time into the customary four eras:
the Triassic (Time of Change); the Jurassic (Period of Giants); the
Cretaceous (more changes, more dinosaurs); and the Early and Late
eras. The land and sea masses of each correspond to those graphically
shown in the chart (pp. 4–5), which also lists time periods. The final
picture shows the land and sea masses as we know them today. (The
continents were all joined in one land mass in the Triassic Age.) Each age
has an introduction that covers the known geography, climate, and biology, and the dinosaurs that lived then. All North American dinosaurs
are discussed under both their Latin and common names. They are
divided according to type—either birdlike or lizardlike hips—and chronologically listed according to when the dinosaur most likely appeared.
This presentation is related to the chronological chart of geological periods (p. 7). The syllabic pronunciation is then followed by a discussion of
the relationships, appearance, and life of the species, where the fossils
have been found, and the purposes, if known, of the body parts.

Thematic Analysis

This book can be appreciated as a title about the ever-popular subject
of dinosaurs among middle-graders. In addition to this natural interest

toward dinosaurs shown by youngsters in grades 2–7, the well-designed, beautifully illustrated book has a readable text and an objective approach that stresses the accuracy of facts and scientific rationality. The difference between theory and natural law is subtly introduced for this age range. Throughout the book, and especially at the conclusion, the various theories of dinosaur extinction are clearly summarized and critically, albeit simply, evaluated. Appropriate controversy within the realm of objective fact is also presented. In the process, the youngster can learn some of the differences between fact and opinion. A final resolution about dinosaur extinction based on known facts cannot yet be made: "We don't know. Perhaps a combination of these theories holds the answer. . . . Perhaps you will find the key." The complex relationship among observable conditions and objective facts, the construction of a theory, and, at length, the formulation of a natural law, which encourages a child's participation, are an invaluable intellectual exercise for the middle-grader. This marvelous oversize work on dinosaurs is a treasure!

Discussion Materials

The book will "sell itself" to those in grades 3–6 by simply mentioning the title, certainly on displaying the book jacket. The first and final (sixth) chapters are recommended for reading aloud. The book will also serve as a reference source for reports. The librarian can make an appropriate packet of transparencies of the graphic pictures of the world's land masses (pp. 4–5); the time chart of the two types of dinosaurs (p. 7); and the double spreads of four well-known dinosaurs: Brontosaurus (pp. 36–37), Stegosaurus (pp. 56–57), Gorgosaurus (pp. 84–85), and Pachycephalosaurus (pp. 96–97) to introduce the book.

Related Materials

Three nonfiction titles can be used here: *Baby Dinosaurs* (Lothrop, 1984) also by Helen Sattler; *Auks, Rocks and the Odd Dinosaur: Inside Stories from the Smithsonian's Museum of Natural History* (Crowell, 1985) by Peggy Thomson; and *The Riddle of the Dinosaur* (Knopf, 1986) by John Noble Wilford. Three fiction titles are: *What Happened to Patrick's Dinosaurs?* (Clarion, 1986) by Carol Carrick, a fanciful presentation of the mystery surrounding the dinosaurs' disappearance; *Dodosaurs: The Dinosaurs That Didn't Make It* (Harmony, 1983) by Rick Meyerowitz, a spoof for middle-graders and reluctant readers; and *Writing on the Wall* (Lothrop, 1983) by Leon Garfield, a story loosely based on the Book of Daniel from the bible. Two other nonfiction titles that may have appeal are *Fish Facts and Bird Brains: Animal Intelligence* (Lodestar, 1984) by Helen Sattler and *Pets, Vets, and Marty Howard* (Lippincott, 1984) by Joan Carris.

Six filmstrips in the Adventures in Dinosaur Land series that are appropriate for grades K–6 are available from Random. Three films that present good information for discussion are: *DNA: Laboratory of Life* (National Geographic Society, 1986); *Aliens from Outer Space* (Films, Inc., 1985); and *Bitz Butz* (Picture Start, 1985).

Stewart, Mary. *A Walk in Wolf Wood: A Tale of Fantasy and Magic*
Illus. by Emanuel Schongut. Morrow, 1980, 148pp.

Since the middle of the twentieth century, Mary Stewart has been writing elegant and popular novels. She has written more than a dozen for young adults and several for children, including *The Little Broomstick*, written in 1971, *Ludo and the Star Horse* (Morrow, 1975), winner of the Scottish Arts Council Award and still in print, and the featured title. A writer and university teacher of English over a long and eventful career, this respected British author has built a solid reputation as a writer of mystery romances for older readers and tales of magic and fantasy for children. Her clear and expressive writing style follows an exemplary British tradition in this genre.

This story features a brother and sister who "slip in time" into a fourteenth-century adventure while on vacation with their parents in the Black Forest (Germany). They reunite a duke and his friend, who has been turned into a werewolf through the sorcery of an evil courtier. At the successful completion of the adventure, the children cross the castle drawbridge and return to meet their parents who are preparing to leave the Wolf Wood. Youngsters ages 9–12 (grades 4–7) will find the dreamlike story engrossing and will be attracted by the presence of a werewolf in the story (albeit one without sensationalism).

The illustrations are by Emanuel Schongut. The full-color painting on the front jacket portrays a ruined, turreted castle framed by woodland trees. The illustration on the back jacket shows a densely wooded portion of Wolf Wood. Schongut did five bordered full-page pictures for the 17 chapters, most with a figure or part of one extending beyond the border, and a half-page frontispiece of the castle set eerily against a large full moon. He also designed 19 oblong panels enclosing a stylized vine; one for each of the 17 chapter heads and one each for the epilogue and the opening page, which lists some of the author's titles. The illustrations are done in ink wash on pale pink paper.

The book was designed by Ava Weiss. Lovely to read and behold, it includes a burnt-sienna script initial at the start of each chapter; thin lines of the same color outline the chapter numeral; and a sienna-colored leaf decorates the page number. The typeface is straight and clear, and the ample ratio of white page to black print makes the book easy to read and view.

John and his younger sister, Margaret (Meg) Begbie, are on vacation with their parents in St. Johann in the Black Forest of Germany. After spending an evening watching the villagers dance in ancient peasant costume, the next morning the children visit the nearby fourteenth-century castle. The family then goes on a picnic to Wolf Wood (Wolfenwald on the map that John and his father examine), and in the afternoon they rest nearby. Father naps, mother returns to the car to knit, and the children decide to follow a track they find in the forest.

Suddenly, a weeping man dressed in royal fourteenth-century clothes passes them without noticing them. As they follow him, they see human footprints merging into animal tracks that John thinks were made by a large dog. They also find a large gold medallion and chain among some fallen branches. On one side of the medallion they see a portrait of a young man with the name Otho under it, and on the back is the word "fidelis," which John translates as "faithful." At nightfall, they find the weeping man's costume in an occupied but empty cottage.

All of a sudden, they see a large yellow-eyed wolf glowering at them in the open doorway. John hurls the medallion at the wolf who momentarily springs away, long enough for the terrified children to escape. They run back to their car, but find the car gone. Feeling desolate, they fall asleep there hoping that their parents will return. But they are awakened by the sound of a horn announcing a hunt. When the man in the lead asks which way the wolf went and Meg points in the opposite direction, the man tosses her a coin with a portrait of an older Otho on one side and on the other a bird and the date 1342. John and Meg slowly realize that they are in the Middle Ages, speaking and understanding a dream language. The nearby castle with flags flying from the turrets is newly built and Otho is seated there as duke.

The children return to the cottage where they find the weeping man sleeping. When he awakens, he tells them that he is Lord Mardian, a boyhood friend and champion of Otho, with whom he sealed his faithfulness in an exchange of medallions years ago when they were boys. Since then Otho had become duke and had a son, Crispin, who is now almost 15, the age of manhood. After Otho suffered a severe battle wound five years ago, Lord Mardian conducted the duke's battles, that is, until two years ago when an envious courtier, Almeric, turned Lord Mardian into a werwolf with a magic spell and turned himself into Lord Mardian's twin. At the end of each day, Lord Mardian flees to the cottage because at night he becomes a dangerous werwolf. The false Lord Mardian who was unable to find the medallion has been continually trying to kill the werwolf.

After relating the story, Lord Mardian tells the children that they can help if they choose, and he leaves while they decide. When he returns, the children have decided to try to help. Lord Mardian calls them Hans and Gretta; finds appropriate dress for them from among old Gulda's trove (she inhabited the cottage when Otho and Mardian were boys); and tells them to say that they are the grandchildren of Lady Gisel, a senile older woman in the royal court. Soon after, it becomes dark and Lord Mardian turns into a werwolf. To protect the children, he leaves to feed his thirst for blood elsewhere.

On his return to the cottage, the werwolf escorts Hans and Gretta to a secret room on the ground floor of the castle where he and Otho played long ago. Once inside the castle, however, the children are soon discovered. Gretta is taken to the women's quarters, and Hans explains his presence to a steward. Hans also quickly discovers that the duke's personal servants are specially chosen pages about Hans's age. Meanwhile, Gretta overhears Crispin and the false Lord Mardian (Almeric) talking in the garden below her new quarters. Almeric is trying to convince the young man that killing the werwolf will restore his father's drastically declining health. Lady Blancheflower, who rode in the hunt, questions Gretta when she sees her in the garden, but fortunately she is distracted by a messenger.

Back in the kitchen downstairs Hans seizes an opportunity to substitute for Justin, a sick ducal page, to bring the duke his nightly posset (drink). Justin is too ill to explain how to concoct the posset, but he is able to exchange clothes with Hans and direct him to Denis, another page, in the private ducal chambers. Avoiding the false Lord Mardian (Almeric) and Denis, Hans convinces the guards to admit him. Duke Otho watches in disbelief as a blow by one of the duke's attendants sends Lord Mardian's medallion spilling from the goblet that Hans carries. The duke then listens intently to Hans's story about Almeric's treachery.

Just as Hans finishes, they are interrupted by a messenger who announces that (the false) Lord Mardian is protecting a young girl from the great werwolf with a knife in the cellar. Gretta had wandered back to the secret room where she was watching the false Lord Mardian who had come there to cast another evil spell. Soon after he catches her, the werwolf arrives. But the duke's soldiers intervene and chain both the false Lord Mardian and the werwolf. The soldiers bring everyone to the porch where the duke has been carried in his chair. As the moon fades, the duke lends the werwolf his royal cloak as covering.

At dawn the chains fall from both prisoners and the amulet of sorcerer's powder hanging from Almeric's neck disintegrates. The werwolf assumes his proper role as Lord Mardian, and the false Lord Mardian permanently becomes Almeric. The duke places the medallion around Lord Mardian's neck and stands to embrace him. For the first time in two years Crispin sees his father well.

As John and Margaret walk across the castle drawbridge, they wave at Lord Mardian and look back at the busy castle. It is once again a ruined fourteenth-century castle. In the distance they can hear their father, who is preparing for the late afternoon trip back to the village, calling their names in Wolf Wood.

Thematic Analysis

That this title should be the final one in the developmental reading ladder is fitting. The book treats ultimate confrontation between good and evil in the human condition, couched in fantasy with "the good" represented as a ferocious werwolf. The text straightforwardly tells the young reader that one must face truth courageously, sensitively, and trustingly, as well as make choices: "Choice is man's right . . ." (p. 50). The elegantly told story delivers its messages in a splendidly designed and illustrated book—one that can be enjoyed and appreciated.

Discussion Materials

The book lends itself to reading aloud or book talking. In either case, use the same introduction: display the jacket, title page, and frontispiece; introduce the child characters, and give the location. For a read-aloud presentation, there are seven affective section breaks: the children find a cottage and see the wolf (pp. 1–26); the hunt and finding the weeping man (pp. 27–42); the werwolf's story and the trip to the secret room (pp. 43–73); the children quickly learn about castle life as Gretta overhears Crispin and the false Lord Mardian (pp. 74–99); upstairs with Hans (pp. 100–111, 123–130); Gretta goes back to the secret room (pp. 112–120, 131–137); and on the duke's porch (pp. 138–148). Use the last episode only if you must.

To book talk, paraphrase the action to the children's first encounter with the wolf (pp. 1–18), highlight the weeping man (p. 2), and be sure to show the picture (p. 3). Then use any of the following episodes: the hunt (pp. 27–36; picture p. 29); the werwolf's story (pp. 43–52); the trip to the secret room (pp. 53–73; picture p. 66); the castle (pp. 74–82); Crispin and the false Lord Mardian converse (pp. 83–92); the duke's private chambers (pp. 100–111, 123; picture p. 101); Gretta and the false Lord Mardian in the secret room (pp. 112–120); and the rescue (pp. 131ff.).

Related Materials

Three fairy-tale books are recommended: *Hansel and Gretel* (Dodd, 1984) by Rita Lesser, illustrated by Paul O. Zelinsky; *Dragon, Dragon, and Other Tales* (Knopf, 1975) by John Gardner, illustrated by Charles Shields; and *Alan Garner's Book of British Fairy Tales* (Delacorte, 1985) by Alan Garner, illustrated by Derek Collard. Robert Louis Stevenson's *A Child's Garden of Verses* (Rand McNally, 1982), illustrated by Tasha Tudor, is also recommended. Three fiction books are suggested: *Wounded Wolf* (Harper, 1978) by Jean Craighead George; *Breadsticks and Blessing Places* (Macmillan, 1985) by Candy Dawson Boyd; and *Dollhouse Murders* (Holiday, 1983) by Betty Ren Wright.

Suggested audiovisual titles include two recordings: Lewis Carroll's *Through the Looking Glass* and *Alice in Wonderland* (both Caedmon, 1958). The kit *Witch of Fourth Street and Other Stories* (Listening Library, 1978), from the book by Myron Levoy, is available, as is the poster "Wreck of the Zephyr" (Peaceable Kingdom Pr., 1983) by Chris Van Allsburg. The film *Castle* (PBS Video, 1983, 58 min.), adapted from David Macaulay's book, is also suggested.

Appreciating Books: Additional Titles

Burgess, Anthony. *The Land Where the Ice Cream Grows.* Doubleday, 1980, unp. (Gr. 2–4)

Doctor DeSoto, by William Steig. Filmstrip, 47 fr. Weston Woods, 1985. (Gr. 2–4)

Doughnuts, by Robert McCloskey. Video, 26 min. Weston Woods, 1984. (Gr. 2–6)

Fisher, Leonard Everitt. *The Statue of Liberty.* Holiday, 1985. (Gr. 3–5)

Gag, Wanda. *The Sorcerer's Apprentice.* Illus. by Margot Tomes. Coward, 1980, 32 pp. (Gr. 2–4)

Garfield, Leon. *Shakespeare Stories.* Illus. by Michael Foreman. Schocken, 1985. (Gr. 5–7)

Geisert, Arthur. *Pigs from A to Z.* Houghton, 1986, 62 pp. (Gr. 3–5)

Giblin, James Cross. *Walls: Defenses Throughout History.* Little, 1984, 128 pp. (Gr. 4–7)

Highwater, Jamake. *Legend Days.* Harper, 1984, 147 pp. (Gr. 5–up)

JAM. Magazine, 6 issues/yr. 56 The Esplanade, Suite 202, Toronto, ON. M5E 1A7 Canada. (Gr. 5–6)

Kennedy, Richard. *Amy's Eyes.* Illus. by Richard Egielski. Harper, 1985, 437 pp. (Gr. 5–7)

Lipman, Jean et al. *Young America: A Folk-art History.* Hudson Hills/Museum of American Folk Art, 1986. (Gr. 5–up)

Lobel, Arnold. *On Market Street.* Illus. by Anita Lobel. Greenwillow, 1981, 40 pp. (Gr. 1–4)

McKinley, Robin. *Door in the Hedge.* Greenwillow, 1981, 216 pp. (Gr. 4–6)

Meltzer, Milton. *The Black Americans: A History in Their Own Words, 1916–1983.* Crowell, 1984, 320 pp. (Gr. 5–up)

Menotti, Gian Carlo. *Amahl and the Night Visitors.* Adapt. by Ann Tobias, illus. by Michele Lemieux. Morrow, 1986, 64 pp. (Gr. 3–5)

Merriam, Eve. *Fresh Paint.* Illus. by David Frampton. Macmillan, 1986, 42 pp. (Gr. 4–7)

Nightingale, by Hans Christian Andersen. Filmstrip, 72 fr. color. Live Oak Media, 1979. (Gr. 3–6)

Peter and the Wolf, by Sergei Prokofiev. Recording, read by Dudley Moore. Polygram Classics, 1985. (All ages)

Raskin, Ellen. *Mysterious Disappearance of Leon (I Mean Noel).* Avon, 1980, 160 pp. (Gr. 5–6)

Rice, Karen. *Does Candy Grow on Trees?* Illus. by Sharon Adler Cohen. Walker, 1984, 32 pp. (Gr. 3–5)

Rogasky, Barbara. *Rapunzel.* Illus. by Trina Schart Hyman. Holiday, 1982. (Gr. 2–4)

Shadow, by Blaise Cendars. Illus. by Marcia Brown. Filmstrip, 33 fr. Weston Woods, 1985. (Gr. 2–4)

The Statue of Liberty. Film, 58 min., also available on video. Direct Cinema, 1986. (Gr. 5–up)

Wind in the Willows, by Kenneth Grahame. Recording, read by David McCallum. Caedmon, 1973. (Gr. 4–6)

DIRECTORY OF AUDIOVISUAL
PUBLISHERS AND DISTRIBUTORS

The following listing is provided as an additional aid in locating the various audiovisual materials that are recommended in the "Related Materials" at the end of each book plot and in the "Additional Titles" at the end of each chapter. This list is as complete and up to date as can be determined at press time.

Agency for Instructional Television
  Box A, 111 W. 17th St.,
  Bloomington, IN 47402

Anti-Defamation League of B'nai
  B'rith
  823 United Nations Plaza,
  New York, NY 10017

Aristoplay
  100 Huron View Blvd., Box 7645,
  Ann Arbor, MI 48107

Audio Book Contractors, Inc.
  Box 40115,
  Washington, DC 20016

Barr Films
  Box 5667,
  Pasadena, CA 91107

Beacon Films
  Box 575, 1250 Washington St.,
  Norwood, MA 02062

Benchmark Films, Inc.
  145 Scarborough Rd.,
  Briarcliff Manor, NY 10510

Bronnimann/Dorsey
  189 Morris Ave.,
  Providence, RI 02906

Bullfrog Films, Inc.
  Oley, PA 19547

Caedmon
  1995 Broadway,
  New York, NY 10023

Calico
  Box 15916,
  St. Louis, MO 63114

CBS, Inc.
  51 W. 52 St.,
  New York, NY 10019

Centre Productions, Inc.
  1800 30th St., Suite 207,
  Boulder, CO 80301

Centron Productions, Inc.
1621 W. Ninth St.,
Lawrence, KS 66044

Churchill Films
662 N. Robertson Blvd.,
Los Angeles, CA 90069

Cinema Guild
1697 Broadway, Room 802,
New York, NY 10019

Coronet
108 Wilmot Rd.,
Deerfield, IL 60015

Cypress Publishing
1763 Gardena Ave.,
Glendale, CA 91204

Direct Cinema, Ltd.
Box 69589,
Los Angeles, CA 90069

Eastman Kodak Co.
343 State St.,
Rochester, NY 14650

The Electic Company
261 E. Fifth St., Suite 318–319
St. Paul, MN 55101

Educational Enrichment Materials
201 E. 50 St.,
New York, NY 10022

Elephant Records
77 Berkeley St.,
Toronto, Ont. M5A 2W5, Canada

Encyclopaedia Britannica Educational
Corp.
425 N. Michigan Ave.,
Chicago, IL 60611

Film Ideas
3080 Scotch Lane,
Riverwoods, IL 60015

Filmakers Library, Inc.
133 E. 58th St., Suite 703a,
New York, NY 10022

Filmedia Studios
10700 Lyndale Ave. S.,
Minneapolis, MN 55420

FilmFair Communications
10900 Ventura Blvd.,
Studio City, CA 91604

Films by Edmond Levy
135 Central Park W.,
New York, NY 10023

Films for the Humanities, Inc.
Box 2053,
Princeton, NJ 08540

Films, Inc.
5547 N. Ravenswood Ave.,
Chicago, IL 60640

Gateway Studios, Inc.
225 Ross St.,
Pittsburgh, PA 15219

A Gentle Wind, Inc.
Box 3103,
Albany, NY 12203

Gerald T. Rogers/Kinetic Film Enter-
prises, Ltd.
255 Delaware Ave.,
Buffalo, NY 14202

Great Plains Instructional TV Library
Univ. of Nebraska,
Box 80669,
Lincoln, NE 68501

GK Hall & Co.
70 Lincoln St.,
Boston, MA 02111

High Windy Productions
Box 553,
Fairview, NC 28730

Howard Hanger, Jazz Fantasy
31 Park Ave.,
Asheville, NC 28801

Indiana University Audio-Visual
Center
Bloomington, IN 47405

International Film Bureau (IFB)
332 S. Michigan Ave.,
Chicago, IL 60604

Jazz Cat Productions
Box 4278,
Sunland, CA 91040

Kids Records
See Silo/Alcazar

Kultur Video
121 Highway 36,
West Long Branch, NJ 07764

KUTV Documentary Division
Salt Lake City, UT

L.C.A.
see Learning Corporation of
America

Learning Corporation of America
108 Wilmot Rd.,
Deerfield, IL 60015

Learning Tree Publishing
7108 S. Alton Way,
Englewood, CA 80112

Listen for Pleasure, Ltd.
One Columba Dr.,
Niagara Falls, NY 14305

Listening Library
One Park Ave.,
Old Greenwich, CT 06870

The Little Red Filmhouse
Box 691083,
Los Angeles, CA 90069

Live Oak Media
Box 34,
Ancramdale, NY 12503

Made-to-Order Library Productions
345 Fullerton Parkway, Suite 1101,
Chicago, IL 60614

MasterVision
969 Park Ave.,
New York, NY 10028

Media Projects
5215 Homer St.,
Dallas, TX 75206

MGS Productions, Inc.
Box 9541,
Austin, TX 78756

Miller-Brody/Random,
see Random House/Miller-Brody
Productions

Mind's Eye/Jabberwocky
Box 6727,
San Francisco, CA 94101

MTI Film & Video
108 Wilmot Rd.,
Deerfield, IL 60015

NAPPS
see National Association for the Pres-
ervation and Perpetuation of
Storytelling

National Association for the Preserva-
tion and Perpetuation of Storytelling (NAPPS)
Box 112,
Jonesborough, TN 37659

National Film Board of Canada
1251 Ave. of the Americas,
New York, NY 10020

National Geographic Society Educational Services
17th and M Sts. N.W.,
Washington, DC 20036

NBC News Archives
30 Rockefeller Plaza,
New York, NY 10020

New Day Films
22 Riverview Dr.,
Wayne, NJ 07470

Nova/WNET
see WNET-TV

Opportunities for Learning
20417 Nordhoff St., Dept. CM75,
Chatsworth, CA 91311

Pathways of Sound
6 Craigie Circle,
Cambridge, MA 02138

PBS Video
1320 Braddock Pl.,
Alexandria, VA 22314

Perspective Films
108 Wilmot Rd.,
Deerfield, IL 60015

Phoenix/BFA Films and Video, Inc.
470 Park Ave. S.,
New York, NY 10016

Picture Start
204 W. John St.,
Champaign, IL 61820

Pied Piper Productions
Box 320,
Verdugo City, CA 91046

Pyramid Film and Video
Box 1048,
Santa Monica, CA 90406

Rabbit Ears and Random
see Random House, Inc.

Random House, Inc.
400 Hahn Rd.,
Westminster, MD 21157

Random House/Miller-Brody
Productions
see Random House, Inc.

Rounder Records
One Camp St.,
Cambridge, MA 02140

RS Records
Box 651
Brattleboro, VT 05676

Sasnett Film
7239 Fox Harbor Rd.,
Prospect, KY 40059

Silo/Alcazar
Box 429, S. Main St.,
Waterbury, VT 05676

Society for Visual Education, Inc.
(SVE)
1345 Diversey Parkway,
Chicago, IL 60614

Spoken Arts, Inc.
310 North Ave.,
New Rochelle, NY 10801

Story Book Starters
Dist. by Opportunities for Learning
20417 Nordhoff St., Dept. CM75,
Chatsworth, CA 91311

Sunburst Communications, Inc.
39 Washington Ave.,
Pleasantville, NY 10570

SVE
see Society for Visual Education,
Inc.

Texture Films, Inc.
Box 1337,
Skokie, IL 60076

Tickle Tune Typhoon
Box 15153,
Seattle, WA 98115

Time-Life Films and Video
100 Eisenhower Dr.,
Paramus, NJ 07652

Tom Davenport Films
Box 527, Rte. 1,
Delaplane, VA 22025

Troll Associates
320 Rte. 17,
Mahwah, NJ 07430

University of California Extension Media Center (EMC)
2223 Fulton St.,
Berkeley, CA 94720

VETS, Inc.
Box 160,
Oreana, IL 62554

Victorian Video Productions
Box 1328,
Port Townsend, WA 98368

Video Associates
5419 Sunset Blvd.,
Los Angeles, CA 90027

Video Learning Systems
1253 N. Vine St.,
Los Angeles, CA 90038

Walt Disney Educational Media Co.
500 S. Buena Vista St.,
Burbank, CA 91521

Weston Woods Studios
389 Newtown Turnpike,
Weston, CT 06883

WNET-TV
356 W. 58 St.,
New York, NY 10019

Wombat Film & Video
250 W. 57 St.,
New York, NY 10019

BIOGRAPHICAL INDEX

Biographical information about authors and illustrators may be found by consulting one of the sources listed here. The abbreviated form preceding the source is used in the index entries. For a few authors and illustrators, information was not available at the time of publication. The following title was used as a preliminary check for all the authors and illustrators listed here: *Children's Authors and Illustrators: An Index to Biographical Dictionaries,* 4th ed., ed. by Joyce Nakamura (Gale Research Co., 1987).

ABYP   *Authors of Books for Young People.* Martha E. Ward and Dorothy A. Marquardt, eds. Metuchen, N.J.: Scarecrow Press, 1971, 1979, and Sup. 1975.

BI   *Biography Index.* New York: H.W. Wilson Co., 1949–1983. Vols. 1–5, 13 (Sept. 1980–Aug. 1984).

CA   *Contemporary Authors.* Detroit: Gale Research Co., 1967–1986, 1987. Vols. 1–117, 120. CA X refers to pseudonym entries which appear as cross-references in the cumulative index to CA.

CGA   *Contemporary Graphic Artists: A Biographical, Bibliographical, and Critical Guide to Current Illustrators, Animators, Cartoonists, Designers, and Other Graphic Artists.* Detroit: Gale Research Co., 1987. Vol. 2.

CLC   *Contemporary Literary Criticism.* Detroit: Gale Research Co., 1973–1986. Vols. 1–15.

CLR   *Children's Literature Review.* Detroit: Gale Research Co., 1976–1986. Vols. 1–10.

DAPF   *A Directory of American Poets and Fiction Writers.* New York: Poets & Writers, 1983, 1985.

FBJA   *Fifth Book of Junior Authors & Illustrators.* Sally Holmes Holtze, ed. New York: H.W. Wilson Co., 1983.

IBYP   *Illustrators of Books for Young People.* Second edition. Martha E. Ward and Dorothy A. Marquardt, eds. Metuchen, N.J.: Scarecrow Press, 1975.

ICB   *Illustrators of Children's Books. 1967–1976.* Lee Kingman, Grace Allen Hogarth, and Harriet Quimby, comps. Boston: Horn Book, 1967, 1978.

JBA   *The Junior Book of Authors.* First edition. Stanley J. Kunitz and Howard

Haycraft, eds. Second edition, revised. New York: H. W. Wilson Co., 1934, 1951.
SA *Something about the Author*. Anne Commire, ed. Detroit: Gale Research Co., 1971–1987. Vols. 1–46. SA X refers to pseudonym entries which appear as cross-references in the cumulative index to SA.
TCCW *Twentieth-Century Children's Writers*. D. L. Kirkpatrick, ed. New York: St. Martin's Press, 1978, 1983.
WD *The Writers Directory*. London: St. James Press; New York: St. Martin's Press, 1976, 1979.
WD-82 *The Writers Directory*. 1982–1984 edition. Detroit: Gale Research Co., 1981.
WD-84 *The Writers Directory*. 1984–1986 edition. Chicago: St. James Press, 1983.
WWAA *Who's Who in American Art*. Jaques Cattell Press, ed. New York: R. R. Bowker Co., 1973, 1976, 1978, 1980, 1982, 1984.

Abolafia, Yossi, SA 46
Adler, C. S., CLC 35; DAPF; SA 26
Allen, Tom, CA X; SA X
Arnold, Caroline, CA 107; SA 34, 36
Avi (Wortis, Avi), CA X; FBJA; SA X

Baker, Olaf, BI 2; JBA
Bang, Molly, BI 13; CA 102; CLR 8
Bauer, Marion Dane, CA 11NR, 69; FBJA; SA 20
Baylor, Byrd (Schweitzer-Baylor, Byrd), BI 12; CA 81; CLR 3; SA 16
Beatty, Patricia (Robbins), BI 7–9; CA 1, 3NR; SA 1, 30; WD; WD-82; WD-84
Bierhorst, John, BI 10; CA 13NR, 33R; FBJA; SA 6
Blake, Quentin, BI 6, 8, 11; CA 11NR, 25R; FBJA; SA 9
Bloom, Lloyd, SA 43
Bottner, Barbara, ABYP; BI 12; CA 8NR, 61; SA 14
Bridgers, Sue Ellen, BI 13; CA 11NR, 65; FBJA; SA 22, 1AS
Brittain, Bill, CA 13NR; DAPF; FBJA; SA 36
Byars, Betsy, BI 8–10, 12, 13; CA 18NR, 33R; SA 4, 1AS; WD; WD-82; WD-84

Cameron, Ann, BI 13; CA 101; SA 27
Cameron, Eleanor, CA 1, 2NR; SA 1, 25; WD; WD-82; WD-84

Carris Joan (Davenport), CA 106; SA 42, 44
Cassedy, Sylvia, ABYP Sup.; BI 13; CA 105; SA 27
Cleary, Beverly, BI 6–10, 12, 13; CA 1, 2NR; SA 2, 43; WD; WD-82; WD-84
Cleaver, Vera and Cleaver, Bill, BI 8, 13; CA 73; SA 22; WD-84
Cooney, Barbara, BI 1, 5–8, 10, 12; CA 3NR, 5; IBYP; SA 6
Cooper, Susan (Mary), BI 9, 11; CA 15NR, 29R; SA 4; WD; WD-82; WD-84
Costabel, Eva Deutsch, SA 45

Dahl, Roald, ABYP, BI 3, 5–6, 8–13; CLR 1, 7; CA 1, 6NR
Danziger, Paula, CA 112, 115; CLC 21; FBJA; SA 30, 36
de Groat, Diane, BI 12; CA 107; FBJA; SA 31
Diamond, Donna, CA 115; SA 30, 35
Dillon, Leo and Dillon, Diane, ABYP Sup; BI 11, 12; FBJA; ICB 67

Egielski, Richard, BI 11, 12; ICB 67; SA 11

Fleischman, Sid, BI 9; CA 5NR; TCCW 83; WD-82; WD-84

TITLE-AUTHOR-ILLUSTRATOR INDEX

Titles fully discussed and summarized in *Introducing Bookplots 3* as well as those listed in "Related Materials" at the end of each book plot and in the "Additional Titles" at the end of each chapter are cited in this index. An asterisk (*) precedes all fully discussed titles. Authors and illustrators are cited for fully discussed and summarized titles only. A dagger (†) precedes names of illustrators.

SUBJECT INDEX

This index is intended to expand the possibilities for reading guidance by providing additional themes and topics for the titles that are discussed fully in this book. Other titles that fit in these categories can be found in the "Related Materials" section that appears in the treatment of the books listed below.

Apartment Houses
Byars, Betty. *Cracker Jackson*, 208
Cassedy, Sylvia. *M.E. and Morton*, 108
Greenwald, Sheila. *Give Us a Great Big Smile, Rosie Cole*, 236

Art, Medieval
Hastings, Selina. *Sir Gawain and the Loathly Lady*, 79

Arthurian Romances
Hastings, Selina. *Sir Gawain and the Loathly Lady*, 79

Astronauts—U.S.—Biography
Haskins, Jim, and Benson, Kathleen. *Space Challenger: The Story of Guion Bluford*, 241

Authors
Dahl, Roald. *Boy: Tales of Childhood*, 71
Yates, Elizabeth. *My Diary—My World*, 270

Aztecs—Religion and Mythology
Bierhorst, John. *Spirit Child: A Story of the Nativity*, 280

Ballet
Bottner, Barbara. *Dumb Old Casey Is a Fat Tree*, 98

Birds
Adler, C. S. *Fly Free*, 199
Arnold, Caroline. *Saving the Peregrine Falcon*, 166
Haley, Gail E. *Birdsong*, 177
Yorinks, Arthur. *Hey, Al*, 89

Birthdays
Hughes, Shirley. *Alfie Gives a Hand*, 43

Bison
Baker, Olaf. *Where the Buffaloes Begin*, 276

Books and Reading
Orlev, Uri. *The Island on Bird Street*, 296

Porte, Barbara Ann. *The Kidnapping of Aunt Elizabeth*, 156
Rogers, Jean. *The Secret Moose*, 194
Rylant, Cynthia. *When I Was Young in the Mountains*, 26
Yolen, Jane. *Children of the Wolf*, 55

Boston Post Road—History
Gibbons, Gail. *From Path to Highway: The Story of the Boston Post Road*, 135

Brothers and Sisters
Carris, Joan. *When the Boys Ran the House*, 11
Cassedy, Sylvia. *M.E. and Morton*, 108
Cleary, Beverly. *Ramona, Forever*, 15
Dahl, Roald. *Boy: Tales of Childhood*, 71
Jukes, Mavis. *Like Jake and Me*, 18
Lowry, Lois. *Us and Uncle Fraud*, 46
McCully, Emily Arnold. *Picnic*, 21
Moeri, Louise. *Save Queen of Sheba*, 152
Rylant, Cynthia. *When I Was Young in the Mountains*, 26
Yates, Elizabeth. *My Diary—My World*, 270

California
Arnold, Caroline. *Saving the Peregrine Falcon*, 166
Beatty, Patricia. *Eight Mules from Monterey*, 2
Brown, Tricia. *Someone Special, Just Like You*, 105
Cameron, Eleanor. *That Julia Redfern*, 8
Gates, Doris. *Morgan for Melinda*, 113
Meltzer, Milton. *Dorothea Lange: Life Through the Camera*, 261

Camping
Lasky, Kathryn. *Jem's Island*, 148

Canada
Danziger, Paula. *It's an Aardvark-Eat-Turtle World*, 37
Mazer, Harry. *The Island Keeper*, 116

Castles
Stewart, Mary. *A Walk in Wolf Wood*, 309